The Migrant's Spirit

THE MIGRANT'S SPIRIT

How Industrial Modernity
Came to the German Lands

BENJAMIN P. HEIN

OXFORD
UNIVERSITY PRESS

OXFORD
UNIVERSITY PRESS

Oxford University Press is a department of the University of Oxford.
It furthers the University's objective of excellence in research, scholarship,
and education by publishing worldwide. Oxford is a registered trade mark of
Oxford University Press in the UK and in certain other countries.

Published in the United States of America by Oxford University Press
198 Madison Avenue, New York, NY 10016, United States of America.

© Oxford University Press 2025

All rights reserved. No part of this publication may be reproduced, stored in a retrieval system, transmitted, used for text and data mining, or used for training artificial intelligence, in any form or by any means, without the prior permission in writing of Oxford University Press, or as expressly permitted by law, by license, or under terms agreed with the appropriate reprographics rights organization. Inquiries concerning reproduction outside the scope of the above should be sent to the Rights Department, Oxford University Press, at the address above.

You must not circulate this work in any other form
and you must impose this same condition on any acquirer.

Library of Congress Cataloging-in-Publication Data
Names: Hein, Benjamin P. author
Title: The migrant's spirit : how industrial modernity came to the German
lands / Benjamin P. Hein.
Description: New York, NY : Oxford University Press, 2025.
Identifiers: LCCN 2025019887 | ISBN 9780197831021 hardback |
ISBN 9780197831038 epub
Subjects: LCSH: Germans—United States—History—19th century | Emigration and immigration—Economic aspects | Emigration and immigration—Social aspects | Industrialization—Germany—History—19th century | Social change—Germany—History—19th century | Germany—Emigration and immigration—History—19th century
Classification: LCC JV8014 .H45 2025
LC record available at https://lccn.loc.gov/2025019887

DOI: 10.1093/9780197831052.001.0001

Printed by Integrated Books International, United States of America

The manufacturer's authorized representative in the EU for product safety is
Oxford University Press España S.A. of Parque Empresarial San Fernando de Henares,
Avenida de Castilla, 2 – 28830 Madrid (www.oup.es/en or product.safety@oup.com).
OUP España S.A. also acts as importer into Spain of products made by the manufacturer.

To my family

Contents

Acknowledgments ix

Note on Translations xi

Preface xiii

List of Figures xv

List of Tables xvii

Introduction: The Migrant's Spirit 1

1. Württemberg, 1817 19

2. New Transatlantic Connections 46

3. Struggles with Impudence 70

4. The Home 92

5. Nation, Incorporated 113

6. The Idea of Deutsche Bank 139

7. Migration-Backed Securities 162

8. Reckoning with the Migrant's Spirit 185

Epilogue: Forgetting America 209

Endnotes 221

Bibliography 295

Index 323

Acknowledgments

This book is based on research I originally did for my PhD dissertation, so I would like to begin my acknowledgments by thanking the Department of History at Stanford University for supporting so many years of graduate study and research. A Charles E. Shepard Scholarship for Graduate Study from Emory University and a predissertation fellowship from the Fritz Thyssen Stiftung paid for language training in Poland, as well as initial trips to the archives in Argentina, Germany, the United States, and Switzerland. The Free University of Berlin sponsored an extended stay in Berlin. The Europe Center at Stanford and a dissertation fellowship from the Mellon Foundation provided funding to complete my studies. The journey from dissertation to book required additional visits to archives that were made possible by the Brown University Department of History, a Richard B. Salomon Faculty Research Award, and a faculty fellowship at Brown's Cogut Institute for the Humanities. Historical research can be expensive, and I am grateful to these institutions and universities for their generosity.

A great deal of what historians do would not be possible without the knowledge and dedication of the scholars and staff who keep the world's archives running smoothly. I would like to take this space to express my deep admiration and gratitude for their work in maintaining a documentary record of the past.

I could not be more thankful to my teachers and mentors for their guidance, wisdom, and patience over the course of years of thinking and writing: Astrid Eckert, Brian Vick, Edith Sheffer, J. P. Daughton, Priya Satia, Richard White, and Norman Naimark. My advisors at Emory introduced me to history and the archives. Edith Sheffer took a chance on me and gave me the courage to pursue the story in those migrant letters. J. P. Daughton taught me how to be a historian not just of Germany, but also of Europe. From Priya Satia I learned about the terrifying power of stories in history. I owe my fascination with the nineteenth century to Richard White, along with much of what I know about political economy and the history of the state. Norman Naimark read the manuscript closely and never stopped talking much-needed sense into me. Without knowing it, my teachers Ran Abramitzky and Kären Wigen were deeply influential in the conceptualization of this project.

Many colleagues and friends at Stanford, Brown, and beyond have read either significant portions of the manuscript or the entire thing, in some cases several times: the anonymous readers at Oxford University Press, Omer Bartov, Holly Case, Bathsheba Demuth, Lukas Dovern, Andrew Elmore, Susan Ferber, Stefan-Ludwig Hoffmann, Nicole Martin, Tara Nummedal, Emily Owens, Steven Press, Lukas Rieppel, Seth Rockman, Michael Steinberg, Jenny Lhamo Tsundu, Brian Vick, Helmut Walser Smith, Natasha Wheatley, and Tara Zahra. I am thankful for their constructive feedback, comments, and insight. I also owe a great debt to Branden Adams, Samuel Huneke, Michelle Lynn Kahn, Vivian Lu, Eda Pepi, George Qiao, Irene Ann Resenly, Stephan Risi, Luca Scholz, James Sheehan, Molly Taylor-Poleskey, Caroline Winterer, and Matthew Wormer for engaging with my work in many thoughtful and illuminating conversations. Last, but not least, this book has benefited in immeasurable ways from the questions and feedback provided by the participants of the History of Capitalism Geballe Research Workshop at the Stanford Center for the Humanities, the Stanford Center for Law and History, the Center for Spatial and Textual Analysis at Stanford, and the European History Workshop at Brown.

I have been fortunate to have a family that has never stopped supporting me in whatever endeavor I have set out to do. They have cared, loved, and listened. They have offered critique and inspiration and assurance. To them, I dedicate this book.

Note on Translations

All translations are my own unless otherwise indicated. In some cases involving unusual semantic complexity or historical significance, the original German was retained (including *Völkerwanderung, Dreistigkeit, Gemütlichkeit, Haus*, and *Sittengesetz*). However, I do not use this approach in all cases. For example, I have opted to translate the word *Auswanderer* (emigrant) into English even though it bears historical significance. I do so mostly in order to be able to accommodate different grammatical constructions. The reader will notice that this choice has yielded phrasing that, strictly speaking, does not correspond to common usage in standard American English. For example, the phrase "the emigrant in America" should read as "the immigrant in America." Likewise, I refer to individuals who "emigrated to America" rather than "immigrated to America." In these and other cases, my intention and guiding principle has been to find a balance between legibility for the reader and deference to the conceptual categories used by historical actors.

Preface

The letters from America were everywhere. I found them tucked inside official government documents and judicial records, reprinted in newspapers, and appended to peasant petitions. Municipal archives had them, as did nearly every ecclesiastical collection and business archive I visited in Germany, Switzerland, Austria, and France.

Initially, I was not sure what to make of the so-called *Amerikabrief*. On the one hand, it was all good news. Personal correspondence of this kind is one of the best sources a social historian can hope to find. Like diaries and other first-person documents, letters offer a fascinating glimpse into the past, shedding light on the lives of ordinary individuals about whom we would otherwise know very little. They are packed with information that is all too often lost to posterity: what people ate for dinner, who they owed money to, what seed they planted that season, who married whom, whose child was recently born, and so on. There are reflections on work and the future, intrigue and love, death and taxes, and everything in between. This is what many a scholar would call a goldmine.

On the other hand, it was not clear to me whether or how I would be able to use this evidence in my work. Letters from America seemed to fall well outside the boundaries of my project, a history of industrialization in the region of Hesse. To justify using Amerikabriefe as primary sources, I would have to contextualize them, and that would require wading into the much larger history of overseas migration, which in Germany is centuries old and global in scale. If the point of my project was to get close to a specific place and its people, it seemed that these letters, rich and fascinating though they were, could only ever be a distraction. So I set them aside.

At least I tried to. But then: here another from California, there one from Quebec City, this one from Australia. Even if there was not an actual letter in the files, people talked about their letters and about the friends and relatives in America with whom they were in touch. At this point, I conceded defeat and decided to allocate a separate chapter to the Amerikabrief. The plan was to open with a brief introduction to the sources as a way of explaining to readers why, despite their seeming distance from Hesse, these letters could nevertheless offer insight into the lives of ordinary Hessians. It was in the course of writing this introduction that I started to wonder: What if these letters did not just offer a unique perspective on the history of industrialization in Hesse, but were also part of that history? Their presence was obviously felt by contemporaries. The authorities always looked on them with suspicion, which was why they were so eager to collect and archive specimens. Businessmen saw in them a resource, a means to get an edge, a way to learn new tricks of the trade. Peasants used them to stay in touch with loved ones and to exchange advice on decisions large and small.

Put another way, the Amerikabrief seemed to have agency, insofar as that may be said of an object. Whether it had enough agency to change the course of history was still unclear at this juncture in my research, but it was a question worth asking. This book is the result. It is no longer solely about industrialization in Hesse. Rather, it is concerned with a burgeoning dialogue carried on in letters and other materials sent across the Atlantic and the unexpected role this exchange played in the triumph of a new, industrial modernity throughout so many of the German lands.

List of Figures

I.1.	*A Letter from America*, by Berthold Woltze (1860)	5
I.2.	Transatlantic mail sailings, 1847–72	6
I.3.	*Telegram from a Better World*, by *Der Kladderadatsch* (1868)	8
1.1.	*Tavern Zum Kranen in Heilbronn*, by Carl Dörr (no date, likely 1830s)	38
1.2.	*Farewell of the Emigrants*, by Carl Wilhelm Hübner (1846)	39
1.3.	*Duke Paul Wilhelm von Württemberg Among the Indians*, artist unknown (no date, likely 1820s)	42
2.1.	*Bride Wagon in Niederwalgern*, artist unknown (ca. 1899–1901)	60
2.2.	Johann Bauer's house in Missouri	64
3.1.	Albert Krause	77
3.2.	A letter from Albert Krause	80
4.1.	*The Weaver*, by Max Liebermann (1884)	95
4.2.	*Geese Pluckers*, by Max Liebermann (1871–72)	96
4.3.	Fighting in the name of the home	107
5.1.	Immigration to the United States, select countries of origin, 1820–70	121
5.2.	Castle Garden, New York	123
5.3.	The Germania Life Insurance Company Building	125
5.4.	Hermann Marcuse	130
6.1.	Friedrich Kapp	145
6.2.	Ludwig Bamberger	146

List of Tables

2.1. US States and Territories Passing Laws or Regulations
to Encourage Immigration, 1845–75   67
8.1. The GmbH by Size of Founding Capital, 1892–98   207

Introduction

THE MIGRANT'S SPIRIT

TO READ THE documentary record left behind by nineteenth-century Germans is to step into a haunted world. Ghosts, spirits, and other supernatural creatures lurk everywhere. Some were harmless curiosities, like poltergeists, the spirits of the dead, or apparitions of the Virgin Mary; others, like national spirits or the specter of communism, were considered capable of enchanting entire societies and shaping the course of history.[1] And so, when a major historical event that was later dubbed the *Industrial Revolution* began to utterly transform the region of Germany around midcentury, observers were fast to spot a spiritual changing of the guard. It was said that a society that had long been possessed by the so-called *Schlendrian*, a good-natured ghost who compelled people to indulge their inner sloth, had succumbed to a new, powerful demon: the "capitalist spirit" (*kapitalistischer Geist*).[2]

What follows is a study of this capitalist spirit: what it was, where it came from, and how it paved the way for Germany's rapid transformation from a relative economic backwater into one of the world's most dynamic industrial economies during the second half of the nineteenth century. The book's claim is that the phenomenon was composed of a set of perspectives, attitudes, and ideas that initially formed abroad, among a burgeoning diaspora in North America numbering in the millions, and that subsequently re-entered communities in Europe via written correspondence and an ever-growing literature about "America." I argue that a significant portion of industrial modernity in Germany, from the timing of its arrival to some of its more recognizable institutional particularities, such as the universal bank model of industrial finance, can be explained as a function of these cultural exchanges across the Atlantic.[3]

Cultural exchange across long distances was one of the hallmarks of the nineteenth century, a period of astonishing human mobility around the world. Driven by poverty, politics, and pessimism about the future, tens of millions of people traversed forbidding sea- and landscapes in search of a better life, moving from India to Africa and Southeast Asia, from Europe to the Americas and Siberia, and from China to Manchuria and across the Pacific. Few contemporary societies escaped the consequences of these vast population movements and the global connections that arose in their wake, and a great many underwent lasting cultural, political, social, and economic change as a result. Germany was one of those places rendered almost unrecognizable: a classic "emigrant nation" like Italy, India, or Ireland. And yet Germany also stood apart because it was one of the first to be engulfed by these globalizing forces and one of the few to have benefited on the whole in terms of its economic development. As such, the country is a case study of the many contingencies that have shaped cultural exchange in the past, as well as a reminder of the deep inequities that attended this great age of globalization.[4]

In pulling back the curtain on the capitalist spirit, I do not mean to suggest that the concept itself can be dismissed as mere superstition. Rather, I think it can offer us clues about the nature of the historical dynamics at play. The notion of a *migrant's spirit* is in this sense less a pun than an attempt to take seriously what contemporaries saw or believed they saw. Let me briefly explain.

Observers in nineteenth-century Germany tended to have little use for another, readily available explanatory metaphor for the events in question, namely, the idea of an industrial revolution, which had been around since at least the 1880s, usually in reference to the English experience.[5] Partly this was because revolutions, at least as they were understood in the nineteenth century, were widely considered to be the work of partisans who shaped history according to well-defined visions of the future. Germany had its fair share of such partisans, but it often seemed as though they were of little consequence. Since at least the late eighteenth century, merchants and businesspeople, reform-minded bureaucrats, and a great many intellectuals had sounded the horns for a modern, factory-centered regime of production, mostly to no avail. After decades of seemingly futile agitating, many of them eventually lost hope, stopped proselytizing, and, in some cases, left the country. Much to their chagrin, it was at this very moment, in the 1850s and 1860s, that a noticeable shift suddenly did take hold in popular attitudes and opinions regarding the new industrial regime of production. Before long, the now-famous period of accelerating economic growth and transformation commenced.[6]

It seems only natural, in hindsight, that contemporaries would try to fill the void with other agents of change: spirits, ghosts, demons.[7] And yet, the supernatural was not just a placeholder. It also reflected a particular understanding of the nature of historical change. Once again, the industrial revolution metaphor was not considered all that useful because it implied a civilizational clash between old and new, with the latter either displacing or destroying the former. Reality looked different to many observers, with familiar people and ideas doing slightly new things. Peasant artisans were heading to the factories, cities, and mines, but they still looked and carried themselves like peasant artisans. Merchants became financiers and titans of industry, but they still looked and carried themselves like the old merchants. Greed became defined as the rational pursuit of one's self-interest, but it still looked a lot like greed. Put another way, there was a great deal of continuity, much more than was implied by a revolution. Spirits did a better job of describing this continuity, because they manifested themselves through, not in spite of, the existing world.[8]

Of course, there was also novelty. Very few observers could or even wanted to deny the importance of revolutionary technologies like the steam engine or the telegraph. The point was more that even minor innovations could have far-reaching consequences for the course of history. "We today can barely imagine anymore the enormous ingenuity that inhered in the idea that one could accumulate money by doing work," wrote Werner Sombart, one of the most influential economists of his day, in his two-volume study on "modern capitalism" from 1902. Not so long ago, Sombart explained, people believed that the sole purpose of working was to earn one's daily bread: nothing more, nothing less. Those desiring wealth and power had to acquire them by engaging in disreputable and shameful activities like plunder, war, treasure hunting, or alchemy. That any of this should come as a surprise, according to Sombart, was itself evidence of the historic significance of this shift in thinking. All it had taken for capitalism to triumph was that such an ancient and ordinary activity like work be devoted to a different purpose than in the past, in this case the accumulation of capital.[9]

Though Sombart is no longer cited, most historians in the early twenty-first century agree with his assertion that economic modernity emerged as a consequence of changes at the margin. Taking a job in a large factory in the city or investing money in an unproven technology like the railroad or telegraph—decisions that, if taken by large enough numbers of people, had immense social, cultural, and political implications—amounted to a relatively minor leap of faith for an individual.[10] It is these minor leaps of faith that fell under the purview of spirits, ghosts, and demons. While the latter never told anyone exactly what to do or even how, they did offer encouragement and purpose. They nudged people along, giving them the confidence to act on choices that, deep inside, they had often already made.

What is interesting about the German case is that here contemporaries had begun, around the middle of the nineteenth century, to turn to a place they called "America" for such encouragement and purpose. Berthold Woltze, a realist painter from Saxony, captured the dynamic in a work from 1860 titled *A Letter from America*. In the painting, an elderly couple, along with a younger woman, perhaps their daughter or granddaughter, pore over a letter that appears to have arrived moments earlier. Their sense of wonder is palpable. The daughter's gaze suggests that she especially is spellbound by the piece of paper. She wants to get closer, to touch and hold it, but she is kept from doing so by the elderly woman beside her, whose hands clutch it firmly. All the while, the man standing in the back struggles to reach past the two women in a vain attempt to point to an overlooked detail.

Woltze, who was partial to the plight of the peasantry, was surely romanticizing his subjects. Still, such scenes of communal reading of the *Amerikabrief* did take place and, indeed, were quickly multiplying at exactly this moment in time. They were the product of a wide range of historical events and developments—some dating to the eighteenth century and even earlier, some more recent—that converged in the middle of the nineteenth century. To begin, there was the explosive growth of the German community in North America since the 1830s and 1840s. Although peasants from the territories of the Holy Roman Empire had emigrated to the Americas (and other destinations in Europe and elsewhere) for as long as anyone could remember, the numbers were considerably larger than they had been in earlier periods. Some seventy thousand people from the region are believed to have ventured to North America via the port of Philadelphia between 1727 and 1775—about as many as might now emigrate in a single year. In the 1840s and 1850s, when several catastrophes struck at once, including a devastating potato blight and a major political earthquake known as the Revolution of 1848, emigration grew to an even greater scale, with up to a quarter million people departing German territories in certain years. The vast majority, well over 90 percent, headed for destinations in the United States, which meant that by the 1860s the German community in that part of the "New World" had swollen to well over two million. Ever

FIGURE I.1 *A Letter from America. Ein Brief aus Amerika* by Berthold Woltze (1860). Oil on canvas, 94 × 77 cm.
Source: Courtesy of the Deutsches Historisches Museum, Berlin.

since, everyone in the German lands seemed to have an "uncle" in America, or at least to know someone who did.[11]

Furthermore, a significant portion of the population in German states and territories was at least partially literate. The product of a quirk of the region's political past, which had seen local rulers regard it as in their interest to invest in primary education, relatively widespread literacy meant that people not only knew someone in America but also could communicate with them via mail.[12] Such communication became even more likely after ca. 1850, when new technologies like the steam engine and steel hull, along with a series of bilateral treaties signed between the United States and central European governments, produced a dramatic drop in the cost of sending a standard, fifteen-gram letter across the Atlantic. As a result, even those of modest means could exchange letters several times a year. And many did. Although mail statistics from this period are patchy, it has been estimated that the volume of private

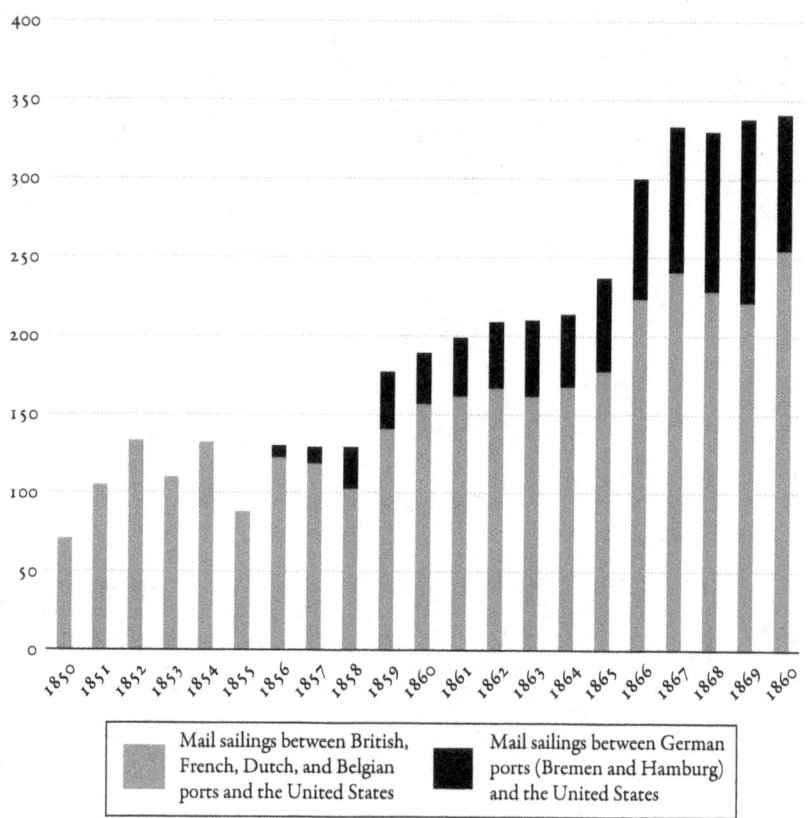

FIGURE I.2 **Transatlantic mail sailings, 1847–72.** This chart shows the number of port calls in a given year made by licensed mail steamers carrying correspondence, newspapers, and packages between European countries and the United States. Such data can offer a more granular picture than aggregate estimates of the growth of transatlantic correspondence after midcentury. Notice that up until the 1860s, most of the mail exchanged between German states and the United States flowed through French and Dutch ports (it was transported overland to and from its final destinations in Germany). Later on new shipping lines based in Bremen and Hamburg started to handle a growing portion of German–US mail traffic.

Source: Calculated by the author based on data in Walter Hubbard, Richard F. Winter, and Susan M. McDonald, *North Atlantic Mail Sailings, 1840–75* (Canton, OH: US Philatelic Classics Society, 1988).

letters arriving in German states from senders in North America grew from just a few hundred thousand a year in 1850 to nearly a million per year by the end of that decade. It continued to rise thereafter, to one and a half million per year in the 1860s, two million in the 1870s, and four million in the 1880s. Such figures were extraordinary by contemporary standards: The United Kingdom, with its much more intensive political, cultural, and economic ties to the former North American colonies, recorded just under two million letters arriving from the United States in the late 1850s.[13]

This great increase in correspondence around midcentury plays an important role in the making of the migrant's spirit. But numbers alone tell only part of the story. Another part has to do with the privileged place that America began to occupy in the imagination of contemporaries in the nineteenth century, when it was increasingly regarded as the epitome of progress, action, movement, and modernity. Some historians have gone so far as to describe the act of engaging with America, whether through migrant correspondence or a burgeoning secondary literature of popular histories, novels, news columns, or business reports, as akin to "traveling into modernity." Woltze's painting certainly can be read in that way, with the lighting and positioning of the Amerikabrief evoking the proverbial window into the future. But the point was also made explicit by contemporaries, for example, in a sketch that was published in 1868 in Berlin's middle-class satire magazine *Der Kladderadatsch*. Titled *A Telegram from a Better World*, it depicted America in its female personification, Columbia, hovering above the clouds, with the United States flag in one hand and the transatlantic telegraph cable in the other. Beneath her, half a dozen hapless European politicians can be found panning for revenue with old-fashioned sieves. Their admiration for America is not the same as that of the three figures in Woltze's painting, but it is there, in their astonishment, irritation, and envy.[14]

The sketch in the *Kladderadatsch* is, of course, a satirical commentary. The magazine's readers would have had vivid memories of a time when neither America nor the people who lived there cast such a spell over Europeans. Well into the nineteenth century, those who left for America were seen as belonging to the dregs of society: criminals, heretics, adventurers, the poor, other good-for-nothings. Contemporaries did not look kindly on these black sheep of society, much less accept their advice on questions concerning the future. Even when members of the respectable classes were involved, such as when long-distance merchants sent their sons abroad to staff remote trade posts, there were few who would have considered insight garnered beyond European shores relevant or applicable to the conditions in the metropole. North

FIGURE 1.3 *Telegram from a Better World*. A satirical commentary on the contemporary fascination with the United States, published in the Berlin magazine *Der Kladderadatsch*. The caption reads, "Newyork. 'The national accounts have grown by ten million dollars since the beginning of June.' (Some European finance minister.) Those fellows, don't even have a standing army, but they want to have a say!"

Source: Courtesy of the Universitätsbibliothek Heidelberg Digital Library.

America was thought to be an especially backward and primitive place. In contrast to much more economically vibrant regions like the West Indies or South America, North America appeared to be nothing more than a refuge for poor pietists, ascetics, missionaries, and coarse woodsmen like the fur-trapping coureurs de bois.[15]

This original disdain for America and for those who absconded there is a useful reminder that the mere ability to communicate across long distances does not necessarily engender a meaningful exchange of ideas. Europeans had long ventured abroad, not just to the Americas but also to every other conceivable corner of the world, and for an equally long time they had communicated, or tried to communicate, with those left behind. But it was not until the nineteenth century, and initially primarily in German-speaking regions of central Europe, that the emigrant's word began to be taken seriously, let alone elevated above other, more local and trusted sources of information. Understanding the migrant's spirit consequently requires more than the identification of movements and connections. What is also needed is an investigation of prevailing perceptions and beliefs about these same movements and connections.

The first two chapters of this book are an attempt at such an investigation. The once-dominant account of Europeans' infatuation with America in this period placed a great deal of emphasis on the events of 1776—American independence and the birth of the US Constitution—as well as the gradual spread of Enlightenment ideals in nineteenth-century Europe.[16] Both developments were, no doubt, important. What they do not explain, however, are the many striking differences in perception that prevailed across different parts of the continent. Why, for instance, did France, arguably Europe's epicenter of emancipatory politics, never valorize its emigrants or America in the same way as did its neighbor just across the Rhine? Understanding these differences requires consideration of local dynamics. Chapter 1 does this by reconstructing the politics surrounding a major exodus from the kingdom of Württemberg in 1817, an event that has long been regarded as one of the starting guns to the great departure that gripped Europe and the rest of the world in the ensuing decades.

What is revealed here is that the moral elevation of the emigrant in North America was propelled by a novel account about the nation's past, present, and future. According to this story, which originated in the turmoil of the Seven Years' War as well as the subsequent confrontations with revolutionary France, the act of emigrating, particularly to North America, was articulated as a uniquely German solution to hardship and tyranny, much like barricades and the guillotine were regarded as uniquely French tools of emancipation. One of this story's leading protagonists, the rabble-rousing Romantic Friedrich Schiller, went so far as to hail the Germanic "spirit of migration and plunder" as an emancipatory agent not just for Germany but also for humanity writ large. Schiller argued that migrating Germanic peoples had long spearheaded the struggle with despotism, whether it was in late antiquity when they toppled a corrupt Roman Empire, or during the medieval crusades, when Teutonic knights descended on the Islamic kingdoms of the Levant. Each act of conquest was an act of pacification: It "prepared the stage" (*Raum ist jetzt gemacht auf der Bühne*) for all the later experiments with good government, including those more recently underway in France. Subsequent writers elaborated on the story by suggesting that Germanic colonizers also defeated despotic regimes in the New World and that their efforts had already borne fruit in the guise of the US Constitution. Many concluded that North America at the time offered the most fertile soils for the blossoming of Germanic ideas about liberty and they began encouraging their poor countrymen to head there whenever circumstances—oppressive governments, poor harvests, unhappiness in general—required it.[17]

What is interesting about this story, versions of which could be found at both ends of the political spectrum, is that it inscribed the act of migrating to North America into the nation's essence. By including emigrants within the national community and by reconceptualizing North America as an extension of national geography—a colonial space in all but name—both acquired a newfound respect and standing in the communities of origin.[18]

This nationalizing logic in turn is key to understanding the immense clout of the migrant's spirit in Germany during the nineteenth century. For one, it shows that the kind of intense engagement with America that Woltze immortalized in his painting did not arise merely from a naive fascination with the "land of freedom." It was also borne out of a sense of responsibility that was felt toward people who could no longer be dismissed as wayward relatives lost to a remote wilderness. Those individuals were instead to be regarded as full-fledged members of the family inhabiting a Germany of their own and, as such, deserving of the same attention, support, and benefit of the doubt as any other kin or compatriot. This did not mean that judgment was withheld or that differences of opinion suddenly disappeared; it only meant that much more effort was put into working through disagreements, maintaining relationships, and perhaps also ensuring a process of cultural reproduction. What was true at the level of the family was also true at the level of state. Many

German rulers in this period, and especially those among them who claimed the mantle of guardian of the nation, found themselves compelled to cater to emigrants in America, both in word and in action, despite their profound misgivings about such deserters and traitors.

For another, the nationalization of the emigrants in America helps to explain their ability to shape opinion on the new, modern economy. In Germany, skepticism about the emerging industrial regime of production derived as much from its novel and alienating effects as it did from its presumed associations with rival national cultures, above all the French and English. Efforts to liberalize labor markets and lift corporate restrictions, so crucial to mobilizing skilled workers for a centralized regime of production (and the subject of Chapter 3), often foundered on an intense hostility toward "French" laissez-faire political economy or the English free-trade "Manchester school." Similarly, the idea of the breadwinner–homemaker model of domesticity, examined in Chapter 4 and constituting yet another ideological pillar of the emerging production regime, was in the minds of many contemporaries associated with just the kind of "dark magic" (*schwarze Kunst*) that only the French mind seemed capable of.[19]

The joint-stock corporation, the focus of Chapter 5, suffered from much the same poor reputation. Often linked to an older and more brutal era of English or Dutch colonialism, especially in light of new expansionist wars pursued by the English East India Company that culminated in the Indian Revolt of 1857, it was not considered a useful model for a nation that prided itself on practicing an allegedly more orderly, less violent, and more respectful form of colonialism. The same was true of the universal bank model of industrial finance, explored in Chapter 6. Understood in the early twenty-first century to be one of the defining characteristics of the German economy as it existed in this period, it was once bemoaned as the legal incarnation of French frivolity and Dutch adventurism—as was the idea of investing capital in fledgling colonial economies in North America and elsewhere, a key precondition to the rapid growth of Germany's rise as one of the world's leading exporters (Chapter 7).

Emigrants and émigrés reporting from North America rarely argued for the straightforward adoption in Germany of these institutions, ideas, and practices. They did not have to. All that was needed to render them transferrable to the German context was to cast them in the idiom of American culture and politics. Some adaptation was still necessary, to be sure. As Chapter 8 reveals, such a process of adaptation could yield entirely novel economic institutions, in this case a bizarre new corporate legal form better known by its acronym, GmbH. But the conceptual gap that had to be bridged was far narrower, because America was not France, England, or Holland. If not an actual extension of the nation, it was certainly much closer in both kindred and spirit.[20]

German nationalism was the most important source of strength of the migrant's spirit. At the same time, it was also its greatest weakness—and a reminder of the limits of the argument in this book. To be susceptible to advice from the diaspora in North America, one had to embrace some version of the national idea. This was hardly a given in the German lands of the nineteenth century, where proponents of nationalism often labored as hard as economic modernizers to persuade the public of their visions of the future. When national consciousness was subdued or lacking altogether, interest in ideas from America was commensurately low—as the renowned political economist and fervent proponent of modern industry Friedrich List famously discovered. List had spent the better part of the 1820s in the Blue Mountains of Pennsylvania, where he had been engaged in the construction of railroads and, more generally, the economic development of Pennsylvania coal country. When he returned to Europe in the early 1830s, hoping to put to use the "higher perspective on political economy" he had acquired in America in an effort to drag Germany out of its own backwardness, he was met with nothing but scorn and ridicule. From Prussia to Saxony to Hamburg and Baden, List's proposals for a national railroad system were brushed aside by businessmen and politicians alike as the crude talk of an American frontiersman. This was not surprising. At the time, the national idea remained suspect in most of these states, a radical political ideology that threatened established political and economic elites. But all that soon changed. By the middle of the century, Prussia especially had begun to loudly assert its ambition to lead the struggle for German national unity. List by this time was dead—frustrated and likely driven to madness by the repeated rejections of what, in hindsight, were genuinely prescient ideas, he committed suicide in 1846—but a second wave of German American émigrés was making its rounds, bearing much the same advice. And this time Berlin listened, reluctantly but attentively.[21]

To argue that "news from America" informed individuals' choices about work, business, and economic governance in the German lands is to make two larger claims about the region's history. The first is spatial in nature: It contends that Germany's path toward a new industrial modernity led, at least in part, through North America and the wider Atlantic world. That this might not strike readers as particularly revelatory is a testament to just how much our understanding of this history has changed in recent years. Until not too long ago, industrialization in Germany was understood as an almost entirely local and, at best, regional event. Leading chroniclers argued that Germany remained an economic backwater well into the nineteenth century, bereft of the Atlantic and global connections that thrust its empire-chasing neighbors to the top of the world economy. More recent accounts tell a different story. Although nobody would deny the importance of local dynamics and factors—this book very much included—it has become quite clear that long before the nineteenth century, the German lands had been deeply embedded in global networks of trade, with people profiting in equal measure from colonial plunder and violence as their counterparts in the traditional European empires.[22] What *The Migrant's Spirit* adds to the newer narrative is attention to the intellectual and even affective impulses from abroad, to the ambitions and desires and ideas about right and wrong that compelled contemporaries to set aside any uncertainties and reservations they might have still had—and hence to embrace a new industrial modernity before it came into full swing.

The second claim that this book makes concerns the character of this new modernity: what it was and what it looked like. Karl Marx, whose view on the matter continues to shape our own, understood it to be a predominantly urban world dominated by imposing factories and terrifying machines. The surrounding rural areas, with their peasants and small-scale agriculture, were to Marx and like-minded others little more than the remnant of a feudal past: a world that, apart from supplying the cities and factories with raw material, human labor, and markets to dump their finished merchandise into, played no role in the next phase of history. This book presents a different picture. Cities and factories, rather than dominating the scene, are ensconced within a broader landscape of villages and rural ways of living. Instead of being a victim of inertia and the idiocy of tradition, this rural world is a lively and forward-looking place, a destination, rather than a place to leave behind. At its center stand the emigrants. Creatures of the countryside, they are people who aspired, if not always successfully, to maintain their rural way of life. It is they who ultimately infused, however unintentionally, the adjacent pockets of smog-emitting industry with their dynamism and meaning.

I recognize that this second claim is somewhat more controversial than the first. It is one thing to argue, as many economic historians do, that a thriving agrarian sector provided the material foundations for an expanding industrial one.[23] It is however quite another to suggest that this agrarian sector furnished the ideas and motivation as well. Yet it appears that most contemporaries understood industrialization less as an end in itself and more as a means to reaching, or building, some kind of agrarian utopia. "Agriculture is the true destiny of man," proclaimed Argentine statesman Manuel Belgrano, in what could very well be described as the guiding principle of the nineteenth century. "Everything depends on and results from the cultivation of the land; without it there are no raw materials for the arts, industry therefore cannot develop, no material can be supplied for commerce." Implicit in such declarations was that industrialization, even in its most intensive phases, neither could nor ever would eclipse the countryside in the manner that Marx imagined, because it was from that countryside that the industrial economy derived both its material inputs and its ideological impulses and justifications.[24]

Belgrano's assertions were, of course, not entirely new at this time. Europeans' fascination with land and agriculture as the backbone of civilization dated to at least the seventeenth century, if not earlier. But the agrarian world acquired new significance in light of the many revolutions that shook Europe and the Americas in the late eighteenth century and disseminated new ideas about government and liberty. According to one such theory, often attributed to the English philosopher and political theorist John Locke, land played a constitutive role in the emergence of individual liberty. By cultivating the soil, individuals acquired wealth and property, liberating themselves from material want and becoming free. The great nineteenth-century liberal statesman Alexis de Tocqueville prodded his government to acquire new land for French peasants to settle and cultivate lest it jeopardize the future of the French republic (he was thinking of Algeria at the time). The same logic inhered in Thomas Jefferson's famous description of the United States as an "empire of liberty." Westward expansion was to Jefferson and to so many Americans of that period an indispensable ingredient of American liberty and democracy.[25]

Jefferson's recasting of what was, in essence, a bloody conquest into an exercise in liberty reveals how this agrarian ideology could justify profoundly dubious policies and institutions. Settler colonies were one of these dubious ideas, but so were key features of the emerging, industrial regime of production. Peasants tended to find it much easier to accept the noxious aspects of city life, mining pits, or factory labor if such experiences could be understood as a temporary phase in life rather than a destination, as a means for salvaging a cherished rural existence and a steppingstone to a homestead and landed independence. In the same vein, a speculative investment in once-unproven technologies like railroads or telegraphs appeared much less speculative—certainly less dubious—when the purpose of the endeavor was to subject more land to the plow and, in so doing, encourage the spread of civilized society and good government.[26]

For contemporaries living in colonial peripheries like Argentina, the United States, or Australia, and for anyone familiar with these exceedingly rural places, the dominance of the century's agrarian ideal was all too obvious. In Europe, however, it was and continues to be much less visible. Because they were short on land and living in an overpopulated world, so the argument went, Europeans could never have entertained the same homesteading dreams as their New World counterparts. The continent, in effect, had no choice but to turn itself into the "workshop of the world"—by force, if necessary. And so it was in Europe that Marx's vision of an urban-industrial society came closest to being realized, as portrayed in the dystopias of Charles Dickens or Émile Zola as crime-ridden urban spaces, monstrous mineshafts, and great halls of child-maiming machinery. Only in Europe could one debate the relative merits of an "agrarian" versus an "industrial" state, as the Germans did at the end of the century, because only there was an exclusively industrial state thinkable and desirable.[27]

The Migrant's Spirit tells a different story. It has been said that nineteenth-century America was exceptional in the world because, although it was steeped in an agrarian ideology, it also boasted a robust industrial heartland. Yet the same was true of Europe, and especially of Germany. This is not just because so many contemporaries still lived in an overwhelmingly rural setting; it is also because they *wanted* to live in an overwhelmingly rural setting. Throughout the nineteenth century and well into the twentieth, the countryside beckoned as a site of emancipation; to its ultimate attainment all else was subjugated.[28] Here, the diaspora in America once more played a pivotal role. Itself the product of the proliferation of agrarian ideals—Schiller's account of the German "spirit of migration and plunder" was full of agrarian imagery—the expatriate community put the prospect of landed independence within closer reach than ever for contemporaries in Europe, mainly by setting up all the networks, knowledge, and resources. Already by the 1850s, the attainment of a homestead in the Ohio valley or in western Texas was nearly as plausible for a Pomeranian peasant as it was for his counterpart in rural New England. Capitalists in Bremen, Stuttgart, or Frankfurt am Main could and did profit in equal measure as the so-called brahmins of Boston from financing the world's next agrarian utopia. Proximity of this kind reinforced the ideal of the age with tangible rewards.[29]

This book's narrative ends in the 1890s, although the process of industrialization in Germany can hardly be said to have run its course by then. What makes the decade a caesura nonetheless is that by then, the agrarian ideal, on which so much of modern industrial society had come to depend, was seriously questioned for the first time. Precipitating this rare moment of introspection was the notorious declaration of Wisconsin historian Frederick Jackson Turner, delivered at the 1893 world exhibition in Chicago, that the United States had completed the conquest of the North American West and the frontier was no more. The idea that America should be closed to further settlement unsettled observers in Germany, who felt that the door to modernity itself had been shut. Some called for the immediate opening of new frontiers elsewhere in the world, such as Africa, South America, and eastern Europe. Others were less sanguine. Max Weber, who in 1904 had completed a tour of the Oklahoma Territory, Wisconsin, and other ostensible heartlands of modernity and was reminded of the fact that America was far more an idea than an actual place, had concluded then and there that no ersatz colonies, whether in Africa or elsewhere, could ever replace it. The Germans had better try to forget the agrarian dream. In "modern capitalism," he wrote, individuals did not work and accumulate in anticipation of landed independence or some other materialist rewards; they worked and accumulated simply for the sake of work and accumulation. A modern capitalist shunned ostentatious displays of wealth and found joy and self-actualization and even salvation in the monotonous grind of his labor. Although such an attitude might seem "irrational" to some observers, to Weber it seemed to be the most plausible way forward.[30]

Forgetting the agrarian dream would, of course, require the Germans to forget an important part of who they were, to absolve themselves of that vaunted "spirit of migration and plunder." As Hans Ratjen, a Hamburg lawyer who shared Weber's misgivings about new colonial adventures and Wilhelmine "world policy" (*Weltpolitik*), put it in a critique in 1908 on the efforts to extend government protection to German settlers overseas, "We should pay tribute to our Germanic heritage, but we cannot go on living exclusively by the laws of our ancestors... who regarded as their home the war barge and not their native soil."[31] Weber agreed, and he found an answer in the history of the Protestant Reformation. As an event that began in Germany and was spearheaded by one of the most pious and patriotic of the Germans, Martin Luther, the Protestant Reformation offered a promising alternative to narrating the nation's past, a new founding ethos that elevated ostensibly more refined Christian ethical maxims over savage pagan ones—one that, as such, might be far better suited to a modern world bereft of the frontiers and wildernesses that once covered the earth. That the capitalist spirit is associated in the early twenty-first century with an ethic of faith therefore has as much to do with Max Weber, the great theorist of capitalism, as it does with the world he tried to move on from, a world that, for much of the nineteenth century, was caught in something of a love affair with its ancient, pagan past.³²

A final note on how this book is put together: What follows is not intended as a comprehensive survey of industrial modernity in Germany, which, after all, encompassed an extraordinarily wide range of political, social, economic, intellectual, cultural, and technological changes and developments. *The Migrant's Spirit* instead focuses on a selection of ideas and institutions that are widely seen as having been essential to the stunning acceleration of growth and transformation that turned Germany into an industrial powerhouse in the 1850s, 1860s, and 1870s. Following two initial scene-setting chapters that excavate and reconstruct the new transatlantic connection that had emerged by midcentury between Germany and North America, each subsequent chapter explores one of these ideas and institutions: the principle of free labor and enterprise, the breadwinner–homemaker model of domesticity, the joint-stock corporation, the universal bank, investment in the New World, and the corporate legal form known as the GmbH. The claim in each instance is that understanding how and why contemporaries came to accept these particular features of the new economy into their daily lives can offer insight into other dimensions of contemporary industrial modernity. If they could pass muster, then so could others—and perhaps by way of similar historical dynamics.

Emphasis meanwhile is placed on individuals. No more than a few dozen people populate these pages, and some chapters center on the life of a single person and their most trusted circle of friends, relatives, and business associates. There are obviously risks in proceeding this way, but I have found that the nature of the problem warrants it. The process by which individuals made decisions about their future work lives, businesses, families, and communities was almost always a profoundly idiosyncratic one. Whereas some made their choices on a whim, others fretted over them for years while they gathered more information, solicited advice, contemplated risks, and labored to reconcile contradictions. It may be impossible to know exactly what went through contemporaries' minds as they confronted a changing world. But I think it behooves us to at least try to understand their thought processes, and the way many historians do this is by zooming in. A close-up perspective allows them to tell a story that goes well beyond the most salient turning points in a person's life: one that encompasses moments not just of clarity and success but also of indecision and disappointment.

This approach consumes a lot of space, which puts a limit on the amount of terrain that can be covered. But the payoff is, I think, considerable. For one, narratives of this kind can shed light on the many contingencies that have shaped the lives of the people of the past. For another, it can give us a sense of the coercive power of uncertainty. Most of the individuals I encountered in the course of my research for this book would have liked nothing more than to skip ahead to the end, to know where they were headed, to understand the meaning of it all. But they could not. It was that feeling of not knowing, of contending with unfinished thoughts, that would have led them to improvise or act on what often turned out to be harebrained advice from the proverbial "uncle in America." *The Migrant's Spirit* is in this sense a book about our everyday struggles to finish unfinished thoughts and how history moves as a consequence.

The Migrant's Spirit: How Industrial Modernity Came to the German Lands. Benjamin P. Hein,
Oxford University Press. © Oxford University Press 2025. DOI: 10.1093/9780197831052.003.0001

I

Württemberg, 1817

THE PEASANT, A certain Christoph Schaar from the village of Weinsberg, in the kingdom of Württemberg, did not strike Friedrich List as a typical emigrant to America. He appeared to be neither rich nor poor—with some land to his name, he claimed about 4,000 gulden in property—and he seemed to be of sound mind. He made no indication that he believed America to be some land of milk and honey, and he never mentioned any divine calling either. And he had not tried to evade List, a royal official there on orders of the king, as an emigrant might. To the contrary, Schaar appreciated "that the government for once comes to see us" and soon launched into an extended monologue about all that ailed him and his family.[1]

All this was a bit unusual, but List appreciated Schaar's honesty. His assignment that May of 1817 was to gather as much information as possible on behalf of the royal government in Stuttgart about the unusually large exodus of people from Württemberg. Schaar at first seemed to make the task easy. Yet the longer List listened to the man, the more puzzled he grew. None of the reasons Schaar cited for going to America made any sense. Schaar complained at length about his taxes and the quartering of soldiers. He detailed a petty dispute with another villager about a maid and her lover. He grumbled about the corruption of the magistrate and about a local official who called him a "rude fellow" and his wife a "quarrelsome broad." And he fumed about a half-hour stint he spent in jail for objecting to such insults, although, interestingly enough, he claimed he would not have minded the jail time if only they had put him in the citizen's tower (*Bürgerturm*) rather than the murderer's dungeon (*Malefizgefängnis*).[2] Schaar was about to carry on about something else when List, growing impatient, burst out, "But that cannot be a reason to leave your fatherland and move to a faraway country"![3]

Suddenly the man went silent. While he did mumble a few more words, about the recent harvest failure of 1816—it had been a tough year, with grain prices doubling and, in some cases, even tripling—and again the taxes, their conversation was, for all intents and purposes, over.[4] List did not mean to offend, and he did not consider Schaar's grievances frivolous. A reform-minded official who cared deeply about the future of Württemberg, List himself had long taken issue with the government's policies, which in his mind depressed commerce and exacerbated the effects of the harvest failures. One of the reasons List had agreed to travel to Weinsberg to speak to emigrants was because he wanted to ensure that the king heard about these issues directly from his subjects.

What List did mean to say was that emigration to America was a rather strange and disproportionate response to the grievances cited. Taxes, corruption, and abusive officials were all important issues, but they were by no means new in Württemberg. Admittedly, some of them had grown worse under Friedrich I. But Friedrich was no longer king at this time, having passed away in October 1816. Sitting now on the throne was his son, Wilhelm I, who, it was rumored, was a much more empathetic man and certainly better liked than his father, because he seemed "able to listen to advice and also follow it." There was a sense in Württemberg that spring that since the young Wilhelm had ascended, the country stood on the verge of a new era. That Schaar would choose this moment to abscond to an "unknown, unimproved, and faraway land" like America seemed puerile, if not altogether mad.[5]

Adding to the puzzle was the fact that America seemed to have so little to offer to someone like Schaar. Even if he and his family managed to survive the Atlantic voyage unscathed—and that was a big if—they would still find themselves alone in a foreign and, as List saw it, primitive country. There would be taxes and village politics there, too, except that as foreigners the Schaars would have even less control over their own fate. If they chose to move to the continent's more sparsely populated interior, they would have to contend with extreme isolation and material deprivation, not to mention hostile Native Americans. Of course, it was possible, and List conceded as much, that he was mistaken about the conditions in America.[6] But even if that were true, it would still leave him with Schaar's rather bizarre claim that the last straw had been the assault on his good name: "That they stuck me in the Malefizgefängnis was difficult for me, as an honorable citizen (*ehrlicher Bürger*), and that was when I decided to leave. Initially it was my intention to settle somewhere else in our district . . . but when good news arrived from America, I decided to join the emigrants. If only they had put me in the Bürgerturm, I would not have made the decision to leave."[7] Granted, the dungeon was a fate reserved for murderers, traitors, heretics, the insane, and other irredeemables. But then, was that not true of emigration as well? One could argue that emigration was worse than the dungeon, given that running off to America also carried the stain of cowardice. Emigrants slipped away under the cover of darkness not just to escape punishment and debtors but also to avoid the judgment and wrath of their families and communities (whom the authorities would likely hold responsible for any outstanding debts). On the rare occasion that their departure took place in public, it was because the authorities wanted to make an example out of them: the banishment of a sinner, the expulsion of an Other.[8]

Needless to say, none of this described Christoph Schaar or, for that matter, any of the other more than one hundred emigrants List interviewed that spring in villages across the uplands just east of Heilbronn. He found that all of them were decidedly respectable members of their communities, honest and hardworking people with families and property to their name. None averted their gaze when he approached them, and most eagerly volunteered their stories. They complained of taxes and corruption, but like Schaar they professed their readiness to "bear it all" were it not for various indignities suffered along the way: verbal insults from officials, bureaucratic chicanery, excessive fines and punishments. The choice to "leave the fatherland" had been "very difficult" and they had shed "bitter tears." Some even demanded to speak to the king because "surely he would help." List was dumbfounded. He wanted to believe them, but common sense suggested he should better not. He began to wonder if they were telling the whole story, whether they had fallen prey to sweet-talking merchants, mendacious letters, or manipulative foreign agents. How else could it be explained that people who had made a point of worrying about their dignity would resort to such an undignified act as emigrating to America?[9]

One way to answer this question—one that List himself never countenanced—was that emigration no longer meant what he thought it meant: that it had shed its wickedness and acquired an aura of respectability, that what was once a mark of shame had been transformed into an act of moral fortitude and independence.[10] Granted, such transformations are rare: It does not happen often that people turn right into wrong and vice versa. But sometimes they do, and when that happens worlds get turned upside down. For that reason alone, the puzzle of Württemberg/1817 is of interest. Another reason is that the event took place at the beginning of an entire epoch of mass flight from Europe. At least twenty-five thousand people left the region over the subsequent two years—an astonishing number for a place that had rarely seen more than a few dozen, perhaps a couple of hundred, leave in any given year. Many more would follow in the decades to come, not just from Württemberg but from throughout the Rhine River basin and, eventually, from the entire European continent. In what has since been described as the "great departure" of the nineteenth century, a vast portion of the European peasantry, numbering in the tens of millions, left, like Christoph Schaar, in pursuit of greener pastures in the United States of America, where the vast majority of them found new homes. The kingdom of Württemberg—along with adjacent principalities like the Grand Duchy of Baden, the Bavarian Palatinate, and several northern Swiss cantons—stands at the beginning of this extraordinary migration of people and was a microcosm of the ideological and political forces driving them.[11]

Thanks in no small part to Friedrich List's meticulous note taking, there are some clues as to what may have transpired in Württemberg in the spring of 1817. But in order to make sense of them, it is necessary to first travel back in time, as well as several hundred miles north across Germany, to the small prince-bishopric of Osnabrück on the eve of the Seven Years' War.

When it became apparent, in the summer of 1757, that Osnabrück would fall to a French army under the command of the duc de Richelieu, Justus Möser, a senior bureaucrat in the small, north German prince-bishopric, felt his heart sink. Möser knew Richelieu. The man was a brute, notoriously indifferent to the plight of those toiling under his command. A period of wanton plunder by his much-abused soldiers awaited the people of Osnabrück. Even those at the court in Versailles expressed their displeasure with what the duc de Belle-Isle, King Louis XV's secretary of war, described as Richelieu's brazen "brigandage."[12]

Even so, Richelieu was only the beginning of the troubles the war might spell for the prince-bishopric of Osnabrück. As Möser soon realized, still more disconcerting was the fact that the French and their allies, the Habsburgs, were planning to "secularize" Osnabrück, which is to say they wished to dissolve it as a sovereign, autonomous entity and integrate it into their own polities. It did not help that the other main party in the present war, a Protestant coalition led by England, Prussia, and Hanover, entertained similar ambitions—if and when it managed to liberate the region. It seemed that no matter who prevailed in this struggle, it would spell the end of Osnabrück.[13]

Möser spent the next few years doing everything in his power to prevent this from happening. The challenge as he saw it was not just diplomatic but also legal-constitutional. Osnabrück's autonomy within the Holy Roman Empire derived from its status as an ecclesiastical territory, one of dozens of dwarf states known collectively as "Germania sacra" whose sovereignty was guaranteed by the Treaty of Westphalia of 1648. The arrangement had served the prince-bishopric well for over a century, repeatedly protecting it from being swallowed up by rapacious neighbors like the Electorate of Hannover, yet it had also tied its existence as a sovereign entity to a peace treaty among Europe's great powers—a peace treaty that, amid the recent hostilities between these same great powers, had come under renewed scrutiny. Möser understood the threat this posed to Osnabrück. Salvaging its autonomy, he explained to a friend, would require establishing a sovereign claim that was separate from its traditional ecclesiastical status, and this in turn would mean writing a "totally new" account of Osnabrück's constitutional origins (*Historie*). Such a Historie would have to extend into a very distant past, preferably into a period when nobody even knew the meaning of *ecclesiastical*. How this could be achieved when everything that had ever been written about Osnabrück came from ecclesiastical sources was unclear. Hunting for new evidence was out of the question while the war raged on. Even finding the hours to write would be difficult.[14]

Nevertheless, Möser was convinced it could be done. He already had a "quite lovely theory." According to this theory, Osnabrück's existence reached all the way to the period of antiquity, when it had been the home of a proud, Saxon yeomanry that had tilled the same soils north of the Teutoburg Forest as its present counterpart in the eighteenth century. Far from the barbarian horde of popular imagination, these ancient Saxon farmers had organized themselves into a remarkably modern commonwealth. While direct evidence of this commonwealth had been lost to the passage of time, echoes of it could be found in the writings of Roman historians like Cornelius P. Tacitus and Julius Caesar, both of whom had studied the lives of these ancient Saxons firsthand.[15] In his famous opus *Germania* (98 AD), for example, Tacitus described a system of government in which "the power of the kings is not absolute or arbitrary." It was something akin to a constitutional monarchy where the sovereign's "prestige" derived more from his "council" than from his raw power, and where "on major affairs the whole community [has] the decision." Elsewhere Tacitus claimed that the "peoples of Germania never live in cities and cannot even bear houses set close together." Previous generations of scholars had interpreted that as evidence of Germanic nomadism, but Möser read it differently. For him, it was evidence of his ancestors' penchant for an agrarian way of life and landed independence, which the English philosopher John Locke had regarded as the very foundation of good government.[16]

That Möser's account should echo Locke's philosophy on the agrarian roots of modern government was no coincidence. By the time the Osnabrücker began committing his thoughts to paper, the military situation in northern Germany had evolved significantly. In early 1758, an English force had landed at the North Sea fort of Emden and, with the aid of Prussian reinforcements, begun pushing the French back toward the Rhine. Möser had promptly set sail for London, hoping to forge a relationship with the war party that now wielded the most influence over Osnabrück's future. Manufacturing a resemblance to Locke's agrarian commonwealths no doubt played a role in those efforts. It may even have been calculated to echo the celebrated philosophe Montesquieu, who once made the provocative claim that England owed its constitutional monarchy to Saxon tribes who had migrated there during the early Middle Ages. Osnabrück's constitutional history in this sense did not just resemble England's: It was cut from the same cloth.[17] Möser's efforts bore fruit. The English soon backed away from their original annexation plans in favor of a close alliance rooted in shared values and perhaps even kinship. George III did appoint Osnabrück's next sovereign—he chose his son, George IV—but the move was largely symbolic since George IV was a newborn. Actual governance, including foreign policy, was put in the hands of the prince-bishopric's first servant and steward, who happened to be Justus Möser.[18]

Möser went on to rule Osnabrück for decades as its de facto sovereign. This happy outcome to the Seven Years' War was hardly a coincidence, and it may well have been his scheme all along. What the savvy bureaucrat did not anticipate, however, was the interest that his lovely theory would garner from an entirely different kind of audience: the German national movement. Contemporary nationalists were especially drawn to the claim Möser had made about the ancient Saxons' agrarian prowess. Nobody, apart from Montesquieu, had ever been brazen enough to make such an argument, and it was widely assumed that the "Old Germans" had been rather incapable of civilized, settled life. They were Europe's original savages, genuine brutes who boasted an impressive physical stature but lacked everything else that made a people great: cities, law, culture, humor, refinement. Proponents of German nationhood consequently believed that their task was far more difficult than that of their counterparts in other European nations. They would have to engage in years of arduous moral education just to "plant thoughts and prospects." In Germany, wrote national poet Johann Gottfried Herder, "philosophers must perform miracles."[19]

Möser's theory, published in 1768 as a book titled *History of Osnabrück*, changed these calculations. If the Osnabrücker was right about the existence of agrarian commonwealths in the ancient German lands, then the task of breathing life into Germany became much simpler, less an act of inception and more one of reawakening dormant spirits. Moreover, if before it was taken for granted that "the only way for us to be great, and if at all possible, immortal, is by imitating the [Romans and Greeks]," now there was no longer any need to borrow from foreigners. All the Germans would have to do is "become acquainted with the spirit of our former condition." A veritable stampede ensued to rediscover this former condition through ancient Roman texts like Tacitus's *Germania*. "Where does the *Germane* begin? Where does he end?," asked Heinrich Heine in a sarcastic jab at what was turning out to be a veritable Tacitus-mania. "May a German smoke tobacco? The majority rules no ... But a German may drink beer, and indeed he should drink it as a true son of Germania since Tacitus definitely mentions German *cerevisia*."[20]

Möser, for his part, had intended none of this. "The idea of writing a history of the [German] fatherland occurred to me very late," he told readers in the first sentence of *History of Osnabrück*. His aim had only been to salvage the prince-bishopric's autonomy. He warned that the work had been rushed and that amid the upheavals of the Seven Years' War he had never had a chance to think deeply about its broader implications. But his warning was to no avail. Herder had already published a glowing review, hailing the book the "first German history [written] with a German head and heart." The story was no longer Möser's to tell.[21]

For Friedrich Schiller, national poet and philosopher, the new infatuation with the nation's ancient past proved to be a godsend. Life had been difficult for the young Schiller ever since he quit his medical studies and left Württemberg in the hopes of becoming a poet, philosopher, and playwright. The issue was always "the damned money." Not even his prodigious literary output—four major dramas and countless poems and short essays in the 1780s alone—sufficed to shore up his finances. Only his historical writings had been worth something. "For my *Carlos*, three years' worth of work, I am rewarded with tepid applause. My history of the Dutch, a work that took five, at most six, months to finish, might well make me famous."[22]

This was an exaggeration, to be sure, but not by much. The piece on Dutch history, part of a compendium aimed at a general audience and titled *History of the Strangest Rebellions* (not "political" ones, as he assured the censors), had earned him greater accolades than any of his literary works to date. It was infuriating. History in Schiller's view ranked far below the refined arts of philosophy and poetry. Though it might serve as a source of empirical material for his plays, he was certain that the past by itself could never enlighten or illuminate. Alas, the public seemed to be of a different mind. At the Leipzig book fair in October 1788, *History of the Strangest Rebellions* proved a genuine success, while in Berlin around the same time it was apparently "making a splash." Most important to Schiller, deans at the University of Jena had taken note of it, which mattered because these deans had been searching for a new lecturer in history and they offered Schiller the post.[23]

It was an extraordinary opportunity. The most avant-garde university of its day, Jena was renowned for fostering an atmosphere of free thought, independence, and interdisciplinarity. It also offered attractive financial incentives. Schiller's new salary paid for a stately three-room apartment with high ceilings, natural light, two comfortable sofas, an elegant gaming table, eighteen red plush chairs, an imposing desk, and an on-call servant to take care of meals and laundry.[24] Never before had the struggling poet lodged so comfortably and respectably. These arrangements gave him a new perspective on the world and on history, which he began to praise profusely. "In [history's] orbit lies the entire moral world," he told an audience of five hundred students and colleagues at his inaugural lecture in May 1789, adding that "there is not one person among you all to whom history should not have something important to teach. Every one of your future paths, however different, will connect to it somewhere; but one destiny you all share in equal measure, that with which you were brought in this world—to educate yourself as a human being—and it is humanity to whom history speaks."[25] The past, he continued, should not be imagined as a meaningless chronology of events; rather, it was a "fertile and expansive field" from which to derive inspiration, confidence, and hope—a place to look up to rather than gaze down at. The crowd roared. "My lecture left an impression," a smug Schiller told a friend the next day. "The whole evening you could hear talk of it in town," and the students "sung an ode to me and cheered 'vivat' three times."[26]

Schiller's triumph did not last very long, however, because that same spring, history was put on trial by one of the greatest rhetoricians of the time: Emmanuel J. Sieyès, a Parisian priest turned intellectual architect of the French Revolution. While Schiller was preparing his lecture in Jena, Sieyès published three earth-shattering essays that, taken together, declared the entirety of history as being at odds with progress and liberty. The past, Sieyès noted, belonged to the nobility. This "caste" of men, "strangers in our very midst," claimed to rule by right of conquest, having descended from ancient Frankish invaders and "other savages from the woods and swamps of ancient Germany" who swept into Gaul more than a thousand years earlier. To emancipate themselves from the descendants of these noble conquerors, the French should "repatriate them to the Franconian forests," forget about the "old" regime, and build a new society from scratch. "Do not let us be discouraged if we find nothing in history to suit our situation." Sieyès assured his countrymen that "a time will come when our outraged offspring will be astounded to read our history and will give that most inconceivable insanity the name it deserves."[27]

The French Revolution posed a major quandary for Schiller and others in the German national movement. While many sympathized with the emancipatory impulses of the event, they could not help but feel anxious about the revolution's frontal assault on a past that, since the days of Justus Möser, they had learned to embrace and cherish. Some, like Herder, regarded the revolution as an assault on the German nation itself. If France's revolutionaries were permitted to define political modernity in opposition to history, then the German people would find themselves relegated to some permanent state of political backwardness. It would turn them into the "negroes" of Europe, Herder warned, the proverbial Other who gave modernity its meaning.[28] Schiller, too, was troubled but nevertheless remained hopeful about the potential for reconciliation between the revolution's emancipatory promise and a past made by the descendants of Germanic kings and peoples. "There can be no question," he wrote in an essay published shortly thereafter, in 1792, "that our present state of bliss"—that is, the emancipatory spirit unleashed by the French Revolution—"ought to be understood as ... the most prosperous that humanity ever enjoyed." Even admirers of the ancients would have to concede as much. The Romans only knew civil rights (*Bürgerrechte*), which were surely a step below the human liberty (*Menschenfreiheit*) that had been called forth by the French people's Declaration of Rights of Man and Citizen of 1789.[29]

The real question, as Schiller saw it, was why it took so long to get to this point. Could humanity not have been spared the savagery of the Middle Ages? France's revolutionaries may have answered with an emphatic yes, but the matter was not so simple. The French, who liked to see themselves as Europe's heirs to Rome, operated on the erroneous assumption that human liberty evolved directly out of Roman liberty. But Roman liberty, however advanced it may have been for its day, was a most parochial idea, one that could only have produced "*Roman* citizens and *Roman* slaves"—so Schiller. As such, it was at odds with human liberty, which, as the name suggested, extended to all human beings. Since Roman and human liberty were in fact at loggerheads, the one could only have triumphed by vanquishing the other. The process would have been a violent one because the "desire for domination clashes strongly with freedom." Anything short of a struggle could only have delayed humanity's great forward march: "Asia provides a case in point. Why did there not emerge any Greek free states in the wake of Alexander's campaigns? . . . Because Alexander conquered with humanity, because his small throng of Greeks dissolved amidst the millions of the great [Persian] king. [T]he local laws and customs, the religion and the state—they were the true victors. For despotically governed states there is no salvation except extinction. Conquerors who spare them merely supply them with seed-peoples, nourishing a decaying body. They can do nothing except to prolong the sickness."

Had Alexander and his men conquered more ruthlessly, they might have avoided "degenerating into Persians." Alas, Alexander was too faint-hearted, or maybe too careless, and Asia fell back under the sway of despots. A different set of events obtained in the "occident." Europe benefited from the exceptional brutality of the Vandals, Suebi, Alani, Goths, Heruli, Lombards, Franks, Burgundians, and various other tribes. Only these Germanic peoples—a "raw genus" (*rauhes Geschlecht*) filled with a "spirit of migration and plunder"— could have broken the "unnatural and nerve-racking quiet," the "weakly slavery," into which Rome had forced the world. "The Scythian wasteland bursts open and a raw genus spills across the occident. Its path is drenched in blood. In its wake, cities crumble into ashes, and in [its] fury it tramples on the achievements of human labor and the fruits of the earth; plague and hunger catch up on what the sword and fire have passed over; but life perishes only so that better life can sprout in its place." So that "better life can sprout in its place" were ominous words, given the murderous turn of events that would grip France during the Terror. But Schiller was writing these lines in 1792, at a time when the revolution remained bogged down in seemingly endless deliberations about a future constitution, and when the yearning for a more sweeping new beginning remained strong. "Let us not count the corpses piled up by the [raw genus], or the cities that were reduced to ashes. They will re-emerge more beautifully under the sway of freedom, and a better people (*Stamm*) will inhabit them."[30]

This was the history of a necessary, thousand-year battle between two titanic forces: the Germanic spirit and Roman despotism. If that was true, it was better to think of past Germanic conquests, from the Frankish invasion of Roman Gaul to the Teutonic crusades in the Middle Ages, as akin to a historical palliative: "people's migrations" (*Völkerwanderungen*). Though the term seemed to mask the violence of these events, Schiller never denied their bloodiness, which he found necessary if humanity was to prevail over a "heart-choking despotism." A Völkerwanderung was to him like a superrevolution that "prepared the stage," clearing away all the rot and corruption and conceit so that more fragile experiments with liberty, like the French Revolution, could have a shot at success.[31]

So there the transformation was: a vice made into virtue, a once-barbaric act recast as a people's pursuit of human liberty. Could this be the solution to the puzzle of Württemberg/1817? One could make the argument. Schiller, after all, was born and raised in Württemberg, and in a town—Marburg—that was quite close to the epicenter of the exodus of 1817. By the 1810s, he was enough of a household name in the German lands, on par with a Wieland or a Goethe, to be known even among the common peasantry. Some may well have read his plays or watched a performance in Mannheim or Stuttgart. Sure enough, his name appears in the correspondence of later generations of emigrants.[32]

But it would be hasty to draw such straight lines from Schiller's ruminations on the ancient Germanic past to the events of Württemberg/1817. More than a quarter century of revolutionary turmoil and war separated the two. Indeed, just months after Schiller had waxed at length about the piling up of corpses and the burning of cities, an armed mob fanned out across Paris and began piling up actual corpses and burning the actual city. The death toll from the September Massacres of 1792 was horrific, with some eleven hundred to fourteen hundred suspected counterrevolutionaries cruelly executed in the streets. The following January, Parisians—along with much of Europe—watched the blade of the guillotine rush onto the neck of Louis XVI. Next, civil war broke out, followed by two decades of total war that consumed millions of lives, in France and the world over. Considering all this bloodshed, much of it committed in the name of liberty, it is remarkable that Schiller's story was not immediately consigned to the dustbin of history.[33]

Granted, some observers always remained unmoved by the violence. Historian Heinrich Luden, who succeeded Schiller at Jena in 1806 and was known for his radical politics, all but parroted his predecessor's apocalyptic rhetoric.[34] But Luden was neither the only one nor the first to indulge in Schiller's Völkerwanderung. A version of the myth also appeared in the writings of Immanuel Kant, a Prussian philosopher and fixture of the Enlightenment in Germany and a consistent critic of liberty obtained by violent means. In *Anthropology from a Pragmatic Point of View* (1798), Kant described a German as someone who "emigrates easily" and is "not passionately tied to his fatherland," and he insisted that this was his "good side": evidence of moral fortitude and a desire for liberty. How exactly Kant arrived at this conclusion is of interest because it reveals something about the appeal of the Völkerwanderung myth-history even amid this new age of gore.[35]

Kant had been commenting on the events in France with great interest. Like Schiller and other leading figures of the German Enlightenment, he sympathized with the revolutionaries' desire to build a better world. He was, however, less excited about the events on the ground, and he especially took issue with the way the revolutionaries used war to foist their ideas on others. While he did believe that human beings had a responsibility to offer their talents "for use to the world," he was quick to add that "the most important thing [in that world] is man himself: he is his own ultimate purpose." There was a reason why such concepts as *esprit*, *étourderie*, or *lettre de cachet* could not be translated into other languages: "because they correspond to the particular sense of the nation that utters them more than the thing they are used to describe." In *Anthropology*—which, not coincidentally, was written in 1796 and 1797, just as Napoleon notched major victories in Italy and began readying an army to liberate Egypt and the Levant—Kant confronted French universalism with a didactic survey about the wide range of human talents and reason that existed. At length, he described how different genders, classes, races, and nations each used their distinct abilities to chart their own path toward liberty.[36]

Given his belief in man's responsibility to focus on improving himself before helping others, it seems that Kant should have been skeptical about the Völkerwanderung, in which Germanic colonizers used scorched-earth tactics to bring human liberty to the world. For Kant, however, the Germans' penchant to emigrate was not inherently problematic. Unlike the Frenchman, the German did not proceed from any expressed desire to enlighten or liberate the world. This was simply because the German, as Kant explained, lacked the ingenuity, wit, and self-confidence—in short, the "genius"—that would have been necessary to indulge in so arrogant an undertaking. He exhibited instead a more "phlegmatic" kind of reason that fostered diligence, patience, frugality, and humility. Cherishing rules and order more than any other nation, the German preferred to find his place within society rather than to topple it. These character attributes, more by happenstance than design, turned the

German into a "man of all lands and peoples." Bereft of national pride to a fault, not to mention desperately short on the genius that distinguished the English or French nations, the German contented himself with working the land or, if he happened to be born into that station, tilling the "field of the sciences" (*Feld der Wissenschaften*). His willingness to belabor even the most barren of wastelands rendered the German a first-rate "colonist"—"such," at least, was the "praise which even the English have for the Germans in N.-America."[37]

This was a very different line of argumentation than the one advanced by Schiller. Kant's Germans were cut from decidedly humbler cloth and as such were far removed from the ruthless barbarian colonizers of Schiller's imagination. If the German nation was prone to migrating, it was not because of some primal urge—there was no spirit of migration and plunder here—but rather because of its penchant for hard work and the back-breaking ordeal of tilling the soil, which gave it a leg up in the important task of colonizing the frontier. The difference was important: It transformed the Völkerwanderung from an apocalyptic struggle between human liberty and despotism—something akin to the struggle France's revolutionaries had been engaged in—into a rather innocuous story about German work mores. Understood in Kantian terms, a Völkerwanderung was in the most literal sense of the word a migration of hard-working people from one place to another, in search of new soils to till, focused on improving only themselves and no one else, making the best of their God-given reason.[38]

Although Kant himself did not invoke the term Völkerwanderung in his writings, the logic he advanced in *Anthropology* and elsewhere informed how others wrote and thought about this history. "Give me soil and space to live!—that was the manifesto of the ancient world," wrote Hans Christoph Ernst von Gagern, a Hessian aristocrat and statesman known for his liberal politics. Von Gagern went on to contend that it was the "most eloquent of declarations, and one against which reason finds no objection." Because, as he explained in *The National History of the Germans* (1813), a fulsome two-volume narration of the "great migrations" since the Cherusci warlord Hermann, these ancients "truly were much more than roaming hordes." The "wagon fort" may have been their fatherland, but "they had laws, sovereigns, and a variety of constitutions. They obeyed constitutional princes surrounded by sages; they idolized freedom, honored women, and already combined... the hunt, animal husbandry, agriculture, and trade."[39] Meanwhile, the Braunschweig historian Ernst Ludwig Brauns, an associate of von Gagern's who wrote on the same topic some years later, distinguished between an ancient, brutal

Völkerwanderung and a "modern," peaceful one. The ancient one was Schiller's: freedom-loving barbarians who had moved west, overthrown Rome, and established the first kingdoms of genuine liberty in Europe (the prime example here being Britain's constitutional monarchy, allegedly founded by Saxon invaders who composed the Magna Carta of 1215). The modern Völkerwanderung was closer to Kant's version of events. It commenced during the more recent age of European exploration, when "younger European nations... mostly of Germanic descent" began to settle "America" and spawn the "most marvelous fruits of culture and civilization." This time they did so in a more peaceful manner. Figures like William Penn, founder of the commonwealth of Pennsylvania, were not to be regarded as wild-eyed conquerors but as men of "energetic reason" who employed the "gentler means of love and peace," always maintaining friendly relations with the Indigenous nations they encountered. That this did not describe the actual history of European settlement in North America did not keep Brauns from casting North America as the most suitable destination for the present-day German Völkerwanderer. As the example of Penn suggested, in North America there was no need to "engage in a bloody struggle over the land"; there, the Germans could "take possession of it peacefully."[40]

As to the Württembergers who assembled to leave for America in the spring of 1817, it is likely that Kant's version of the Völkerwanderung appealed more than Schiller's since it was more in line with traditional peasant mores that lionized labor and impugned idleness. "They just wanted to be given the opportunity to work so that they could earn their bread," Friedrich List wrote of his interviewees in Weinsberg and Heilbronn. "Charity they did not want, they were men capable of working." They had decided to leave Württemberg because they were deprived of the dignity of labor. "Seven weeks ago, the seigneur [*Herrschaften*] solicited bids for a dam," explained one of List's interviewees, carpenter Jakob Strähle in the village of Egolsheim near Ludwigsburg. "[Our] mayor purposely did not make a public announcement, and so nobody showed up other than the mayor and his comrade." This was how the "mayor wins all the auctions for land leases and street-building and other contracts." That Strähle would seek remedy in a place as "unknown, unimproved, and distant" as America makes much more sense when read in the context of Kant's musings on national character. Its very remoteness and lack of cultivation would have rendered it attractive to a good German.[41]

"To a good German" was, of course, the crucial point. A national frame of mind was essential if one was to derive any assurance at all from the myth-history of the Völkerwanderung, be it Kant's or someone else's. Herein lies another piece of the puzzle that is Württemberg/1817. At the dawn of the nineteenth century, a national frame of mind was by no means a given, at least with respect to the peasantry. If such awareness did exist, there was little reason to identify with the nation in public. In a world that continued to be governed by dynastic rulers who derived their legitimacy from paternal myths and presumptions—and the German lands in the 1810s were such a world—there would have been little to gain from posturing as a good German and invoking national idioms. To the contrary, any embrace of national identity was more likely to attract unwanted interest from the authorities, not to mention from neighbors and relatives who cherished their local identity far more than their belonging to the still rather abstract idea of Germany.[42]

The kingdom of Württemberg was no exception—until, that is, the spring of 1817. The timing turns out to be significant, because at that moment the national idiom made an unexpected cameo in Württemberg, at the behest of none other than the king himself.

Wilhelm I of Württemberg first grew acquainted with the awesome powers of nationalism around the time of the Battle of Leipzig in 1813. Still a crown prince at the time, he had been appointed to lead the chase of Napoleon's defeated army back across the Rhine, which he did, all the way to Paris. When he returned to Stuttgart in June 1814, he was received by a cheerful crowd draped in national colors. Leipzig was already known as the "battle of the nations": a historic moment when, according to later chroniclers, the Germans finally overcame their petty differences and fought as one, proud people, with princes like Wilhelm leading them in their struggle.[43]

Ever since that summer, the crown prince could be heard talking up his German roots and those of the old Reich, so much so that some began to suspect he desired to one day be crowned "kaiser of the Germans." In truth, Wilhelm had no such ambitions. He knew that the chalice was poisoned; what concerned him was only his future as the sovereign of Württemberg. Leipzig revealed a remarkable harmony between German nationalism and royal authority. "Our fatherland has nothing in common with that of the Spaniard," explained a booklet from 1820 written at the behest of Wilhelm. The German people were "not revolutionary," it continued, because in Germany it was usually the most "resolute and loyal adherents of order" who most "sincerely love their fatherland." The politics were unusual, but then so were the historical circumstances in which Germany found itself: divided into many sovereign kingdoms, united by a common language and culture. It seemed that in Germany national politics might very well underwrite, rather than undermine, royal legitimacy.[44]

The reason Wilhelm was pondering questions of royal legitimacy is that for some time he had been watching his father, Friedrich I, struggle mightily with the issue. The challenges facing Friedrich were many, but nearly all could be traced back to his controversial alliance with Napoleonic France, which had lasted from 1801 to 1813. Although borne of defeat, the partnership with Napoleon had served Friedrich well. In exchange for providing the French with a steady supply of auxiliary forces, he had been generously rewarded with titles (including that of king) and vast swaths of new territories (mostly former Habsburg lands in Swabia). With Napoleon's backing, he had carved out a powerful position for himself domestically, which enabled him to go on the offensive against local stakeholders and to concentrate all administrative, fiscal, and judicial authority in his own hands. Thus, in 1806 Friedrich moved to abolish Württemberg's old regime constitution and with it the many privileges enjoyed by local notables, including guildsmen, town patricians, clergy, and the nobility.[45]

The waning of French power following the Battle of Leipzig in 1813 had called all this progress into question, and before long a powerful coalition of "old constitutionalists" (*Altrechtler*), a good number of them former Habsburg subjects in the new Swabian territories, began demanding the restoration of their customary rights and privileges. Initially, Friedrich had managed to buck these Altrechtler; having switched allegiances early enough in the wars with France, he had staved off intervention by the Great Powers, especially a revanchist Austria that entertained vague ambitions to have its former Swabian territories restored to the House of Habsburg. He had also continued to enjoy the support of other important factions in Württemberg politics, like merchants, liberal professionals, intellectuals, and much of the royal bureaucracy, all of whom shared his dislike of the estates and the Swabian nobility. Real trouble for Friedrich only arose in 1815 when these latter groups suddenly turned their backs on him. Their rebellion had started with a rumor according to which Austria and Prussia, who at the time were deliberating the postwar order at the Congress of Vienna, were planning to force member states of the German Confederation (*Deutscher Bund*), which included Württemberg, to restore their prerevolutionary constitutions. Terrified, Friedrich had cobbled together a counterconstitution and rushed it before Württemberg's version of an estates general (*Landtag*), expecting that it would gain swift endorsement. Much to his chagrin, his proposal failed because his allies had crossed the aisle and joined the Altrechtler in refusing their support.[46]

The affair had been disastrous for Friedrich and the monarchy. What was originally intended as a legal stumbling block for his enemies, at home and abroad, had suddenly turned into a millstone around the king's neck. Having spearheaded the return to constitutional government in Württemberg, Friedrich could not simply drop the matter. He now required a constitution to govern, and to put such a constitution in place, he would need to go back to the Landtag with an amended proposal that could win endorsement—a costly and humiliating endeavor. All the while, the attacks on his person were multiplying: Friedrich, the French-made tyrant, engaged in the "characteristically French vice" of mandating constitutions, "like decrees."[47]

Then, in October 1816, Friedrich suddenly passed, leaving a messy and seemingly intractable situation to his son Wilhelm. But the latter quickly grasped the gravity of the situation. Recalling the lessons of Leipzig, Wilhelm pushed back against the charges of Bonapartism by emphasizing his German heritage. In March 1817, making the best possible use of his first speech as king before the Landtag, he declared his intention to govern from the "higher perspective" of a "German prince," not just as protector of Württemberg. He then put forth his own proposal for a new constitution, which, he explained, was conceived both with an eye to Württemberg's time-honored institutions and in deference to the "higher demands that the culture of the German people places on constitutions." Put another way, he had no intention of yielding to his enemies. As the "resolute defender of German independence" that he was, he would accept nothing less than complete loyalty from his subjects—including every Altrechtler before him.[48]

The assembled were furious, and understandably so. For months they had been led to believe that the young king would be more cooperative than his stubborn father, that he was a practical man, a negotiator. Instead, Wilhelm assumed a most antagonistic posture and all but commanded them to accept a constitution that was scarcely different than the one proposed by his father back in 1815, save for the fact that it was wrapped in a new story: a *German* constitution. Yet little could be done in response. Wilhelm's appeal to the nation had put his adversaries on the back foot. On the one hand, he had challenged the Altrechtler on their own terms, because to invoke ancient Germanic law was to argue that only the king could rightly call himself an "old constitutionalist" since the law proposed by his adversaries dated to much more recent times, at best the sixteenth century.[49] On the other hand, no Altrechtler could accept the "higher demands" that Germanic law placed on them, even if he wanted to. Germanic law as commonly imagined in this period, particularly among standard-bearers of the Holy Roman Empire, was the law of shepherd kings and their hapless flock; it did not recognize men of privilege to act as interlocutors between princes and the people. Whatever authority might have accrued to them in the past derived solely from their function as administrators; assertions to the contrary were arguably tantamount to treason.[50]

To be sure, this was not the last word in Württemberg's constitutional standoff, which carried on for another two years at least. But it was a pivotal moment in the struggle between the monarchy and the privileged orders because now the Altrechtler had to justify their own authority.[51] Württemberg's eventual constitution, ratified by the Landtag in 1819, still represented a compromise between the king and his adversaries, but one that clearly favored Wilhelm, who went on to rule the kingdom of Württemberg as its undisputed sovereign for another half century. That he managed to hold on to power for so long, and in a period in the nineteenth century when royal authority everywhere was increasingly under siege, was a testament to his formidable political talents and to the cunning way in which he pressed the nation into the service of his crown.

There can be little doubt that the king's speech in March 1817 made an impression. As for the exodus that ensued just two months later, it was perhaps its siren call. By embracing the nation in so grand a manner, Wilhelm had in effect endowed Germanness with a respectability and power in local politics that was practically unheard of. Yet by being rather coy about what exactly was meant by this Germanness and by German law, he had granted that same respectability and power to anyone hoping to emigrate to America, because ever since Schiller and Kant, there was an argument to be made that emigration to America was a quintessentially German endeavor, a modern Völkerwanderung. Wilhelm of course had no intention of sanctioning the mass flight of his subjects. He was probably just as stunned by this brazen appropriation of the nation's ancient past as the Altrechtler had been when he confronted them as a German prince.

To be clear, the king's speech itself did not send anyone across the Atlantic. The catastrophic harvest failure of the previous fall, along with myriad other challenges to Württembergers' material future that arose with the end of the Napoleonic Wars and the transition to peace, was the foremost driver of the events in 1817.[52] What Wilhelm did with his declarations before the Landtag was to lower the threshold of action. Those who had long contemplated leaving Württemberg but had so far hesitated, fearing the consequences to themselves and their loved ones, suddenly found themselves presented with an opportunity: to leave for America without turning themselves and their families into targets of ridicule, harassment, or retaliation—as had been common in the past. That, in turn, opened up the possibility of a more orderly and dignified departure: no fire sale of their property, no slipping away under the cover of darkness, no passing over proper farewells and sharing plans and routes with family and community. It was even conceivable that the authorities might support their endeavor by, say, intervening on their behalf against a vindictive landlord or bitter magistrate, or by permitting them to claim property left behind at a later date. As the German prince he claimed to be, sensitive to German instincts and desires, the king would have to think twice about getting in their way lest he undermine his own pageantry.[53]

What exactly went through these emigrants' minds as they embarked on their journey is of course difficult to say. But given what is known about the patterns of peasant politics in this place and time, it would be surprising if such strategic calculations had not informed their thinking. Experience had long taught the people of Württemberg, as it had taught peasantries across the Holy Roman Empire and elsewhere in Europe, that by indulging their paternal rulers' conceit they could hope to acquire at least a modicum of control over their lives. Fawning acts of deference and soaring tributes to the traditions, symbols, and rituals of power allowed individuals to assert their place on the public stage and to acquire "the power of comprehensible speech." Using such standing and power, they could stake claims, carve out autonomy for themselves, or—as was true most of the time—simply remind a ruler of his own duties toward them. Just as his subjects behaved themselves, he, too, was not to forget his *buena maniera*—those "good manners" with which every good shepherd was to treat his flock. In the past, politics of this kind had proven especially effective in Württemberg, since Württemberg's peasantry had long been subject to multiple competing layers of authority, from local landlords and magistrates to princes, ecclesiastical powers, and the ruling cadres of the Holy Roman Empire. Within this world of overlapping control, much of which remained intact even after the empire was dismantled in 1806, a demonstratively loyal subject wielded considerable power: With some deft signaling he or she could even hope to broaden the scope of paternal responsibility by pitting different authorities against one another.[54]

The events of spring 1817 bear all the signs of such "wily maneuvering," only with the particulars no longer reflecting the paternal idiom and instead turning on a national one. To begin, there was the extraordinarily public character of the event and the desire to be seen and heard that this implied. As Friedrich List's report of the proceedings makes clear, everything took place in plain view of the public and royal authorities—who were present in the person of List and his assistants—and with the purpose and destination of the endeavor known far and wide. Over the course of roughly two weeks, the prospective departees said their farewells, gathered their belongings, loaded everything onto carts and horses, and began making their way to the port of Heilbronn on the Neckar River, ten miles to the west. Once there, they unloaded everything and allowed the harbor crane to lift it onto eight barges brought in for just this purpose. While waiting, they loitered among the crowds at the loading dock or sat for a conversation with List at the Heilbronn harbor tavern "Zum Kranen." There and everywhere, they recounted their stories and shared their regrets. And they reminded List, the royal attaché, that their grievances pertained more to their local tyrants than to the king— who they believed would "surely help."⁵⁵

FIGURE I.I *Tavern Zum Kranen in Heilbronn Gasthof zum Kranen in Heilbronn* (no date, likely 1830s) by Carl Dörr. Lithograph, 9 × 13.5 cm. According to his report from May 1817, Friedrich List interviewed prospective immigrants to North America at the tavern depicted on the left side of the image. Notice the loading crane and the Neckar River in the background.
Source: Courtesy of the Städtische Museen Heilbronn.

In his report of the events, List seized on these grievances to argue for political and social reform. Yet it was not reform that these emigrants were interested in. Nothing, they averred in their testimonies, could compel them to change their plans. What they appeared to desire was only safe passage out of Württemberg, to be shielded from the harassment, intimidation, and shame that traditionally awaited those who absconded. Thus, what mattered was less what they had to say about the state of affairs in the kingdom and more what impression their departure made on those who witnessed it. The potential for evocative imagery was undoubtedly there. On a clear day—and List's report suggests that the weather was tolerable enough—it would have been possible to watch from afar as a large procession of people with their luggage-laden wagons, their children, and their livestock cascaded down the highlands in Württemberg's northeast, where the emigrants' villages were situated, and from there crisscrossed fields and meadows on their approach to Heilbronn. Such imagery would not have been so different from the way in which contemporaries imagined the great people's migrations of the distant past, as, for example, in the majestic panorama paintings of Hungarian genre painter Árpád Feszty. Up close, their demeanor and posture would have rounded out the portrait, with some emigrants enacting the part of the weeping father who stands at the center of Carl Wilhelm Hübner's *Farewell of the Emigrant*: aggrieved and solemn yet also determined and resolute, just as one

FIGURE 1.2 *Farewell of the Emigrants. Abschied der Auswanderer von ihrer Heimat* by Carl Wilhelm Hübner (1846). Oil on canvas, ca. 70 × 100 cm. Genre paintings like this one are often interpreted as reflections of the artist's romanticism, but they can also be interpreted as capturing an elaborate pageantry by the subjects themselves. Notice the luggage-laden carts in the background, as well as the two uniformed observers on the left-hand side who seem either unable or reluctant to intervene in the drama before them.

Source: Courtesy of the Nasjonalmuseet/Høstland, Børre.

might expect of a German people whose decision to leave their homeland sprang not from any premeditated design but from instinct, from the nation's esprit.[56] "It truly was a spectacle throughout all the villages," wrote a witness to a similar scene of departure years later and a bit further southwest, in Alsace. He may have intended the remark in a literal sense, not just a stirring visual but also an event with a storyline, the so-called modern Völkerwanderung.[57]

The theatrics would have been quite useful. Ever since Wilhelm's provocative speech at the Landtag in March, his opponents had tried to recapture the initiative by seizing on rumors that a mass exodus was to take place imminently from Heilbronn. Such an event was easily cast as an indictment of the king's arrogance and, by the same token, as an endorsement of the Altrechtler's steadfast opposition to his constitutional proposal. A perceptive observer of these politics would have recognized that, if such arguments were to win the day, it would be a major embarrassment to the king and would likely compel him to intervene as much as possible in his subjects' planned departure, if only to save face. It behooved the emigrants to communicate as clearly as possible that they regarded themselves in the king's column that spring of 1817, not in that of his political adversaries. By carrying themselves in the manner that they did, they could complicate the Altrechtler's efforts to use them as pawns in political attacks against the king. By echoing the king's pageantry and suggesting that their departure was merely a manifestation of their character as the German subjects of a German prince, the emigrants could hope to strengthen the king's hand, hence putting him in a position where a permissive attitude toward their departure would not undermine him and might even be regarded as being in his interest.

Given the king's posture toward the mass flight that did eventually take place in early May, he seemed to have read the situation in just this way. Thus, he declined to take steps to discourage, sanction, or otherwise interfere with the emigrants' departure (although he continued to harbor concerns, given that his kingdom could scarcely afford to lose so many able-bodied and propertied subjects).[58] Then, in early June, not long after the events in Heilbronn had gotten underway, he went even further and dismantled various administrative hurdles to emigration, for example, by abolishing the customary 10 percent tax on any property emigrants took with them. While he clearly did so from a position of weakness, it was no coincidence that he announced this change in policy on the very same day—June 4, 1817—that he took the extraordinary step of unilaterally dissolving the Landtag and asserting de facto absolute authority in Württemberg. The timing is significant, as it suggests that Wilhelm discerned a connection between his political fortunes and a public endorsement of emigration. "I will give the people (*Volk*) their rights and liberties right this moment," he had declared in a thunderous speech that same afternoon, immediately before announcing a major overhaul of Württemberg's tax code—including abolition of the emigration tax.[59]

In the months and years that followed, the king continued to lean into his German-national pageantry, having discovered its usefulness for shoring up royal authority. As before, he would not be remiss to pay his tributes to the emigrants, and in fact he began to incorporate the issue into an ever more intricate pageantry casting him as heir to the shepherd-kings of an ancient Germanic tribe, the Alemanni people.[60] He did not retreat from his permissive stance on emigration as soon as his authority was secure but, rather, inscribed it into the heart of his constitution. His original proposal from March 1817 had already contained permissive language regarding his subjects' "freedom of movement" (*Freizügigkeit*), but this was boilerplate as far as constitutions went in this period and was more likely a gesture toward progressive and liberal constituencies. In the final version of the document, completed in 1819, much more explicit language was introduced: the "freedom to emigrate" (*Auswanderungsfreiheit*), standing alongside other foundational civil rights like the freedom of press or faith. This was an extraordinary concession by contemporary standards, one that effectively burdened the king with novel, far-reaching, and potentially dangerous responsibilities, since to guarantee this kind of liberty, he might very well be forced to interfere in the domestic affairs of whatever country his subjects chose to settle in. For that reason, few governments in the nineteenth century, including the most liberally inclined, dared to incorporate such language into their constitutions. Nor did they wish to put the idea of leaving the polity in their citizens' minds, which they very well might have done had they given it formal expression in the law.[61]

Wilhelm thought differently about the matter. As he explained some years later, "It is not the soil (*Boden*) on which we live that makes the Heimat a fatherland; there is a spiritual land where our customs and virtues and our souls reside, and only insofar as this land becomes one with our Heimat do we have a fatherland."[62]

This was not just rhetoric. Tens of thousands of Württembergers abandoned Wilhelm I in those years, greatly exacerbating a demographic crisis in the kingdom that had begun years earlier, amid the deadly wars with Napoleonic France.[63] As to the emigrants themselves, significant hardship awaited them.

FIGURE 1.3 *Duke Paul Wilhelm von Württemberg Among the Indians. Herzog Paul Wilhelm von Württemberg bei den Indianern*, artist unknown (no date, likely 1830s). Gouache on paper, 54 × 65 cm. Visible at the center of the image is Duke Paul Wilhelm of Württemberg, a cousin of King Wilhelm I and a renowned naturalist and explorer of the Americas, during a trip in 1822–24 to what is now the US state of Kansas. In 1828, the king gifted a historic castle in Bad Mergentheim to the duke who, in turn, used to it exhibit his impressive collection of zoological, botanical, and ethnographic items from North America, then one of the largest of its kind in Germany. The exhibit, which included this gouache painting, further reinforced the nationalist political pageantry of King Wilhelm I, in that it cast the royal family as a patron of knowledge about North America, by then widely recognized as the primary destination of a "modern" Germanic Völkerwanderung. Although the duke's vast collection was eventually scattered to other museums across Germany, this particular gouache painting remains on exhibit at the Residenzschloss Mergentheim.
Source: Elfriede Rein, Staatliche Schlösser und Gärten Baden-Württemberg.

Lives were upended; families and communities were left behind, never to be seen again.

But this is precisely why the pageantry mattered: It would have given all this pain and suffering a certain meaning and purpose and direction. It is impossible to know whether things would have turned out differently in Württemberg had there not been the story of the Völkerwanderung—history offers no such counterfactuals. However, the kinds of hardships that afflicted the Württembergers in these years were addressed in very different ways elsewhere. In France, respectable peasants, instead of marching off to America, marched into the public squares of their villages. They broke into church towers and rang the bells outside the normal service, and when the authorities called in the cavalry to disperse them, they put up barricades, not just because barricades were an effective means to obstruct the movements of soldiers but also because they were a recognizable symbol of French nationhood. Those who built them could not so easily be dismissed as an angry and illegal mob; they had to be engaged with and listened to as sovereign members of the body politic. The only difference vis-à-vis Württemberg was the fact that there, on account of certain interpretations of the nation's past and character, asserting belonging in the body politic could very well mean emigrating to North America.[64]

There is, then, a universal aspect to the story of Württemberg/1817, one that can offer insight into the nineteenth century's great Atlantic migrations more generally. Instead of understanding this extraordinary event—some 5.4 million German speakers would emigrate from Europe to North America by World War I, along with nearly 30 million other Europeans—as merely the consequence of privation or some mass delusion about the New World, it can be seen as a dynamic linked to the triumph of the national idea. This would help explain why the geography of America-bound migration was so spotty at first, why it focused on only a few specific regions, most of them home to populations that associated with German culture and language: the Hesse states and the Grand Duchy of Baden, for example; or the Swiss cantons of Berne, Aargau, and Graubünden; France's Haut- and Bas-Rhin departments (Alsace); or the Dutch provinces of Gelderland, Overijssel, and Drenthe. What all these places had in common, aside from the fact that they all struggled with similar crises of subsistence, is that they were among the first on the continent where the respective ruler, or ruling gentry, appealed to the nation for purposes of shoring up their own legitimacy. As was true of Württemberg, the exodus overseas, mostly to North America, tended to follow in short order, and in similarly public and theatrical fashion.[65]

The fact that regions that in theory lay outside the German lands proper, like French Alsace or Switzerland, were part of this story, even as ostensibly German states like Austria or Saxony were not, is a reminder that the issue is not some essential feature of German national life but, rather, local politics in a new key. The Alsatians who emigrated to Texas in the early 1830s may have identified more with the French nation than with the German one; being bilingual and bicultural, however, they chose to play up their German heritage because doing so promised to ease their departure from France. For the sovereign—in this instance the unapologetically nationalist King Louis Philippe I—the statement "I am emigrating to America" may well have read as an assertion of local autonomy, urging the king to respect the rights and dignity that accrued to a coequal nation residing within his territory. In other cases, neither subject nor ruler needed to drape themselves in German national colors. After all, German national myth-history was far from the only one in Europe that could inadvertently legitimate emigration and the colonization of distant lands; Scandinavian and east European nations, in their own glorification of Vikings, Magyars, and other Nordic barbarians, had the potential to offer just as powerful an endorsement, as did Britain's "Anglo-Saxon" mythology. The fact that so many European nations ultimately traced their lineage to the barbarian peoples of late antiquity goes a long way toward explaining why migration out of Europe was never just a German phenomenon in the nineteenth century, why it was an event that, with the rise of national politics everywhere, eventually gripped nearly every corner of the continent.[66]

A second insight that can be derived from the events in Württemberg regards the nineteenth century's peculiar preoccupation with North America. In prior periods, and certainly in the eighteenth century, North America had been just one of many destinations that beckoned, and in matters of attraction to would-be settlers it lagged well behind the El Dorados of South America and the West Indies, as well as the fertile soils of the Banat (modern-day Romania) or the Volga valley in the Russian Empire. Most Europeans in this period imagined North America to be a rather cold, sterile, and inhospitable place, a refuge for puritan fanatics, a giant poorhouse of the English Crown, a threatening wilderness inhabited by fearsome Native Americans and boorish French fur-trappers. The Württembergers who dared to venture there were either ardent pietists or poor indentured servants who identified with Protestantism, which meant that they could rest assured, as well as reassure their lords, that although they were leaving their homes for good, they at least remained a part of the greater Protestant world. That nineteenth-century North America suddenly became a destination for many of Württemberg's Catholics as well, even though they had long preferred Habsburg, Russian, and South American dominions (the greater Catholic world), can once more be explained in terms of the introduction of the national idiom into Württemberg politics. This national idiom, which identified North America as the most fertile soil for the modern Germans' work, was constructed around an ancient and pagan people. In an environment that assigned sovereignty on the basis of this kind of secular identity, the old confessional divide, though it was hardly erased and continued to shape communities in Europe and abroad, no longer mattered in the same way it once did.[67]

Part of America's attraction was, of course, America itself, as many a booster of the great "land of freedom" emphasized. And yet, the point should not be overstated. Throughout the nineteenth century, reliable knowledge about this corner of the world remained scarce in Europe, as evidenced by a burgeoning literature of emigration guides in the 1820s and 1830s that struggled to educate readers about what life there was like. The events in Württemberg demonstrate once more that America was above all a trope, a place that beckoned not because of any intrinsic merit but because of stories that contemporaries in the German lands told about their own past and future as a people. It should come as no surprise that the events of 1776 or 1783, when the United States declared and won its independence, did not immediately change minds in Europe regarding the suitability of the region for settlement. From a German-national point of view, the turning points came only later, in 1803 and 1814, when Americans claimed and won "millions of fertile acres . . . awaiting humanity's plow," first by completing the Louisiana Purchase and then by defeating Britain and its Indigenous allies, the powerful Haudenosaunee (Iroquoian-speaking) Confederacy, in the War of 1812. In each instance, a long-dreaded barrier to the "peaceful" settlement of America's bountiful west—on the one hand the French Empire, on the other the British—dropped away, which meant that North America could increasingly be regarded as the most suitable destination of the modern German Völkerwanderer. As von Gagern put it in his comments about the remarkable exodus of 1817, "Nothing seems more practical, more German, more righteous," than emigrating to America.[68]

The Migrant's Spirit: How Industrial Modernity Came to the German Lands. Benjamin P. Hein, Oxford University Press. © Oxford University Press 2025. DOI: 10.1093/9780197831052.003.0002

2

New Transatlantic Connections

JOHANN BAUER CAME to America in 1854 for the same reason that so many of his compatriots made the daunting voyage in these years: to acquire land and become a farmer.[1] It was, as the twenty-six-year-old explained, one of the few "advantages" that "one does not have in Germany." Born in Heidelsheim, a small town in the northern wine-growing region of Baden, Bauer felt he had everything he needed to turn his dream of a homestead into a reality. He already knew how to cultivate fruit trees, especially apple trees. He never missed a prayer and did not swear like his "godless" brother Georg. He possessed the discipline of a devout Lutheran and knew that success would require that he not be "too anxious to become rich quickly." Most of all, Bauer was an industrious man with no time to lose. His plan following arrival in New York was to immediately begin the twelve-hundred-mile trek to Chicago, even though it meant traveling in the middle of winter. He wanted to get to Illinois before the spring thaw to have enough time to identify a suitable plot of land and prepare for planting his first seed of the season.[2]

Bauer did make it to Chicago in time, in January 1855, but he soon discovered that determination and faith alone were not enough to buy him a farm on the Illinois prairie.[3] Only money could do that and, as Bauer realized, "in the beginning quite a bit of money is required": some $300 to $500, or about three to four years' worth of wages for an ordinary farm laborer in Germany.[4] It was the kind of money Bauer did not have, and so his "plan to start something right away could not be carried out." He was not alone. Many young emigrants from Europe made this discovery upon arrival in the United States. Although they all agreed that in America "you have your free will, you are not dependent on anyone, you can start whatever you want," they also learned that "unless you have the means to do it, you will have to dance to other people's tune here, too."[5]

Still, the situation was not hopeless. Aspiring farmers in this period could choose from several options to raise the necessary start-up capital. One increasingly popular solution was to take out a mortgage. Here, all Bauer had to do was come up with a down payment—guidebooks cited an average $150 for the initial deposit—plus the interest that accrued over those initial few months before the first harvest was sold.[6] Though this was still a substantial sum of money, it was rather more manageable. Bauer might work for another farmer for a few years and save his wages, which is what many immigrants did in these years. He could also ask an acquaintance in Philadelphia or his brother Georg in Albany for a small loan. As a German speaker, moreover, he could seek help in one of the hundreds of predominantly German settlements that dotted much of the landscape of the Midwest, in addition to the German immigrant neighborhoods of larger cities like St. Louis or Chicago.[7]

Bauer, however, chose none of these solutions. In contrast to generations of German emigrants before him, Bauer showed little interest in relying on relatives and friends in New York or Philadelphia, and he seems to have intentionally shunned the German American communities in the Midwest. Bauer instead began to write long, effusive letters to his parents and siblings back in Heidelsheim. He inquired about their well-being since his departure, described his progress in learning English, gushed about the "fertile prairies" of Illinois, debunked myths of American backwardness—"you might call America a wilderness [but] in terms of religious faith (*Religion*) it far surpasses Germany"—and, finally, asked for money.[8]

As Bauer kept writing letters, money appeared. The first bill of exchange from his parents, for $61.64, arrived in 1860. Bauer wrote again. In 1868, another bill of exchange for $80 showed up. Still more arrived in 1872. Apparently the last one, the largest so far at $150, had been sent against his father's will, with the senior Bauer letting on that he believed the family in Heidelsheim "needs the money" and that "Johann has gotten enough help already." When his father died a few years later, in 1877, Bauer wrote more letters. He offered his condolences and prayers, assured his mother and siblings that he had never "worked a day less in the hope of an inheritance," and noted that he would "thankfully accept anything that comes my way and put it to good use."[9]

It was a novelty of the period that an immigrant like Bauer could reasonably expect financial support from a family that lived halfway around the world. In the decades prior to the 1850s, such transatlantic credit relationships were uncommon, if not altogether unheard of, among families of middling means like the Bauers. Most remarkable of all was the fact that Bauer genuinely expected to be able to claim a share of his inheritance in Europe. Previously, the enormous geographical distance, which included not just the

Atlantic Ocean but also thousands of miles of difficult, if not altogether treacherous, terrain—mountains, rivers, and swamps—in both Europe and North America had made claiming inheritances back in Europe a logistical nightmare that few contemporaries deemed worth the effort. Claims on inheritances and dowries were especially difficult to assert since they often required the sale of physical assets like livestock, plots of land, artisanal tools and equipment, or furniture—in no way a simple task, even for heirs and brides who were physically present. In cases of inheritance disputes, emigrants like Bauer were left with no choice but to issue powers of attorney to a trusted sibling, friend, or neighbor, knowing full well that relatives had an interest in prioritizing their own stakes over those of a sibling, son, or daughter who emigrated decades earlier. Those who left their hometowns for the United States during the early nineteenth century had, for all intents and purposes, forfeited their claims to any property they left behind.[10]

Starting in the early 1850s, all this began to change. Emigrants appeared more confident than ever in staking their future in America on continued support from home. "I don't like to write to Hickory," Albert Krause demurred in response to his parents' suggestion in 1860 that he reach out to a relative in the United States for help with finding employment. "Our paths probably go in a very different direction." Like Bauer, Krause aspired to become "king on his own property," and he deemed friends and relatives in America to be a nuisance rather than helpful in that endeavor. Upon receipt of a new loan from home, Krause added, "Besides, here in America one must not rely on such acquaintances—one gets ahead best on their own!"[11] One thing that made propositions like these possible was reliable and regular transatlantic communication. In the 1850s, technological innovations in maritime travel, including the introduction of steam engines and steel hulls, dramatically reduced the length, cost, and risks of transatlantic voyages and, in so doing, revolutionized communication. An expanding and increasingly densely interwoven network of railways, canals, and improved rivers in both the United States and European states expanded inland access to overseas ports, connecting even the most remote of communities, including Bauer's hometown of Heidelsheim, to the Atlantic world. The cost of sending a fifteen-gram letter from continental European states to North America consequently dropped from the equivalent of 1.66 marks in 1835 to only 0.25 marks in 1871. Affordable postage meant that Bauer could keep in close touch with relatives in Europe, send frequent updates about his personal progress, describe his hard work and setbacks, and inquire about the well-being of family. In short, he could attend to all the filial duties necessary to keep his name in his relatives' wills.[12]

Of course, better communication alone could not assure Bauer that his claims to an outstanding estate would be honored. The expectation that an inheritance would materialize on the other side of the Atlantic only became plausible in light of the emergence of new legal and financial institutions that acted as transatlantic intermediaries on behalf of emigrants like Bauer, such as banks or attorneys who were well-versed in both American and German law. Some of these institutions had long existed, but they had served a mostly elite clientele. Banks, for example, tended to be operated by Atlantic merchants in the interest of Atlantic merchants. The closest equivalent of a transatlantic attorney's office—a consulate or equivalent diplomatic outpost—tended to be preoccupied with carrying out commercial espionage on behalf of merchants back in Europe. These officials, often members of merchant families themselves, possessed neither the resources nor the will or even awareness to help people like Bauer with their comparatively small financial transactions.[13]

Starting in the early 1850s, novel legal and financial institutions that catered to the lower middle classes and even the migrating peasantry began to pop up across North America, complementing this existing structure of merchant banks and consular offices. These institutions were an unexpected consequence of the Revolution of 1848 in Europe. The failure of the revolution sparked the sudden exodus of some three to four thousand well-heeled professionals to the United States: lawyers, doctors, bankers, and businessmen. These men, and less often women, went on to establish a robust network of attorney's offices, savings banks, and mutual aid organizations. It was these enterprises that enabled immigrants like Johann Bauer to draw on property that they might otherwise have been forced to forfeit and, in so doing, to pursue their dreams of landed independence.

Among the leading causes of the failure of the Revolution of 1848 in Germany, according to one popular obituary at the time, was the extraordinary aloofness of the revolutionary leadership. While national delegates inside the Paulskirche in Frankfurt am Main, host to Germany's National Assembly, engaged in seemingly endless oratory about a nation-state that did not yet exist, indulging what detractors ridiculed as a debilitating 'speech craving' (*Sprechsucht*), their enemies conquered the streets. This was nonsense, of course—an example of the bitter disappointment and scapegoating that tends to follow on the heels of defeat. Nevertheless, there was a kernel of truth to the story. Many of the Frankfurt parliamentarians were passionate and talented speakers, not to mention brilliant legal minds and skilled debaters, able to command the podium for hours on end and often without notes of any kind. Such skills were not just useful but also necessary, because in the weeks and months that followed the initial street fighting in March 1848, which had brought the National Assembly into existence, the task at hand was not to build more barricades but, rather, to think through the legal and practical challenges of turning revolutionary slogans into actual institutions and lived realities. Moreover, because the Frankfurt Parliament enjoyed the support of Germany's princes—a unique distinction when compared to other revolutionary bodies in this period—there was in fact little need to worry about securing the streets: The princes' regulars were already doing that work. Of course, when these princely praetorians eventually did turn on the revolution in the spring of 1849, the decision not to have spent more time and resources raising an independent, revolutionary army began to look like a grave strategic error. But such is hindsight; the politics of the moment were more complicated.[14]

After this, many of the Frankfurt parliamentarians and their allies emigrated to the United States, where they once more proceeded to demonstrate their gift for oratory. Many of these so-called forty-eighters quickly found their way back into politics, founding influential newspapers, standing for elections to local office, and rising through the ranks of the Republican Party in particular. Rhineland radical Carl Schurz, for example, served not just as a trusted advisor to the Lincoln administration but also as a US diplomat, a Union general, a US senator for the State of Missouri, and later as secretary of the interior under President Rutherford B. Hayes. Women, too, carried on the struggle: Feminist writer and journalist Mathilde Franziska Anneke embarked on an illustrious career as one of America's leading proponents of women's rights, forging a close friendship with like-minded trailblazers like Elizabeth Cady Stanton and Susan B. Anthony. This was no mean feat. The newcomers had to quickly master a foreign language, along with all the other challenges facing an outsider in a foreign world. In the 1840s and 1850s, powerful nativist currents had begun ripping through the sea of American politics, mostly in response to burgeoning immigration, generating growing support across this society for the fiercely anti-immigrant and anti-Catholic Know-Nothing Party. Figures like Anneke and Schurz—the latter having been born to a Catholic family in Cologne—managed to hold their own by taking advantage of the opportunities arising from America's ongoing struggle with the institution of slavery. They recognized that the effort to dismantle the institution of slavery created a pressing demand for anyone who could speak cogently and eloquently about the blessings of a free society and who could detect and snuff out the many specious arguments that were being advanced in support of human bondage. It was first and foremost by placing themselves at the vanguard of the emancipatory politics of the day that these forty-eighters transformed themselves into a fixture of American political life for decades to come.[15]

To be sure, not all forty-eighters succeeded by entering the ring with slavery. Some found a home in the so-called copperhead movement—northern Democrats who sought a negotiated settlement with the partisans of slavery, opposed conscription and the bloodshed of war, and represented mostly agrarian interests in midwestern states like Ohio, Indiana, and Illinois. Others again tried to steer clear of politics altogether: Friedrich Kapp, a young lawyer born in 1824 in Hamm near Münster, Westphalia, conceded that after the humiliations of '48 he no longer had any "desire to be doing something in public affairs." Initially swept up in revolutionary politics while studying law at the University of Heidelberg, Kapp had been among the first to head to Frankfurt following the seating of the Frankfurt Parliament in June 1848, posing as a journalist to gain entry to the gallery of the Paulskirche and hence witnessing the making of history. But like so many observers of the proceedings, Kapp soon grew impatient and disenchanted. While the politicians were deliberating, he complained to his uncle in August 1848, "The reactionary mindset is once again on the front foot in the countryside," and it appeared that the sheer "inertia (*Schlaffheit*) of the people will rob us of what little was won on the barricades [in March]." His premonition became a reality in the late spring and summer of 1849, when revolutionary armies in Baden and the Palatinate briefly skirmished with Prussian forces before suffering a complete and humiliating defeat. Kapp, who had witnessed some of the battles himself, still remembered the swiftness with which the recruits of the revolutionary army tossed away their weapons and began running for the hills. It was then and there, he claimed, that he lost whatever faith he still had in the people. "I was stupid to trust the noblesse of wage-laborers, and in the end I became a laughing stock."[16]

Kapp never did lose his interest in politics, and he eventually found his way back into the midst of it through the antebellum Republican Party. Yet for the time being, the twenty-six-year-old preferred to join the circles of the American "moneyswanker" (*Geldprotzentum*). Channeling one of his childhood mentors, humanist philosopher Ludwig Feuerbach, a fierce critic of the Romantic idealism that colored so much of German politics during the years immediately prior to the Revolution of 1848, Kapp rationalized his decision to focus on his business life by arguing that "one does well to first establish a healthy, economic basis." Remunerative work not only was a more "practical activity" but also could serve as a "positive objective." America appealed to Kapp because, he explained, Americans "appreciate the proper role of money-making and material means in achieving spiritual and moral purposes." It was a shame that intelligent men like his friend Karl Friedrich "Fritz" Anneke, the husband of Mathilde Anneke and an ardent and lifelong socialist with close ties to Marx and Ferdinand Lassalle, failed to secure even a "bearable material existence" following their exile from Germany. Anneke's heart was in the right place, Kapp thought, but he was also profoundly ineffective.[17]

It was one thing to talk about joining the moneyswankers in America and quite another to actually do it. In his native Westphalia, Kapp's law degree from the University of Heidelberg would have earned him a relatively comfortable existence, but in New York the law profession at midcentury offered nothing comparable in terms of remuneration or stability. Even if Kapp managed to gain admission to a state bar, he would find himself in a fiercely competitive world. It comes as no surprise, therefore, that the attorneys' offices that Kapp and two forty-eighter associates set up at 47 Chatham Street, just off the Hudson River landing docks in Hoboken, New Jersey, failed to generate any business whatsoever. And so, after a few weeks of allegedly staring at the flies on the windows, the three young men decided to change course. They would do what "nearly everyone who had something to sell" in 1850s New York did: "make money off of immigrants."[18]

When Kapp arrived in New York in the early months of 1850, the Castle Garden immigrant facilities had yet to be constructed. Immigrants still entered the city directly via landing docks along the Hudson River. As they disembarked crowded sailing vessels and entered the bustling streets of New York, Europe's poor and wretched were immediately swarmed by so-called runners—agents, solicitors, and, in many cases, thieves who sold fake railroad tickets and shuffled newcomers into exorbitantly priced boarding houses. Immigrants who did not speak English—and in the 1850s these were predominantly Germans—were especially vulnerable. Although guides warned readers to "protect themselves against fraud," an unsuspecting newcomer might mistakenly take such advice to apply only to English speakers. Kapp and his associates were different, however. They did not attract attention as potential fraudsters because they sported posh attire, bourgeois mannerisms, and a high German dialect. Their demeanor inspired confidence in their countrymen who, as one claimed, "literally knew not a single being in New York or elsewhere to whom I might have looked for advice or help."[19]

There is no way to know for sure whether Kapp exploited emigrants or whether he was of genuine help to them, as he liked to claim.[20] What is certain is that Julius Fröbel, one of his original partners, quit little more than a year into their new venture because "I did not want to speculate with the settlement of German emigrants." Fröbel would not stand for earning "blood money" by "selling souls" and turning compatriots into "white slaves." His colleagues seemed less fazed by ethical concerns. Kapp went so far as to complain that the job was, in fact, "scarcely remunerative." Unless it was conducted "on a grand scale," the math just did not add up. Few emigrants carried much change on them, and even if Kapp managed to coax every last dollar out of them before they boarded trains to Cincinnati or Chicago, it would never earn him the fortune he was after.[21]

The silver lining was that Kapp got to know many of the emigrants personally. The lessons he learned from listening to their stories proved quite valuable in due time, both for himself and for the people whose interests he claimed to represent. His first discovery was that many emigrants were hardly as destitute as their wallets suggested. Once, he recalled some years later, he watched an "old farmer and his three adult sons" disembark at Castle Garden. When officials inquired about cash and valuables, the father and his sons "opened their pocket-books, counted the contents of each, and hesitatingly declared it to be about $25." Kapp remembered being skeptical. "I interposed and explained to these people... the reason of the interrogatories, whereupon the old farmer showed me a bill of exchange of $2,700 on a New York banker, and remarked that each of his sons had about the same amount with him. These men had been entered as having about $100 together, while in fact they ought to have been credited with about $11,000."[22]

It was surely an exceptional case, if it happened at all. Few German emigrants disposed of this kind of cash, even if they were generally better off than, say, their Irish counterparts. Kapp's point was nonetheless abundantly clear. German emigrants wielded substantial resources, certainly more than the average $68.08 that officials calculated in 1856. It is not difficult to imagine why this was so. Unlike the Irish, who in the late 1840s and early 1850s were fleeing from famine, German emigrants in this period enjoyed the advantages of a more orderly departure. Even if they did not have much, at the very least they enjoyed the luxury of picking the moment of departure, allowing them to sell whatever livestock, tools, shops, houses, or plots of land they did own. Migration, Kapp learned, had the potential to transform even the lower classes like tenant farmers, peasants, apprentice artisans, and journeymen into temporary wielders of significant sums of money.[23]

While running the Hudson River landing docks, Kapp also learned that some emigrants, especially when they were young and came without family or dependents, held title to property back in Germany: claims to an inheritance, dowry, or minor debts owed to them by fellow villagers. It was likewise common for emigrants to still own plots of land in Germany, plots too small to support a family but nevertheless worth a certain sum of money. This was indeed the situation in which Baden native Joseph Ignatz Scheuermann found himself. Practically penniless when he first arrived in New York in 1872, Scheuermann initially took a job with a local German brewer. Yet he soon quit the position—although it paid quite well, "20 dollar per month, dollar is 2 fl. 30"—to do what he had come to America for in the first place: to purchase land, in his case a $350 farm in Kentucky. It turned out that the job at the brewery was merely a means to sustain him while he waited on the proceeds of a land sale back home. "Dear brother," he wrote in a letter to his family in Altheim, "I now have a big favor to ask. I have bought a farm and wrote Liebrot 3 letters that he sell my [parcel of land], and send me my money by the 15th today is the 14th and it is still not here." He had managed to secure a "judicial" extension, but "if my money does not arrive by the end of the month...I will not be able to complete the purchase and lose my deposit. Think of my grief...and help me get at my money." Scheuermann was lucky: His parents were able to advance him some cash by December, but a dispute over his alleged capital of 3,600 gulden (presumably tied up in a plot of land) dragged on for years in the local courts in Baden.[24]

The situation was much the same with Auguste Witte, who sailed on her own to New York in 1860. Soon after arriving, she wrote her mother of her plans to marry a fellow emigrant by the name of Friedrich Betke. Though he was a hard-working young man, Betke possessed little capital: He had lost all his belongings, including an alleged 400 talers in cash, when his Hamburg steamer *Austria* suffered shipwreck due to a fire on the lower decks. Witte pleaded with her mother for help. "You wrote of a bill of exchange of 300 thalers or 198 Dollar," she noted. "This sum would definitely be sufficient to set up an ordinary household here." And what of the dowry of 2,000 talers "that would be due to me as a girl of legal age in cases of marriage"? She assured her dithering mother that the money would "likewise be safe here" and "instead of 5 percent can get 10.20 to 25 percent."[25]

These varied forms of property—inheritances, dowries, savings—were worthless to an emigrant in America unless she could somehow lay claim to them. None of this was lost on Friedrich Kapp. He told a friend back in Germany that, starting in 1852, "we have altogether sworn off all immigrant promotion business." Instead of exploiting the masses for their pocket change, Kapp began focusing on personalized legal and financial services to German emigrants hoping to settle in America. His firm would discount bills of exchange, prepare powers of attorney, and furnish legal documents concerning inheritance claims, dowries, and other illiquid assets in Germany. Finally, Kapp would offer legal representation to emigrants hoping to sell real estate back in Germany, however modest it might be, so that they might be able to assemble the minimum capital necessary to purchase a farm and "live independent of anybody" in America.²⁶

Kapp once likened his work to that of a "consul of German culture in foreign lands."²⁷ It was a made-up title; he never held an official consular assignment from a German government. He himself probably did not think much of it, since it all sounded prestigious enough and seemed like convenient shorthand for his activities in New York. Nonetheless, the comparison was a bad one and was not even in Kapp's own interest, given the many differences between what he did and what a European consular office did.

Starting in the late 1840s, when European migrants like the Irish and Germans first arrived in large numbers, a sophisticated system of support institutions cropped up in both European and American port cities. Mutual aid societies, recreational clubs, German-run boarding houses and bars, hospitals, and savings banks abounded. These institutions aimed to protect the newcomers from exploitation and fraud upon arrival. For a temporary period, they offered food and shelter, a sense of community, rudimentary health services, small loans at low interest, and a place to safely keep and deposit valuables.²⁸ This patchwork of mostly charitable institutions was paralleled by an increasing number of honorary "consuls" who operated on behalf of German principalities and city states. The idea of a consul was not new: European governments had long dispatched consuls across the world to represent their commercial interests and support their merchant diasporas. In the context of the new migrations of the nineteenth century, however, these consuls' responsibilities gradually expanded to support not only influential businessmen who traded overseas but also the much larger class of peasants that was settling abroad permanently. Besides preparing annual reports with updates about price movements and foreign politics, ordinances, and tariffs, consuls were thus responsible for an increasing variety of notary tasks. On a commission basis, they were asked to record marriages, births, and deaths; keep track of property; offer postal services of sorts; and exchange currency.

Much like Kapp's offices, some dealt with claims on inheritances and other kindred property.[29]

Given the similarity of their activities, it may seem that commission-based lawyers like Kapp were competing with these institutions, especially the consulates, but this was not at all the case. Kapp's offices complemented rather than replaced the charitable organizations and the consulates. Charitable organizations for their part offered stopgap measures concerning the overseas voyage and the first weeks of arrival; Kapp, by contrast, supplied legal and financial services, often for long periods of time. But the main difference between Kapp's offices and consulates boiled down to the direction of their workflows. Because consuls worked in the interest of authorities in Europe—whether a monarchy or the city council of a free imperial city like Frankfurt am Main or Hamburg—they tended to process claims that originated in European courts and with European officials. Consular cases almost always concerned an individual in Europe who asserted a claim to an outstanding debt or on the estate of a deceased emigrant in the United States. Kapp's offices, by contrast, worked in the opposite direction. His clients, who were very much alive, were emigrants in the United States who sought to claim their own property or the estate of a deceased relative in Europe. If consulates facilitated a transfer of capital from the United States to Europe, Kapp did the same in the opposite direction, from Europe to the United States.

In theory, nothing kept an emigrant from approaching his former state's consul for help with staking claims on property in Europe. But there were good reasons to avoid this route. As the overseas deputy of a sovereign, a consul was all but set up for a negative relationship with the emigrant; his primary role was to apply the law and enforce the claims of lenders in Europe. Some consuls were even tasked with tracking down deserters, thieves, and other troublemakers. Approaching the consul of a German state thus all but invited trouble; Kapp's private law offices offered an alternative, a more discreet path to accessing capital in Europe.[30]

The records of Kapp's Manhattan-based law firm did not survive, but the mechanisms of its operation can be extrapolated from the activities of other lawyers who modeled their businesses on Kapp's original firm. Paul Schulze, for example, was trained in German law and emigrated to the United States in 1868. Schulze, who knew Kapp personally, probably after meeting him in New York upon his arrival, went on to run a notary office in Portland, Oregon. As part of his day-to-day work there, he accepted commission-based jobs for the San Francisco–based General Consul Adolph Rosenthal. Schulze's correspondence with the German consulate reveals that his main responsibilities involved identifying German emigrants throughout Oregon, finding out whether they were still alive, and collecting outstanding debts or inheritances on behalf of heirs in Germany. His workflow with the San Francisco consulate was therefore mostly one-directional: He received assignments from Rosenthal and carried out individual jobs in exchange for a commission. During the period for which records are available, between 1876 and 1883, there was not a single instance in which Schulze forwarded an emigrant's claim to the consulate.[31]

Rather than relay claims to Rosenthal, Schulze corresponded directly with European lawyers and bankers with whom he seems to have had a preexisting relationship, including the Karlsruhe-based "bank and commission bureau" of Heinrich Müller, the Würzburg attorney "Lenk," and the prestigious banking house Gebrüder Sulzbach in Frankfurt am Main. These business associates, in turn, connected him with local courts and attorneys in the respective German towns in which an emigrant held title to a plot of land, a savings account, or an inheritance. In a process that could take anywhere from a few months to several years, Schulze furnished powers of attorney, submitted lawsuits to German courts, supplied information about transactions costs, and processed bills of exchange. The key was that officials like General Consul Rosenthal would no longer be privy to the business of transatlantic monetary exchange.[32]

It could be a profitable business, with many other potential upsides for those with a bit of entrepreneurial spirit. Thus, in addition to the legal fees and commissions that could be earned, and that ranged anywhere from 1 percent to 2.5 percent, there was the opportunity to serve emigrants as real estate brokers, insurance agents, and savings managers. Intimate knowledge about their clients' financial condition could be leveraged into remunerative pursuits with local business interests. For example, for years Schulze acted as a land agent for the Oregon & California and Northern Pacific Railroads. Kapp, whose offices were situated in Manhattan, did not have any land to sell to his clients, but this did not keep him from finding ways to monetize his insider perspective, such as by investing in insurance companies and, in later years, making brazen speculations in western railroad corporations.[33]

Although "semi-legal patrons" such as Friedrich Kapp tended to be narrowly preoccupied with their own accounts, their work proved to be of far-reaching consequence.[34] To begin with, much like other technological innovations that lowered the risks of long-distance migration, including the steamship or the railroad, the emergence of institutions dedicated to facilitating microfinancial transactions across the Atlantic turned emigration into an ever more predictable and routine undertaking. This not only swelled the numbers of those who left for America but also, crucially, changed the socioeconomic and demographic composition of migrants. Thus, German emigrants arriving after the middle of the nineteenth century tended to be much younger and less affluent than previous generations and for that reason were less likely to be accompanied by children, spouses, and other dependents.

Another significant change pertained to the emigrants' geographical origin. Starting in the 1850s, an increasing proportion of them hailed from places like the eastern provinces of Prussia, the Thuringian highlands, or Saxony, regions in Germany that had previously largely been spared a mass exodus of their residents and, in some cases, had no history of migration across the Atlantic. Any shift in the geographic locus of migration would have had many driving forces, but it is worth noting that Prussia in those years had been loudly asserting its leadership in the movement for a unified Germany and, in so doing, imbuing emigration with new meaning and political power, similar to what had happened in King Wilhelm I's Württemberg during the 1810s.[35] Yet the presence of ever larger numbers of poor Prussian peasants among the emigrants was at least in part attributable to the fact that the act of settling abroad was no longer so contingent on access to the established transatlantic networks and to the deep generational knowledge that had been so important to emigration from southern Germany and other localities across the Rhine River basin. "[Their] prime purpose was the betterment of their material condition," lamented a proponent of a more communal approach to long-distance migration, such as migration cooperatives or formal, government-sponsored settlement societies. As this observer went on to contend, the new arrivals of the 1850s and 1860s no longer exhibited any loyalty toward their countrymen in America. "A depressing spirit of the *Kleinelei* peculiar to the sons of the *kleinstaatliche* Deutschland...dominates many of their actions. They were distrustful and often unjust and so increased the labors of their officers and retarded the progress of their undertaking." Whether the newer generation of emigrant really was more given to insubordination and "blighting jealousy" is difficult to say, but there clearly was a paradox here that demanded an explanation. At just the moment when the number of emigrants from Germany reached record highs—in the 1850s the movement was so large that it occasionally surpassed even Irish emigration at its own peak during the potato famine—a great many of the German ethnic enclaves and settlements across the United States found themselves starved of new arrivals and suffering from high rates of attrition. More people of German cultural and linguistic background than ever lived in America, but outside large cities like New York, Chicago, or St. Louis, the idea of a German immigrant community was quickly becoming a thing of the past. Shifting attitudes were part of the reason, but so were the new modes of financing resettlement to America that had emerged in the wake of 1848.[36]

Another consequence of the institutions built by Kapp and others like him concerned the purpose and character of migrant correspondence. It should come as little surprise that, even as the emigrants in the United States grew more alienated from each other, their dependence on, and sense of connection to, families and communities back in Europe grew in proportion. This, in turn, shaped how they approached their letter-writing duties: what they chose to share, when, and with whom. If previously the purpose of a letter to Europe had been to relate logistical information about the voyage and desirable destinations to other prospective emigrants, its function now shifted toward the author asserting belonging in the family and community that had been left behind. Thus, it has been said about migrant letters from this period that they tended to be "wordy" and disorganized and that often their message was drowned out by copious amounts of seemingly irrelevant detail: the number of acres that an emigrant had cleared in a season, the weight in pounds of their individual livestock, the price of items at the local convenience store, the vagaries of the weather, the many "formulaic contemplations about faith" and "endless enumerations of persons to be greeted." But if the point of such correspondence was to maintain relationships, not to mention to keep one's name in a relative's will, then wordiness of this sort was key. Details mattered—the more the merrier—as did the frequent use of formulaic prose: Both fostered a sense of intimacy, familiarity, and trust.[37]

This new function of correspondence, or more specifically the crude, material concerns that seemed to motivate them, was not lost on contemporaries. "No, we are not waiting for your death," exclaimed an embarrassed Regina Kessel, an emigrant who had settled and married in Illinois, in a letter to her "dearest parents!" composed in the winter of 1863–64. Kessel went on to explain that the reason she had inquired with her ailing "dear father" about "how much capital you possess" was that she and her husband Fritz hoped to purchase a farm in the "Mississippi valley"—just as she had intended when she originally decided to emigrate to America. Once they were ready to proceed, she sought to determine what they might be able to afford, and in this regard the prospect of their inheritance had come up.[38] "Dear father, we

FIGURE 2.1 *Bride Wagon in Niederwalgern. Brautwagen in Niederwalgern* by unknown author (ca. 1899–1901). Black-and-white photograph. A wagon carrying the dowry of Katharina Rupp in Niederwalgern near Marburg, which includes furniture and other household items. Transatlantic intermediaries like Friedrich Kapp helped emigrants negotiate the sale of similar household items and family heirlooms, usually to relatives who remained in Germany, so as to gain access to at least a portion of their equivalent cash value. The ability to claim financial resources from an ocean away transformed the logistics and patterns of transatlantic migration, emboldening younger people to strike out on their own in the United States and incentivizing more regular and sustained communication between members of the family.

Source: Courtesy of Anni Dienstbach, Weimar/Lahn-Roth.

cried after receiving your letter, not because of the money, no, we cried because we were touched after hearing from you and from mother as well.... We wish that you live a long life, and we are happy to hear that you have been so brave and sprightly. May the Lord give you strength and bless you and bless you double for this new year 1864." Kessel may be forgiven for her forwardness; money is rarely a pleasant topic among loved ones, especially when the availability of funds is contingent on a relative's passing. But circumstances required that the matter be discussed, and given the constraints of the written letter, there were bound to be a few jarring juxtapositions here and there between what may well have been an innocent inquiry into a family member's health and a question about the business side of things. Kessel did promise to avoid any further "distasteful" questions, but in truth there was not much she could do: When money was involved, even the most carefully crafted letter could not avoid at least an appearance of impertinence.[39]

To be sure, most families understood this, and indeed it was rare for any contretemps to lead to estrangement—certainly no more so than would have been true had these families still lived under the same roof or in the same village. In fact, tensions of this kind point to an awareness among all parties that they were ultimately bound to one another as members of the same family, notwithstanding their all but permanent separation from each other, and that this recognition of kinship came with responsibilities and obligations. That Regina Kessel's father rushed to conclusions suggests that the issue was already very much on his mind and that he had not written his daughter, who he could not have expected to ever see again, out of his will. On the European side, this meant indulging the requests of the pesky relative in America, no matter how forward or dubious; and it meant that many more members of the family took an interest in the "news from America," even if they had no desire or plans to go there, because the presence of another brother, sister, or cousin bore directly on their own claims to the family's estate. On the American side, meanwhile, the emigrants continued to pour their hearts out onto the page, carrying on their filial duties as best they could by sharing whatever fit on the pages of a standard fifteen-gram letter about the weather, the size of the apples in their orchard, the most recent scandals in American politics, how frugally they lived and hard they worked, and the number of pigs they had managed to sell to the local butcher. Johann Bauer maintained correspondence with his family for nearly four decades, from 1854 until 1891, an extraordinary length of time by contemporary standards. Bauer did so, he explained, not because he expected to see his relatives again but, rather, "so that I can assure you that with every year I have made a step forward."[40]

There was one final consequence of the businesses established by the forty-eighter generation that is worth noting: the German immigrant community's relationship with native-born Americans. With the support he received—some $290 in total, in addition to an unspecified amount he collected when his stepfather died in the 1870s—Bauer was able to progress not merely in steps but in leaps and bounds. In the first ten years following his arrival in the United States, he transformed the $180 he reported in cash in 1860 into a 60-acre farmstead worth some $3,000. A decade later, he claimed to have doubled the size of his farm to 120 acres, with six horses and twenty cows, and with annual revenue flows of between $400 and $500. That Bauer managed to do all this during one of the most tumultuous periods in American history was bound to impress not just his relatives in Europe but also his neighbors in Adair County, Missouri. The latter likely wondered about his ability to "always improve my situation a little bit," no matter the circumstances. Without knowing the whole story of his success, they may have concluded that he was simply an accomplished farmer and enterprising businessman.[41]

Perceptions of this sort were worth their weight in gold, especially in midcentury America. Given the politics of this period, there was a dire need for people like Bauer: free men of European stock who could get ahead quickly, and seemingly on their own, in remote frontier regions like Missouri. It was in this context that German emigrants and their native-born compatriots in America forged new connections with one another—bonds that would ultimately bring the regions of North America and the German lands closer together than they had ever been before.

When Frederick Law Olmsted began working as a correspondent for the *New York Daily Times* in 1852, he did not have any plans to write about German immigrants. A aspiring journalist at the time, before his career change to landscape architecture, Olmsted intended to weigh in on the nation's discordant "discussion of slavery." His position was antislavery, which is to say he took the more moderate stance that slavery needed to be abolished not because it was morally indefensible, as abolitionists insisted, but because it was unproductive and "not less disastrous in its effects on industry [than] gambling." Slavery endured, Olmsted argued, because Southern plantation owners found it to be "fashionable," much in the way that the English wore top hats, the Arabs coveted their horses, and the Chinese preferred the "queue." The *New York Daily Times* furnished Olmsted with an opportunity to dig a little deeper into the matter, which he did by embarking on a years-long horse trip across the American South and visiting slave plantations large and small.[42]

Although a tour into these corners of the country did prove illuminating in many respects, it soon dawned on Olmsted that once he had seen a few slave plantations, he had seen them all. He decided to broaden his investigation to include properties whose owners did not rely on enslaved labor to do their planting, if only as a reference point, to show what was possible without slavery. It was with this goal in mind that he turned his attention toward the Germans, including those living in the foothills north of San Antonio, Texas, an area with both plantations worked by enslaved people and freeholds worked by immigrants and other homesteaders. Olmsted already knew, via his introduction in New York to several prominent forty-eighters of the day, that the larger portion of these immigrants strongly disapproved of slavery and that many of them possessed no "instinctive prejudice of color." As generally poor immigrants, moreover, the Germans seemed unencumbered by the "prestige [of] accustomed dominance over...slaves, of language, capital, political power, and vociferous assumption." All they seemed encumbered by was diligence, hard work, and an ardent desire to make America their home. If Olmsted could document their success in getting ahead without resorting to enslaved labor, his mission would be completed.[43]

His first opportunity to do so arrived during his approach of San Marcos, a small community some thirty miles south of Austin. There, Olmsted noticed a local man strolling along the side of the road. He stepped down from his horse and began to question the man about the area and, more to the point, about "his experience...with regard to the character of the Germans." The man answered that he found "no reason at all to think of them as bad neighbors." Olmsted decided to press a little further, commenting, "But I understand that they are in rather wretched condition and are hardly able to get their living in this country," to which the stranger responded, "Why, most of [the Germans] seem to be very poor people...but they are getting along very well, I should think, for poor folks; they are every year improving about their houses and building new houses which are more comfortable than the old ones. [Those] that came here poor must be getting along very well—at any rate they say so, and it looks so."[44]

Olmsted requested to be shown one of these dwellings and was duly pointed in the direction of New Braunfels, the largest German community in the area. Riding south on San Antonio Road, its main thoroughfare, he found himself admiring the modest but handsome structures lining the streets everywhere, all "trim-built with pink window-blinds."[45] He noted, "The singular composite character of the town is palpable at the entrance. For five minutes the houses were evidently German, of fresh square-cut blocks of creamy-white limestone, mostly of a single story and humble proportions, but neat, and thoroughly roofed and finished. Some were furnished with the luxuries of little bow-windows, balconies, or galleries."[46]

These homes were a sight to behold, but what most struck Olmsted was the contrast between them and some of the other dwellings he passed by next: "From here we enter the square of the Alamo. This is all Mexican. Windowless cabins of stakes, plastered with mud and roofed with river-grass, or 'tula'; or low, windowless, but better thatched, houses of adobes (gray, unburnt bricks), with groups of brown idlers lounging at their doors."[47] This was to be expected, so Olmsted wrote, since Mexicans were "only a step above the negroes."[48]

FIGURE 2.2 *Johann Bauer's house in Missouri*. A photograph of Johann Bauer's property in Adair County, Missouri, taken in the early 1900s. Architectural designs like these appealed to northerners like Frederick Law Olmsted.

Source: E. M. Violette and C. N. Tolman, *History of Adair County, Together with Reminiscences and Biographical Sketches* (Kirksville, MO: Denslow History Company, 1911), 656.

In his view, what really proved the Germans' superiority was a comparison with white Texans. In another conversation Olmsted struck up with locals later on during his visit, this time with two "German settlers," he had learned that they "purchased, about a year since, the cabin they lived in, 100 acres of land, some cattle" from an "American." Intrigued, he had requested to inspect the cabin—and was immediately struck by how well the two men had fixed it up: "They had taken up the rotten wooden floor of the American, preferring to it a hard earthen floor. They had prepared the roof, and, with a stucco, which they formed by mixing grass with a calcareous clay, had made tight and smooth walls inside and out.... They had put glass sashes into the windows, and had made new doors, swinging easily on their hinges, and furnished with wooden latches."[49] It did not occur to Olmsted that renovating a Texan frontier cabin in so splendid a manner was an undertaking that likely required substantial capital and that said capital may well have been summoned from an ocean away, possibly with the help of a German attorney in San Antonio or Austin. What mattered to him was only that they had done "all the work themselves." They had not employed any enslaved labor, and there was no sign of domestic help. And yet "evidently they lived in greater luxury than most slaveholding Texans."[50]

By 1856, Olmsted had seen enough. Energized and flush with notes, he hurried back to New York to write three book-length accounts of his observations, to be published between 1857 and 1860. Although these books, along with short articles and opinion columns in the *New York Daily Times*, were unlikely to have had much of an impact on the debate over slavery and free labor as had been intended—ultimately, there was not much new that Olmsted added to that particular discussion—they did prove to be of far-reaching consequence for the German immigrant community about which Olmsted had drawn an unequivocally positive portrait. Here was a group of enterprising individuals, he argued, who out of sheer "force and character" had managed to erect admirable farmsteads despite their initial poverty. Such praise came at an opportune moment for the Germans. Within the toxic anti-immigrant atmosphere of the 1850s, it could help to disarm attacks from nativists like those in the Know-Nothing Party, which stood at the peak of its influence in that same decade.

Olmsted had advanced a powerful endorsement of German immigrants' alleged qualities as settlers, frontiersman, and, in particular, builders of homes. With their supreme homes, the Germans in west Texas "inaugurated almost a new era for humanity," he claimed, at least as compared to what Texans who held enslaved men and women had so far managed to achieve, and so it behooved his fellow Americans to finally "acknowledge the Germans as their equals as pioneers." He did not stop there. Given their track record in places like Texas, Olmsted continued, the Germans deserved the strongest consideration in any future attempts to "settl[e], at the least cost, and in the best manner, the vast territorial regions that still are awaiting the pioneer's fences" in the North American West. Such advocacy mattered, since amid the torrent of events that followed, above all the outbreak of the Civil War, both the federal government and a proliferating number of US states developed a voracious appetite for just the kind of "patient and well-directed muscle" that "is the first demand of a new country."⁵¹

Efforts to recruit European immigrants to frontier states were not new, and in some cases they long predated the Civil War. Since at least the 1840s, abolitionists and antislavery activists, followed by small armies of land speculators and railroad men, had sought to introduce "free labor" of European background to the region in hopes of complicating the spread of slavery beyond the South.⁵² Prior to the Civil War, however, recruitment of this sort tended to be sporadic, to arise from private initiative, and to focus on a few specific places, most notably Kansas and Missouri. The war catapulted the issue to the forefront of government agendas across the country, starting with the federal government, which began to regard the rapid settlement of western territories as a military-strategic necessity. In 1862, President Abraham Lincoln signed into law the Homestead Act, granting anyone—regardless of citizen status—title to 160 acres of farmland in the West, free of charge, after five years of residence and relatively basic improvements to the property. Two years later, Lincoln's Republican Party introduced further incentives to settlement by passing into the law the Pacific Railway Acts. As part of these new laws, which expanded on similar land-grant legislation at the state level, tens of millions of acres across the American West were issued to large railroad corporations to build new rail lines and to assist the government with the recruitment of settlers to the region. (Since much of the land in question was not under the control of the federal government at the time, being inhabited as it was by Indigenous peoples, the administration also agreed to provide US Army support to both the railroads and the homesteaders in case they should encounter resistance along the way.)

Individual states soon followed suit with similar policies and programs—though not always with similar motives. Ohio established its first foreign immigrant recruitment office in Cincinnati on April 12, 1863, largely to address wartime manpower shortages in its factories; Kansas and Minnesota did the same in February and March 1864, less with the hope of defeating slavery and more because their denizens feared a large influx of emancipated Black people after the war. Similar concerns compelled the South to enter the fray. "It can only be by the importation of white men," editors at the *New Orleans De Bow's Review* conceded, "to stand shoulder to shoulder with white men in perpetuating a white man's government, and checkmating Yankee ingenuity to drive the Southerner from his home, and inviting negro rule, and with it ruin, and giving them an excuse to people it with the minions of their power." In 1865, Missouri and Tennessee became the first states affiliated with the Confederacy to initiate immigrant recruitment efforts, with Alabama, Louisiana, South Carolina, and Virginia joining the following year. All in all, the number of states and territories that devoted funds to immigrant recruitment jumped from just three in the entire antebellum period to twenty during the decade between 1860 and 1870.[53]

The Civil War did not just stimulate an increase in immigrant recruitment activity. Another notable shift concerned the particular groups that such efforts targeted. If before the war immigrant recruitment had been primarily a regional affair, with most governments and railroad corporations concentrating their activities on the large cities along the Atlantic seaboard, in the

Table 2.1 US States and Territories Passing Laws or Regulations to Encourage Immigration, 1845–75

1845–49	1850–54	1855–59	1860–64	1865–69	1870–75
Michigan (1845)	Wisconsin	Minnesota	Iowa	Alabama	Alabama
		Michigan	Ohio	Arkansas	Colorado Territory
Michigan (1849)			Kansas	Dakota Territory	Iowa
			Minnesota	Florida	Maine
			West Virginia	Georgia	Nebraska
				Louisiana	North Carolina
				Michigan	Oregon
				Missouri	Tennessee
				South Carolina	Texas
				Tennessee	Virginia
				Virginia	Washington Territory
				Wisconsin	West Virginia
					Wyoming Territory

Source: Assembled by the author based on data in Ingrid Schöberl, *Amerikanische Einwandererwerbung in Deutschland 1845–1914* (Stuttgart: Franz Steiner Verlag, 1990).

wake of wartime disruptions and an unprecedented slaughter on the battlefields of the South recruitment efforts increasingly began to targeted Europeans. Priority tended to be given English immigrants, traditionally regarded to be the best "class of foreign immigrant."[54] Apart from these, however, there was also an interest in "northern Europeans" more broadly, including Dutch, Germans, Swiss, Norwegians, and Swedes. In 1865, Ohio became the first state to dispatch a separate recruitment agent to Germany. Others followed in short order; by the early 1870s, no fewer than ten states supported "at least one" permanent representative in Germany—double the number that maintained an agent in the British Isles. In the United States, meanwhile, German speakers were elevated to influential positions such as immigration commissioner or land department commissioner. Michigan hired two German Americans for such positions as early as 1859; native Prussian Frederick W. Horn ran Wisconsin's immigration offices in the 1860s; Louis

F. Schade, a forty-eighter resident in Burlington, Iowa, carried out commission-based immigrant recruitment for the state and several of its railroads; German American Hermann Bokum served in Tennessee as immigration commissioner; Westphalian Francis A. Hoffmann split his time recruiting German immigrants for the state of Illinois and for the Illinois Central Railroad since at least 1862; and Friedrich Kapp was appointed in 1867 as New York's commissioner of emigration and oversaw the Castle Garden immigration facilities, the busiest in the nation.[55]

Often this tack toward immigrants from "northern Europe" was justified using tropes quite similar to those invoked by Olmsted regarding the Germans' alleged prowess as farmers and frontiersmen. George S. Harris, land commissioner of the Hannibal & St. Joseph Railroad Company in Missouri, put it this way: "I have so poor an opinion of the French & Italian immigrants for agriculturalists that I shall not issue any circulars in their languages. My efforts will be most confined to Germans, Scandinavians, English, Welsh and Scotch, as they make good farmers together with all I can induce from the Northern and Eastern States & the British Provinces of America."[56] Tennessee Governor William G. Brownlow agreed. Although just a few years earlier Brownlow had disparaged European immigrants as "paupers and convicts," after the war he could no longer emphasize enough the "vast importance of a large emigration to Tennessee from…Germany and Switzerland." Louisiana planter W. C. Denegre similarly praised "my Germans," to whom he had turned in lieu of enslaved men and women, for their "untiring zeal" and "patient industry, energy, and careful preparations of the soil," and described their "plowing [as] thorough and their preparation of the land careful beyond anything I have ever seen." William G. LeDuc, an influential figure in Minnesota politics and the US commissioner of agriculture under President Rutherford B. Hayes, argued that the Germans and Scandinavians "bring with them not only the means of reaching their respective destinations, and establishing themselves in some honest, if humble occupation, in our cities, towns, and inland counties, but also that they bring what is incomparatively more valuable, honesty, sobriety, persevering industry, and mental cultivation."[57]

Once again, the politics behind such statements tended to be complex and reflect local and regional concerns more than anything else. In the South, interest in immigrants from northern Europe was often less than sincere, given that most observers were well aware of Europeans' reluctance to settle there, and was usually intended as political cover for ongoing efforts to reclassify as "immigrants" those brought under coercive conditions resembling slavery, especially Chinese and Indian indentured servants to whom Southern planters looked as more plausible replacements for their emancipated Black workforce.[58] In the North and West, meanwhile, an ever-evolving "alchemy of race" awarded wide-ranging privileges to some immigrants while rather arbitrarily excluding others. Here, assumptions about a distant kinship between "Anglo-Saxondom," which sat atop the social and political hierarchy of midcentury America, and people regarding themselves as "Germanic" or "Teutonic" went a long way in securing favorable treatment for those who could plausibly claim to belong to these categories.[59]

Myths of kinship mattered, but so did the fact that, as novelist Herbert Quick put it, the Germans in so many cases had "money enough to build the finest farmhouse in the country."[60] Such circumstances, which reinforced stereotypes and created grounds for new political alliances, usually went unexplained. Then and now, it has been a commonplace to say that the Germans of nineteenth-century America were better off than other immigrants, like the Irish, who fled circumstances far more dire than those prevailing in the German lands at virtually any time in the nineteenth century. There is a great deal of truth to such generalizations. But it is also only part of the story. Another part had to do with the struggles of individuals like Johann Bauer, who put a life of hard work into their dream of landed independence. And yet another part had to do with the failure of a revolution, the disillusionment of a professional elite, and the money that began to materialize from halfway around the world.

The Migrant's Spirit: How Industrial Modernity Came to the German Lands. Benjamin P. Hein,
Oxford University Press. © Oxford University Press 2025. DOI: 10.1093/9780197831052.003.0003

3

Struggles with Impudence

In the fall of 1859, Johann Carl Leuchs sat down at his desk to add the finishing touches to a new manuscript. It was his fifth book and yet another milestone in his lifelong struggle to educate the public about the "blessings" of *Gewerbefreiheit*, that is, the freedom to enter and practice any trade one wished. Ever since he published his first prize-winning academic essay at the age of fourteen, Leuchs had written on this topic. More than one hundred pamphlets, essays, and books on Gewerbefreiheit bore his name.[1]

At the core of this prodigious publication stood one key principle: that the liberalization of commerce promotes economic growth. Like almost everyone who considered themselves a liberal in this period, Leuchs believed that only "full and pure" freedom in all aspects of economic life, including in the spheres of work, marriage, and residency, could create the conditions in which commerce and agriculture might thrive. For too long, he warned, an impenetrable thicket of "flawed laws" had sprawled across the German legal landscape, protecting noxious "special interests" and "privilege" at the expense of the German nation as a whole. Cutting back on all the rules and regulations, Leuchs argued, would immediately release the nation's entrepreneurial energies, especially those of the middling classes and the peasantry. Fewer of them would leave for greener pastures, like North America, and deprive Germany of its productive powers. It was all basic "common sense" (*Vernunft*); anyone who considered the question at some length, Leuchs wrote, "cannot decide [it] differently."[2]

Still, Leuchs knew that change remained an uphill battle. The problem was not just the rules and regulations themselves, or even the powerful vested interests like the guilds and local authorities. In Leuchs's view, the biggest obstacles to advancing his economic reform agenda were "stupidity" and "indolence," both all too prevalent among the very class of people he wanted to empower: the small peasant proprietor, the young journeyman, the manufacturing worker, the struggling artisan. After all, so Leuchs, only stupidity could compel people to oppose policies that improved their lives, swept away "patronage," and created the conditions in which they might build more prosperous communities.³

To make matters worse, since the Revolution of 1848 stupidity and indolence had spread to state bureaucracies. For decades—indeed, ever since the Napoleonic period—so-called enlightened monarchies across the continent had been liberalism's staunchest allies, implementing sweeping reforms in an effort to expand their control over local institutions of power, boost their economies, and grow their tax bases. The revolution, not surprisingly, drove a powerful wedge between liberals and their princely partners. As soon as the barricades had been cleared, princes everywhere took steps to preempt another uprising by ingratiating themselves with local institutions of power, including the guilds, communities, and churches. This political alliance proved devastating, at least in the eyes of liberal reformers. Backed by state bureaucracies, communities across German Europe embarked on what has been described as "the strongest program of communal restoration they had ever undertaken."⁴ Not only were pending reforms from the prerevolutionary period shelved, but also, far worse, from Leuchs's perspective, the princes and communities appeared determined to reverse decades of progress by re-establishing the corporate order and, in some cases, even expanding its reach. By the end of what liberal observers decried as the "conservative fifties," prospects for an expanded freedom of enterprise across German Europe had moved farther out of reach than ever before.⁵

But at the very moment when it seemed as though things could not get worse, winds began blowing in a new direction. In a stunning break from decades of stalled reform, starting around 1860, almost every German state introduced sweeping reform packages aimed at dramatically reducing or altogether abolishing local rules governing commerce, business, and citizenship. Most remarkable was that the shift came about completely organically, beginning with the explicit backing of the communities and guilds. In the 1860s, indeed, it was master artisans—traditionally one of the staunchest defenders of the corporate order—who demanded more "freedom" in all corners of social and economic life. It was these people, not men like Leuchs, who were behind the so-called New Era (*Neue Ära*), who saw through the most sweeping liberal reform program in half a century.⁶

Against all odds—or so it seemed—Leuchs's lifelong vision suddenly became a reality. As one of those liberals who always retained his faith in ideas and education, Leuchs could think of only one good explanation for this sudden turn of affairs: Reason, at last, had triumphed over stupidity, just as he always knew it would.

Historians have since interpreted the unlikely shift in favor of economic liberalism as the crowning achievement of persistent efforts by bourgeois journalists and other proponents of progress. Men like Leuchs "gradually managed to pull public opinion onto their side" after years of "untiring agitation" in books, pamphlets, newspapers, journals, and other forms of writing. Such tenacity paid off because "around 1860 the turnaround was complete: once and for all, the public had been won for the idea of economic liberalism."[7] Other observers have trod more carefully, realizing that "the pendulum of public policy swung…so violently as to seem historically and politically improbable." How was it that after 1860 Leuchs suddenly found an audience, even among his most recalcitrant adversaries like small-town artisans? How did he and other liberals accomplish a feat that had remained elusive for half a century and that not even an unprecedented uprising like the Revolution of 1848 had managed to bring about? Still more remarkable was that Leuchs had changed nothing about his argument. In the manuscript he was finishing in the fall of 1859, he explicitly ruled out the need to rethink his position: "It would be superfluous," he scoffed, "to waste another word on explaining the blessings of Gewerbefreiheit and the disadvantages of the old system." The new book would focus on simply providing "more facts."[8]

The issue, of course, was never a shortage of facts. Work encompassed a broad array of meanings and purposes. Some believed that work was nothing short of the "key to the entire human universe." Work earned a wage, but it also earned respect and dignity because "it is not success or profit that matters but the moral deed in one's work." To some, like small-town artisans, work was a "calling." To others, like tenant farmers or field hands, it was a "prime masculine virtue."[9] Critics of Gewerbefreiheit often dwelled on this point, contending that proponents of the policy failed to "grasp the full scope of consequences." Nobody opposed the idea of economic growth; to the contrary, by the middle of the nineteenth century growth had found an enthusiastic following, even among once-fervent skeptics. But growth could still mean different things to different people and, besides, there were larger "political-moral" issues that needed to be taken into consideration. Corporate institutions were the glue that held society together: They ensured social peace, stability, continuity. While they limited competition, in so doing they also guaranteed a more equitable distribution of resources. They upheld a certain social inequality, through paternal authority, gender norms, and customary morality (*Sittengesetz*), but the purpose of all this was first and foremost to prevent "mischief." What to Leuchs looked like an "overreach of regulations" was so much more: an ingenious web not just of actual laws but also of an unwritten and even unspoken coda, a web so strong it supported the weight of an entire way of life. Cutting its strings would send society into free fall: It would "undermine [our] moral and physical power, our existence."[10]

If Leuchs was aware of such objections, he seemed either unwilling or unable to take them seriously. He mocked his compatriots for mourning what looked like an overly romanticized version of the past, suggesting that the triumph of Gewerbefreiheit was as inevitable as that of modernity itself. Even Karl Marx, whose sympathies for the working classes went considerably further than Leuchs's, demonstrated little patience for those who valorized the more holistic conception of work, which he maintained was just another way in which the bourgeoisie exercised control. "The bourgeois have very good reasons to attribute to work supernatural creative capabilities," Marx explained. "For it follows just from the dependency of work on natural resources that Man, who does not possess any other property besides his own labour power, has to serve as slave to other Men, who have made themselves proprietors of the material conditions of work, under all social and cultural circumstances."[11]

There was some truth to this. A corporate understanding of work did imply a social hierarchy, atop which stood the bourgeois owners of the means of production. But it did not help Marx's cause to write with such contempt for the people in whose name he claimed to speak. To the contrary, it only widened the chasm between well-intentioned writers like himself and his audience. As a spokesman of Lübeck's artisans put it in 1861,

> In times of economic growth and mighty development, such as we witness today, it may be frowned upon to oppose this fresh and freewheeling life with a cool and calculating mind. But while there have been efforts to discredit us, we who have not shown ourselves to be captivated by and ecstatic about those great social ideas that have moved the world; to attribute our words and actions to personal interest; to chastise us as heartless and obstinate; or to detect in us a fearful and weak laggard; and yet, here we are, daring to speak up against an idea... that has led many to dream of a golden age.[12]

Statements like these suggest that, by the 1860s, the debate over Gewerbefreiheit had devolved from a discussion about merits of policy into a caustic exchange characterized more by personal insult than by substance. Standing in Leuchs's way were neither stupidity nor indolence, but powerful identity politics. No wonder Leuchs's books had failed for decades to reach their intended audience: They probably evoked only disdain, if they were even read in the first place.[13]

In August 1861, excitement broke out at the home of the Krause family in Borzykowo, a small village just outside the town of Wreschen (Września) in the overwhelmingly rural East Prussian province of Posen. A letter had just arrived from "Quebeck in Amerika." The handwriting on the front left little doubt that it was from Albert. Several postage stamps, placed unevenly along the right side of the letter, evidenced the enormous distance it had traveled: from "West-Canada" to New York, then across the Atlantic Ocean and on to Hamburg, from there to Berlin, then to Posen, and finally to Wreschen and Borzykowo. The Krauses had good reason to be excited. It was the first sign of life from their son and brother since his decision in January to emigrate to America.[14]

It is easy to picture what might have happened next. In a manner reminiscent of genre painter Berthold Woltze's depiction of a communal reading scene in *A Letter from America* (1860), the entire Krause family likely gathered around to read and listen to Albert's letter. One of the parents may have sliced open the envelope and shaken out its contents. Eight wide-eyed children—Albert had two younger brothers and six sisters—likely watched in anticipation as the elder Krause began to read.[15] "Once, in thick fog off of the coast of Newfoundland," it began, "our ship was almost smashed by an iceberg that was three English miles long and as tall as the mast of our ship. The helmsman only saw it when we were barely three boat lengths away." A wild, last-minute maneuver staved off disaster, preventing the mighty three-masted *Gellert* from plunging to the bottom of the sea. In what Albert described as "Lorenzbai," off of the coast of Prince Edward Island, "100 whales" swam right beside the *Gellert*, each the "length of a ship." Next, he recounted the train ride from Québec City to Ottawa. It was crowded and uncomfortable but exhilarating all the same because it took him past the most breathtaking monuments and landscapes he had ever seen in his life: across the "famous Victoria-Bridge," "the largest bridge in the world," and through the "North American jungle," which during that spring of 1861 was apparently "brimming" with so many of "the most beautiful red raspberries, you only had to reach for them."[16]

The Krause children likely savored these communal readings of their brother's adventures in America. Having grown up in the home of tenant farmers and part-time proprietors (there is evidence that Krause Sr., besides working the fields of sugar beets and potatoes, ran a tool repair workshop), it was unlikely that they enjoyed access to the kind of entertainment readily available to the middle classes, like adventure novels, travel stories, and other popular writings about North America.[17] Nor were they likely to have the leisure to engage with such long-form writing. Although in many cases they were able to read and write, thanks to Prussia's well-established elementary school system, children of tenant farmers in midcentury Posen still spent most of their time by their fathers' sides in the fields. Albert's sisters were almost certainly occupied from a young age as maids in either their own household or another nearby.[18] The letters they received from their brother Albert in America consequently took on a form of entertainment that was affordable and comfortably slotted into the daily routine of a working family. Never longer than a few pages, they could be read alongside dinner or before the children's bedtime.[19] Since it was their own brother Albert who was the protagonist, the siblings could insert themselves into the narrative by scribbling a question or two at the bottom of their parents' next reply to Albert. "You ask, dear Elise, how things are with my eyes?" Albert once responded to his younger sister in a letter from Baton Rouge, Louisiana, where he was serving in the Union Army in 1863. "They are not very well, even though I am otherwise healthy and strong. The southern sun and heat have a poor effect on my face."[20]

Granted, not all members of the Krause family were interested in Albert's letters for their entertainment value. His father always wanted to know more about "what sort of plan" Albert had set for himself to "make a living."[21] The point of his son's emigration to America had not been simply to roam the world as an adventurer and storyteller. It had been to help his family escape their increasingly untenable situation in Borzykowo, where growing competition from Polish seasonal migrant laborers was depressing wages for the German tenant farmer families (*Instfamilien*).[22] Albert was to acquire land that their family could call its own and that would be large enough to sustain them all. Once Albert had identified a suitable plot, he was to "build a house on it," "furnish it," and after "one year," the rest of the family would "follow and run the farm."[23] From the very beginning, Albert's father sought reassurances on these matters; he wanted to know that his eldest son was not "living aimlessly into the future" and forgetting his "oath" to his family.[24] If land was too expensive in the beginning, as Albert pointed out in late 1862, then he needed to think about starting an apprenticeship instead, rather than languishing in odd, menial jobs that paid the rent and nothing more. Years of difficult training lay ahead. What was Albert waiting for?[25]

Albert retorted that he was waiting to "take advantage of an opportunity." He had discovered that in America people took a different approach. Nobody settled on a single line of work so early in their lives, and few followed in the exact footsteps of their fathers—which in Albert's case would have meant farming combined with petty craftwork. "In such a sprawling country as the United States," he explained, "the poor foreigner has such a large and varied choice of the most diverse lines of business that it would be hubris to think that one could choose the most advantageous one in such a short time as I have been in this country."[26] Moreover, he added, in the United States "the choice is made all the more difficult by the fact that in no other country each profession is subject to such rapid changes in pecuniary remuneration.... As a result, here artisans especially learn many different businesses at the same time—if one no longer works, then they do something else. This changing of professions takes place frequently, at least by European standards, and to the most unnatural degree, doctors become blacksmiths, painters, and shoemakers and they, in turn, become doctors, pharmacists, attorneys, etc."[27] Albert had a point: People were much more at liberty to pursue different trades in the United States than in East Prussia at this time, even if he was exaggerating the differences. But his father seemed unimpressed and indeed chastized Albert for entertaining "illusions" about America. Of course, one had to "be prepared for the worst" when trying to make it in a foreign world. But a good job and income would not simply fall into Albert's lap, as he seemed to think; it required discipline and the "most strenuous of efforts."[28]

Albert kept pushing back. His father had misunderstood; he had a plan, even if it was a bit unconventional. "My plan is and has been to earn myself some money and then invest it in land at the right moment," he claimed. He knew full well that "the farmer lives happiest and most independent," and it was his intention to become one. In fact, in a few months' time he would head for "western states where it will be easier for me to familiarize myself with the agriculture" and where he could learn the ropes of American farming by working "in the agrarian factories of Milwaukee, Chicago, and St. Louis"— just as one might in an apprenticeship back in Prussia. "That is why, dear father, trust my words," he pleaded. "In just a few years already I will be all satisfied with my situation! Until then, of course, you my loved ones must take care of yourselves with whatever you can. Dear father I ask you once more: do not fret the matter, trust the future and give me your blessing in all my decisions!"[29]

Struggles with Impudence 77

FIGURE 3.1 **Albert Krause.** A reproduction of an original photograph of Albert Krause during military service in the US Civil War. Krause served at the rank of sergeant in the VIII Corps of the Union Army.
Source: Courtesy of the Forschungsbibliothek Gotha, Universität Erfurt.

Albert's struggles with his father offer an alternative vantage point from which to make sense of concomitant debates in Prussia (and elsewhere in German Europe) over reforms such as Gewerbefreiheit. For the Krauses in Borzykowo, Albert's letters from America offered a personal and, by all accounts, more positive perspective on these reforms—in stark contrast to the books and articles of Johann Leuchs, who lived more than 400 miles away in the equivalent of a foreign country, the kingdom of Bavaria. For those who spent twelve hours a day, and sometimes as many as fourteen, planting and harvesting sugar beets on a Prussian lord's manor, Leuchs's writings were inaccessible and unrelatable.[30] Albert's letters were neither; not only were they read by every member of the family, but also they were vigorously discussed. This did not mean that ideas about freedom suddenly become celebrated values in the Krause home. Tensions lingered, as evidenced by Albert's repeated requests for his father's blessing. It would take Albert years, if not decades, of writing letters to assuage his family's concerns. Again and again he explained why his new vagabond life was, in truth, no vagabond life at all: why it was the right thing to do, why it demonstrated character, persistence, even filial piety—and why, in the end, it was the family's best hope of achieving their dreams of a prosperous farm safe from the uncertainties of an emergent, modern economy.[31]

There can be little doubt that intimacy furnished pen-wielding emigrants with considerable advantages vis-à-vis social reformers like Johann Leuchs. But the reasons why Albert Krause proved so much more effective also went beyond the basic trust enjoyed by kin. One was that Albert, quite cognizant of his new role as cultural translator, possessed a knack for anticipating the indignation and apprehension that his letters might prompt back in Borzykowo. Far from dismissing such concerns, he spent considerable effort, along with plenty of ink and paper, to acknowledge them. "Of course I have become more American," he conceded in one letter from 1865, some four years after his departure from Prussia. He was responding to accusations that his family no longer recognized him, particularly as they learned more about his unusual choices with regard to his work life. Albert insisted that he remained quite aware of his Prussian roots and that his moral compass was still fully intact. "Sometimes," he assured his mother, "I myself am surprised by my own impudence [*Dreistigkeit*]."[32]

Albert was referring here to a specific incident that had taken place in Buffalo, New York, the previous summer. Short of the kind of cash he needed to move west and buy a homestead, he had been roaming the streets of Buffalo for weeks in search of gainful employment. Finally, he had found a job with a local patent agent who paid him "6 taler per week" to create drawings of machines for which the agent was submitting a patent application to the US Patent Office in Washington, DC. Drawing on his years of schooling back in Prussia, Albert had impressed the agent with his knowledge of perspective drawing, which apparently none of the other job candidates understood how to do. "They looked at me and were stunned," he wrote. "Everyone admired my work," and soon thereafter the agent raised his wage to "12 taler per week." Meanwhile, Albert confessed that he had never expected to "earn my daily bread" with an activity that "back in Prussia" constituted little more than "doodling."[33]

But the most controversial part had yet to come. Within months, Albert's workload at the patent agency began to decline, and soon enough he was once again in search of a job. This time, he found one right away, at a "windmill-factory called John T. Nay, the largest here in America." It was a "firm that constructs windmills in all parts of the United States," and Albert's task consisted of drawing up the necessary blueprints. Once again, his ability to draw in perspective proved invaluable because he needed to imagine "how to distribute machine parts in the most advantageous way in a building so that everything fits." His drawings would determine the "details of the parts the factory produces and then ships to the construction sites," which meant that a "large responsibility... rests on my shoulders." Not long thereafter, Albert reported that he had started his own engineering business, preparing drawings for local developers and contractors. In Buffalo, "there now hangs a sign on one of the largest houses in the best business district in town: 'Albert Krause, Mechanical Draughtsman.'"[34]

For the son of a tenant farmer in Borzykowo, East Prussia, this was a remarkable transformation. What might have taken years back in Prussia took Albert less than six months, a period during which he not only completed his training as an "engineer" but also established his own business. That Albert would choose the word *dreist* to describe these experiences made good sense. It was a word that might be translated into English as "brazen" or "daring," but it also carried more negative connotations: impudence. It was the kind of brazenness one needed to defy authority, like one's social betters or, more broadly speaking, experience, wisdom, and learning. By practicing as an engineer without first subjecting himself to years of training and vetting in someone else's workshop, Albert had made a mockery of the engineering profession.[35]

He knew that there was something fundamentally wrong about accepting a job for which he was patently unqualified, given his prior technical training as well as his age and social background.[36] Eager to preempt what seemed like an inevitable reproach from home, he opted to confess. "Think about it," he wrote, reflecting on his deeds as if they were someone else's. "I had never seen a mill before, definitely had no idea of its different components, and now I was to draft blueprints for the largest mills [in the country]." He explained that, at the time, "my head was spinning, and I doubted myself, subconsciously knowing that I had been overly confident in my own abilities."[37] But then life got in the way. An empty wallet had left him with little choice but to go through with his charade: "I reminded myself of the consequences of what would happen if I gave up on this position, and so I put to work what little brain I have as best as I could; and that helped; I compared

FIGURE 3.2 **A letter from Albert Krause.** An excerpt from one of Albert Krause's letters to his family in Prussia dated May 10, 1863. Krause occasionally included small drawings alongside his writing. He claimed that his ability to draw "in perspective" enabled him to embark on a new career as a "Mechanical Draughtsman."

Source: Courtesy of the Forschungsbibliothek Gotha, Universität Erfurt.

different blueprints in order to get a clear picture of the inner setup of these mills, and because I know my way around scale and mechanics, before long I figured it out."[38] It was in the context of real-life experiences like these that Albert implored his family to think differently about his choices. What he had done might be considered dreist on some level, to be sure, but it might also be interpreted as a sign of healthy self-confidence and survival instinct. "Instead of being shy," he wrote, "it is better to say that you know how to do this and that, too, even if you have no idea how to do any of it, because then they will take you." Being "*dreist* and boastful" did not just imply a lack of moral judgment. In America, at least, it was also a well-respected strategy for "finding work."[39]

In fact, he argued, his family might think of Dreistigkeit as a skill in its own right. Aware of customary Prussian Protestant deference for anyone who possessed the discipline of honing a craft for years, he explained that Dreistigkeit was not the inevitable consequence of poor moral judgment. It, too, required practice and learning. "A hundred times before I tried to be dreist," Albert wrote. But it "is entirely at odds with my nature," and every time "I made as timid an impression as before so that people were convinced that I did not understand what I was doing." Yet nothing could have been further from the truth. "And guess what happened! It turned out that I knew better how to draw blueprints than any of the others... four weeks I worked for 8 taler, then I finally had the courage to ask for 12. No American would have done that, already after a week they would probably have asked for 15 taler."[40]

"Thanks to my mathematical knowledge," he continued, "I am now widely considered a proficient engineer." It was an achievement worth celebrating and proved a larger point that Albert had been trying to make all along regarding the "blessing of freedom":

> The work is very interesting, and I have the most beautiful opportunity to train myself as an engineer. That is the blessing of freedom! Would I have ever been allowed out there in Germany to take on such work, even if I knew what I was doing? There, they would first ask: Have you completed the necessary, required studies, do you have all the mandated certificates? etc etc. Do you have the permission of the government? Here nobody asks for that stuff. Here they only ask: "Do you know how to do it?" and "If you know how, then do it."[41]

One can only marvel at Albert Krause's presence of mind. Perhaps it was just who he was: young, ambitious, bold, and perhaps also a bit naive. Traits like these may well have been what brought him to America in the first place. Emigrants tended to self-select in this way; real gumption was required to leave everything behind, to board a creaking and crowded ship, to plunge into the unknown. Dreistigkeit may not have come naturally to Albert, but he did sport an immigrant's knack for striving.

There can be little doubt that people like Albert stood apart. And yet to explain their experience in terms of personality traits alone would miss the forest for the trees. Albert's embrace of Dreistigkeit, not to mention the urgency with which he sought to persuade relatives to do the same, was not just a function of his personal ambitions or idiosyncratic nature. It was also a reflection of the world he came to inhabit, its politics and values. Thus, when Albert first arrived in America, he found himself in the midst of one of the most tumultuous decades in US history. This was a time of war, marked by the utmost brutality and hatred and destruction, yet also by soaring ambition and optimism. As a prolonged struggle over the freedom and human dignity of millions of enslaved Black men and women, the decade was revolutionary in every sense of the word. It would be no exaggeration to say that the United States of America that Albert arrived in in 1861 was just then undergoing a second founding. These events bore directly on Albert's life, and not just because he spent years serving in the armed forces of the Union. The most significant development from his perspective was that the legal definition of US citizenship changed in a fundamental way. Before the 1860s, citizenship was governed by the Naturalization Act of 1790, which stipulated that only "free white person[s]" should be eligible for the privileges of citizenship. After the Civil War, and with the passage of the Fourteenth and Fifteenth Amendments, it became illegal in America to discriminate on the basis of race or skin color. US citizenship consequently became more widely accessible than ever before.[42]

One would think that expanding the rights of people of color would be of little concern to German immigrants whose own legal status remained unchanged. By and large, that was true. Yet there were unexpected consequences to the revolutionary changes in US citizenship law that followed in the wake of the Civil War. The previous regime, in which whiteness had constituted an explicit legal category, had given rise to a particular set of assimilatory and immigration strategies, all of which now ceased to make sense and, in some instances, were even rendered counterproductive. Thus, during the antebellum years, German immigrants as a rule did not invest much effort into assimilating into American society, not least because attainment of American rights and privileges had been contingent only on being white, not on being American. Asserting their Germanness was, consequently, just as effective a strategy for making it in their new environs as was asserting Americanness or Englishness or even Irishness. All met the whiteness threshold.[43]

The events of the 1860s put an end to this logic. When the Naturalization Act of 1790 was amended and whiteness was abolished as the basis of citizenship and belonging in the United States, the ambiguous and shape-shifting category of Americanness assumed its place, and this was a development that did not bode well for any immigrant alien, including the Germans. The change created new pressure to change tactics and, more to the point, to embrace assimilation as one's path into American society. "Naturally, one's behavior & the way one conducts oneself as a gentleman determine the degree of good will one gets," observed Emil Kuhn, in a letter he composed not long after his arrival in New York in 1867. It mattered now more than ever, he urged, that the Germans act "more dignified and manly" and do more to counter Americans' "antiquated prejudices" against the "fawning, toadying, crawling…Dutchman."[44]

As Kuhn went on to explain, the stakes were quite high. On the one hand, there was the possibility that the Germans would fall from their privileged perch in America, that anti-immigrant nativists might well succeed in their ongoing campaign to deny the Germans entry into the country or demote them to some second-class status. Something of the sort was already happening to the Irish; more recently, it had been done to Black freedpeople who, despite having finally won their liberty, were still denied citizenship and the right to vote. In an ominous sign for the Germans, the rationale often cited for Black disenfranchisement was that the recently enslaved population suffered from too "servile" a mindset to qualify for the full array of civil privileges. It would take time for them to unlearn the slavish indolence that a life in chains had inculcated in them.[45]

On the other hand, at just the moment when the Germans' standing in America seemed more tenuous than it had been in decades, the privileges associated with belonging to the American nation multiplied. In 1862, Congress passed the Homestead Act, part of a slate of wartime legislation that aimed to secure western territories for the Union by settling them as quickly as possible with "free" Americans. The law offered 160 acres of free land to any free man willing to live on it and improve it, and it also promised that the US Army would protect him from harassment by Native Americans. In the meantime, great sums of public money were made available to lay new railroad tracks across the continent and to connect all the new homesteads to the markets of the east and to the world.

The opportunities were there there, but the Germans, Kuhn advised, needed to wise up. Lest they be "spurned" like a "lowly...subject" and lest they be denied the fabulous bounties of North America, they should immediately shed their "dandyish, all-subservient" behavior. It was not too late; "there is still space for many thousands." Time was of the essence, and there would have to be sacrifices. It would no longer suffice to learn a bit of English, for instance, or to make minor adjustments here and there. They would have to compensate for their Germanness. They would have to be double the gentleman they might otherwise have been, more American than the most American patriot. Their self-confidence would have to be greater, their showmanship bolder, their mobility more unbridled, their contempt for authority louder. In a word, they would have to perfect the art of being dreist.[46]

Kuhn had little doubt that they would do it, and without protest, because any price, no matter how steep, was worth a homestead on the edges of the American West. "I pity all the poor country folk at home who year in and year out must endlessly till that meagre plot of land they call their own, just in order to earn their gangly bread & as a reward for all their effort at the end of the year they can only expect new toil in the next.... How richly their work would be rewarded here, on lush ground that does not need any fertilizer and that on top of it all is so cheap that you can almost call it free."[47] Kuhn himself had already become someone he never thought he would be. He had changed jobs countless times, moved from place to place with astonishing frequency, "saddle[d] over, as they like to say here." He had adjusted his stance on the question of liberty, informing relatives that "I would be lying if I said that I agree with [equality for Black Americans], despite all my views on freedom...once the negro is clean of the feces in which slavery has kept him, then one may give him citizen rights, but we are not there yet." And he had started to drink less beer, "at most three glasses a day." A year later, he reported drinking only "water, tea & milk" which, he remarked, "taste pretty good once you get used to them."[48]

Given the one-sided nature of Albert Krause's surviving correspondence—the letters he received from Borzykowo have been lost—the question of what exactly the family thought of their son and brother's conduct in Buffalo can be difficult to answer. Still, it is not altogether impossible. On the one hand, Albert usually organized his letters by first paraphrasing the questions and concerns raised by his family in a previous letter, a practice that had the effect of turning his letters into a kind of transcript of their exchange. On the other hand, it is possible to infer some forgiveness, maybe even tacit acceptance, in light of the fact that the correspondence continued for many years, lasting at least another decade or so. Albert succeeded insofar as he managed to retain enough credibility so as not to be shunned or cut off entirely.

Whether he managed to change minds and inspire others to emulate him is a different question. As far as his parents were concerned, his persuasive powers appear to have been limited. Thus, there is evidence that the two elder Krauses, a devout couple, stayed true to what they would have described as a Prussian Protestant morality that emphasized honesty, truth, humility (*Demut*), and self-discipline. When Krause Sr. suddenly passed away in December 1862, Albert found few words to say but to praise the old man's ardent commitment to a "moral life." His letter from that time reads like an exercise in finding synonyms for "righteous." "From his youth on," Albert wrote, his father had shown himself "diligent, honest, virtuous, and upright." Never had he dared to "test his luck," and never had he chosen the easy yet ethically questionable path. Of course, what reads like a heartfelt eulogy to his father's "strong EXECUTION OF HIS NOBLE, unwavering will" may also have been a subtle jab at the obstinacy of the departed. Albert never capitalized words in his letters; it was an indicator of the deep frustrations that may have built up in him over a father who refused, until the very end, to acknowledge the righteousness of his son's activities in America.[49]

Krause Sr. seems to have taken his skepticism to his grave. But it was a different story with Albert's siblings, especially his younger brother Aurelius. At the time of their father's passing, Aurelius, as the second oldest son in the family, inherited the responsibility to feed, house, and clothe an aging mother, a younger brother named Arthur and six sisters. Though he was only fourteen years old in the spring of 1863, Aurelius was suddenly forced to grow up. Under these circumstances, it would have been customary for Aurelius to quit school immediately and take his father's place on their tenant farm, in addition to keeping up the family's tool repair workshop. But that is not what happened. In a remarkable show of defiance—call it Dreistigkeit—Aurelius told his grieving mother that he planned to leave Borzykowo as soon as possible and become a sailor. For a son of tenant farmers in one of the most rural parts of Prussia, some 185 miles inland from the nearest seaport, this was an unusual, not to mention jarring, ambition. Not only was Aurelius abdicating his filial responsibilities in pursuit of what sounded like a selfish thirst for adventure, but also he was doing it at the worst imaginable moment for his family.[50]

Of course, Aurelius was not simply the son of peasant-artisans. He was also the brother of an emigrant who lived in America and wrote letters that ceaselessly touted the "blessings of freedom." In the wake of their father's death, Aurelius may have felt emboldened to act on dreams nurtured by Albert's letters. Was it surprising that he, a teenage boy, would find appeal in his brother's adventures, in stories about floating icebergs off the coast of Newfoundland or the "ship-long" whales near Prince Edward Island? Albert had urged his siblings to take the initiative ever since he arrived in America in 1861: Do not commit to any one path right away, he advised. Wait for "an opportunity." Try to "see the world." In the spring of 1863, Aurelius was given an opportunity, and he seemed ready to take it.[51]

There is other evidence that Albert's letters were part of the mix of motives that set Aurelius on the path toward his unexpected decision: namely, the fact that his mother unsure how to tame Aurelius's seafaring ambitions, turned to none other than Albert in America for advice and help.[52] She seemed to believe that Albert had Aurelius's ear and that he might therefore be in a position to talk sense into his younger brother. She suggested that, if Aurelius refused to change his mind, Albert could back her up in insisting to Aurelius that at the very least he should enlist in the Prussian navy, not the merchant marine. In the navy, he would receive proper accommodations and provisioning and, in exchange for committing to a certain period of service, would have access to an education in a specific skill or craft at the naval academy in Berlin. He might also learn some discipline and respect for authority, both of which he evidently lacked. And, if Aurelius was forthright and diligent, he might climb the career ladder and one day become an officer. The merchant marine offered none of these advantages. Aurelius would likely suffer the worst of conditions on poorly equipped merchant ships; he would have no opportunity to gain useful skills, let alone proper discipline; and he would have to contend with all the vagaries in remuneration that came with working in a risky business like maritime commerce.[53]

Albert sympathized with his mother's concerns. He, too, was taken aback that Aurelius "so desires to become a sailor," and he urged his brother in the same letter to give the matter "thorough thought." At the same time, he contradicted his mother by adding, wryly, "I prefer he join the merchant marine." It was doubtful, for one, that the navy's "accommodations, treatment, and provisioning" for sailors were that much better than on merchant ships, even if the navy "may be better organized." Far more disconcerting to Albert was that Aurelius's "entry into the service of the state" would essentially require him to surrender his "personal freedom." And that, Albert warned, would constitute "too great a sacrifice."[54]

What worried him most was that the Prussian navy was unlikely to afford his brother opportunities to rise through the ranks. Albert predicted, despite never having served in the Prussian military himself, that Aurelius "will be passed over" by those with "rich and noble parents, regardless of their scant ability." He would be forced to "quietly endure" this "injustice" because if he dared to "speak his opinion or express his views in any way he will fall out of favor with his officers and his service will become so much more difficult." He might attempt to curry favor with superiors by employing "cajolery," as others did, but that route was hardly "worthy of a decent man." It certainly did not instill the kind of values that their mother expected of her sons. And so Aurelius, "possessing too much honor" to brownnose himself to a promotion, would have to recognize that there was "no straightforward, lawful way" to the top in the Prussian navy. In the end, he would be an "unhappy person" throughout the entire "twelve years of service to which one is obligated."[55]

No, Albert concluded, enlisting in the Prussian navy was the last thing Aurelius should be thinking about. Returning to his mother's original dilemma, he proposed an alternative solution. What if his brother came to live and work in the United States for a few years? A one-way ticket would cost Aurelius no more than "50 dollars," which in any case was "a sum that in Germany would not even suffice to learn a suitable profession." During the voyage, Aurelius would have the opportunity to experience the life of a sailor for himself, and "on top of it all he would have the advantage of seeing a beautiful part of the world, expand his knowledge, and meet people." After crossing the Atlantic Ocean, his brother could decide whether he still wanted to become a sailor or whether he might instead look to learn "a craft, a trade, or some profession"—that is, a steady line of work that would help him support his family.[56]

If Aurelius chose the latter, Albert continued, it was still best that he come to America. After all, in the United States he could get his certifications much more quickly "than over there in Germany," certainly in less than twelve years as "a slave" in the Prussian navy. It might even be possible "that he can start his own business here" and run it "with me, hand in hand. Two people can do it much better than one, and we both would be able to rely on each other." Meanwhile, Albert reassured his mother that, of course, "I am not saying that Aurelius should stay here in America forever." But if Aurelius was going to earn good wages as soon as possible to support his mother and siblings, it was perhaps most advantageous for him to get his start in America, where it is "noticeably easier to get ahead."[57] At the very least, Aurelius was to "think on it and write me how you judge it." All he expected from his brother was "hard work, good will, and courage," in exchange for which he promised "all the help and support I can offer."[58]

In the end, Aurelius never did join Albert in America. What, then, did he choose to do?⁵⁹ Did he stay in Borzykowo, supporting his family and running the farm and workshop? Or did he stick to his plans for a "life at sea"? Given what is known about the lives of tenant farmers in the Vistula delta in this period, the answer to both questions was probably no. A study published in 1892 found that at midcentury there had been a distinct "tendency among the indigenous [agricultural] worker" of this region "to either switch into another trade or to emigrate." In regions just north of Borzykowo, for example, government officials detected a dual pattern of "heavy emigration" and "an almost routine switching of careers amongst the children into either other trades [or] into factories, as in the coastal estuary."⁶⁰ It was possible that, rather than emigrate to America or join up as a sailor, Aurelius opted to stay in or around Borzykowo while leaving his father's tenant farm and pursuing a new line of work, perhaps a trade or a factory job in a larger urban center like nearby Bromberg (Bydgoszcz) or Danzig (Gdańsk).

In the context of the conversations taking place among the Krauses in the summer of 1863, this seems like the most plausible outcome. To begin with, Albert's relentless arguments against the Prussian navy idea probably appealed not just to Aurelius but also to his mother. Besides losing twelve years of his life, Albert warned, "it seems to me that the education Aurelius will receive [from the navy] can only have a damaging effect on the later character of a young man." Officers would attempt to inculcate in Aurelius a strong sense of "servility." His confidence would be undermined; he would "think less of himself." Ultimately, he would lose all capacity for "free thought, judgment, and speaking his mind." These problems would have struck Aurelius as quite familiar, since what Albert was describing was not unlike the "education" their late father had tried to instill in his children.⁶¹

Albert had further warned that a "servile" mentality was especially "damaging" at this very moment in history, in the 1860s. The world was changing quickly, he warned. "The most magnificent Revolutions, both in political and societal respects," were underway. Though vague as to what precise revolutions he was referring to, Albert predicted that new "lines of business" would soon emerge as a result of these changes, along with substantial "earnings that derive from them." He warned Aurelius, and his mother, that the kind of "lowly thinking" they were teaching in the Prussian navy would leave "a young man" like Aurelius woefully ill-prepared to take full advantage of these opportunities.⁶² These arguments, too, would have made sense to Aurelius as he debated his future in Borzykowo with his mother and siblings. In 1863, the Kingdom of Prussia had been experiencing a rapid ascent for years, both politically and economically. Free commerce had been on the rise across the central European map. Perhaps Prussia, too, might soon introduce Gewerbefreiheit. Whether Aurelius would take advantage of these changes is anyone's guess. Certainly he was well informed about their promise.

There is another perspective from which to reflect on Aurelius's thinking and fate, and that is by considering the experience of those who could not point to a relative in America and his urgent endorsements of the "blessings of freedom." One such individual was the Hessian tanner Julius Caesar, who was born and raised in the village of Maxsain in the heart of the Westerwald Forest, then a part of the Duchy of Nassau.

Apart from the fact that he did not enjoy the benefit of news from America, Julius Caesar seems to have had much in common with Aurelius Krause. Born in 1835, he was about the same age, and he also had many siblings, six in total, among whom he was the second oldest after his brother Karl. Like Aurelius Krause, Caesar did not take much liking to his lot in life. While it was the expectation of his father that he would carry on the family business and become a master tanner, especially after Karl, who was supposed to inherit the workshop, passed away prematurely, it was obvious to Caesar from a young age that the business of tanning was not just loathsome but also did not match his strengths and talents. Those laid elsewhere: with reading books, with artistic endeavors like sketching and drawing, and with learning foreign languages like English and French. Caesar dreamed of finishing secondary school and believed that one day he would "make my luck abroad."[63]

At times, there had been opportunities to escape the burden of expectation and, "free as a bird," to pursue his passions and "see the world." One of these came along in 1854, when Caesar was eighteen years old. After his father had unexpectedly passed away the previous winter, he had been hurried off by his family to Göttingen, known for its master tanners, to complete his apprenticeship so that he could take over his father's business. But after just one week on the job, he had been let go by his overseeing master, who he remembered had been an "unfriendly man" and who had taken issue with the poor quality of his work, as well as his apparent lack of discipline (as Caesar himself admitted, he had arrived drunk on the first day of work). Suddenly finding himself free of the watchful eye of a chaperone, as well as out of sight from his family and any acquaintances who might recognize him, he had decided to take his chances and to set off for the port of Bremerhaven on the North Sea. What exactly he had hoped to do there he did not say. Yet the thought of leaving for America must have crossed his mind, given that in 1854 Bremerhaven was a central node in what was then the largest exodus of emigrants ever recorded from the region, with an estimated quarter of a million emigrants from the German lands arriving on American shores that year.[64]

Whatever Caesar's ambitions in the great North Sea port, they came to naught. Traveling to Bremerhaven in those days required boarding a steamboat in Bremen and sailing roughly 35 miles down the Weser River.[65] Although Caesar had expected it to be a short and straightforward trip, things had turned out differently. Delayed at departure, his vessel had missed its high tide window and sat stranded on a sandbank for hours. Hoping to head below deck to escape the frigid North Sea breeze, he had found himself immediately turned back by the "suffocating, putrid air" inside the ship and by the sight of a vast crowd of wretched "emigrants...who sought their new home (*Heimat*) in America." By the time the vessel reached its destination, he had caught a "nasty cold" and, it seems, cold feet as well. "The sight of the great port, and of the sea, about which I was so excited, now only made me feel sad," he wrote. Within days, he had left Bremerhaven again, not to pursue more adventures but to search for a master tanner who would accept him without a letter of recommendation.[66]

The rest of Caesar's life story unfolded in a more or less predictable manner. He did eventually manage to convince Carl Dittmann in Ludwigslust in the Grand Duchy of Mecklenburg-Schwerin to offer him an apprenticeship, which he completed without further incident.[67] When he subsequently returned to the Westerwald, he did not go back to school, pick up any books, practice his English or French, or return to sketching and drawing. Instead, he used his inheritance to set up his tannery, married and had children, and in general learned to make the best of his lot in life. "It is quite a pleasant thing when a young man who has long depended on others for his daily bread becomes independent, when he can arrange his home as he pleases," he concluded, adding that it "goes without saying that he should not entertain any desires that would exceed his means." His household was "simple but nice and orderly," he loved his wife, and he went to work always "in high spirit."[68] Nonetheless, he never seemed to have stopped wondering what might have been, for he decided to sit down in the twilight of his life, in 1879, to craft an autobiography that all but set the record straight. Its subtext was obvious: Whatever one might make of his choice to become a tanner in his native Westerwald, it did not reflect on who he actually was, namely, a complicated and conflicted individual, a student of life, a man of many talents—indeed, a figure who was not so different from his namesake, the great Roman emperor, who everyone knew was a brilliant general by day and a gifted man of letters by night.[69]

It was an autobiography that wrestled at length with the fateful decision he had made all those years ago, during his brief time at sea on the way to Bremerhaven. A litany of explanations and rationales were presented, as he insisted that it was not just his sense of filial piety that had compelled him to "set aside" his dreams and to "wet my fleshing knife." Another important factor in his decision was sheer common sense. "Every young person would be well-advised, once he has settled on his calling, to pursue it with diligence and perseverance, so that he may learn to perfect it as much as possible; because otherwise, in a world of ever-multiplying demands, it is impossible to succeed." Yet another explanation for the choice he had made was the fact that "getting ahead in the world" demanded a certain amount of "courage, energy, and plucky confidence"—all traits that he, Julius Caesar, "very much lack[ed]" and that no person could have "acquire[d] on his own." Yet being as "lonely in the world" as he had been in his youth and young adulthood, this was precisely what he would have had to do. The many tragic and premature deaths in his family had robbed him of the mentors and role models who might have changed his life. His mother had passed away when he was three, his older brother and stepmother when he was ten, his father when he was eighteen, and sometime along the way four other unnamed siblings. He either barely knew or did not trust his extended family, and being a "shy and awkward" person, he could count few friends. He had little regard for churchmen, and he was even less impressed by the many do-gooders associated with the Revolution of 1848, which he dismissed as that great "freedom fraud" (*Freiheitsschwindel*).[70]

It is on the question of guidance and mentorship that the story of Julius Caesar makes for an illuminating contrast to that of Aurelius Krause. One does wonder whether his trajectory would have been any different if he had had an intrepid older brother who walked him through the virtues of impudence and of "saddling over" into another line of work. Having no such person in his life, Julius Caesar simply did what he thought was the right thing to do. He let himself be guided by the moral universe that existed around him and learned to embrace, find solace, and derive certainty from its wisdoms and virtues. Aurelius may well have reached the same conclusions, his brother Albert and the letters from America notwithstanding. But the chances that he would have done so were scarcely the same as they were for Julius Caesar.

4

The Home

THERE IS SOMETHING endearing about a figure like Albert Krause who, having tried "a hundred times" to adopt an impudent approach to his work life, ended up confessing that he could not master the act because it was "entirely at odds with my nature." Even after all the possible strategic and cynical motives behind his claim have been considered, it still seems that Krause's feelings of shame were genuine and heartfelt. There is a certain comfort in the idea that dishonesty is an acquired habit that ultimately may be at odds with human nature.

It could very well be that this is what Albert meant to say: Impudence was against his nature as a human being. However, there is another way to read the phrase "my nature": his nature as a man. For it turned out that so many of the behaviors and affects Albert was wrestling with—the blustery self-confidence, the disregard for decorum and authority, the resort to mendacity as a means of survival—were in fact traditionally associated with women, at least in most European societies. As daughters of Eve, the great temptress of the Old Testament, women were supposed to have some natural inclination toward deception and connivance. Men, by contrast, were expected to be pious, humble, honest, peaceful, and loyal; it was their responsibility to tame and guide women because, much like Adam himself, they were believed to be closer to God, blessed with much greater moral fortitude, and able to control their passions. Good men were moral shepherds; they exuded a "pastor's gravitas" (*hauspriesterliche Würde*) and guarded their honor with stubborn ferocity, not out of vanity or some inflated sense of righteousness but because male honor was the only thing standing between order and chaos. Albert Krause's feelings of guilt could be explained in just this way: They were a function of his creeping realization, one he dared not articulate, that in his embrace of *Dreistigkeit* he was in some way abdicating his duties as a man. Worse still, he was behaving like a woman.[1]

Such an explanation is less far-fetched than one would think. The tropes of Adam and Eve can seem overly stylistic, but they were also reflected in the lived reality of this period. Women certainly had good reasons to slip into the role of Eve. Whether by law or by custom, the types of productive activities that common women in Europe could engage in remained severely restricted well into the nineteenth century, leaving them to seek their fortunes in the most reputable trades, trades in which their alleged shamelessness and loud confidence might be considered an asset rather than a liability. The sale of perishable foodstuffs like milk, eggs, fruit, vegetables, and fish had long been considered a woman's business because these items tended to lose value over the course of the day, putting their sellers at a significant disadvantage and practically requiring them to employ more hard-nosed sales tactics. Men, by contrast, kept to selling more durable goods, like leather- or earthenware, that tended to retain their value over time and hence did not require excessive haggling. Arguably, all one had to do to be reminded of the biblical tropes about the two sexes was to visit the weekly market.

Similar dynamics could be found in the domestic sphere. Male patriarchs often felt inclined to leave money matters to their wives and daughters, wagering that they might employ their feminine wiles to secure better prices or credit terms. Whatever autonomy accrued to women as a result was but a small price to pay. A financially independent and self-sufficient woman was useful to her husband because she supported herself and her children. Laws governing marriage, divorce, and women's access to property mirrored this logic. In a world in which men frequently died or disappeared, whether as a result of disasters like war or because they were unable (and sometimes unwilling) to support their dependents, the authorities proved all too willing to grant women access to divorce, expansive rights to property, and even custody of their children to keep them and their kin from falling burden to society. "The excellent woman is she who, if her husband dies, can be a father to their children," Goethe reportedly once said.[2]

Therefore, the difficulty, and stakes, of Albert Krause's efforts to recast his impudent conduct into something good may have been far greater than meets the eye. If Dreistigkeit was a womanly affect and morality a manly one, then a man's foray into impudence would have been tantamount to challenging the very order of things. Success on Krause's part would require some degree of rethinking the nature of the sexes, in particular a disentangling of femininity from Dreistigkeit.

Fortunately for the Albert Krauses of this period, they were not starting from scratch. Long before the arrival of "news from America," attempts had been made, in the German lands and elsewhere, to rethink the nature of man and woman. One effort, part of an ambitious endeavor to reimagine the family from the ground up, dated to the early nineteenth century. It was spearheaded by a small but influential group of reform-minded civil servants, bureaucrats, clergymen, physicians, intellectuals, and entrepreneurs who had grown concerned with—and in some cases terrified by—the dramatic rise in alcoholism, illegitimacy, poverty, and disease, as well as begging, petty theft, and vagrancy, that accompanied the Napoleonic Wars. While the root causes of these problems were many and complex, it was decided that the most promising site of intervention would be the domestic sphere. The reason was that ever since the revolution in France, most of the traditional institutions of moral and spiritual and civic edification, like the guilds, churches, confraternities, and other corporate institutions, had either been abolished or seen their influence severely diminished. Efforts had been underway to restore many of these institutions, but this often took time and, in any case, was not always practicable or even desired. The domestic sphere in this context emerged as a key site—if only because it was the only remaining site—of moral edification; by design or default, it was one of the only places where proper norms, manners, principles, and virtues were being conveyed to future generations.[3]

The reformers did not take issue with this trend. Most were inclined toward a liberal kind of politics and, as such, welcomed the elevation of the family as the nation's primary educator.[4] However, they were also discovering—much to their chagrin—that the homes of so many of their compatriots were exceedingly ill-equipped to handle this great new responsibility. To begin with, there was the frightful physical condition of so many dwellings. Whether they were centuries-old, dilapidated structures or makeshift shelters built more recently, the homes of the peasantry all seemed, and often were, dark, wet, crowded, and generally filthy places. Dirt, grime, and animal droppings covered the floors. Windows were small, few, and far between, and like the walls, roofs, and doors, they leaked for want of maintenance and repairs. The furniture was primitive and sometimes lacking altogether: a stool or bench here and there, a barrel "doing service as a table," a single chest holding everything from linens and clothing to family heirlooms, perhaps a Bible, and kitchenware. Beds consisted of woolen mattresses, sometimes mere straw, usually placed directly on the floor and separated from livestock by a simple screen. An open hearth provided warmth, the opportunity for boiling water or preparing soup, but was otherwise ill-suited for extensive cooking.[5]

Widespread poverty was chiefly to blame for this state of affairs. But there was also the fact that these homes were rarely intended to provide comfort and conviviality to their inhabitants. They were first and foremost sites of sweat and toil, and people tended to treat them accordingly. Furniture, decorations, and other domestic essentials were kept to a minimum to make room for all the tools and machinery: spinning wheels, handlooms, and work benches, along with livestock and much else. Cleanliness was a concern, but only insofar as it ensured the functionality of the work environment; anything beyond the bare minimum cut into a person's productive hours and rendered those rare moments of respite even rarer. The din of hammers clobbering, spindles whirring, and feet tapping on pottery wheels was interrupted only by occasional shouts to discipline the children or servant-folk (*Gesinde* or *Ehehalte*): spinster and orphan maids, apprentices, field hands, day laborers, and others who toiled away for little more than room and board and, of course, paternal guidance. Meals were rarely consumed together; community was found elsewhere: in town, at the tavern, at the market, or in the commons. It did not surprise reformers that vices like alcoholism, adultery, illegitimacy, theft, and vagrancy had grown so rampant. Rather than providing a much-needed anchor in a person's life, these homes—bereft of comfort and love and community (*Gemütlichkeit*)—exerted powerful centrifugal forces that greatly exacerbated people's sense of alienation and despair.[6]

FIGURE 4.1 *The Weaver. Der Weber* by Max Liebermann (1884). Oil on canvas, 57 × 78 cm. The equipment required for the manufacture of yarns and other textile products tended to be bulky and take up a significant portion of the interior living spaces of the peasantry.

Source: Courtesy of the Städel Museum, Frankfurt am Main.

FIGURE 4.2 *Geese Pluckers. Gänserupferinnen* by Max Liebermann (1871–72). Oil on canvas, 118 × 172 cm. Nineteenth-century reformers argued that even the poor could have comfortable and clean homes if only they embraced a more distinctive division of labor of male breadwinners and female homemakers.
Source: Courtesy of the Deutsches Historisches Museum, Berlin.

One obvious solution, at least to those who defined the problem this way, was to make the domestic sphere more attractive to everyone in the family. Here, there was some cause for optimism. It seemed that improvements to homes could be made relatively quickly and without great expense by instituting a stricter domestic division of labor. Even a little extra time spent washing, cleaning, cooking, and caring for children could go a long way in turning these disorganized dungeons into virtuous homes. Since housework of this sort was customarily a woman's purview, it seemed only natural that wives and mothers and sisters should be the ones to take it on. Ideally, the women would be relieved of all their other onerous work—spinning, weaving, stitching, working in the fields, and so on—to be able to focus entirely on mothering and homemaking. Husbands and fathers would make up for the lost wages by reducing the time and money they spent at the tavern, on the favors of other women, or on frivolous luxury items like clothes and pocket watches. They might also seek employment outside the home, taking advantage of the higher wages that could be earned in nearby factories, mines, and cities, which would also obviate the need to bring Gesinde into the home and thereby remove a key source of vice and depravity.[7]

It was a promising proposition—seemingly simple to execute, far-reaching in its results. Not only would this new family of breadwinners and homemakers transform the peasantry's homes, these wretched incubators of vice, into what the Saxon physician and poet Leopold Schefer touted as "heaven's temple," but also it would prepare the way for various other poverty-fighting policies, including efforts to promote commerce and modern industry. To run the modern factories that manufacturers and governing authorities were envisioning, skilled workers would have to be recruited, and most skilled workers were men who were rather reluctant to leave their domestic parishes unsupervised, even for higher pay. The revamped domestic space would reward these men with a clean and comfortable refuge from the travails of factory life, not to mention more loyal and devoted wives, better-educated children, and sumptuous home-cooked meals. "That's why," explained advocates of the new domesticity,

> The home is the most sacred of places!
> Love's altar and heaven's temple,
> For the finest celebration of all its wonders,
> For the most blessed enjoyment of all its charms,
> Even if the house is the poorest, smallest hut.[8]

Needless to say, the matter was never quite so simple. While few reformers seemed to notice or care to admit it, the new division of labor they were touting presupposed what amounted to a minor revolution in contemporary thinking about sex, particularly about the nature of femininity. While it was true that the new family model merely asked men and women to focus more on what were already understood to be their proper roles within the family, it also assumed that women could be trusted to shoulder a much-expanded role—not despite their womanhood but because of it. Now it was her nature as a mother and housewife, not her ability to act like a father, that justified a woman's claim to independence.[9]

In the context of the nineteenth century, this was nothing short of extraordinary, and perhaps for that reason the idea of breadwinners and homemakers largely failed to generate the kind of immediate enthusiasm that reformers had hoped for.[10] There certainly was handwringing among many men, who wondered about the wisdom of ceding so much of their authority to anyone not explicitly acting in their name. It did not help that memories were still fresh of the horrific violence that overcame France when it executed its father,

King Louis XVI, which meant that even a minor infringement on patriarchal power could raise eyebrows in this period.[11] Beyond the politics, there were practical concerns. It just did not seem prudent, at least financially speaking, to tell half the members of a household to stop working. Sound domestic political economy—some would say common sense—dictated that the more individuals who were engaged in remunerative activities, which did not include domestic labors like cleaning, cooking, and mothering, the better.[12]

Women, too, were often skeptical. The new role of dedicated homemaker may have constituted a promotion within the family hierarchy, but for those accustomed to the relative mobility and independence afforded to them under the old *Haus* model of domesticity, the costs seemed immense: much greater domestic confinement, increased financial dependence on men, and a new vulnerability to spousal violence resulting from said dependence, along with general feelings of worthlessness and boredom.[13] "I am earning half of our income without ever missing a chore," boasted Therese Huber, an author and the daughter of a renowned academic in Göttingen, in a letter to her son Viktor Aimé in January 1817. Huber refused to reduce herself to a "small woman" (*kleine Frau*) engaged solely in housewifery; "true German womanhood" to her meant doing everything all the time and never tiring along the way.[14] By comparison, the domesticized femininity espoused by the reformers appeared prude, uninteresting, even unsettling. "There are times...when even the most beautiful garden can frighten us," warns the character Charlotte in Johann Ludwig Tieck's novel *Der Junge Tischlermeister* (The young cabinetmaker). Other critics, like the children's book author Heinrich Hoffmann, preferred a more humorous approach. With his satirical illustrations in *Der Struwwelpeter* (The shaggy-haired Peter), a wildly popular children's book, Hoffmann skewered the tedious morality of the new family. Picky eaters are made to starve, and those who are sloppy and distracted suffer horrific punishments, including death.[15]

And yet, for all the skepticism and mockery being lobbed at it, the idea of a breadwinner–homemaker family never went away completely. Around the early 1860s, it started to win a growing following.[16] This was because, on the one hand, there had always been a genuine interest in the domestic *Gemütlichkeit* that reformers had promised, and the most sought-after improvements ultimately outstripped the resources and abilities of even the most industrious women.[17] On the other hand, by midcentury the idea was powerfully boosted by the diaspora in America. Emigrants in America, especially the women among them, turned out to be enthusiastic practitioners of breadwinning and homemaking. Though they, too, were often skeptical at first, many of them quickly embraced the two new roles and began reporting with palpable excitement the various advantages of their new domestic arrangements. Indeed, so prominent was the new family model in writings from and about America that by the 1850s it was no longer even associated with any local reform efforts but, instead, was referred to as the "North American" model of domesticity. "We do not yet have to fear North American conditions," wrote Wilhelm Heinrich Riehl, a vocal critic of the new arrangements, in a well-regarded critique of "the family" from 1854. Riehl took comfort in the fact that German marriages had not yet devolved into the "very strict, secluded marriages [of] North Americans"; that *Gesinde* remained an integral part of German families, loyal and content with nothing but "room and board, at most some gift money"; and that German men were not yet "go[ing] to the market, basket under their arms" because they thought it unbecoming of their wives to leave the home. But change was in the offing, as Riehl himself seemed to acknowledge: "The German people," he wrote, "no longer really [know] what a German *Haus* actually look[s] like."[18]

All this would have been crucial for someone like Albert Krause who was attempting to recast Dreistigkeit as something good and virtuous. In a world of (at least aspiring) breadwinners and homemakers, an affect like impudence would no longer be so gendered, which meant that it was ripe for new meaning and significance. For that, Krause had others to thank: on the one hand, an entire generation of *bürgerliche* reformers and, on the other, his fellow emigrant writers in America, especially the women among them.

"It's strange that in California people don't know anything about pottery," Sophie Meinecke wrote to relatives in Germany from Vallecito, a remote mining town in the foothills of the Sierra Nevada, in the late 1850s. "That sort of business would do well here, there are places where there is clay" and one could "raise all sorts of things in pots." But in California, things were different; there, people just bought everything they needed from the store. "It is not easy to get used to this," she admitted, "to be buying every little trifle for the household, back home we made many things ourselves, and I think in comparison to over there, here everything is much more expensive."[19]

But there were upsides, for example, the fact that "in most families fresh meat is served three times daily." The novelty here had as much to do with the quantity of meat served as with its freshness. Meinecke, like most German emigrants in this period, was accustomed to cured and smoked meats, which were flavorful and paired well with the staple food of the day, bread and potatoes. They also required little to no cooking, a key advantage at a time when detached cooking spaces were a rarity in the homes of the peasantry. Once more, things were different in California, said Meinecke, since here the "cured meat is terribly bad," the "bacon we don't like at all," and smoked meat "I don't think they have." Freshly butchered meat was abundant but came in just one variety, beef, which meant that it needed creative preparation. Fortunately, Meinecke reported, her new home in America featured a modest kitchen "attached to the stillroom," with a "small stove on which you can cook and bake wonderfully." This was something special. "I used to think that in these houses there is too little room [for a kitchen] but I now have to admit that you don't need a more spacious house, you can do very well in here."[20]

It would be Meinecke's responsibility to cook and clean the dishes, three times a day, since the men in the home—her husband Fritz and her brother-in-law Wilhelm—agreed that her cooking "tastes much better" and "washing bowls is the worst." Meinecke would have liked to spend more time in her garden raising vegetables, but "Fritz said to me that besides some salad, some soup cabbage, a few flowers it is not worth it" and that they "could buy the vegetables for the same price." Though Meinecke maintained that California vegetables "do cost quite a bit," they went on buying them anyway because Fritz earned good money running a "milk shop" with Wilhelm, along with various other business in Stockton, a larger town just a few dozen miles further west in the Central Valley. If Meinecke chafed at her domestic confinement, she did not let it on. "I like it very well," she assured relatives, "even if it is lonely here, the house is cutely and comfortably furnished… in front is a cute porch [and] the rooms are elevated, pretty spacious, both have a good view." A few lines later she wrote, "So far I have not regretted that I don't have anything here with respect to socializing, and that I'm confined entirely to the house."[21]

To be sure, she may have had little choice in the matter. In a remote community like Vallecito where physical distances were great, an isolated lifestyle was the norm. And yet, interest in the new household arrangement could also be found among big-city dwellers. When they first arrived in Baltimore, Wilhelmine Schlüter and her husband Christoph, of the town of Liebenau near Hannover, worked side by side as tailors. But because business was slow and because "our eyes suffered too much," Schlüter wrote, the couple "decided to arrange our things differently." They set aside their stitch work, converted one of their street-facing rooms into a retail store, and began peddling wholesale "fabrics like calico, woolens, socks, tissues." With Christoph attending the store, it was up to Schlüter to "do the housework." Similarly, Angela Heck, who emigrated to New York in 1854, had been living on her husband's wages ever since setting foot on American soil. "We had to buy all sorts of things, what we needed," she remembered of those initial weeks in New York City, but Nikolaus "earns a dollar a day" at a store "making all sorts of coats for men" and "all the money gives us courage." Heck wrote, "I neither have to nor need to work, other than my housework."[22]

Heck was brave to share this information because in touting her homebound life she risked appearing indolent to her interlocutors in Europe.[23] "You may think at home that I don't do any work. You must not think that; I always help [Nikolaus] with the sowing." Sophie Meinecke did not help her husband with his milk business but she, too, made sure to recount her backbreaking daily responsibilities: the constant washing, cooking, baking, and cleaning, along with the bearing, raising, and—too often—burying of children. This was not just parrying charges of indolence; it was also pushing back against suspicions about her femininity, that she had not surrendered a woman's customary independence, her determination, her refusal to fall prey to others. When her husband was drafted to serve in the Civil War, Angela Heck boasted that "[Nikolaus] sends me all his money every two months," along with "a letter per week." As the administrator of the household ("I already have a big capital together"), it was in fact Heck who was in charge: "And when he finally comes back, I want to treat him and allow him to visit Germany, even if a few hundred are out the window."[24]

The role women like Heck and Meinecke and many others were carving out for themselves was indeed approaching that of a matriarch. When they first arrived in America, many women tended to be confined, and may have confined themselves, to the postscript of men's letters. But that hierarchy was soon turned on its head. Women, especially married women, kept up the lion's share of correspondence and, in a patriarch's manner, wrote not just about the family but also in its name. They dispensed advice, instruction, and moral support, and they urged relatives—especially breadwinning husbands, fathers, and brothers—to build the calluses needed to prevail in the bare-knuckle fight that was the marketplace. They pushed their men to overcome a man's pride of place and craft, furnished rationalizations of men's indecent working lives, acted as character witnesses, and stepped in when men felt so conflicted about their impudence that they "can't talk much about my doings here."[25] This at least was how Anna Maria Schano, a native Württemberger who arrived in New York City in the 1850s, approached her correspondence. When her brother Daniel weighed a decision to follow his sister to America,

Schano urged him and others at home to adopt an open mind as to the way he would make his living: "Daniel, his profession, is not the best and he can't rely on it, tailor or shoemaker is better.... But not to worry, here many [men] don't practice their profession and learn other professions in addition or they do other business."²⁶ This was sound advice and also a subtle way to prepare relatives for the news that her husband, Franz Schano, had been changing jobs in New York at a record clip.²⁷ Franz himself rarely spoke in their correspondence, leaving his wife to account for his activities, to persuade the family that there was a lot to gain from changing jobs, and that men seeking their fortunes abroad would succeed if only they were flexible in their choices regarding work.²⁸

Sophie Meinecke took a more subtle, though no less effective, approach to supporting her husband, often simply reproducing, almost verbatim, Fritz's rationales and adding commentary about his inner moral wranglings.²⁹ When Fritz decided to abandon his milk business in Murphys, California, to take up wheat farming in Stockton, Meinecke commented that "a move has always awaited me because Fritz has long planned [it] and it will be better then."³⁰ When Fritz changed his mind again a few years later, this time proposing to speculate in land and precious metals mining near San Joaquin—a plan that almost certainly would have raised eyebrows back home—Meinecke did not question him.³¹ Instead, she recounted a story of "just how boldly the American speculates," making Fritz seem almost prude by comparison:

> About 8 to 10 months ago someone tried to sell a few shares...in the copper mines. They asked for 10,000 dollars per share but could only sell one share for 7,500 dollars in San Francisco. An accountant in one of the most distinguished businesses in Stockton...had a great inclination to buy in, but his fortune was not bigger than 1,000 dollars. His principal, who thought highly of him, lent him 9,000 and he bought in. Three months later news came in that the ore alone which was sent to England was worth 7,500 dollar per share, and some English came over to look at the mines for themselves and to buy in. Now they offered this man 100,000 dollars for his share, which he still rejects. In the worst of cases he would have had to work for 10 years to pay back the 9,000 dollars.³²

Whatever truth there was to this, the story itself was likely Fritz's, not Meinecke's. The latter rarely left their farm, after all, and these were not the kind of stories one read in the newspaper. Fritz, however, spent a great deal of time on "unpleasant business tours" in Stockton and as far as San Francisco, and so he had numerous occasions to hear about "promising" opportunities for speculation in San Joaquin.³³

That the story should come from Meinecke's hand may have been a deliberate strategy. "Since Sophie is still such a good daughter," Fritz explained to relatives in a rare instance of firsthand writing, "then you will hopefully forgive me, if only for her sake; after all, did God not promise to spare Sodom & Gomorra for the sake of just five righteous souls?"³⁴ Sodom and Gomorrah were the twin cities of sin in the Old Testament: According to the story there, if the patriarch Abraham could identify but a handful of innocent souls, God would spare them. Meinecke undoubtedly played the part of the five righteous souls, but she also sought to use that role to redeem her erring husband. Her next letter home began not with matters of money or with the San Joaquin affair, but with happier news of their infant son, who had just started walking. It continued with inquiries about the well-being of various distant relatives; went on to observe that "this morning Fritz brought me a beautiful bouquet of flowers from the garden"; and finally shifted to the heart of the matter, namely, that "there is not just gold here but also silver, copper, and coal in immense quantities" and that "Fritz thinks it is promising."³⁵ It made little difference, in the end, that the San Joaquin speculation did not pan out, like so many of Fritz's ill-considered endeavors in California. Sophie could vouch for him, turning her husband's poor gambles into responsible investments.³⁶

It cannot be ruled out that at least some of this writing by emigrant women was produced under duress. Moving across the Atlantic and settling in a foreign country would have been a humbling experience for anyone, but it was especially fraught for women. Removed from networks of kin and community, women found themselves reliant on the protection and goodwill of their male companions, at least for the duration of the journey, which could take weeks, if not months. Often their dependence continued after they had reached their destinations because most of the opportunities that had been available to them in Europe to earn a bit of money on their own simply did not exist in mid-nineteenth-century America. The sale of homemade yarns, cloth, knitwear, pottery, and baskets—activities in which women tended to predominate in Europe—presupposed well-integrated local and regional markets, operated by large numbers of middlemen who competed for and could absorb inventory both in good times and in bad. Outside the large metropoles along the Atlantic seaboard, sophisticated markets of this kind were only just beginning to emerge in colonial societies like the United States. It left women with few choices but to focus on their domestic responsibilities and to support their men unconditionally in all their breadwinning endeavors.[37]

Yet it would be wrong to understand emigrants' embrace of housewifery solely as a function of the widespread lack of alternative opportunities for female employment. Earning their own income was just one tactic among many that women could turn to in order to carve out autonomy for themselves and to evade the heavy hand of a male chaperone. Another, arguably more effective, strategy was to try and rebuild their social networks and communities of support. Often, that meant stepping outside the social circles of the German immigrant community: learning English, developing familiarity with local customs and values, in general assimilating to an American way of life. And here it is worth noting that in middle-of-the-century America, the breadwinner–homemaker model of domesticity—known there simply as the "home"—was understood to be much more than a practical solution to primitive market conditions or, as in Europe, a clever means for improving the domestic sphere. It was, first and foremost, a cultural institution. That mattered, because it suggests that the eagerness with which these emigrant women embraced their new role as homemaker could also be a reflection of efforts to reconstitute their social networks, whether it was out of a desire for community or to keep their patriarch at arm's length.[38]

One reason that the new model of domesticity long failed to catch on in Europe is that it became closely identified with a particular kind of *bürgerliche* way of life. Its proponents had tried to avoid this, always stressing the model's universality. They had done so by focusing on the material rewards of breadwinning and homemaking, which on its face was a smart choice. Whereas the promoters' own motives (which ranged from a paternalist concern about peasant immorality to bold visions for a modern, factory-based economy) were politically controversial, in the early nineteenth century the prospect of greater domestic bliss was quite popular. However, the problem with focusing on the material promises of the home was that it drained the concept of meaning and urgency. Skeptics of the new division of labor within the family consequently felt at liberty to ignore the idea altogether, on the grounds that it was just one solution among many to a common problem: the solution of an estate (*Stand*) to which they did not belong, with its own peculiar notions about sex, womanhood, morality, and authority. In the United States, by contrast, the idea of the home always transcended class and regional boundaries, which is notable because America's loudest promoters of the home tended to hail from the same bourgeois social background as their counterparts in

Europe, with similar paternalist attitudes and, in many cases, similar stakes in the emerging factory-based economy. In part, this had to do with the United States' political past and its revolutionary heritage. In a republican system of government where only propertied men were deemed rights-bearing citizens, a breadwinner–homemaker model could be—and often was—interpreted as mirroring the gendered character of civic life and the law. Some proponents of the home went so far as to regard the home as a civic institution in its own right. Woman homemakers were not just appendages of the sovereign male individual; rather, they were "Republican Mothers" endowed with a range of rights and responsibilities. They governed a sovereign space of their own: an "empire" of the home. As Barbara Meister, an emigrant in Spring Bay near Peoria, Illinois, summed up the distinction, "Here one is a different woman (*Frau*) than in Germany, you rarely are called a broad (*Weib*)."[39]

The republican heritage was key, but even it paled in importance when compared to a second ideological current that filled the home in America with meaning: namely, the nation's alleged manifest destiny to conquer, civilize, and improve the American West. This gave the home concept a dual purpose. On the one hand, it served as a symbol of American civilization, distinguishing white settlers' ostensibly more refined domestic lives from the "horse and mule fashion" of domesticity that was allegedly practiced by the Indigenous nations encountered along the way. On the other hand, many settlers appreciated a breadwinner–homemaker division of labor as a practical instrument of colonization, on par with their firearms, hatchets, horses, cattle, and plows. War had always forced families to adopt a starker domestic division of labor, with men usually heading into battle and women administering the household during their absence. The colonization of the American West was in effect a long-simmering war stretched out over many decades, characterized by near-constant armed skirmishes and confrontations between the newcomers and the peoples already inhabiting the region. Amid the isolation and extreme deprivations of the frontier, moreover, the task of maintaining even a rudimentary home was magnitudes greater than in the communities of the east—no "little Domestick affair," but a full-time occupation. "If the American women of the East merit the palm, for their skill and success as accomplished housekeepers," wrote Catharine Beecher, a daughter of the renowned New England preacher Lyman Beecher and one of the period's most vocal champions of the home, "still more is due to the heroines of the West, who, with such unyielding fortitude and cheerful endurance, attempt similar duties, amid so many disadvantages and deprivations." For Beecher, women's work in frontier homesteads was as integral to America's great calling to pacify the West as the pioneer's slashing and burning of the wilderness: a "manifest domesticity" to match its manifest destiny.[40]

Just how potent a cultural symbol the home was in nineteenth-century America was made evident by the fact that not even the struggle over slavery could displace it from its privileged perch. Since at least the 1830s, abolitionists and antislavery partisans, intending to drive a wedge between slaveholders and American civilization, had argued that the institution of slavery was fundamentally incompatible with the home. It was not just that paternalist slaveholders conducted their households in accordance with the same despised "horse and mule fashion" attributed to Native Americans and people in Mexico (and, for that matter, European aristocrats). It was also the fact that enslaved labor, especially when applied to domestic tasks, denigrated and marginalized women. Household chores and the work of mothering were, so the argument went, no mere nuisances; they were how women came into their own, how they claimed their independence and sovereignty, how they contributed to the political and moral order of society. To leave such labor to enslaved individuals was to deprive all women, not just Black "domestics," of their path toward self-emancipation. Only by abolishing slavery could domestic work serve its liberating function, which was to say, only by abolishing slavery could Americans begin to build actual homes and, by extension, civilization.[41]

Slaveholders might have tried to parry these attacks by taking aim at the home itself, portraying it as some northern, New England fixation and articulating their own, alternative vision of civilized domesticity. But they did no such thing. On the question of the home, supporters of the slave system refused to cede even one inch. They countered abolitionists and antislavery partisans by arguing that enslaved men and women, far from an impediment to the home, were in fact its most important corollary, arguably a foundation, in that much like draft animals helped a farmer till his field or a hammer helped the carpenter build his frame, so enslaved individuals "build our houses."[42] In reality, so the claim, it was antislavery stalwarts who were guilty of hypocrisy. In a world in which men did not earn the kind of wage needed to support a family, people had no choice but to rely on enslaved labor. Nowhere was this more true than on the western frontier, the proslavery partisans continued. While abolitionists like the Beechers put the onus on women, demanding of them the impossible, to be nothing short of "heroines," slavery advocates claimed to understand the back-breaking work that was involved. If a pioneer was to tame the wilderness and not have to force his wife and children to work to do so, he would require affordable "help." That the presence of strangers—enslaved Black men and women, no less—inside the home was not ideal was readily acknowledged by slaveholders and was usually addressed by arranging separate living quarters for their enslaved individuals and in general keeping a "prudent distance."[43]

In 1861, Americans went to war with one another in one of the more violent and seismic conflicts of the century. While the underlying issue was slavery and its expansion to the new territories in the west, it is telling that many understood themselves as fighting "in the name of the home."[44] President Abraham Lincoln had already declared, in 1858, that "a house divided against itself cannot stand," and like most northerners he was determined to ensure that the West would not be turned into a giant slave plantation, that instead "the wild lands [be cut] into parcels, so that every poor man may have a home." Confederates, meanwhile, clung to the institution of slavery because it provided them with those "thousand comforts of life that crowd our happy homes." An attack on slavery was an attack on the home, and that was a cause worth fighting for—no matter the cost. "We lack arms & ammunition," wrote a plantation mistress in Georgia just a few months into the war. "In that respect they have the advantage over us but our men are fighting for liberty &

FIGURE 4.3 **Fighting in the name of the home.** A flag stitched by Catharine Heth Morrison, a supporter of the Confederacy, for the Virginia Infantry (1861). Morrison claimed to have sacrificed her wedding dress to make it.
Source: Courtesy of the American Civil War Museum, Richmond, VA.

Homes, the Federalists fighting for a name." And another in Louisiana: "The North has more towns and villages, she has a greater population, but Southernors when called to fight for their homes, for their liberty will they not prove superior to fanatics whose zeal will soon cool?"[45]

This was the world that emigrants like Sophie Meinecke, Anna Maria Schano, and so many others stepped into. It was a world in which the idea of the home was everywhere and where indifference to the matter presented a grave risk to life and property. To make it in this home-obsessed America, many emigrant women and men came to believe that they had better embrace the idea, regardless of its practical advantages or even where in America they happened to find themselves, and that they go about it with an urgency and zeal that matched if not outdid that of their American counterparts.

Marriage had always been somewhat of an afterthought to Johann Jonas, a resident of Howell, Michigan, who was originally from Jammelshofen in Westphalia. In 1862, when Jonas married an eighteen-year-old Michigander ("She comes from Baden [but] speaks better English than German"), it took him seven paragraphs to broach the subject in a letter to his family in Germany. "I don't know many other news to write you, except that on January 19th this year I married in a Catholic church." He then devoted another five paragraphs to topics like the weight of his four pigs ("I think each will soon weigh 400 [pounds]") before he shared his new wife's name: Elisabetha Ridinger.[46]

Not all emigrant men spoke this casually about their spouses, but Jonas's account was not entirely unusual. Marriage, childbirth, death: These events received short shrift in the European household, if only because women and children were deemed first and foremost a source of labor that sustained the patriarchal household. This is not to say that all marriages were devoid of love or that parents had no affections for their children. But child mortality remained quite high, even at this stage in the nineteenth century. Marriages still began as practical endeavors, serving spouses' material interests and their legal coming of age before turning into loving relationships later. Jonas considered marriage a necessary milestone in his pursuit of independence, which he defined as becoming the patriarch of a household that served his needs and interest above all else. "I think that I have a good wife. She is loyal, hardworking, clean, and frugal, and that is all I ask of her and can ask of her."[47]

There were other circumstances that could explain Johann's terse treatment of Ridinger in his letters home. One was that Jonas lived in a foreign country, with little family and few friends, which meant that his wedding could not possibly have evoked the same reaction as it might have had he still lived in Jammelshofen. "There were many people at the wedding but nobody I have anything to do with. I had invited those Germans who I got to know since I started living in this town. Still, it was not as when I was able to see you." Then there were all the expenses. Johann was accustomed to a world in which brides came with all the essentials they required; some bachelors could even expect marriage to enrich them. That was decidedly not true of Jonas's American bride. "My in-laws gave me lots that is necessary for a household. And still this marrying cost me over 50 dollars. I bought an oven that cost me 20 dollars. And many more things that I can't write you all." He also was compelled to rent a house at nearly four dollars a month "until I can build or buy one."[48]

What Jonas was paying for were the trappings of a new domestic arrangement, one still unfamiliar to him but, as it turned out, one that was growing on him. "I and my wife live alone in [our] house in peace and unity, as married people should," he wrote. Better still, "I now live more cheaply than I did before I married, and am much calmer and more content. And I feel more as though I was at home than I did before I married. I also don't have so much homesickness." Ridinger and her rather expensive American household may have come with a great deal of trouble and a hefty price tag, but in the end, Jonas deemed both well worth his money.[49]

Henry Baumberger in San Antonio, Texas, drew a similar conclusion about Americans' domestic arrangements and division of labor. "It is a strange life here," Baumberger began. He went on to recount all the usual clichés about the land where "money is God," but all this was less interesting to him than the fact that "the female sex has many privileges." A "fine American woman" never ate the same meal twice. (She also refused to "enjoy any part of the head or the innards of butchered livestock" and "the feet are also thrown out.") She could not be disciplined by her husband ("If, for example, a man would beat his wife even just quietly, she could get him jailed for as long as she wishes") and, most astonishing of all, she enjoyed considerable control over the household's financial affairs ("for example, no man can sell his home without the approval and signature of his wife"). However, Baumberger did not mind any of it. He explained that in Europe creditors "can take away everything a man needs for himself and his [family] to get on." Yet in America "a man can have so and so much debt," but he went scot-free so long as he had a wife and children to his name. "If I had a farm and house, along with 10,000 talers in cash, and I owed someone 20 talers, he could not force me to pay" because everything belonged "forever to his wife and children." "These laws," he found, "are quite right."⁵⁰

Baumberger evidently had never had to deal with an American debt collector. Nevertheless, his account is illuminating because what he was describing were not any actual laws but a broader moral economy—a set of norms, assumptions, and established practices that governed American homes. If European creditors were permitted to "coerce and pressure" a man "until he pays," it was because he was not presumed to be a breadwinner. His wife and children were thought to be financially self-sufficient, at least in theory, and this implied that collecting his debts would have little bearing on their livelihoods. The opposite was true of Baumberger's America. Because by custom, and at times by law, family property belonged to husbands, it was logical and even expected that men should share some of it and use it to support their dependents—in practice, it was never really theirs to have.⁵¹ Many a self-respecting patriarch might have deemed this a bridge too far, but Baumberger knew better. Handing over the fruits of his labor to his family; withholding the beatings, even "quiet" ones; consulting his wife on financial decisions—all this was better than dealing with creditors. And so, Baumberger happily embraced the role of the American gentleman, as did so many of his compatriots. Fritz Meinecke bought Sophie flowers after returning from work. Johann Jonas accessorized Elisabetha's household. Christoph Schlüter mourned his wife Wilhelmine, who passed away in 1864, as a "diligent housewife, of which there are only few, and daily I realize just how much I have lost in her." And Nikolaus Heck, writing to Angela Heck from the battlefields of the Civil War, bragged about his wages and promised to send her "all his money."⁵²

Johann Thie of Langförden, a community in the Grand Duchy of Oldenburg, was growing tired of all the moralizing and (mostly) unsolicited life advice from his relatives in America. In a recent, "cold-hearted" letter from "Milikrick" near Cincinnati, Ohio, his brother Anton Thie had admonished him for taking advantage of their sisters (rumor had it that they were unsatisfied with their pay and "would like more money" for working Johann's farm in Oldenburg). "As if you in America know better than I in Germany," Johann fired back. "I know very well that I, along with all my sisters and brothers, must stand before God's judgment." Anna Maria, Elisabeth, and Gertrud "are loyally helping me with my work, and I care for them every day as I do for myself. [Y]ou don't need to write me from America what I should pay [them]."⁵³

Evidently, advice from abroad was not always taken kindly. Tensions often simmered just beneath the surface and between the lines, and every once in a while they burst into the open. Just "be glad you didn't receive the last letter," one writer told his relative in America, because "in that one you got a real scolding."[54] The stakes were indeed high. Johann Thie resented Anton's lectures not just because of their patronizing tone but also, more important, because Anton's critique implied a fundamentally new kind of family. To pay their sisters meant to exclude them from their household, and this was an idea that Johann struggled to come to terms with. He made this clear in his letter when he went out of his way to emphasize that he was speaking for the "entire household, from the youngest to the oldest." "Dear brother," he explained, "we together with our entire household hope [that] you are healthy and cheerful."[55] Similarly, a letter written by Heinrich Pape of Mascherode, in the Duchy of Braunschweig, to his brother-in-law in America, read, "You write that in America you have acquired a different belief about how to treat my sister." Pape's skepticism was palpable. He had just learned that his sister had "sinned" and yet his brother-in-law refused to properly discipline her, citing American custom. "Remember," Pape warned, "God has made you the head of your family and that you are responsible for taking care of all affairs. [F]orgive as Christ wills it...and then through love, patience, instruction, reprimand, and strictness lead her onto the right, faithful path."[56]

So there it was: the clash of two worlds, the old Adam-and-Eve story and the new domesticity gospel. And yet, the differences were not irreconcilable. Even though families like the Thies and the Papes engaged in heated arguments, they rarely broke off communication altogether. To the contrary, they continued to debate the various pros and cons of each approach, sometimes for years. Pape may have fretted about his brother-in-law's unorthodox methods in dealing with his sister's "boorish, stubborn will," but he still asked that "next time you write, please explain what you mean." Pape's curiosity outweighed his disappointment, and he was far from alone. There was always a voracious hunger for "news from America," and the emigrants knew it. It is why they spoke so openly in the first place. They even warned relatives: "I know you are interested in hearing about these things."[57]

Not everything about the American home was controversial or foreign.[58] Patriarchy in America had many features that were dubious to Europeans, but it was patriarchy nonetheless. Domestic labor and childrearing fell to women, whether they were American or German. The self-disciplining of the American "gentleman" had its limits, just as the "goodness" of the father did in Europe, and ultimately both remained in charge. Even when there were meaningful differences, they were unlikely to have struck readers as such. Much of what the emigrants were saying recapitulated ideas and advice that had long been dispensed by Germany's own domesticity apostles. The words were different, and so was the tone and the context, but the message was the same.

This, too, explains why advice from America was regarded as being so useful. There simply would not have been a need to introduce new ideas; all that had to be done was to gesture toward an older, somewhat dated, discourse about the home. What the emigrants did was imbue that dated home ideal with a fresh sense of novelty, along with a detailed blueprint and practical advice on how to turn it into reality.

The Migrant's Spirit: How Industrial Modernity Came to the German Lands. Benjamin P. Hein, Oxford University Press. © Oxford University Press 2025. DOI: 10.1093/9780197831052.003.0005

5

Nation, Incorporated

DURING A TRIP to England in the fall of 1838, twenty-three-year-old Gustav Mevissen, soon to be a leading financier of German industry, found himself in luck. The representatives of Marshall & Co. in Holbeck near Leeds, one of England's largest textile manufacturers, took an immediate liking to the samples of flax fiber that Mevissen had brought with him from his native Dülken in the Rhineland. In fact, they had liked his samples so much that they immediately placed a large order. They also generously offered to give Mevissen a tour of their factory grounds, which was no minor gesture. It gave him an opportunity to view up-close some of the company's most proprietary technology, including its patented wet-spinning process, a stunning recent invention that had given Marshall & Co. a decisive edge over competitors abroad, including in the Rhineland. This was indeed one of the main reasons Mevissen had come to England: to learn more about how flax, a notoriously recalcitrant fiber, could be subjected to a mechanical spinning process. Thanks in no small part to the apparent carelessness or perhaps hubris of the Marshall representatives, Mevissen left Holbeck with a much clearer sense of what was needed to replicate the process in Germany.

Getting his hands on English industry secrets was important but, as Mevissen knew full well, it was only part of a larger puzzle. Turning blueprints into market share would also require money, and gauging by what he saw in Holbeck, the initial outlay would need to be quite large. Four mills, each rising five or more stories high, towered above a sprawling compound of warehouses, mechanics workshops, offices, dry houses, and cooling ponds. Some 1,250 workers (many of them children, Mevissen noticed) toiled amid endless rows of mechanical looms and massive Boulton & Watt steam engines. Construction was underway on a fifth mill. Nicknamed "the Temple," it was the largest yet on Marshall's grounds, expected to triple the company's workforce within a decade and reportedly costing some £300,000 to build. This was an astonishing figure, one that far exceeded the cost of any textile establishment in Germany at the time. Of course, any firm hoping to compete with the English would need much more than even this sum, not just to match the Temple investment but also to pay for all the auxiliary equipment, warehouses, and an expanding payroll.[1]

Still, Mevissen remained hopeful. While it was probably true that German capital could not match the financial muscle of its counterpart in England, by one account "the greatest moneyed country in the world," Germany was not exactly a poor country. Pockets of wealth existed throughout the region, not least in the Rhineland, home to historic mercantile cities like Cologne and Düsseldorf, and also to smaller but still quite affluent towns like Crefeld, the center of a storied silk industry, or Düren, an important paper-manufacturing town. The question was not where the money would come from, but rather how it could be made more accessible to a new generation of industries—how, as English financial journalist Walter Bagehot put it, funds could be made more "borrowable" for the benefit of "new and great undertakings." And on this point, Mevissen already had an answer: the joint-stock corporation (*Aktiengesellschaft*).[2]

The institution had obvious advantages. Although it was of foreign import—at the time joint-stock corporations were more common in places like England and France, and to a lesser extent Belgium and the Netherlands—it seemed all but tailor-made for the German context. Quite apart from the better-known features, like the principle of limited liability, what was perhaps most appealing to the Germans was the joint-stock corporation's capacity to transcend political, social, and cultural boundaries. Experience had taught Mevissen that his homeland was a place where local pride was fierce, distrust and jealousy were endemic, and political autonomy was regarded as sacred. If German entrepreneurs had difficulty finding investors, so Mevissen thought, it was less because of the economic risks associated with their enterprises than because of the "petty philistinism" and "narrow subjectivity" of their countrymen, which could turn even the soundest investment into a political liability. The joint-stock corporation afforded investors anonymity, enabling those with a shared interest in the furtherance of their nation's "material progress" to pursue that patriotic endeavor without having to worry about blowback from spiteful partisans. Most important, the joint-stock corporation stood ready for use today rather than tomorrow. In contrast to other mechanisms for financing industry—one might have considered replicating England's well-integrated system of local, regional, and national banks, for example—the joint-stock corporation did not require any changes in the German political map to serve its purpose.[3]

Mevissen had been thinking about these issues even before he visited England in 1838. But it was the sight of the textile mills of Marshall & Co. that filled him with a sense of urgency and purpose.⁴ In 1841, he decided to leave his family business in Dülken and move to Cologne. There, he helped found a new newspaper, the *Rheinische Zeitung*, and threw himself headlong into the then-ongoing debates over tariffs, railroads, and other measures with which to support Rhenish industries in their struggles with English manufacturers. His stance on all these issues was the same: Success required more cooperation among the Germans. Only by finding ways to better associate German "capital and spiritual powers" could the region's industries prevail. And in Mevissen's view, there was no more promising mechanism of association than the joint-stock corporation. The institution, he predicted, had a "bright future" in Germany.⁵

That prediction turned out to be prescient. The joint-stock corporation would indeed play an essential role in the financing of modern industrial enterprises in Germany, more so than even in England, where private banks long furnished the lion's share of industrial credit. Initially, however, the promise of the joint-stock form was far from obvious, and skepticism in Germany ran deep.

One of the most common retorts was that the joint-stock corporation lacked many of the mechanisms that businesspeople thought to be essential to the operation of a profit-maximizing enterprise. The absence of personal liability, for example, was regarded as especially problematic, encouraging profligacy among individuals, diminishing productivity, and ultimately cutting into the bottom line. Similar problems arose from other hallmark features of the institution, like the division of ownership and management and the principle of legal perpetuity. Mevissen himself acknowledged these shortcomings. The joint-stock form, he observed in 1856, had so far only found acceptance in those "branches of industry where capital plays the leading role [and] the actions and abilities of the individual are of secondary importance," such as transportation and mining companies, as well as financial institutions like banks and insurance companies. Though he remained confident that the joint-stock form was still on track to becoming the "defining feature of our time," it was evident that the road ahead was rockier than anticipated.⁶

Other obstacles abounded. Apart from the concerns about incentives and profitability, there was a profound lack of trust in the institution owing to its long and checkered past. As the organizing principle of the great overseas trading companies of the seventeenth and eighteenth centuries, it seemed to many observers to be part and parcel of a darker period in European history when merchants armed to the teeth carried out their trade at gunpoint; when respectable men in business seemed to have few qualms about dealing in human beings, alcohol, and weaponry; and when corruption and greed were the order of the day. Mevissen's rejoinder to these concerns, that such backward business practices had long ago given way to more rational methods and honest accounting—that the joint-stock corporation of the nineteenth century was but a phoenix that had risen from the "ruins of a bygone era"—seemed somewhat naive, and perhaps even disingenuous, given that one of the worst offenders, the English East India Company, very much carried on its fiendish rule in South Asia. Recent campaigns in Afghanistan (1838–42), Sindh province (1843), and the Punjab in northwest India (1845–46, 1848–49) hardly inspired confidence. To the contrary, they reinforced all the assumptions and prejudices about the greed and brutality of the English enterprise.[7]

Granted, most observers likely agreed with Mevissen that the East India Company was a unique case: that it had been allowed to continue its backward ways only because of the steadfast support of the British Empire. But a more recent crop of joint-stock corporations did not inspire any more confidence. A case in point was the Société Générale de Crédit Mobilier, a joint-stock bank founded in France in 1852 to considerable fanfare. Hailed as the harbinger of a more modern, democratic, and meritocratic age in banking—it was designed in part to break the allegedly monopolistic stranglehold of the Rothschild banking dynasty on European capital markets—the bank fell well short of expectations, at least in the first decade of its existence, when it struggled with poor management, ill-timed investments, and several close brushes with bankruptcy. The lesson once more was that the joint-stock corporation was susceptible to abuse by dilettantes, adventurers, and speculators, in short, by the "dirty crowd of little men." The problem was not just the consequences for an enterprise's own bottom line but, rather, the systemic threat this posed to society writ large. The East India Company made an entire subcontinent suffer from its greed and incompetence, while the Crédit Mobilier in France was often blamed for greatly expanding the breadth and depth of the financial crisis of 1857, which had wreaked havoc on the wider business and financial worlds.[8]

Uptake of the joint-stock model was accordingly slow in Germany. Entrepreneurs, leery of ceding control over their businesses, continued to impose wide-ranging restrictions on the rights of stockholders, in effect negating many of the features that distinguished them as joint-stock corporations.[9] Concerns about the risks posed to the wider economy also undermined efforts at reforming the state concession system, which required entrepreneurs to petition the government for formal approval of their enterprise, and which in light of many governments' wariness about the "money-power of the joint-stock corporations" remained one of the main obstacles to the institution's broader adoption. To be sure, the concession system had many vocal critics. In Prussia especially, the process of attaining a concession was widely perceived as patronizing, intrusive, and overly bureaucratized, with the government often inserting itself directly into the writing of company bylaws and even dictating business strategy. But there was never sufficient consensus among the critics on what exactly might replace this system because very few within the established business community supported the adoption of general laws of incorporation that would have cut the government out of the process altogether. Even Mevissen refrained from going there, calling instead for only modest changes to the ways in which the government conducted its vetting process. As he explained his thinking, "the joint stock corporation is still too young" and there were still too many "uncertainties in the present" to dismantle a regulatory regime that provided at least a modicum of protection from mischief and abuse. More time would have to pass before the joint-stock form could be trusted to "reveal its full potential."[10]

When the joint-stock corporation's fortunes finally did turn a few years later, they did so quite abruptly. In June 1870, the Prussian government broke with long-standing practice and abolished the concession system, replacing it with a remarkably lenient law of general incorporation. The new rules, which soon were extended to the entire German Empire following its creation in 1871, put the joint-stock corporation on an entirely new trajectory. In the first five years after their introduction, well over eight hundred new enterprises with a nominal capital of 1.3 billion talers were registered in Prussia—more than double the number that had been established over the entire past century and well in excess of the estimated one billion talers raised since the seventeenth century. While railroads and mining corporations predominated, as they had in the past, for the first time other types of businesses began to take advantage of the institution in numbers: textile establishments as well as tool and machine manufacturers, food and retail businesses, real estate developers, and even portions of a still-nascent chemical industry. Whereas prior to 1870 these industries never accounted for more than 5 percent of the total capital raised by joint-stock corporations in Prussia (before 1850 the figure was even lower, just 2 percent), now it reached almost 15 percent. Added to this were a proliferating number of joint-stock banks, which, in a remarkable renaissance of the recently discredited Crédit Mobilier model, threw themselves headlong into the business of financing the nation's next generation of industrial enterprises.[11]

Few observers in these years doubted that they were living through a watershed moment in the financing of industry, with the joint-stock corporation at long last assuming the pivotal role within the economy predicted by Mevissen. What they were less certain about, however, was what exactly had precipitated the sudden shift in policy in the first place. Efforts to reform the concession system were not exactly new in 1870 and, once again, the fact that most previous attempts had gone nowhere—only a handful of small states, mostly Hanseatic cities like Hamburg and Bremen as well as a few South German principalities with cultural and political connections to France, had done away with it—had had as much to do with the intransigence of German governments as it had with a business community that generally preferred to err on the side of too much state oversight than none at all. Hence, it was unlikely that, as a vocal chorus of critics would later argue, the Free Incorporation Act of 1870 constituted some kind of capitulation on the part of the Prussian government to business interests or, worse still, to French laissez-faire dogma.

What, then, could have accounted for the Prussian government's decision to do away with the state concession system? One way to approach this question is to place the state's interest, not those of protagonists like Gustav Mevissen or the liberal political establishment, at the center of the story. In this version of events, Berlin was moved primarily by its own strategic calculations and turned to the politics and language of liberalism only secondarily, probably in an attempt to legitimize what was, after all, a controversial policy change. It would not have been the first time it had done so. For much of the preceding period, the Prussian government's approach to joint-stock corporations—and more generally to an ascendant liberalism clamoring for greater influence over economic affairs—had been to press them into the service of its own, often quite narrow strategic interests. This was why for many years Berlin had been all too willing to grant joint-stock concessions to railroads and mining companies, even as it dragged its feet on proposals from companies in other sectors of the economy. Iron rails and coal played a critical part in the monarchy's attempt in this period to bolster its military capacity and, in particular, to enable the Prussian army to fight wars on multiple fronts, as indeed it would during the wars of German unification against Denmark (1864), Austria (1866), and eventually France (1870–71).

Viewed from this angle, the question that needs answering is not why Berlin succumbed to political pressure from businesspeople and modernizing reformers but, rather, how its military-strategic interests might have shifted in 1870 to justify the wholesale abolition of the concession system. Was the policy change motivated by war-planning concerns rather than newfound convictions about liberal economic governance, as had often been the case in the 1850s and 1860s? The timing of the events—the Free Incorporation Act of 1870 was introduced mere weeks before the outbreak of hostilities with France—suggests as much. Sources from within the Prussian government can offer further clues, but they also leave many questions unanswered owing to Berlin's time-honored practice of disguising its true intentions using the idiom of liberal reform. Still, there are ways to peer past the subterfuge. One is to consider parallel events and developments in what may at first seem like an unrelated context: antebellum New York City.

Business was booming at the law offices of Kapp, Zitz & Froebel in New York. It was 1852, and the three German attorneys—all of them recent arrivals to the United States, part of the so-called forty-eighter generation that left German states in the wake of the failed Revolution of 1848—had just moved their offices from Hoboken, New Jersey, to a more central location in Manhattan, at 4 Wall Street. The firm was making "daily progress" and, according to one of its partners, Friedrich Kapp, it had managed to capture an "ever-expanding circle" of clients, including several "large merchants, bankers, and importers." But success came at a cost. "This constant running, chasing, and pushing... dulls the spirit," Kapp confessed. Not only were the long hours at work preventing him from engaging in other interests, like history, philosophy, and writing, but also they made it difficult to spend more time with his children, whose education and cultural refinement Kapp worried deeply about in this country of "the small and ignorant farmer who knows of no ideal except to chomp on his daily bacon."[12]

The grind was relentless, but it was not the only thing weighing on Kapp. His exhaustion was made worse by a nagging feeling that his business, which consisted of helping German emigrants stranded in America settle financial and legal claims back in Europe, resembled a monument of sorts to an old and ever-worsening malady afflicting his native Germany: emigration.[13] About a decade earlier, Heinrich Heine, the famed national poet, had described emigration using language that, at the time, seemed overly dramatic and perhaps was intended as such: a "great stream of blood," Heine had called it, "gushing from the wounds of the fatherland." From the vantage point of the 1850s, Heine's words no longer seemed so over the top. "For weeks at a time, and for many years in a row," Kapp recalled some years later, "I watched 6,000 to 8,000 people arrive daily in [the] port of New York, and I stood right beside them as they landed at Castle Garden." It was hardly an exaggeration. In the five years since Kapp had arrived in the United States, the authorities registered some 1,800,000 immigrants, or about twice the population of Paris in 1850. Not all of them were Germans, of course—many spoke Irish, Scottish, English, Swiss German, French, and other languages—but a good portion were: In 1854 alone, some 215,000 claimed to come from Germany, according to the official statistics.[14]

The numbers were terrifying, and not only because they dwarfed those of the past. A migration of this scale also made it difficult to dismiss it as a movement of mere paupers, adventurers, madmen, criminals, and other good-for-nothings. For years, observers in Europe had derived reassurance from such a presumption, even going so far as to argue that emigration constituted a blessing in disguise. The spectacle in New York offered the strongest evidence yet that the argument was quite simply wrong. Even if it were possible to round up all the dregs of German society, it was unlikely that the numbers should have added up to match those now being recorded by US authorities. Kapp, for his part, knew very well, based on what he saw day in and day out at his law offices, that a good portion of his countrymen in America were neither poor people nor madmen or idle loafers. They were hard-working, honest people who only sought to claim the share of their family's possessions that they were entitled to by birth and to use the money to found a business, purchase a homestead, or otherwise create an existence for themselves. At times, it was Germany's best and brightest who found themselves on American soil: men like Friedrich Wilhelm von Steuben and Johann Kalb, for example, two German officers who fought valiantly alongside the colonists against the English yoke during the American Revolution and whom Kapp paid tribute to in two well-received biographies published in 1858 and 1862.[15]

Perhaps the most frightening aspect of Heine's image of the gushing wound was the fact that there seemed to be so little that could be done to stanch the bleeding. A unified nation-state in Europe, long considered a panacea for all that ailed Germany, had failed to materialize in '48 and now appeared at least decades away.[16] Parallel efforts during the 1830s and 1840s to establish a "new Germany" in the form of ethnic enclaves and settler colonies had likewise come to naught. Even the more successful ones, like the "Hermann" settlement on the Osage River in Missouri, led by the competent Westphalian physician Bernhard Bruns, failed to attract and keep enough

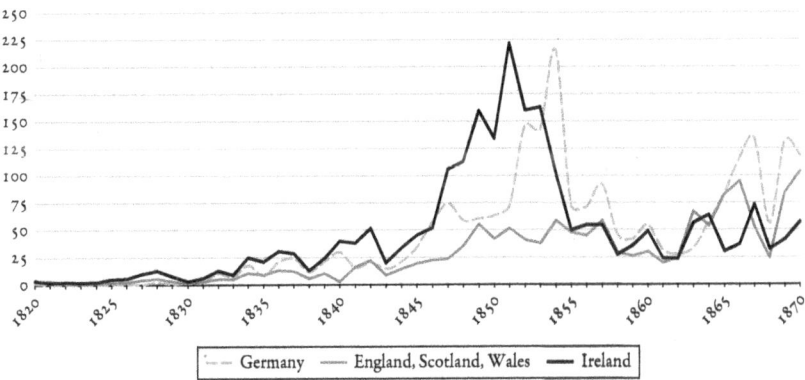

FIGURE 5.1 Immigration to the United States, select countries of origin, 1820–70 (in thousands)*

The so-called gushing wound was mirrored in US immigration statistics. In the 1840s and 1850s, emigration from Europe, especially Ireland, Great Britain, and Germany, reached unprecedented scale. The vast majority of the newcomers arrived by ship in northern ports like New York, Philadelphia, and Baltimore and to a lesser extent in Savannah, Georgia, and Galveston, Texas.

* The US government did not employ a consistent method to collect data on immigration in this period. Between 1820 and 1870, for example, statistics on immigration were assembled primarily from passenger lists on inbound vessels, so-called ship manifests that captains were required to provide to US customs authorities upon arrival. While these passenger lists offer details on every passenger's name, age, sex, occupation, and "country to which they severally belonged," they also exclude important information, such as whether an individual intended to stay in the United States permanently or only temporarily. Further complicating the picture is the fact that the definition of countries of origin varied over time in accordance with shifting political boundaries in Europe (thus, prior to 1861, Austria went unreported, with passengers from that region likely citing Germany as their country of origin). Because of these and other limitations, the data should be interpreted with caution, and primarily to gauge general trends over long periods rather than an accurate count of immigrants to the United States in a given year.

Source: Based on tabulations in Susan B. Carter, *Historical Statistics of the United States: Earliest Times to the Present* (New York: Cambridge University Press, 2006).

settlers to stay viable in the long run. On the one hand, better opportunities always beckoned elsewhere, in larger American cities or in the gold mines of California (Bruns himself left Hermann in the 1850s and moved to nearby Jefferson City, Missouri, mostly for economic reasons). On the other hand, intense competition among the various German settler projects encouraged an active rumor mill about the horrors experienced by emigrants who had been left stranded in remote, desolate wildernesses by conniving or incompetent patrons, thus compelling subsequent generations of emigrants to proceed with extra caution or to avoid German colonies altogether. Making matters more difficult still was that by the 1830s and 1840s the United States had firmly asserted its own claims over those territories in North America that German colonists coveted as most suitable, climatically and otherwise.[17]

The growing provenance of the United States on the North American continent, whether real or merely aspirational, forced ardent German patriots to find new ways of organizing the national community in North America. Carl Heinzen, a forty-eighter known for his radical politics and ties to communist circles, proposed that rather than starting a new state from scratch, the German community might take control of existing American governments, infiltrating them and turning them into quasi patrons of German culture. But this approach, too, had proven difficult. It would have required the Germans to form a unified voting bloc—an elusive endeavor, as Heinzen and his associates were forced to discover, given the fact that the Germans of North America were every bit as divided as the Germans of Europe. Not only did old suspicions and jealousies survive the transatlantic voyage, but also new ones were added upon arrival, especially on divisive issues like the institution of slavery. So alienated were the Germans from one another that not even the specter of nativism sufficed to bring them together: In 1857, Carl Schurz, a good friend of Kapp's and a tireless spokesman of German interests, found himself on the short end of a very winnable Republican primary contest in Wisconsin, losing by a mere forty-seven votes to his openly nativist opponent. Schurz and his allies were furious about their countrymen's failure to show up when it counted.[18]

It was all too apparent that if not even a political talent like Schurz could rally the Germans, and on so urgent an issue as the struggle with nativism, then probably no one could. It certainly would not be Kapp: Although he was a keen spectator in the political battles raging across antebellum America— Kapp was firmly in the antislavery and "free soil" camps—he lacked the skill, patience, and statesmanship required to forge larger political coalitions. After some years of observing American politics from the sidelines, moreover, Kapp had fallen on the belief that the approach was flawed for another, more structural reason. It might have made sense back in Europe, he explained, to attempt to influence or gain control of the reins of government, since in Europe "all civilization, education, and even industry is introduced to the people from above via the organs of the state." But in the United States, politics worked differently. The US government played at best a peripheral role in the making of society: Its influence on American political life, Kapp mused, was about as great as that of a German university on German "spiritual life," which was to say that it was almost nonexistent. It followed that even if the Germans managed to assert themselves within the halls of American government, it would likely be of no consequence.[19]

FIGURE 5.2 **Castle Garden, New York.** *The Labor Exchange—Emigrants on the Battery in Front of Castle Garden, New York.* Wood engraving, 18 × 24 cm (1868). Like so many German forty-eighters, Friedrich Kapp owed his business and public persona to his patronage of German immigrants, many of whom entered the United States via the Castle Garden immigrant processing facility in New York.
Source: Courtesy of the Wallach Division Picture Collection, the New York Public Library.

But what, then, could be done about the nation's gushing wound? For years, the question was a source of profound anguish for Kapp and a growing circle of like-minded forty-eighters in Manhattan. In the conversations that ensued, and in which Kapp reportedly always stood "at the center," various solutions were considered. One proposal that eventually gained traction was a mutual life insurance company, to be established on the basis of a joint-stock corporation model. Given the nature of the problem at hand—a national community uprooted, dispersed, and divided, and for those reasons increasingly vulnerable to dissolving itself into American culture via assimilation— the advantages seemed all too obvious: Through the sale of ownership shares and life insurance policies on an individualized and anonymous basis, the enterprise would assemble the nation and its formidable financial resources under a shared, institutional roof, a national home of sorts. Crucially, it would do so without recourse to politics, namely, by appealing to the material interests of each individual instead. (In a mutual life insurance model, policyholders were also stakeholders, entitled to privileges similar to those of investors, like dividends earned on the company's capital reserves.) For Kapp, who never tired of emphasizing the "role of money-making and material means in achieving spiritual and moral purposes," the project was an exemplar.[20]

It was also not exactly new. In fact, when the Germania Life Insurance Company of New York opened its doors for business in the summer of 1860, it was doing so in a crowded field of life insurance companies, including genuine pioneers of the industry like the New York Life Insurance Company and the Mutual Life Insurance Company of New York, both of which dated to the 1840s. In Europe, too, the concept had already made inroads. Half a dozen life insurance companies were formed in the 1850s in Prussia alone, and some even shared the Germania's explicit appeal to a national clientele, like the similarly named Germania Life Insurance and Savings Bank for Germany in Cologne, established in 1849 by none other than Gustav Mevissen. The parallels were not surprising because many of the figures behind these endeavors either knew each other personally or moved within the same social and political circles. For example, Hugo Wesendonck, a dry-goods merchant from the Rhineland who served as the first managing director of the Germania in New York, grew up in a prominent family of textile merchants near Düsseldorf—just as Mevissen had. Moreover, prior to leaving for the United States in the wake of the revolution, Wesendonck had been an influential voice in German national politics, partaking in the same debates as Mevissen over railroads and tariffs and other policies aimed at fostering national economic development.[21]

Still, the Germania in New York stood apart. While it might have shared a national ethos with its competitor in Germany, it was ultimately driven by a very different set of ambitions. The contrast to Mevissen's venture in Cologne is particularly revealing. For Mevissen, and for European advocates of life insurance more generally, a life insurance company was part of a broader collection of novel economic institutions that could be used to encourage growth and modernize the nation's commerce and industries. Apart from offering yet another powerful mechanism for aggregating capital, for example, life insurance supported a modern and mobile workforce. Companies like Mevissen's did not just supersede local institutions of risk management, thereby facilitating people's movement into cities, mining districts, and factory towns. They also enabled ordinary working people to benefit from the efficiency gains and financial upsides promised by modern actuarial science.[22]

The German Americans, by contrast, pursued no such macroeconomic agenda. Though they always touted their use of modern management tools and actuarial science, the raison d'être of their enterprise had more to do with

FIGURE 5.3 **The Germania Life Insurance Company Building.** *N.Y.C. Avenues—Broadway, 17th–20th Streets*. Photograph (no date). The Germania Life Insurance Company Building, constructed in 1911, is visible in the back on the right-hand side. The building is known in the early twenty-first century as West New York Union Square.
Source: Courtesy of the Milstein Division, the New York Public Library.

anxieties about the loss of capital and people to a foreign country. These New Yorkers aspired above all to stop the proverbial bleeding of the nation's body, both by offering an institutional home to German people in America and by protecting individuals from falling on unexpected financial hardship, widely regarded as an accelerant of assimilation into American culture. Justified or not, the implications of this narrative for the business were far-reaching. To promise guardianship against the loss of national life and treasure was to change the metrics for the company's success in a fundamental way. Once more, Mevissen's enterprises offer a revealing contrast: Whereas Mevissen often found himself compelled to answer to critics about his choice of incorporation, still seen by fellow businesspeople as an inefficient and backward way to organize a business, the men behind the Germania in New York did not need to justify their use of the joint-stock model. Partly, this was because they had made no attempt to articulate the purpose of their endeavor using the idiom of modernity, as Mevissen had, and partly it was because a good portion of the German American community seemed to agree, or at least tacitly accept, that the joint-stock corporation was the best institution available to tend to the nation's gushing wound.[23]

Beyond this, there was the context of antebellum America and its politics. It was no coincidence that at this same moment in time, in the 1850s, Americans had begun to dramatically rethink the meaning and purpose of joint-stock corporations and that they had done so in ways that closely echoed the German Americans' fixation on national loss. Thus, in decades prior, most Americans were inclined to think about joint-stock corporations—if, that is, they thought about them at all—in a manner more similar to that of Gustav Mevissen, namely, as instruments of economic development and modernization: "internal improvements," in American parlance. The perception dated as far back as the nation's founding in the eighteenth century, when figures like Alexander Hamilton advocated for the use of joint-stock corporations in everything from churches to schools, municipalities, and commercial infrastructure. The link between the joint-stock corporation and modernization further crystallized amid Americans' subsequent push into western territories in the 1830s and 1840s. Whether it was familiar enterprises like canals, turnpikes, and railroads or novel types of businesses like life insurance companies, the joint-stock corporation was understood to be a useful and essential tool in efforts to "improve" the allegedly backward western wilderness.[24]

In the 1850s, however, this long-standing association of joint-stock corporations with development, improvement, and modernity began to give way to a new preoccupation with crisis and national decline. What set this shift in motion was the then-intensifying struggle over the institution of slavery and, more specifically, the fierce debates that were had in these years about whether slavery should or should not be allowed in the still-"unorganized" territories west of the Mississippi River. Because most Americans by this time had come to view that region as the place where the nation's heart, soul, and future resided, the question of whether settlers moving there should be allowed to bring enslaved persons with them struck a deep nerve. Both pro- and antislavery partisans regarded it an existential question, one in which failure to prevail over the opponent was likely to be interpreted as the very end of America's experiment with liberty.

Joint-stock corporations—and railroads in particular—loomed large in the discussions about how to save the West from being gobbled up by the other side, especially after Congress set off a furious and bloody stampede to populate western territories with partisans by passing the controversial Kansas–Nebraska Act of 1854. During the Civil War, the new narrative around joint-stock corporations fully came into its own. Congress's Pacific Railway Act of 1864 granted unprecedented financial resources, rights to land, loan guarantees, and outright gifts to so-called transcontinental railroad corporations like the Union Pacific, which were to lay track into some of the most remote parts of the continent. To be sure, government largess of this kind was partially owed to the prevailing atmosphere of corruption and to a Congress that had managed to "combine...recklessness with ineptitude" in unparalleled ways. Yet it also reflected the profound ideological stakes in play. To prevent the West from falling into the hands of "Slave Power," Washington would have to do more than just prevail on the battlefields of the South. It would also have to rush "free labor" to western territories and create stronger ties to vulnerable and remote regions like California and the Pacific Northwest, forging what became quite literally an iron bond to the nation's soul.[25]

The men behind the Germania Life Insurance Company, many of whom were fiery antislavery partisans themselves and also no less covetous of western territories, shared this crisis sentiment. They also seemed to draw inspiration from it because the Germania soon embarked on its own mad dash across the North American continent in the 1860s, establishing no less than 138 general agencies in just the first five years of its existence. Only seven American life insurance companies—out of an industry numbering in the hundreds—operated this many agencies, and all of them serviced far more life insurance policies than the Germania. As had been true of the transcontinentals, a significant portion of the Germania's agencies were established in exceedingly remote locations across the far West and the South, as well as in the Caribbean and Central and South America. As early as 1862, an office was established in distant San Francisco, then home to a relatively modest community of 6,346 German Americans and reachable only via a twelve thousand–mile voyage around the southern tip of South America or by an arduous wagon trek across Native American territory on the Great Plains.[26]

There was no business rationale or actuarial imperative for an agency in San Francisco or, for that matter, in Havana, Cuba, or Valparaíso, Chile—a point frequently made by the company's own actuaries. But for years, these warnings were simply ignored. Partly this was because they *could* be ignored, since the continuous arrival of German immigrants in New York City furnished the company with a reliable source of new business that was usually enough to compensate for the money-losing agencies west of the Mississippi. And partly it was because the stakes of the enterprise were deemed too high, the services rendered to the nation too essential, to pay much attention to cost or the bottom line. Where German capital and souls stood to be saved, the extra expenditure associated with an office on the far side of North America was thought to be but a small price to pay.

As it turned out, the price to pay was not small at all, but rather significant. As soon as German immigration to the United States entered a temporary lull in the 1870s, directors were forced to retreat from the ambitious expansion of the early years. By this time, however, many of Germania's founders had long moved on from the company. Galvanized by Prussia's impressive victories over Denmark and Austria in 1864 and 1866, which were viewed as monumental steps toward the unification of Germany, they had decided to return to Europe to witness and partake in these historic events. All this meant that they were spared a reckoning with the Germania's ill-conceived approach to the life insurance business. Left with the impression that the company they had founded in New York was a singular success, they took it upon themselves to gather all "the experiences and knowledge...won in America" and, as Friedrich Kapp put it, to use it to "enlighten the continental philistine."[27]

Toward the end of March 1869, representatives of some of Frankfurt am Main's most prominent banking houses, including Johann Goll & Söhne, Alexander Gontard & Sohn, Gebrüder Schuster, and D. & J. de Neufville, gathered to draw up a plan for a new joint-stock bank. With a target capitalization of twelve million taler, the venture would be more than double the size of the Frankfurter Bank, heretofore the city's largest joint-stock bank. The ambitious size of the project was thought to reflect the immense business opportunities at hand. In the spring of 1869, America's first transcontinental railroad, the Union Pacific, was fast approaching completion. The Frankfurters bet that linking the Atlantic and Pacific Oceans would usher in nothing less than a new era in global commerce. Not only would the long-hailed bounties of the North American continent finally be made accessible to the world, but also a new, more direct trade route would be opened between Europe and the rich markets of the Far East. With their Deutsch-Amerikanische Handelsgesellschaft, or German American Trade Company, the Frankfurters sought to position themselves to take advantage as soon as the Union Pacific's "last spike" was driven into the ground on May 10, 1869, at Promontory Summit in Utah.[28]

Of course, the Frankfurters were not alone in spotting the upside. The competition promised to be stiff: Rumor had it that dozens of similar projects were in the making near and far, from London to Amsterdam, Paris, Zurich, and Vienna. (By the summer, according to the *Frankfurter Zeitung*, Frankfurt's leading financial daily, no fewer than forty new bank projects dealing with "overseas commerce" had been founded in Vienna alone). But the bankers who assembled in Frankfurt in March 1869 were filled with confidence. They had just secured one of the most experienced and highly regarded names in transatlantic trade and finance to lead their enterprise as managing director, a certain Hermann Marcuse of the renowned Wall Street firm Baltzer & Marcuse.[29]

Marcuse's resume was impressive and, it seemed, tailor-made for the Deutsch-Amerikanische. Born and raised in Hanover, Marcuse had left Germany as an adolescent, taking an apprenticeship in Manchester, where he learned about the cotton trade and other Atlantic world commodities. In the 1850s—when he was still in his twenties—Marcuse emigrated to the United States. He established his own cotton-trading firm, which, in light of what observers described as his prodigious "intelligence and business acumen," quickly acquired a reputation for excellence. During the Civil War, Marcuse did what so many New York cotton merchants did at the time: He shifted out of commodities and into finance. He began trading in US treasury bonds, helping to underwrite a booming sovereign debt market for the Union, both in North America and in Germany, while also spearheading the founding of the Germania Life Insurance Company. With some $32 million in life insurance policies in force by 1870, the Germania was already one of the largest life insurance companies in the world, with a strong presence across the Atlantic, from Berlin to New York, Cincinnati, Chicago, New Orleans, and San Francisco. From the Frankfurters' perspective, this experience was invaluable. Not only did Marcuse have a track record of serial business success, but also the companies he had run over the course of his career had operated in precisely those places where the Deutsch-Amerikanische was poised to exploit new opportunities. With Marcuse on board, the Frankfurters could expect to hit the ground running.[30]

Some roadblocks remained, however. One was that Marcuse, as a condition of accepting the offer of managing director, insisted that the new bank be organized as a joint-stock corporation.[31] This turned out to be a tall order for the Frankfurters. A few years earlier, in 1866, their city had lost its autonomy as a "free city" when it was annexed by the kingdom of Prussia and made subject to Prussian law. Now Berlin would have to approve the Deutsch-Amerikanische and grant a formal concession before business could commence—an "almost impossible" prospect, as Wilhelm Hohenemser, a spokesman for the Frankfurters, quickly recognized. The Prussian government had a reputation for taking a cautious approach toward joint-stock corporations, and that was especially true of financial institutions like banks, on the grounds that they could devolve into a Crédit Mobilier of sorts and, as such, threaten the stability of local financial markets. Only one bank had ever received a joint-stock

FIGURE 5.4 Hermann Marcuse. A photograph of the cotton merchant and financier Hermann Marcuse, ca. 1883.

Source: Henry Villard Photograph Album, Baker Library, Harvard Business School.

concession in Prussia, the A. Schaaffhausen'scher Bankverein in Cologne back in 1848, and that was during an exceptional moment of crisis, when Berlin looked for help from private investors as it sought to bail out the strategically important Ruhr industrial region. Making matters more complicated still, relations between Frankfurt and Berlin in these years were frosty, to say the least. Historically, the city on the Main felt closer to southern Germany and Austria, both rivals of Prussia, and for years it had provided them with everything from generous loans to diplomatic support. Berlin, fully aware, mistrusted the Frankfurters, and the feeling was mutual.[32]

To be sure, there was a workaround. The Deutsch-Amerikanische could have opted for an alternative corporate form that did not require formal approval from the government, namely, the Kommanditgesellschaft auf Aktien. Though closer in form and content to an ordinary partnership—the

Kommandit did not offer limited liability protections to owners—this form of incorporation offered at least some of the advantages of a proper joint-stock corporation, such as the ability to raise capital on financial markets through the sale of nonvoting stock. The route had been taken before, by the Disconto-Gesellschaft in Berlin, an enterprise founded in the 1850s by the Aachen wool merchant and financier David Hansemann. But it was not the route the Frankfurters would take, if they even considered it. Instead, they proceeded with attempting the "impossible" and making their Deutsch-Amerikanische the first-ever bank since the Schaaffhausen'scher to win a concession to operate as a joint-stock enterprise.

It was a sign of Marcuse's obstinacy on the matter, as well as the importance that the Frankfurters attached to his presence at the enterprise. They might have considered his insistence on the corporate form irritating and perhaps even bizarre, but they did not dare to question it.[33] Beyond humoring Marcuse, however, the decision not to pursue the much easier and faster Kommandit route was also indicative of the extraordinary confidence they seemed to have in their proposal's promise, the fact that it would not just withstand scrutiny but also win swift backing from Berlin. There were at least two explanations for such confidence.

The first had to do with the Frankfurters' apparently nuanced understanding of what actually stood behind the long-standing reluctance on the part of the Prussian government to grant permission to new joint-stock corporations. An uninformed observer might have presumed that Berlin was simply too reactionary in its politics, too jealous of its own authority, too timid to take a chance on a change. Reality was more complicated. It was certainly true that some people within Prussian officialdom sought to prevent the formation of joint-stock corporations at all costs, usually to protect the interests of the communities and those of existing commerce. These voices were most commonly found among the lower-level bureaucracy, which maintained close relationships to local stakeholders like magistrates, guilds, ecclesiastical institutions, and landed gentry.[34] However, closer to the upper echelons of the bureaucracy, and especially at the ministerial level, opinion often tended in the opposite direction. Typical here was the figure of August von der Heydt, a progressive merchant from Elberfeld who in the 1850s and 1860s served in various ministerial roles, including the ministries of commerce and public works and of finance. Von der Heydt was not shy about his enthusiasm for joint-stock corporations: "Enterprises of modernity" is what he hailed them as, useful not just for purposes of building new infrastructure or financing new industries but also for endeavors as wide-ranging as "raising [levels] of agricultural production" and improving the "capital value of real estate."[35]

Now, the fact that the king and his deputies, in accordance with their ultimate decision-making authority on the matter, often sided with the lower-level officials rather than with the August von der Heydts had little to do with reactionary politics or a backward view of economic affairs (to the contrary, given how vocal von der Heydt had been about his plans to modernize the Prussian economy, his appointment signaled royal support for the reform and modernization factions within the government). Instead—and this is what the Frankfurters understood quite well—the choice had to do with the Crown's broader strategic interests. Empowering local officials was good politics, and not just as a matter of building popular legitimacy for the monarchy. It also promoted loyalty among a class of state servants that was much larger in number, and therefore much more difficult to replace, than the ministers. Furthermore, by siding with the opponents of joint-stock corporations, the government could extract financial concessions from any new ventures for purposes of funding public infrastructure like churches, schools, and parks—an apparent win for all sides. From the perspective of Deutsch-Amerikanische, meanwhile, these strategic calculations were very good news. As a company devoted solely to "promot[ing] and facilitat[ing] commercial relations between Germany and North America, especially the United States," it promised to have only a slim footprint on local Prussian businesses and communities. And that was a significant advantage if the key to earning a joint-stock concession in Prussia was to secure the blessing, or at least the indifference, of local stakeholders and their allies in the Prussian government.[36]

The second explanation for the Frankfurters' confidence about winning approval from Berlin was that they seemed to genuinely believe that the Deutsch-Amerikanische was a different kind of enterprise—that it was not just another bank in the mold of France's Crédit Mobilier. They demonstrated this belief by describing a bank much more in the mold of the Germania Life Insurance Company in New York. There was a conspicuous absence in the bank's initial proposals of references to modernity, economic growth, or heightened productivity—outcomes that stood at the forefront of how most aspiring joint-stock corporations justified their existence. Although the Deutsch-Amerikanische did promise to both "promote and facilitate" (*fördern und vermitteln*) trade between Germany and North America, the narrative that was presented placed decided emphasis on the second term, that is, on the bank's stewardship of extant trade relations. Commerce between German states and the United States was quite old, so the argument went, having emerged in tandem with decades of large-scale German emigration to the United States. Given the German-national character of this business, it was only in the best interest of the (Prussia-led) North German Confederation that a powerful financial institution be created to ensure its "preservation" (*Erhaltung*) and "care" (*Pflege*)—even more so since a good portion of it was currently being facilitated by French and English intermediaries and because in recent years some key sectors, like the export of machine tools and other manufactures from northern Germany, had been experiencing a "regretful decline." (What exactly precipitated the decline was not spelled out, but the earlier references to English and French intermediaries left little doubt about the likely culprit.)[37]

How exactly the Frankfurters had come about this rather unusual formulation of the purpose of their enterprise is difficult to say based on the proposals alone. The echoes to the Germania were certainly there and, given Marcuse's active role in the project, they were not entirely surprising. But it was also possible that the Frankfurters, who claimed to have "long thought about" spearheading this bank project, had conceived the pitch entirely on their own—and for that very reason had managed to attract Marcuse to their project. Either way, the narrative they presented held strategic advantages with respect to navigating the politics of joint-stock corporations in Prussia. Not only did the idea of preserving and caring for the nation's overseas trade relations appeal to a Prussian state that had long committed itself to a leadership role in German national politics, but also, more important, it distanced the Deutsch-Amerikanische from the politically fraught modernization agenda of an August von der Heydt, casting it instead as a champion and guardian of existing commerce. In so doing, the Frankfurters gave Berlin useful political cover to approve the project. A vote in favor of the Deutsch-Amerikanische could very well be regarded as a vote in favor of local stakeholders and, by the same token, a rejection of the controversial modernizing agenda of the von der Heydts and proponents of the Crédit Mobilier's model of development.[38]

Filled with such confidence about their arguments, the Frankfurters immediately put wheels into motion. Within days of their initial meeting in late March 1869, Wilhelm Hohenemser sent out feelers to his associate, Joh. Jac. Sauerländer, an influential cotton merchant and broker in Vienna. Sauerländer in turn approached his contact, Prince Gebhard Bernard Carl Blücher von Wahlstatt, a descendant of the celebrated general Gebhard Leberecht von Blücher, who helped defeat Napoleon at Waterloo and had intimate access to the European diplomatic world, including to Baron Carl Anton von Werther, the top Prussian diplomat in Vienna and a close confidante of Otto von Bismarck. Blücher instructed von Werther to "inform the chancellor in advance of our intended démarche...and induce His Excellency to exercise favorable influence on the appropriate ministers." Von Werther obliged; on April 20, he informed Bismarck of the project, adding, for good measure, that if the chancellor was not inclined to entertain the idea, then the Frankfurters, whose loyalties to Berlin everyone knew were wanting, would likely work with Vienna, "where, as you know, the administrative rules are exceedingly lax." Despite this rather blatant attempt at blackmail, the chancellor proved receptive. On April 25, Bismarck submitted a circular to his deputies recommending that the Deutsch-Amerikanische be given special consideration as being "politically and commercially useful." As long as there would be an "upper limit on the speculative activities" to prevent the bank's "degeneration" into a "so-called Crédit Mobilier," the Frankfurters' new joint-stock bank was "worthy of sponsorship."[39]

Things appeared to be going exactly in the way the Frankfurters had hoped. Soon, however, the momentum seemed to escape them. Although de facto approval had already been secured, subsequent negotiations with ministers and lower-level officials about the exact language of the new company's bylaws—there was still some disagreement about how exactly to achieve the chancellor's upper-limit directive—dragged on for much longer than anticipated. When the paperwork was finally completed in September, a new obstacle emerged. On October 8, 1869, officials in Wiesbaden, the Prussian provincial capital of Hesse-Nassau, informed the Frankfurters that they could not proceed with final approval of the company's bylaws. Citing the Notary Ordinance of 1512, they were told that they would need all founding members of the new enterprise to be present in Wiesbaden for an oral reading of the documents, followed by a clearly audible "yes" from every founder of the Deutsch-Amerikanische.[40]

Heinrich Goll-Platzmann, a spokesman for the Frankfurters, was stunned. The 350-year-old notary ordinance was entirely "antiquated," he fumed. "[It] dates from a time when almost nobody knew how to read or write."[41] Goll-Platzmann's frustration and anger were understandable. Assembling the leading shareholders in Wiesbaden, on short notice and with winter on the doorstep, would be difficult; at the very least, it would require time, and time was something the Frankfurters no longer had. The competition was not going to wait: Rumor had it that fall that at least two more foreign trade bank projects, one in Hamburg and the other in Berlin, were on the verge of being approved by their respective governments. On January 26, 1870, the Frankfurters received the worst possible news in the form of a letter from Hermann Marcuse. Their star manager and frontman was writing to inform them that "following up on our earlier verbal communication, I have the honor of sending word today that I have joined 'Deutsche Bank,' recently founded in Berlin, as a member of the administrative board. Since this enterprise was created based on the same motives and since it pursues the same purposes that were intended by us in the Deutsch-Amerikanische Handelsgesellschaft, it will be easy to understand that I can no longer contribute to and partake in the latter."[42] This was devastating, and not just because the Frankfurters had now lost the man on whom they had pinned so much of their hope for the project. Marcuse did not exaggerate the extent to which Deutsche Bank echoed the business model of the Deutsch-Amerikanische. According to Deutsche Bank's application for a joint-stock charter, submitted just weeks later, on February 8, the new bank aimed to protect German commerce around the world and to put an end to the Germans' "humiliating" tributes to foreign financial intermediaries, especially the English and French. Informed observers estimated that the Comptoir d'Escompte in Paris earned a staggering 4,250,000 francs in "interest and profit," most of it on trade between German business and their German clients overseas. Much as the North German Confederation served as the German nation's "protecting power" in Europe, Deutsche Bank would ensure "security and confidence" among Germans around the world, especially "on this side and that side of the Atlantic."[43]

On March 10, the king of Prussia, Wilhelm I, awarded the first joint-stock concession to a bank in over fifteen years, and only the second in the kingdom's history. It was an extraordinary development and, as time would tell, a turning point in the monarchy's handling of joint-stock corporations—just as the Frankfurters had predicted it would be. Yet it was not they who received the honor, but a rival in Berlin, Deutsche Bank.

The Deutsch-Amerikanische Handelsgesellschaft eventually did receive a formal concession from the king, on April 25, 1870.[44] It was too little, too late, however. Not only did the Frankfurters struggle to find a replacement for Hermann Marcuse, but also many of the company's initial investors had already followed the German American to Deutsche Bank in Berlin. And so, an enterprise that had seemed so promising, with the potential to stand at the very top of a budding new world of commerce, was reduced to little more than a footnote in the historical record.

That, at least, is how the Frankfurters, still seething over the whole affair, saw it. But the Deutsch-Amerikanische was much more than a footnote. It mattered, first, because it had made the exact same arguments that eventually earned Deutsche Bank its nod for a joint-stock concession, only it had made them almost a year earlier. Subsequent chroniclers of Deutsche Bank would argue that the reason they had managed to win the government's approval so quickly was because of the renown of the persons backing the enterprise, along with what was by then a widely recognized need for a German financial institution devoted to protecting national commercial interests overseas. The claim was not lacking in merit. At the time of its founding, Deutsche Bank did boast a star assemblage of German merchants, bankers, and financiers. Yet it was also true that by the beginning of the year 1870, the Prussian government was already familiar with both the rationale Deutsche Bank cited on its behalf and some of its most important personalities, above all, the sought-after Hermann Marcuse. Bismarck surely experienced something of a déjà vu when, in February 1870, he received yet another proposal for a joint-stock bank claiming to serve the nation in ways he had already been made aware of by the Deutsch-Amerikanische and headed up by the same Marcuse who he already had been told was the "sole person appropriate" for the job. Though it would hardly have been a consolation for the Frankfurters, their arduous work over the preceding ten months or so likely paved the way for the swift approval of the Deutsche Bank project, soon to be one of the largest and most consequential financial institutions in the German Empire.[45]

Second, the Deutsch-Amerikanische mattered because it helped set the stage for an even more remarkable event that transpired just a few months later, namely, the passage in early June of the Free Incorporation Act of 1870. For those familiar with the story of the Deutsch-Amerikanische, and in particular with the circumstances of its failure, the Frankfurt enterprise offered a valuable lesson in how a venture that carried the written endorsement of no less an authority than Otto von Bismarck could nevertheless founder because of a relatively minor administrative technicality. What exactly had motivated the Wiesbaden official's bizarre insistence on the letter of a 350-year-old notary ordinance is not clear, but regardless of the intention, it was obvious that the matter created enough delay to torpedo the entire project. This was an important insight from Berlin's perspective. It revealed that if circumstances ever arose in which the government was pressed for time and, for strategic reasons, needed to move swiftly in approving an enterprise—and such a scenario no longer seemed all that remote, given the new, defensive rationale for joint-stock corporations that had been articulated by the

Deutsch-Amerikanische and its successor, Deutsche Bank—there was a nontrivial chance that the effort might fail on account of unanticipated administrative delays. The adoption of a general law of incorporation in 1870 closed this loophole and ostensible threat to national security: By transforming the joint-stock form from a privilege into a right, any influence that local officials might have wielded over the process was rendered null and void.

Granted, this was precisely the reason why Berlin so far had resisted the shift to general incorporation: It had no reason to sidestep local officials, whose support and loyalty were needed and valued, who served as convenient boogeymen in controversial cases, and who in any case could be overruled if necessary. But those strategic calculations were changing in early 1870, largely in light of Berlin's intensifying campaign at the time to bring about the unification of the German states under Prussian leadership. In what turned out to be a fast-evolving diplomatic and geopolitical crisis, time was suddenly of the essence, raising the stakes and urgency of changing the existing rules governing joint-stock corporations.

Thus, since at least February 1870, Bismarck had been engaged in a series of diplomatic maneuvers aimed at paving the way for German unification under Prussian leadership. His efforts had focused on France especially, where the government of Emperor Napoleon III had long regarded the creation of a unified German nation-state as a significant threat to French national security and therefore something to be opposed or at least delayed at all costs. To soften France's stance, the chancellor had tried to isolate the war hawks within Napoleon's cabinet while elevating the doves. The strategy had shown some signs of success, not least because the French public at the time had been weary of Napoleon's hawkish foreign policy, which it blamed for France's humiliation following a botched military intervention in Mexico in 1867. But then, in May 1870, Napoleon called a plebiscite on his rule, scoring an unlikely victory in the final tally. With his domestic political position strengthened, the emperor was suddenly at liberty to return to his preferred hawkish foreign policy.[46]

Needless to say, this turn-around in the political winds in France created a serious dilemma for Berlin. Although Bismarck at this point was not concerned that Napoleon would go to war—though the chancellor made it clear that if such a war ever came about, the Prussian army would be ready—he was well aware that any further step taken toward German unification was but an invitation to the swaggering French emperor to respond forcefully, including by imposing diplomatic and perhaps even economic sanctions. Indeed, Napoleon had already made gestures toward that end. Shortly after winning the plebiscite, he had installed Antoine Alfred Agénor, the Duke of Gramont, as his new foreign minister. Gramont was known in European diplomatic circles as a hard-liner and foreign policy hawk, as well as a fervent supporter of a closer economic union between France and Austria—a union that Berlin (rightly) interpreted as a thinly veiled attempt to isolate Prussia economically and cut off its access to foreign markets, both in Europe and overseas. The message behind Gramont's appointment was clear: France had the power, quite apart from waging war, to inflict serious pain on Prussia should it continue its vain endeavor of unifying Germany.[47]

Bismarck eventually found a way to extract himself from the bind, most famously by manufacturing a faux diplomatic crisis that goaded Napoleon into unilaterally declaring war on Prussia, which served Berlin's interests because it gave Europe's other great powers—London, Vienna, and St. Petersburg—the diplomatic cover they needed to stay on the sidelines in the ensuing conflict. But there was an intermittent period, from May through early July 1870, during which the chancellor very much felt boxed in by Paris, recognizing that anything he might do to advance the German national cause could provoke costly sanctions, especially with regard to Prussian commerce, on the part of France. That Berlin introduced the Free Incorporation Act of 1870 at this moment of strategic weakness was, in this sense, no coincidence.

To be sure, the new rules surrounding joint-stock enterprises were not exactly an elegant solution to the strategic dilemma raised by France's threats to Prussia's overseas trade interests. As subsequent critics would point out, it was a rather crude and "hastily cobbled together" piece of legislation. In effect, Berlin had used a sledgehammer where a gentle nudge would probably have sufficed. Still, this did not change the fact that, at least functionally speaking, the reforms of 1870 could help preempt French aggression in the economic arena, allowing for the rapid formation of new joint-stock enterprises to help Berlin protect its commercial interests in case of an armed conflict with France. And that was something, especially for a government that had always prided itself on a sober, utilitarian approach to politics.[48]

The Migrant's Spirit: How Industrial Modernity Came to the German Lands. Benjamin P. Hein,
Oxford University Press. © Oxford University Press 2025. DOI: 10.1093/9780197831052.003.0006

6
The Idea of Deutsche Bank

THE TAUNUS MOUNTAINS of central Germany were known to nineteenth-century contemporaries as a place of respite, relaxation, and entertainment. The reasons were both old and new. In Roman times, the region was recognized for its energizing natural hot springs, and the many spa towns that subsequently emerged attracted convalescents from around Europe for centuries. In the eighteenth century, the region's gentle peaks and mild climate began attracting enlightened Europeans who, driven by their faith in man's capacity for self-improvement, sought to take advantage of the spectacular hiking opportunities. They were followed by the Romantics of the early nineteenth century who hoped to discover themselves in the Taunus's calming pine forests and amid the ruins of its medieval castles. Starting around the middle of the century, the Taunus began drawing a more raucous crowd of pleasure-seeking aristocrats and nouveau riche who came to mingle at the horse tracks, botanical gardens, casinos, salons, grand hotels, and gun ranges that began cropping up at this time, especially in the regional capital of Wiesbaden, known then as the "Nice of the North."[1]

Among those making their way to the Taunus in these years was Hermann Marcuse. Like so many German Americans who made their names and fortunes abroad, Marcuse sought to retire in Germany, and to that end he had purchased an estate in Walluf, a town just six miles south of Wiesbaden, in the early 1860s. Given its proximity to Frankfurt am Main, an important financial center, Walluf combined the seclusion of an alpine village with the sophistication and cosmopolitanism of a major metropole. Many of Marcuse's old business associates were based there, so if he ever desired to re-enter the business world, his networks were nearby.

That, in essence, was how Marcuse came upon the Deutsch-Amerikanische Handelsgesellschaft in Frankfurt. News of the imminent completion of America's first transcontinental railroad in the spring of 1869 prompted his Frankfurt friends to try to retrieve him from retirement. He answered their call, albeit reluctantly, on the condition that the new bank be organized on his terms, namely, as a joint-stock corporation. When a government concession for such a company proved elusive, he appeared to lose interest. He had reached a stage in life at which he could afford to be selective in his business undertakings.²

It was puzzling, therefore, that just a few months later Marcuse decided to join Deutsche Bank in Berlin. Granted, this project stood a much better chance than the Deutsch-Amerikanische of acquiring a coveted joint-stock concession. But that alone was unlikely to have moved Marcuse. Quite aside from the fact that Berlin was nowhere near Walluf, the city's financial scene was terra incognita for him. He had never done business there, so he had few friends or connections. Unless he scrapped his retirement plans and moved to Berlin, he was unlikely to overcome this outsider status and likely to get sidelined on all the decision-making. For someone of Marcuse's stature and fortune, being sidelined on anything was unacceptable. That was especially true since he invested a formidable sum of his own money, some 314,000 talers, enough to make him Deutsche Bank's largest individual shareholder.³

Something else must have intrigued Marcuse about the Berlin project. One possibility was that Deutsche Bank, at least as it was described in an early blueprint from 1869, promised to be an unusual and quite innovative financial institution—it certainly seemed to be something more than just another foreign trade bank. In addition to financing (and "protecting") Germany's overseas commerce, it also proposed to establish an investment banking business, serve as an underwriter of sovereign debt, and offer a wide range of retail and consumer banking services, and it endeavored to do all this in locations around the entire world. It was a grandiose plan but, so the argument went, a necessary one in light of the circumstances. The diasporic scattering of the German people across the globe demanded an correspondingly global institution, one that offered the full catalog of financial services lest Germans overseas be forced to continue their reliance on French and English bankers who favored their countrymen.⁴

And this was only the beginning. Aside from emancipating the Germans from an English and French financial infrastructure, Deutsche Bank also promised to put German capital to German uses. Thus, it was argued that when Germans banked with foreigners, their deposits, along with any interest earned in short-term investments, were effectively lost or, more to the point, went into the pocketbooks of English or French bank directors. Deutsche Bank would be a more patriotic financial steward. It would pool all the capital and funnel it back to Germany, where it could be employed in the financing of trade, industry, and technological innovation. In so doing, Deutsche Bank would help to supercharge the nation's economy.[5]

A venture of such scale and patriotic purpose was bound to resonate with Marcuse. After all, he had founded a business of this nature before, namely, the Germania Life Insurance Company in New York. Like the proposed Deutsche Bank, the Germania endeavored to protect Germans who lived abroad from discrimination and favoritism by American competitors, and it too endeavored to pool what was considered the nation's scattered resources. Like Deutsche Bank, moreover, the Germania turned to innovative methods, in this case actuarial science, in an attempt to finally solve the nation's peculiar, geographic dilemma—that is, the fact that this was a people with a notorious tendency to wander, to settle in diverse places around the world, and in general to eschew the confines of a more traditional nation-state.

The resemblance between the two projects was indeed uncanny, and it helps explain why Marcuse was not the only Germania veteran who joined the Deutsche Bank project in January 1870. Half a dozen others can be found among the new bank's initial investors and board members.[6] All were close friends or former business associates of Marcuse's, and all were then re-emerging from what had been an early retirement in Germany. Their presence and participation, too, may explain Marcuse's interest in Deutsche Bank. Far more than the Deutsch-Amerikanische in Frankfurt, the Berlin venture constituted a kind of homecoming for New York's German American business community.

There is however another way to tell this story. In this version, the resemblance between the Germania and Deutsche Bank was not just happenstance, and Hermann Marcuse and his German American entourage were not just unwitting bystanders swept up in the patriotic bluster of a new bank project in Berlin. They were instead the main act. They went to Berlin to continue the work they had commenced in New York, to place their hard-won insights and experiences from overseas in the service of their country. They did not just join Deutsche Bank; they were Deutsche Bank.

Such an account is odds with how the story of Deutsche Bank is usually told. According to that narrative, Deutsche Bank is the "archetypical" German bank. Its rise to dominance in the late nineteenth century both paralleled and mirrored Germany's own rise as one of the great industrial nations of the era. From its earliest days in the 1870s, the bank's boosters exploited this coincidence to construct a lucrative brand according to which Deutsche Bank was synonymous with German modernity. It was always a myth, of course, but it was a powerful myth nonetheless, and it arguably survives to this day. Part of the reason is that the business model that Deutsche Bank popularized, what would eventually be known as *universal banking*, was well suited to the needs of German industry at that specific moment in time. Many a historian has concluded that only a homegrown company with intimate knowledge of local conditions could have done this.[7]

And yet, there are signs everywhere that Deutsche Bank had German American roots. Numbers tell part of the story. Marcuse's 314,000-taler investment was a statement, but he was not the only Germania veteran to commit large sums of money to Deutsche Bank. Altogether, the seven German Americans signed for a full 30 percent of the bank's original stock, enough to hand them control of nearly a quarter of the seats on the company board. It was a commanding share, bigger than that of any other group of investors, including those from Berlin, and it may as well have been a majority since the remaining shares and board seats were divvied among much smaller investor collectives from Bremen, Cologne, Stuttgart, and elsewhere.[8]

Then there was Deutsche Bank's unorthodox business plan. Even the bank's own spokesmen thought it too innovative to have been conceived of by a German banker of that period. The issue was not so much a lack of ambition, or patriotism, or even worldliness—German bankers in the nineteenth century were well endowed with all these traits—but rather a far too keen sense for money-making. No one in Germany had ever thought of doing what Deutsche Bank aspired to do because the approach was a recipe for financial disaster. To begin, the idea of using consumer deposits to finance other bank business, like loans to industry, was at the time considered a guaranteed money loser. A version of the concept had been tried in France in the 1850s by the Pereire brothers. It took just a few years for their Crédit Mobilier to run out of liquidity—and this in a country that boasted one of the largest and most affluent middle classes in Europe. Why the results should have been different in Germany was not clear. Years later, Karl Helfferich, a Deutsche Bank executive in the 1890s and one of the bank's first chroniclers, remembered how nobody "cared for and paid attention at all to the deposit business" because everyone knew there was "no profit in serving households."[9]

A similar disconnect arises with respect to Deutsche Bank's ambition to emancipate German trade from foreign financial institutions by duplicating the latter on a global level. To many contemporaries, this proposal was outright bizarre. While they could appreciate its patriotic impulses and often judged it "correct in principle," they tended to be put off by the immense scale and cost of the undertaking, warning that "you [still] needed to earn money in order to pay dividends to shareholders." The world's existing financial infrastructure had been developed and fine-tuned over centuries. It may have been in the hands of French, English, and Dutch bankers, but like it or not, it was still the most efficient, cost-effective way to do business, including for German industry. Why not formalize a partnership with the French or English and capitalize on their know-how and networks? The point of a bank was to make money; "how that was going to happen interested nobody."[10]

The explanation usually given is that Deutsche Bank was initially run by outsiders, men who possessed little or no prior experience in banking. The most frequently cited example in this regard is Georg Siemens, one of Deutsche Bank's first managing directors and the man who is most often credited with its meteoric rise in the nineteenth century. Just thirty years old when he was hired, in 1870, Siemens had never worked at a bank and had not studied the business in any systematic manner. His youthful ignorance was considered an asset because, so the argument went, it liberated him from the crushing weight of custom and convention.[11] Meanwhile, those among Deutsche Bank's leading figures who did wield prior experience in banking tended to downplay its importance. Ludwig Bamberger, who alongside Adelbert Delbrück was one of the bank's original founders, and who prior to Deutsche Bank spent nearly two decades working as a banker in Paris, once claimed that deep within, he always loathed being a banker. He thought it a "stupefying" profession. "My abilities did not tend toward any business talent," he confessed in his memoirs. "I never fancied any speculations, possessed no divination for them."[12]

Character portraits like these are not exactly wrong. Siemens really was a novice when it came to banking, and an unabashed one at that. Deutsche Bank was a success, he once told a colleague, "<u>because</u> I am *not* a financier."[13] Bamberger, too, meant what he said, judging at least by the fact that he quit Deutsche Bank almost as soon as he had founded it. The problem with these accounts is that this was not where they began and ended. One crucial fact is missing, which is that both men, who together have been cast as embodying the idea of Deutsche Bank, also happened to have a very close relationship to Marcuse and the German Americans, and to one man in particular, Friedrich Kapp.

The spring of 1869 was a stressful time for Ludwig Bamberger. On June 3rd, the second session of the "Customs Parliament" (*Zollparlament*), the legislative body of the German customs union (*Zollverein*) in Berlin, was to commence.

Judging by the prior year's session, another round of contentious debates on trade and fiscal policy awaited him. Law proposals needed to be read and speeches written. The evenings, too, would be busy with receptions, dinners, and late-night strategy sessions with colleagues in the National Liberal Party.

Then there was the disappointing letter from Kapp in New York. "My move back to Germany is all set for May 1870," it began, before pivoting to the bad news: Kapp would not be able to join Bamberger in Berlin. Various schemes meant to finance his move to the Prussian capital, where the two men had planned for years to reunite, had failed to materialize and he was no longer sure "whether my means and... income suffice to settle down in that nest." His brother-in-law had recommended an alternative, Wiesbaden. What did Bamberger think of that idea? Wiesbaden was a "gambling den," but then again "one can live decently, study, work, and drink a nice glass of wine in the evenings anywhere."[14]

Bamberger, in all likelihood, took this change of plans with a heavy heart. He regarded Kapp as one of his closest friends and confidantes. They had known each other since at least the 1840s, when they attended law school together at the University of Heidelberg. At the Walhalla Heidelberg fraternity, they had practiced their oratory and honed their radical bona fides by debating the works of French socialist Pierre-Joseph Proudhon. When the revolution broke out a few years later, they had thrown themselves headlong into the fray. After the revolution's fortunes began to take a turn, they had fled to Switzerland. On the shores of Lake Geneva, they had shared a bottle of wine—white wine, naturally, not an "un-German red"—and plotted their next move. Kapp had wanted them to go to America; his idea had been to set up an attorney's office in New York together with Julius Fröbel and Franz Heinrich Zitz, two mutual friends. But Bamberger had declined. His family duties required him to stay in Europe; London and then Paris would be his chosen exile. Still, the two friends stayed in touch, always maintaining a "busy correspondence." What kept them close was not just memories of their youth but also a shared passion for history, politics, and prose. "Since Heidelberg we were good comrades, always of the same mentality," Bamberger recalled in his memoirs. There were "few people [beside Kapp] who so delighted my heart from the first to the last hour."[15]

A shared mindset no doubt deepened their friendship, but so did their differences. Bamberger was evidently the more reserved and timid of the two. He hated taking unnecessary risks and was discerning to a fault. Born into a wealthy family of merchant bankers in Mainz, the Bischoffsheims, he inherited

The Idea of Deutsche Bank 145

privileges that he would not have dared to squander. Kapp was unencumbered by such anxieties. The son of a gymnasium teacher in a rural corner of Westphalia, he could only ever aspire to Bamberger's fortune. He thrived in America precisely because he was everything that Bamberger was not: confident, gregarious, opinionated, prone to confusing prejudice with common sense.[16] And yet, far from driving them apart, these differences brought them closer together. At times, it was as though they lived vicariously through one another.[17] Kapp's abiding problem was that his noisy showmanship, an asset in America, was generally a liability in Europe. More than once he was dismissed as a tactless, loud-mouthed American, and he always yearned for some of the respect accorded to his more refined, more diplomatic friend.[18] Bamberger, in turn, could not contain his admiration for Kapp's courage to speak his mind, his "original wit." He also could not help but notice Kapp's "trim, blond, and blue-eyed" physique. Given his own modest stature, he saw the "mighty head on broad shoulders" as evidence of an "ur-strong manliness."[19]

FIGURE 6.1 **Friedrich Kapp**. From Ludwig Bamberger, "Der Bürger zweier Welten," *Die Gartenlaube: Illustrirtes Familienblatt*, 22 (1869), 341.
Source: Courtesy of the Bayerische Staatsbibliothek München.

FIGURE 6.2 **Ludwig Bamberger.** Photograph by J. Braatz (no date). Reproduced in Paul Nathan, ed., *Erinnerungen von Ludwig Bamberger* (Berlin: Georg Reimer, 1899).
Source: Courtesy of the Universitätsbibliothek Trier.

The fact was that they trusted each other, and not just on matters of work or politics. Kapp was at least part of the reason why Bamberger had come to Berlin a few years earlier, in 1867. That was around the time of the Battle of Königgrätz, in the summer of 1866, when Prussia notched a decisive victory over Austria and, at long last, succeeded in settling the German question in its favor. Upon hearing the news, Kapp promptly made plans to move to the Prussian capital "no matter what," and he urged his friend to do the same. Bamberger hesitated. It was not for lack of enthusiasm; he had long thought about relocating to Germany, even before Königgrätz, because he knew his destiny was in politics. Holding him back was his wife, Anna, who could not countenance trading the elegance of Paris for the grubbiness of Berlin. Bamberger sympathized with that view; France had grown on him, too. He told Kapp that he had come to believe that perhaps he could better serve

The Idea of Deutsche Bank

Germany by staying in Paris and using his reputation there to rally French support for the fatherland.[20] His friend would have none of it: "You may have a certain...influence" in Paris, he fumed; it mattered little, however, because in the end the French "will never allow a foreigner to acquire renown." It was time to act. "Give up your bank business, go to Germany and engage yourself in literary matters and especially in politics," because "now we *can* become a nation if only we *want* to become a nation." Not long after that, in January 1867, Bamberger had indeed acted. He had quit his bank career and left for Berlin. Anna stayed in Paris; it was, as her husband confided to his diary, "le commencement de la fin."[21]

Presumably, the episode was still fresh in Bamberger's mind two years later, in February 1869, when he learned of Kapp's own wavering. Now it was Bamberger's turn to lift spirits and stiffen spines. He rushed to finish a spotlight article for *Die Gartenlaube*, the most widely read print publication in the country, which he had promised Kapp over a year earlier but never finished. Titled "The Citizen of Two Worlds," it was so full of praise, casting Kapp as nothing less than a German Garibaldi, that it embarrassed his friend. It was too much "mutual admiration," Kapp remarked. The "personal element" distracted from what was, ultimately, an "objective portrait."[22]

Undeterred, Bamberger redoubled his efforts and scoured his networks for opportunities. One promising one, he thought, was a new foreign trade bank that was then in the process of organizing, called the Deutsch-Amerikanische Handelsgesellschaft. It seemed like a good fit. Not only were German American financial relations Kapp's forte, but also—as far as Bamberger knew—the project was being spearheaded by their mutual friend, Hermann Marcuse. But alas, it was not to be. On July 6, a despondent Kapp sent notice that, after contacting Marcuse "right away," he learned that the project had stalled and Marcuse himself "seems to have already given up on [it]." For the time being, it would have to be Wiesbaden.[23]

All these events relate directly to the story of Deutsche Bank's founding because around this same moment, in the early summer of 1869, Bamberger was approached by Adelbert Delbrück, a fellow National Liberal delegate at the *Zollparlament*, about the founding of a new foreign trade bank to be established in Berlin (the eventual Deutsche Bank). A renowned Berlin financier, Delbrück had probably read the headlines from May about America's first transcontinental railroad. He would have immediately spotted the upside but been prevented from taking advantage because he lacked the know-how in international finance to get the project off the ground. Hence, he reached out to Bamberger, whose reputation in the area preceded him, to make a proposal to work together.[24] Bamberger's answer was—reportedly—an unequivocal yes, which seems a bit odd given that just two years before he had sworn off being a banker. This, along with the fact that he put together a business plan within weeks, suggests that he may have been motivated, at least in part, by a lingering hope that Kapp would join him in Berlin after all. Certainly, by the time he received word that the Deutsch-Amerikanische opportunity had fallen through, Delbrück's proposal would have looked more attractive. Delbrück, after all, was a powerful man; the scion of a notable Prussian family, he boasted valuable connections in government and Berlin's banking circles. He also offered to take on the more tedious side of founding a new bank, like lining up investors and garnering government approval. All Bamberger would have to do was to craft some inspirational language while tailoring the whole business to Kapp's expertise and liking.

Whether this was in fact his thinking is difficult to say, but it is also a moot point because less than a year later, Kapp did indeed join the board of Deutsche Bank and moved to Berlin.[25] A year after that, in 1872, he also won a seat in the Reichstag, allowing him to serve his nation alongside Bamberger. He even had enough money left over to purchase a summer residence in the spa town of Charlottenbrunn (Jedlina-Zdrój) in the foothills of Lower Silesia. Apart from these later developments, there is the memorandum that was produced in July. While it was drafted by a commissioned associate (the Dutch financier Gustav Dufresne had been hired to write it up and fill in the details), it nevertheless carries signs of a similar story, namely, that one of Deutsche Bank's two founders was in fact channeling the ideas, insights, and experiences of his good friend in New York.[26]

To begin, there is the document's preoccupation with the geographic dispersion of the German people and with the challenges this posed to the nation's political and economic future. Anxieties of this nature were not completely unusual in this period; Germany's political geography, or rather its lack thereof, had long been a topic of debate in nationalist circles. Still, there was always an implicit consensus that the question was a European one, that it was a matter of deciding between a Prussian-led, "little" Germany (*Kleindeutschland*) and a "greater" Germany (*Großdeutschland*) inclusive of Austria. Few factored into the equation the German-speaking communities in, say, Russia or North America or elsewhere, even as it was becoming more and more difficult to ignore them completely.

The memorandum takes a notably different perspective on the matter. Its focus is squarely on the "German element" that lived outside Europe, in places as diverse as Bombay, Singapore, Réunion, New York, and Rio de Janeiro. While this was partly a reflection of the fact that the bank's business was to be foreign trade, it was also taken to an extreme. The city of Berlin, the bank's ostensible headquarters, barely warrants a mention. Vienna and Paris, both home to large German-speaking populations, and both crucial conduits for German trade with the rest of the world, are ignored. The one European city that is given any attention at all is London, and that is only because London remained the "trade metropole of the world."[27]

There was a subtle critique here of the way the German question was framed at this time, of its continental bias. This critique likely originated in the burgeoning expatriate communities of the Americas, from the Rio Grande do Sul in Brazil to Galveston, Texas, and New York. Kapp, for his part, had been making this argument ever since he arrived in the United States in the early 1850s—to Bamberger and anyone else who would listen. It was one of the reasons he so yearned to return to Berlin; German America badly needed a spokesman in the nation's capital.[28] Besides, he often added, there was "*one more point, and that is the financial one.*" Aside from bodies, considerable sums of money were at stake. "Here in NY there are more than a dozen [Germans] with an annual income of more than one million dollars." He had heard of at least one "poor German brewer" who acquired a fortune so vast that he decided to donate $500,000 to a girls' school—a frivolous cause, in Kapp's mind. Granted, not all Germans in America were spendthrift millionaires, but that was not the point. The point was that they were nothing like the impoverished masses of popular imagination; they had money—lots of it.[29]

In fact, he had calculated just how much money they had. In a book on the "capital value" of German emigrants in America—published, incidentally, in 1869—he estimated that the Badeners were worth the most, at "245 florins, or $98 gold." Next came the Brunswickers, at "136 thalers, or about $96 gold, each," and the Bavarians with "233 florins, or $93.20 gold." Everyone also carried "apparel, tools, watches, books, and jewelry," which meant that, if one assumed an average of $150 "per head," the 258,989 emigrants who passed through Castle Garden in 1869 were worth a grand total of $38,848,350. It was an astonishing sum, but even more money was received after the emigrants settled down. That was when they called in the real money: inheritances, dowries, outstanding debts. Kapp knew this because he had witnessed it firsthand, not just at his "overseas business bureau" in Manhattan, but also while serving as the US commissioner of emigration at Castle Garden.[30]

There can be little doubt that Bamberger took a personal interest in all this, if only because his own experience with the German expatriate community in Paris had been so different. "Petite Allemagne," as it was called, had nothing in common with New York's "Little Germany." Those who made fame and fortune in Paris were, like Bamberger himself, already famous and fortunate when they arrived. Everyone else was and remained poor, living in what could only be described as squalor. Itinerant, seasonal workers all, these destitute migrants had been hired by Parisian authorities to sweep the city's streets, and they were more likely to remit their meager wages than to receive money from Germany.[31]

The memorandum, in its fixation on the overseas arena, reflects these divergent experiences. On the one hand, it recognizes the financial opportunities arising from the large-scale migration of Germans into the world, the way that their movement unlocked a spectacular store of national wealth, and to that end it proposes that the bank should offer personal checking and savings accounts. On the other hand, it distinguishes between the German diaspora of Europe and that of the rest of the world, proposing at once to establish a global network of subsidiaries while offering no plans for branches in Europe—apart from London. New York is identified instead as the most promising site to commence the business, followed by branches in South America and East Asia at a later stage. This order of priority reveals once more what, or rather who, Deutsche Bank was really for. The text states that branches in Shanghai or Buenos Aires would not be set up right away for want of "requisite personnel." No such obstacles seem to stand in the way of New York, a location about which Kapp's knowledge was, according to Bamberger, "second to none."[32]

Finally, there was the question of what to do with all the capital that was expected to accumulate in New York and other overseas branches. The Deutsche Bank plan was to aggregate these resources and, in the spirit of France's Crédit Mobilier, direct them toward other bank business, including financing German industry and trade with the world.[33] But this turned out to be easier said than done. One nagging problem was the considerable spread in the interest rate that prevailed in different parts of world, in particular the higher returns that could be earned overseas compared to Europe. High interest rates abroad incentivized the branches to hold on to their deposits and to invest them locally. If any capital at all was to be pooled, Deutsche Bank would have to curtail or even prohibit investment activity by the branches, which meant forfeiting returns. This was why an early group of investors who were given a glimpse of the memorandum from 1869 were so puzzled by it: Real money was at stake. Nor was it simply a matter of short- versus long-term horizons. The rationale offered in the memorandum, namely, that even greater windfalls could be expected once the bank managed to establish itself as the premier German trade bank, had always rung a bit hollow. Investment in a high-yield colonial context was the bread and butter of the very same French and English banks, like the Comptoir d'Escompte or the Hongkong and Shanghai Banking Corporation, that Deutsche Bank was supposed to replace. Everyone knew it was what made them rich in the first place.

Some degree of incoherence is to be expected in such documents. Business proposals of this kind rarely present finished ideas: By design, they are focused on the bigger picture, with the details left to be hashed out at later stages. But that is exactly the problem with the Deutsche Bank memorandum. It does not leave these controversial details to be hashed out at another time; to the contrary, it places them front and center. This suggests that there was more to the policy, that it played another, albeit implicit, function in the larger endeavor that was Deutsche Bank.

Once again, Bamberger's conversation with Kapp offers some clues. A few years earlier, Kapp had been working on a book titled *The German Princes' Mercenary Trade in America, 1775 to 1783* (1864). He and Bamberger had discussed it on several occasions and Bamberger had helped with some of the research in Parisian archives. The book told the story of eighteenth-century German princes who, in their ostensibly innocent pursuit of profit, turned to "selling" their soldier-subjects to serve as cannon fodder in the British Empire. Though the book was mostly devoted to exposing the profound immorality of the princes, Kapp also advanced a more ambitious claim about political economy, namely, that the whole business had crippled Germany's national development. Proceeds earned from selling good men into Britain's global wars had furnished the princes with windfall profits, which they used to consolidate their tiny fiefdoms and, in so doing, prevent the emergence of a unified German nation-state.[34]

As might be expected, Bamberger admired the work a great deal and soon published a gushing review of it. With his characteristic verve and sharp tongue, Bamberger explained, the famous German American had cut through all the nonsense and "exposed" the culprit behind the "many-colored absurdity that is the German political map." But the princes were just the beginning. Kapp's "exhaustive" research revealed that many of the soldiers themselves were complicit in the same wretched philistinism. They had abandoned their fatherland and risked their lives in a foreign power's war games. The historical record offered not a single instance of how the German people might have "erupted in indignation" over being sold across the Atlantic, like the enslaved subjects of the "king of Dahomey." Adam Smith famously argued that self-interest was the road to the "wealth of nations," but Kapp had turned that logic on its head: In the German lands, self-interest only led to national impoverishment.[35]

The argument was not solely Kapp's. Although the relevant footnotes were missing, it was in fact a version of a well-known critique of Smithian political economy undertaken years earlier by the Württemberg bureaucrat and political economist Friedrich List in his *The National System of Political Economy* (1841). Smith may well have been right about the English case, List had argued there, if only because England was the context from which Smith extrapolated his theories in the first place. By the same logic, List had written, it made little sense to try to apply Smith's insights to other nations, like Germany, then "still in the first phases of [its] development." Context mattered, but more important, there was the fact that commerce was not just the product of imbalances in supply and demand. It was also a power-political contest, a struggle between nations. It followed—so List had argued—that genuinely free and mutually beneficial trade could only happen in cases where there was parity of "culture and power" between two contracting parties. Only once a nation had "completely and harmoniously developed in all its parts, perfect in itself, and politically independent," could it expect to benefit from an embrace of Smith's principles. Before then, engaging in free trade simply locked it into a state of dependence on the more advanced English.[36]

The memorandum on Deutsche Bank seems, on the whole, to echo List's critique more than Kapp's. It insists that historical circumstances matter, that commerce is as much a function of power as anything else, and that German industry, if it is to engage with the world on equal footing, requires a commensurately "powerful" national patron.[37] It is in the specifics that Kapp's version played a role, for example, in the conspicuously distrustful stance toward Deutsche Bank's own overseas subsidiaries. Rather than consider them extensions of the bank, seamlessly connected like limbs to a torso, the proposal portrays them as autonomous actors who, not unlike the German princes of old, pursued their own, subversive agendas. Part of this may have been inevitable; each branch had to be granted some degree of autonomy to exploit opportunities on-site whenever they arose. Yet the memorandum also describes an apparent need to guard against deception and sabotage. "By no means may high interest...be used to justify the accumulation of capital at the branches," it stipulates. "Long-term investment of capital" at the branches is to be "carefully avoided," especially if "the funds originate from local deposits." Anything short of such cautionary measures is presumed to undermine the whole endeavor—just as, one might say, the princes of eighteenth-century Germany once undercut the nation with their pursuit of profit.[38]

Bamberger, for his part, believed that there was a great deal of useful information to glean from *The German Princes' Mercenary Trade*. It should be every patriot's "vademecum," he insisted—their pocket guide. "It should lie open like a bible on the kitchen table of every family," with a "chapter to be read to [every] child at the youngest age for its edification." Maybe this was just his usual hyperbole with respect to Kapp. What is certain is that the German American was on his mind that summer. If there was one unifying idea in the memorandum on Deutsche Bank, it was the idea of strength: how Germany did not have it; how it was required to succeed in modern, global commerce; and how the bank would manufacture and use it. In Bamberger's eyes, there was nobody who knew more about strength than Kapp. Years of "struggle with insolent North America" had taught him everything there was to know on the matter, had "reinvigorated" his sense of self and bolstered his "mature, ur-strong manliness." Kapp did not submit to the profit motive; it submitted to him, and he used it for whatever purpose he so desired.[39]

Once more, it is worth remembering that ideas in a business proposal are usually a far cry from business practice. Not too much stock should be put into the aspirational statements of founding entrepreneurs. The purpose of these documents is first and foremost to tell a gripping story, to entice and lure in investors. What happens later is usually another matter.

But Deutsche Bank was not a usual business. In its case, the dynamic was reversed. While investors cared little about the grand economic-political (*wirtschaftspolitische*) mission that had been laid out in the memorandum from 1869 (indeed, they were more likely to be put off by it), the men who ran the bank tended to take it quite seriously. That turned out to be a major problem because as a business strategy, the memorandum made little sense, at least not in the near term. First, it was very capital intensive: Setting up branches and subsidiaries would require significant upfront investment. Second, it depended on optimistic assumptions about the future development of global trade (many of which failed to hold). Dogged efforts to implement the sales pitch anyway almost brought the bank to its knees several times. Had it not been for timely interventions by sober minds ready to jettison the sales pitch, Deutsche Bank might have collapsed within a few years.

To be sure, initially things did follow the usual pattern. Thus, almost as soon as the memorandum was completed, it was shelved away. Delbrück, who hoped to use it to line up investors and government approval, quickly discovered that it raised more questions than it answered.[40] By the time he and Bamberger began crafting their application for a joint-stock corporation charter, in the winter of 1869, they had reduced their pitch to the least controversial aspects of the project, like the mission to wrest German trade away from English and French banks. After the initial public offering in March 1870, any need to tout or explain the bank's unorthodox economic-political mission dropped away.[41]

And yet, as soon as it commenced actual business in 1871 (a planned start in 1870 had to be postponed because of the outbreak of war between France and Prussia), Deutsche Bank implemented the plan almost exactly as it had been laid out in the beginning. The story of how this came to pass began—once more—with a letter from Kapp to Bamberger. This one dated from September 1869 and was a reply to Bamberger's proposal from earlier that summer suggesting that Kapp inquire with Marcuse about a management position at the Deutsch-Amerikanische. Kapp told his friend that, after some reflection, he had decided that he no longer sought a full-time position. The purpose of returning to Germany was to "live according to my own purposes and study," not to "devote myself solely to business." Besides, he added, he could "more easily make relatively good money here" than in Germany. If he was ever going to join Deutsche Bank, it would have to be in an advisory capacity, perhaps as a member of the board.[42]

Bamberger's response to Kapp's letter did not survive, but it seems that the news embarrassed him, because he scrambled to find a suitable manager for Deutsche Bank. The first candidate, Wilhelm Platenius, proved a complete disappointment. A former Atlantic cotton merchant who spent years in the United States, Platenius may have seemed a promising candidate because he was a fellow German American. However, like Kapp, Marcuse, and all the other Germania men at Deutsche Bank, Platenius was semiretired. He had returned to Germany at the end of the 1860s and lived in Stuttgart, nowhere near the bank's offices in Berlin. It is quite likely that Platenius only accepted the position as a favor to Marcuse, a business associate from his days in transatlantic trade.

Platenius quit after just a few idle months on the job, as did the man Bamberger subsequently brought in to replace him, a certain Privy Councillor

Mölle who previously worked as a bureaucrat in Prussia's finance ministry. Mölle apparently was even less impressive: "The man was neither stupid nor inexperienced," Bamberger wrote in his remembrances years later, "but I have never come across a greater degree of incompetence." These early departures proved of great consequence because they created an unexpected opening for Georg Siemens, hired in 1870, to manage Deutsche Bank during its inaugural period. It was Siemens who turned out to be the source of much of the bank's woes in those years, because he embraced the original economic-political mission and implemented it with a devotion that, while evidencing the strength of his character, nearly bankrupted the bank many times over.[43]

Siemens was always an unconventional choice for managing a bank, even an unconventional one like Deutsche Bank. He possessed no prior experience in the business, knew nothing about transatlantic trade and its financing, and had never been to New York or anywhere else in the Americas. What he did have, aside from pedigree, was his youth and temperament. In the eyes of Deutsche Bank's board, his age more than compensated for his lack of experience. He might have known little about transatlantic finance, but for that same reason he was probably also too young to be encumbered by traditional German business methods. His temperament was that of a showman, not unlike the German Americans on the board: "Though I understand little of…banking, I nevertheless try to look very erudite, give the occasional shrug, grin from ear to ear—this is my sneering smile—and secretly refer, when I get home, to my encyclopedia or dictionary on 'How to become a banker in 24 hours' when I want to find a word I didn't understand. I've already just about grasped the difference between ask and bid."[44] Most importantly, Siemens indulged in the same chauvinism and carried himself with the same braggadocio that Bamberger so admired in Friedrich Kapp. He once joked, in reference to Deutsche Bank's first shareholder meetings, "When twenty-four people want to run a bank, it is the same as with a girl who has twenty-four suitors. Nobody marries her, but in the end, she is pregnant!" Siemens oozed with confidence, and he promised strong leadership.[45]

To be sure, not everyone was impressed. Delbrück always thought Siemens just "a bit too green" and warned that the board would have its work cut out trying to "tame his exuberance so that he doesn't commit us to any bad business."[46] To win Delbrück's endorsement nonetheless, the decision was made to hire yet another managing director with a bit more experience. Hermann Wallich, who joined the management of Deutsche Bank later that year, was a seasoned foreign trade specialist who had previously worked for the Comptoir d'Escompte in the East Asia markets.[47] Bamberger had known him from his days at Bischoffsheim & Goldschmidt in Paris; he could vouch for Wallich's competence and, perhaps more important, for his much more measured, businessman-like temperament. Wallich took his fiduciary responsibilities seriously. He was in the business to make money, not to pursue vanity projects ("By the way I had been brought up," he once wrote, "I would like to be rich one day," to which Siemens reportedly responded, "And what will you be then? Just a rich man!").[48] While Wallich did not shy away from the occasional high-risk, high-reward investment, he understood full well that in banking the real money was usually made with more tedious and boring projects. His very first business proposal was commensurately uninspiring: He recommended investing a significant portion of Deutsche Bank's capital into 5 percent North German Confederation treasury bonds.[49]

This, of course, was not what Deutsche Bank's board had imagined to be Deutsche Bank's business, and Wallich was duly asked not to speak again unless he came up with a better idea.[50] As a result, for the time being, Wallich played second fiddle to Siemens, who used his much more brazen proposals to turn the board into what Wallich decried as a "powerful pro-Siemens lobby."[51] Thus, Deutsche Bank's "first order of business," according to an early plan likely conceived by Siemens, would be the "establishment of the planned New York branch, which would carry the name 'Germanische Transatlantische Bank in New York.' Using this template, one would create similar institutions in New Orleans, Havanna, Rio, Buenos Aires, Montevideo, Valparaiso... All of them would view Berlin as their epicenter and converge their operations in the Deutsche Bank. In this way, the latter would centralize all the business of the above-mentioned institutions [and] Deutsche Bank's mission as a global institute (*Weltinstitut*) will have been achieved."[52] Reality did not turn out this way, but at Siemens's unrelenting urging, it came quite close. The first overseas branch that Deutsche Bank established was in London because, as everyone grudgingly acknowledged, London remained Europe's financial gateway to the world. Next came offices in Bremen and Hamburg, Germany's own world gateways. Only after these initial, more local forays into the branching business did the bank's focus shift overseas in line with Siemens's proposal. In 1872, the New York subsidiary was established, "in a way...the very foundation" of the bank. This office was managed by Paul Lichtenstein, Kapp's son-in-law and Marcuse's nephew. Branches in Shanghai and Yokohama opened the same year. A $1 million investment for a one-third stake in the Belgian-led Deutsch-Belgische La Plata Bank followed in short order, with locations in Buenos Aires and Montevideo.[53] Thanks in no small part to Siemens's energetic and uncompromising efforts, Deutsche Bank's ambitious economic-political mission was off to an auspicious start.

The rapid expansion overseas that Siemens had spearheaded was impressive, a remarkable achievement for someone who by all accounts was still new to the business. Although Siemens never worked alone, with Hermann Marcuse and other members of the advisory board always personally involved, and with his colleague Wallich doing much of the legwork, he was widely regarded as the "mainspring of our...business."[54] And yet, the breakneck speed with which Siemens went about the matter raised eyebrows in some corners of the bank. Already in 1873, shareholders in Bremen and Stuttgart had started to wonder whether management was expanding across the globe less in search of dividends than in spite of them. Given that year's cascade of stock market crashes, along with the concomitant freezing of global credit markets, they questioned the wisdom of tying up so much liquidity in subsidiaries that, at least for the time being, generated no returns at all.[55]

For some time, Siemens remained insulated from this criticism. He still enjoyed the backing of most of the board. There was also the unintended upside to the frenzied branching activity, which was that the work had so preoccupied him that he found neither the time nor the capital to pursue much "bad business," like investments in railroads or real estate. Consequently, Deutsche Bank was able to weather the crisis of 1873 quite well—at least initially. But as the financial crisis wore on, and as the entire world economy slid into recession, a process that was greatly exacerbated by the adoption around the globe of an unprecedented level of trade protectionism, the drawbacks of Siemens's "appetite for business which did not always have due regard for the available resources" came into full view.[56] None of the overseas branches turned a profit in the 1870s, and more than a few required new infusions of capital, whether it was for a lack of business (Shanghai) or incompetent management (New York). It seemed only a question of when, not if, Deutsche Bank would begin liquidating these subsidiaries. Siemens himself acknowledged that he was no longer sure "where the money will come from."[57] Things came to a head in September 1875, after the decision was made public that Deutsche Bank would indeed liquidate some of its branches, starting with the failing East Asian offices (at a combined loss of $103,000), and that the dividend for the year would have to be cut. Soon, the bank's stock price began a precarious slide. In November, 112 Bremen shareholders broke into open revolt. They demanded a reduction in the bank's capitalization from the current 15 to 10 million talers, to "restore confidence" in the bank and its stock. The heedless branch founding of the past few years suggested that management had "several millions of thalers" too many on their hands. The Bremeners were not interested in financing "irregular, reckless business."[58]

This was a serious challenge. Reducing the capitalization of a bank in the midst of a bear market was a sure-fire way to destroy public confidence in its stock—a "suicidal" proposition, as one insider put it.[59] Around this time, more sober minds at Deutsche Bank decided to intervene. Hermann Wallich was suddenly asked to take the lead as the board gently nudged Siemens to step back from the business.[60] While an irritated Siemens went off to Heidelberg for an extended vacation (ostensibly to attend his doctoral diploma ceremony), an eager and appreciative Wallich worked overtime to put Deutsche Bank back on track. His first move was to go to Bremen to quell the revolt, or at the very least, to present a new face of earnest management. Next, he executed a lucrative government contract that Delbrück had arranged, using his family connections, which involved the sale of Germany's silver reserves to East Asian markets ahead of the country's adoption of the gold standard in 1876. Wallich did well; the deal generated enough liquidity to enable Deutsche Bank to avoid further, reputation-damaging branch closures for the time being. That same year, moreover, the board resolved to take over two struggling local banks in which Deutsche Bank held major stakes, the Berliner Bankverein and Deutsche Union-Bank. (They were the only ill-advised domestic investments that Siemens had made in the early 1870s, no doubt because he had the backing of the board, with Kapp also on the board of the Bankverein.) Once more engineered by Wallich, this double acquisition proved a boon. It staved off embarrassing write-offs on the Bankverein and Union-Bank investments, while proving an expeditious way to "grow" Deutsche Bank's domestic business. Such growth in the middle of a major economic crisis that saw dozens of competitors fail was crucial to the bank's image, imbuing Deutsche Bank with an aura of invincibility. It also became a welcome distraction from the botched foreign trade business.[61]

All these interventions helped put Deutsche Bank on track for its later successes. Having weathered the crisis so well, or at least appearing as if it did—as Wallich later remarked, "the public, of course, were quite unaware of our weakness [but] I, who did recognize [it], was tired of being a party to this incessant brinkmanship"—Deutsche Bank was admitted into the prestigious "Prussia consortium." This admittance gave it the privilege of underwriting Prussian sovereign debt and thus ensured a reliable stream of revenue while

The Idea of Deutsche Bank

the bank absorbed write-offs from Siemens's ill-fated branching bonanza. The stake in the struggling German Bank of London, Deutsche Bank's first attempt at an overseas subsidiary, was sold at a loss of $28,000. The New York branch was liquidated in 1882, by which time it became known that the branch had "either lost or mismanaged" some $600,000. The Deutsch-Belgische La Plata Bank locations in Buenos Aires and Montevideo hung on a bit longer, through 1885, mostly to keep what were likely even bigger write-offs off the bank's balance sheet. Yokohama and Shanghai had been closed years before. Deutsche Bank had survived, but its vision to become a Weltinstitut, as Siemens put it, appeared to be in shambles.[62]

It can be tempting to see this as the end of the German American chapter of Deutsche Bank's history. Only by abandoning the economic-political mission laid out in the memorandum from 1869 and by reverting to tried-and-true methods did the bank weather the storms of the 1870s. Kapp, for his part, was disgusted. "I have the opportunity to observe the innermost activities of a bank and the entire world of trade," he told a friend in 1877, and "in all seriousness...if I were you I would sell [my bank stock] at the first opportunity for a good price." He himself would rather "quit Deutsche Bank today rather than tomorrow."[63]

Kapp never did quit, however, because he still needed the money. And that summed up the idea of Deutsche Bank, which, as originally conceived, had never really been about the scheme laid out in the memorandum of 1869: not about the branches, not about the diaspora, not even about Germany's foreign trade. Rather, it had been about the whims and wishes of the people behind it. The memorandum proposed to emancipate the German nation from foreign financial intermediaries like the French and English; in reality, it simply emancipated the bank's founders, not just from financial insecurity but also from the longing for a friend, the weight of history, the discipline of markets, business as usual, and even their own grandiose plans.

The idea of Deutsche Bank was, then, a German American idea in the sense that in business one should do as one pleased. If that meant setting aside the bottom line and constructing an expensive, global network of retail banks, with the patriotic but also rather ambiguous goal of unifying the "German element," then so be it. If it meant prioritizing profits over patriotism, that was fine, too. Doing a little bit of both was also acceptable. Marcuse, for example, was perfectly willing to accept the liquidation of the East Asian offices on the rationale that they were losing money, even as he objected to doing the same with the New York branch, which was losing even more money. "[We must] allow the New York firm to take its path," he instructed Wallich, and stop "making its existence difficult and restricting it too much in its operations." The German American had no doubt that the "gentlemen" in New York—like his nephew and Kapp's son-in-law—"will not only work their way out of these losses but also generate good returns if Deutsche Bank would refrain from restraining the credit of its own subsidiary." None of this was hypocrisy: It was a manifestation of strength, of what Bamberger might have described as a masculine approach to doing business.[64]

This was also what Siemens got so wrong about Deutsche Bank when he first started working there. He may have been a blowhard like the German Americans, and he may, like them, have sneered at his philistine countrymen. But he was not one of them. In contrast to them, he had developed his attitude not because of any "struggle with insolent America," as was true of Kapp, but because he came from money and grew up in the shadow of his famous uncle, the brilliant inventor-entrepreneur-industrialist Werner von Siemens. Deutsche Bank was how Georg Siemens would make his own mark in the world, and the grandiosity of the memorandum of 1869 was just what he needed to create a stir. The only difference between Siemens and other rebellious prodigy was that, in his case, rebellion ironically meant sticking to the plan.[65]

It was only after Siemens had committed Deutsche Bank to a global branching drive that he began to realize that genuine independence would require him to emancipate himself from the memorandum, too. While his ambitions to one day run a Weltinstitut remained unchanged, he went about it in a new way, one that did not just deviate from the original memorandum but also, at times, turned its basic logic on its head. He continued to push toward a universal banking model, insisting that the hidden riches of the nation be mobilized and exploited through the establishment of a sprawling branch network, except that now he focused those branching efforts on Germany's domestic arena. He also returned Deutsche Bank to the business of foreign trade finance in the 1880s, but this time he avoided capital-intensive subsidiaries and, instead, entered partnerships with English, French, Dutch, and American banks. Through these collaborations—a strategy that was entirely at odds with the economic-political mission outlined in the memorandum—Siemens's Deutsche Bank began to invest heavily in foreign railroad companies, steamship lines, mining ventures, plantations, and manufacturing. In effect, he was funneling German domestic savings overseas instead of gathering the diaspora's capital and channeling it toward industrial enterprises in Germany.[66]

He did this because it was better for the bottom line and because it put him at the head of a Weltinstitut. One might say that he had developed a German American sensibility for business, turning Deutsche Bank into something that served his own ambitions rather than the other way around.[67] He certainly received mentorship along these lines from the German Americans on the bank's board, chief among them Friedrich Kapp, with whom Siemens grew quite close over the course of the crisis-ridden 1870s. It was in no small part through Kapp's connections, including another one of his protégés, the journalist-turned-financier Henry Villard, that Siemens notched his first genuine success in the sphere of international finance. Through Villard, Deutsche Bank would acquire a major stake in the Northern Pacific Railway Company, one of the most high-profile transcontinental railroads in the United States. The investment did not always pay the dividends that had been promised, but it carried considerable prestige and secured Siemens and his Deutsche Bank their name in a budding, global *haute finance*. Arguably, it was during this grandiose act of funneling "German" capital abroad, to the plains of the North American West, that Deutsche Bank came into its own.[68]

The Migrant's Spirit: How Industrial Modernity Came to the German Lands. Benjamin P. Hein,
Oxford University Press. © Oxford University Press 2025. DOI: 10.1093/9780197831052.003.0007

7

Migration-Backed Securities

FOR CARL FÜRSTENBERG, a railroad aficionado and managing director at Berliner-Handels-Gesellschaft, America had always been a sure bet. One inevitably suffered the occasional headache when working with scheming American financiers, "masters of stock market ambushes." Nevertheless, he wrote years later, "it was obvious" that the United States "was in more than one way the land of the future" and, as such, deserved special consideration. Even in times of uncertainty, such as the devastating Crisis of 1873, "I did not think it was right to stay away from the American business, to the contrary I thought one needed to expand it as much as possible." The result of such thinking, prevalent in continental Europe during the second half of the nineteenth century, was one of the most extraordinary transfers of capital in modern European history. Before 1860, total European capital invested in the United States rarely surpassed $200 million, but that figure had surged to $938 million by 1868 and then reached $1.5 billion in the mid-1870s. Within a dozen years or so, America had become "the world's greatest debtor nation," a title it would retain through the World War 1, thanks in no small part to the exuberance of men like Fürstenberg.[1]

Fürstenberg's faith in America may sound familiar in the early twenty-first century, perhaps even justified. But as late as the 1860s, few affluent Europeans, including the Germans among them, possessed much confidence in the future growth of the United States. Most would have imagined it was stuck in what some called the "hillbilly stage," a place inhabited by "small and ignorant farmer[s] who know no ideal but to chomp on [their] daily bacon."[2] Only with the Civil War did that attitude change.[3] The new interest in the economic future of the United States was especially palpable in the German-speaking regions up and down the Rhine River Valley. Between 1863 and 1869 alone, German, Dutch, and Swiss capitalists purchased an estimated $600–$700 million worth of American securities, enough to pay back the entire sovereign debt of the kingdom of Prussia, not just once, but twice. By the middle of the decade, cities like Amsterdam, Frankfurt am Main, Stuttgart, and Geneva—

among the most conservative financial centers on the continent—had emerged as the most exuberant speculators in America's future. This was not a temporary mania. For the remainder of the century, Amsterdam and Frankfurt would rival London, still the world's financial epicenter, as key nodes in a new era of transatlantic capital relations.[4]

What compelled economically conservative German bankers to develop such confidence in America's future? The rationales for investing in America ranged widely, from sympathies for the country's republican institutions to the lure of high interest rates, to a sense of paternal responsibility toward the New World, to sheer naiveté. But these sentiments prevailed among all European elites. Far more important for understanding the German-centered geography of transatlantic finance since the 1860s may have been that region's unique access to information about America. Sustained emigration since the 1810s and 1820s had generated a burgeoning print culture about the region, consisting of everything from adventure novels and travel diaries to business reports, news media, and feuilleton articles, all of which kept the spendthrift middle classes on the edges of their seats. "German investments were much larger than those of the French," it has been argued, "because Germans knew about America. They had countrymen in this nation, whom they trusted."[5]

Access to information was undoubtedly important. But it, too, leaves key questions unanswered because it assumes that in the 1860s, America's subsequent status as the world's largest and most dynamic economy was somehow "obvious," as Fürstenberg put it. Others, including more seasoned French and British bankers, remained deeply skeptical.[6] In 1870, the United States was still reeling from one of the most destructive wars in recent memory; its debt had swollen to a seemingly unsustainable $2.8 billion; its political institutions were far from healthy, which the corrupt machinations of New York's "Boss" Tweed readily attested to; and its businesses continued to earn their traditional reputation for fraud and financial malpractice. Arguably, the more one knew about America in this period, the fewer reasons there were to be enthusiastic about its future.[7]

Still, men like Fürstenberg stubbornly clung to their faith in "the land of the future." Understanding why they did so is important, not just for what it can reveal about the extraordinary quantity of capital that was being sent across the Atlantic in this period. Equally crucial is what this story reveals about both the character and the trajectory of the emerging industrial economy in Germany. Although the activities of Fürstenberg and others like him were mostly confined to portfolio investments (in other words, the purchasing of stocks and bonds) and as such they were one degree removed from the economy proper, they were nevertheless crucial to German industries' growing presence on, and eventually dominance of, global markets. In particular, such investment fostered new personal and institutional relationships between financial institutions in the German Empire and the United States, relationships that turned out to be convenient conduits for business expansion, especially for fledgling enterprises that might otherwise have struggled to gain a foothold abroad. "Through their manifold connections in the United States," wrote a contemporary observer, "German financial institutions created a capacious overseas information and news service" that was ready to be exploited by their "domestic clients" for purposes of market research, the identification of local retailers, or the navigation of a foreign legal environment. With the cost of doing business in the United States effectively subsidized, it became possible for even small German companies with little experience in foreign trade, and with no meaningful comparative advantages, to tap into one of the fastest growing and most lucrative markets in the world.[8]

Such relationships proved even more important after around 1880, when new barriers to trade emerged around the world in response to a devastating economic downturn unleashed by the Crisis of 1873. Confronted with new tariffs on all fronts, particularly in the United States, the "motherland of modern protectionism," German industries nevertheless maintained their presence on the world stage, and in some cases even managed to expand their business, by leaning on their financial institutions to set up subsidiaries and forge new partnerships with local businesses. Many household names of modern German industry followed this path. The electricity company Allgemeine Elektricitätsgesellschaft—sometimes described as the German equivalent of America's General Electric—began in 1883 as a joint venture with Thomas Edison, facilitated by none other than Deutsche Bank and its transatlantic intermediaries. The Frankfurt-based manufacturer Metallgesellschaft, a global behemoth in the metalworks industry founded in 1881, gained access to American markets and technological expertise via Frankfurt bankers and their New York–based partners, the investment bank Ladenburg, Thalmann & Co. The chemical concern Merck of Darmstadt, by 1913 one of the most influential pharmaceutical companies in the United States, turned to the same Frankfurt banks to establish its first New York subsidiary in 1887. Similar dynamics characterized the early history of such iconic names in German industry as AGFA, Farbwerke Hoechst, Degussa, and Mannesmann.[9]

To be sure, these companies still owed the bulk of their business to markets in Europe, not the United States. Although in the second half of the nineteenth century the Americas did account for a sizable portion of German exports (16–17 percent), a much bigger and in fact growing share (around 70 percent in 1880, rising to 75 percent in 1913) continued to be sent to more immediate neighbors in Europe, especially Great Britain, Austria-Hungary, Russia, France, and the Netherlands. The significance of access to American markets had more to do with the fact that it enabled individual businesses to become competitive in their own backyards. As a de facto extension of the domestic German clientele, the US market created incentives for German firms to pursue new economies of scale; served as a hedge against volatility at home; and, crucially, justified investment in the kind of product differentiation and brand development that was required to take on much larger, more established competitors. It is in this sense that the story of how Germany managed to build such a formidable export economy and compete with some of the most advanced industrializers of the day, including Britain and France, begins in the 1850s and 1860s, with men like Fürstenberg and their astonishing faith in a place that to most reasonable observers of this period spelled nothing but chaos and fraud.¹⁰

When, in 1872, German American immigrant Henry Villard visited Zweibrücken, a Rhineland spa town on the Schwarzbach River, he was in luck.¹¹ He had come to sell American securities, in this case a batch of crisp new Wisconsin Central Railroad Company first mortgage bonds. According to reports in *Bankers Magazine of London*, the Germans had recently shown a "voracious desire for all things American."¹² This was good news for Villard, who at the time was still new to railroad finance and so was trying to make sense of all the financial jargon: preferred stock, bonds, coupons. He knew little about what gave the paper its value, which did not bode well for fielding questions from potential customers. In 1872, however, it seemed as though he might not have to.¹³

Villard guessed that German investors' excitement about American bonds must have had to do with the stories so often told about America's breathtaking landscapes, its natural resources, the precious minerals of California and Colorado, the endless prairies of the Dakota Territory, and the dark, fertile soils of Iowa and Kansas. He had first witnessed for himself the natural treasures of the North American continent when he was a "pioneer in Colorado" in 1858 peddling guidebooks to gold rushers at Pike's Peak. "An encounter with original nature has a truly elevating effect," he later claimed, adding that one could not help but "marvel at the natural wonders, rejoice in the landscape." He reasoned that the profits of land-grant railroad companies like the Wisconsin Central came from the sale of their land, along with the returns that accrued from bringing to market resources like timber, minerals, and agricultural products.[14]

Land, minerals, and agricultural products were important, but apparently they were by far not the most compelling selling point. That at least is what Charles L. Colby, a Boston financier and Villard's associate, kept reminding him of. Colby repeatedly explained to Villard that the "timber and iron and lands" surrounding the Wisconsin Central were of "great value," but that they were really only "so much extra." As "I have stated to you heretofore, apart from these [resources]" the Wisconsin Central "will unquestionably be a very paying road." Rising traffic would generate all the revenue needed for the company to meet its interest obligations to stock- and bondholders. Even if there were "no land grant or iron interests," the company and its bonds would be "worth double the amount of them."[15]

Ever since the Civil War, this kind of railroad bond math had become commonplace in the United States. It derived from grand designs, conceived of during the war, to encourage the rapid colonization of the western half of the North American continent. The idea of expanding to territories west of the Mississippi was not new, but during the Civil War it acquired additional political and ideological urgency. The Lincoln administration, for its part, sought to encourage the swift settlement of these lands to preempt the spread of slavery westward should the Confederacy gain the upper hand. But even after the defeat of the Confederacy, westward expansion retained its heightened ideological currency. In the wake of the devastating destruction wrought by half a decade of war, the colonization of the western territories had evolved into a rallying cry for the injured nation. Here, on the lands between the Mississippi and the Pacific, Americans would start anew. As early as 1862, the Homestead Act symbolized Washington's vision for a future in the West, offering 160 acres to all free Americans willing to head west and "mend the pioneers' fences."[16]

The national-political motives driving the Homestead Act were reinforced by the Pacific Railway Acts of 1864, whereby the federal government issued vast tracts of land in western territories not to individual settlers, but to individual railroad corporations. Railroad land grants, which often measured in tens of millions of acres at a time, were a quintessential example of republican economic policy in the 1860s. Rather than take up the complicated and arduous task of coordinating the settlement of the West itself, the government believed it could save itself money and administrative headache by leaving the matter to private enterprise. All that was required was to set the right incentives. Congress would offer corporations bountiful loans to finance construction (usually consisting of treasury bonds whose principal and interest it guaranteed) and then promised that, with every new mile of track it laid, a given corporation would become eligible for full title to 12,800 acres of public lands alongside the track, plus "any coal or iron they contained." Thus incentivized, so the argument went, entrepreneurs would race to construct iron rails across the West, thereby drawing new traffic to the region and "creating value." Both the government and the corporations stood to reap the benefits of gradually selling landholdings to future settlers—and in the process achieve the federal government's original objective of colonizing the West.[17]

Against lawmakers' expectations, however, constructing a railroad in the overwhelmingly arid and mountainous territories west of the Mississippi proved a difficult and costly endeavor. Few of the transatlantic railroad operators of the 1860s and 1870s were able to lay enough track to qualify them for full access to the land grant they had been promised, which meant that—at least initially—they rarely sold any actual land to any actual settlers (especially west of the ninety-eighth meridian). For the new generation of railroad financiers after the Civil War, including men such as Collis P. Huntington, Jay Gould, and Leland Stanford, the land grants came to serve a categorically different purpose: They functioned as collateral against which to borrow money from financial markets in New York and London (and, ultimately, continental Europe). This, in essence, is what led financiers like Colby to declare the land that their companies had been granted as "just so much extra." Thanks to the bond market in New York, the Wisconsin Central could use the land grant to raise money even without selling any of it to settlers.[18]

At the same time, this logic of railroad finance shifted the focus of railroad corporations away from the land itself and toward a different measure of value: population growth. Since the size of a railroad's land grant was set by law, railroad owners were left to maximize the book value of their collateral, namely, the land grant they had been promised, by boosting estimates of the price per acre. The Northern Pacific Railway Company, for example, might increase its collateral if it simply multiplied its fifty-million-acre land grant by, say, $3.00 per acre rather than $2.50. The price of land was, of course, contingent on demand for it, which is why railroad owners concluded "that *people* along [our] line will be of vastly greater value to [us] than land." It usually mattered little where exactly those people came from or where they chose to settle: "It does not matter very much to the Company," R. M. Newport of the Northern Pacific wrote in 1881, "whether settlers locate upon our lands, or upon lands purchased from us, or upon government lands. What we want to do is to secure the rapid settlement and development of the lands tributary to our line." Overall population growth implied that land prices would rise, and that was generally sufficient to boost the collateral value of a land grant.[19]

This was how aggregate population growth emerged as the single most important measure of value for American railroad corporations in the 1860s—and, by extension, for the federal government, which itself was raising money in this period on the premise of a future hinged on the colonization of the West. Every brochure, every guidebook, every advertisement, and every sales pitch uttered by the postwar booster marshaled impressive statistical enumerations about the region's overall population growth, usually lifted from the decennial US census, as their most important sales point. And to be sure, during the middle decades of the nineteenth century, there was some cause to tout America's demographic transformation. Although growth always unfolded unevenly across the country (it was fastest in middle western states and generally sluggish and even nonexistent in the far west), on the whole America's population was expanding at a pace unprecedented in recorded history: 2.83 percent per annum between 1820 and 1870, a rate that implied a doubling of the entire population every twenty-five years. This pace dwarfed Europe's own population explosion, often hailed as historically unprecedented in its own right (it averaged 0.76 percent per annum over the same period). No wonder Colby urged his young associate Villard to sell America to Europeans on account of its demographic story: Who would doubt that such spectacular population growth was well sufficient to "take care of [the interest on] its bonds" within a "very few years"?[20]

I was not just the logic of America's growth that made Villard's sales pitch such an easy one. He also found that he rarely needed to introduce clients to the promise of America's demographic transformation because a good many of them were already more than familiar with life in North America. Since the 1850s at least, and arguably even earlier, a sprawling literature ranging from adventure novels to emigration guides to newspapers and academic studies offered no shortage of opportunities to learn about and engage with America.[21] Undergirding this prodigious literature was another key source of information: emigrant letters. Transatlantic correspondence, whose volume had grown exponentially since the introduction of regular steam-powered mail services in the late 1850s, proved crucial because it provided an intimate, trusted source of information with which to fact-check the larger print-based discourse about the United States.

Writings on America were always diverse and wide-ranging, but the theme of population growth ran like a red thread through virtually every novel, newspaper, and letter. "Probably no country on earth has so splendidly refuted the theory of Malthus as the United States," marveled the former consul Eduard Wiss in his 1867 exposé of American progress. If in Europe population growth had been known to cause social strife and poverty, in the United States it had proven a harbinger of "national wealth." Westphalian emigrant, businessman, and Chicago politician Francis A. Hoffmann agreed. In his reports to some thirty-two banks in German states and elsewhere in Europe, he found that "hopes for Chicago's future have not failed to materialize" and offered, as proof, "imposing columns of numbers" detailing the city's rapid growth in population.[22] Meanwhile, emigrants like Johann Bauer explained to relatives, friends, and neighbors in Heidelsheim, Baden, that his community in Missouri "progresses in constant step forward, ever since we have the railroads, & very many immigrants are coming; that is the reason that the land which one could buy for 10 dollars two years ago now costs 20 dollars.... When America declared itself free the population stood at 3 million, now it is over 40 million, what will it be in 100 years. The changes that have occurred only since I arrived! Places where 10 years ago a huntsman shot deer from his wild horse...are now filled with people." Bauer, like most contemporaries living through these historic times, expected that "once this gargantuan land is settled," it would be "difficult to fathom" just how much "influence the country will have on politics & religion."[23]

Still, knowing about American demography did not necessarily mean understanding it. Ironically, the sheer abundance of information available could sometimes obscure key details and causal relationships in ways that overstated America's population growth potential even more. As late as 1877, Prussian native and emigrant Albert Krause felt compelled to explain to his relatives that they were quite mistaken in their understanding of America's growth story: "One cannot deny that America has long advanced past the 'hillbilly stage,' indeed in many...respects has surpassed the other nations, but it is equally true, that not the Yankees but the immigrants, especially the Germans, and particularly those Germans who have emigrated from over there, have contributed the lion's share."[24] Krause was flattering himself, to be sure, but he was also on to something: namely, that a substantial portion of

America's demographic transformation was due to global forces, including unprecedented levels of immigration, which may have accounted for close to a third (32 percent) of the US population's growth in this period. Indeed, it was immigration, not merely natural increases in America's own population, that transformed the United States into what has been described as the "most exciting demographic story of the nineteenth century."[25] Ultimately, this failure to place population growth in the context of the concomitant transatlantic migrations played a key role in whipping up German enthusiasm for American securities in the 1860s. By falsely crediting America's transformations to local dynamics alone, the growth that Europeans ostensibly knew about was bound to seem even more remarkable than it already was.

One reason why so many people who ostensibly knew a lot about America could still be so wrong about it was the tendency of chroniclers to assume the role of distant and detached observer. Take the periodical *Westermann's Illustrirte Monatshefte*, a Berlin-based culture and politics magazine that specialized in reporting on North America. In 1872, *Westermann's* dispatched a correspondent to write a story about the state of Minnesota. The resulting article offered an account that would have been quite familiar to readers in Berlin at this time:

> As beautiful and as varied as [North America's natural environment] may seem—she alone does not draw our attention. We are spellbound by the most magnificent drama of our age, standing at the midst of the torrents of mass migration. The pioneers of Minnesota pass by us; here a train of wagons harnessed up with oxen; the wagons are packed with everything that belongs in a household, stove and stovepipe, furniture and farming tools, beds and dishes.... Men, women, children, all of them hurry toward a new home, everyone endures the hardships of a short journey in the hope for better days.[26]

Notwithstanding his close attention to detail, this North America correspondent showed little interest in the origin of the migrants he watched passing by him. On the one hand, this may have had to do with efforts to maintain a safe distance, both physically and rhetorically, from the "torrent of migrants" thus witnessed. On the other hand, it likely resulted from a mistaken interpretation of America's demographic transformation. The reference to a "short journey" suggests, for example, that the migrants passing through Minnesota hailed from eastern states, perhaps the Atlantic seaboard, certainly not from halfway around the world. For this reporter, as for so many German Americans who informed their national compatriots at home, American growth was, in essence, an American story.[27]

Of course, most print media was not designed to help Europeans make informed choices about American securities. But even standard business reports offered little information on the role played by foreign immigration. In 1873, bankers in Frankfurt am Main sought to evaluate the future viability of the struggling Oregon & California Railroad Corporation, which operated a line running north to south along the Oregon coast. Paul Reinganum, a leading attorney in Frankfurt and an expert on American railroad finance, was dispatched to Oregon to inspect the property and construction site. Reinganum's diagnosis was simple: The road was behind on its payments because Oregon suffered from a "shortage of human beings [*Menschenarmut*]." The state's largest city, Portland, counted barely 20,000 inhabitants and further immigration was only "progressing slowly." Still, Reinganum was optimistic. He had already crunched the numbers and, given the road's current fixed costs, he estimated that, if Oregon's population could be augmented by "200,000 people," the railroad would "probably" be able to resume its interest payments. Who these people were or where they would come from, Reinganum did not care to explain.[28]

If information received from America was incomplete, it was scarcely possible to fill in the gaps using evidence from European sources. As perceptive contemporaries sometimes pointed out, as late as the mid-1860s still very little was known about the precise magnitude of emigration from continental Europe. The so-called age of mass migration had only been underway for about two decades, and during most of this time it affected just a few key regions on the British Isles and in the upper Rhine River basin. Even in these areas of concentrated emigration it would have been difficult to discern a "mass" movement because most emigrants left in sudden bouts, which lasted no longer than several weeks at a time. Further compounding problems accruing from the spotty pattern of emigration was an even spottier statistical record about it. Before the 1870s, few European governments kept systematic track of emigration, and those that did, like Prussia, were almost certainly underreporting. Prior to the construction of a robust railway network, emigrants relied on riverine transportation to reach the ocean, which meant that the movement as a whole was dispersed across numerous ports along the North Sea and Atlantic Ocean coasts (and, later in the century, the Mediterranean coast as well).[29]

Flawed, incomplete information was an important barrier to understanding, yet equally important was what investors chose to do about the dearth of information: for the most part, very little. Bankers rarely pressed their informants, including railroad boosters Francis A. Hoffmann and Eduard Wiss, for an in-depth analysis of the causes of American growth: not because they simply took Hoffmann's grandiloquent claims at face value but rather because they already knew everything there was to know about demographic change. This is because, like so much of the European bourgeoisie and nobility, they had read and studied the works of the most influential demographer of this period, British political economist Thomas R. Malthus.[30]

The problem with Malthusian thought was simple: Malthus did not engage at any great length with the issue of immigration. He considered only the phenomenon of emigration, how it reduced social pressures that he believed were a function of excessive population growth. That migration could also fuel demographic growth elsewhere seemed neither plausible nor of immediate interest to Malthus at the time of his writing, in the early 1800s. Movement from Europe to the Americas was too negligible in size to have any discernible impact on the host society, especially places deemed as vast and allegedly empty as North America.[31] These conceptual barriers to understanding America's population growth helped make that growth credible and mythical all at once—especially in German Europe, which profited from a deluge of information about the United States. Here, bankers and investors rested assured in the fact that they knew America. It was this false confidence, the idea that one knew better than others because of privileged access to information, that may have convinced the German investor, more than his French or Austrian counterpart, that America's future was different and that he could trust the reassurances of that traveling bond salesmen Henry Villard.

The first stack of railroad bonds that Villard ever held in his hands were for the Grand Rapids and Indiana Railroad Company, a line that aimed to connect the cities of Grand Rapids, Michigan, and Cincinnati, Ohio. In 1869, a Boston businessman had handed him the paper at a meeting of the American Social Science Association, a gentleman's club where businessmen, academics, and politicians socialized and deliberated "the discovery and application of the immutable laws governing man and his social relations" and where his marital connections had landed Villard the job of secretary. At the time, he did not yet know that the bonds he had just been handed were essentially worthless. The Grand Rapids and Indiana was one of those American railroad corporations that spent most of its existence in the hands of receivers. Villard, however, felt as though he had just won the lottery. As he would later recall, those ornate Grand Rapids bonds marked his triumphant entry into what he described as the "*Eisenbahnsekuritätenbranche*," or "railroad securities business," and with it, a giant step forward in his long-running chase of the American Dream. If all went according to plan, those bonds would enable him to transform a devastating string of failed pursuits in law, journalism, and writing into an inspiring rags-to-riches life story.[32]

Things did not go according to plan. As it happened, nobody in Boston or New York or anywhere else along the northeastern seaboard would put money into the Grand Rapids and Indiana. Villard spent almost two years trying to place the bonds in the United States before he finally decided, in May 1871, to reach out to an old acquaintance, the prominent German American Friedrich Kapp, for help. Villard knew Kapp from his years as a Civil War correspondent and, before that, from an unsuccessful immigration scheme he had spearheaded in Kansas in the 1850s. They had not spoken for some years, but it was a well-known fact in New York's German American community that Kapp had recently decided to return permanently to Germany. In Berlin, Kapp had already established himself well: He sat on the boards of two new banks, the Berliner Bankverein and Deutsche Bank, and rumor had it that he aspired to a seat on Berlin's municipal council. Villard ventured a guess that Kapp might know at least some investors who would have an interest in owning the debt of the Grand Rapids and Indiana.[33]

Kapp's reply, arriving two months later in July, gave Villard hope. According to his friend, Berlin's new generation of joint-stock banks would have "reached for an issue like the Grand Rapids with all ten fingers." Berliners, he added for emphasis, were "hungry for a new American bond issue like the devil for a soul." He explained that, ever since the unification of the German Empire, local bankers were driven by an extraordinary level of "envy, jealousy, and ambition": They wanted to assert themselves on an international stage and seemed willing to do so at all costs. Moreover, Kapp added, it was obvious that "the Americans need money," that "the Europeans have it," and that these imbalances of supply and demand left upsides to be chased. "If you want to make money in railroads," Kapp advised, "find ways to connect the stock market [in Berlin] with a company over there."[34]

This was good news, but things got better still. "I just thought to myself," Kapp continued, "you should become the primary liaison between America and Germany." The more he thought about it, the more it all made sense. The current glut of money in Berlin and the simultaneous shortage of capital in the United States made it seem "imperative that a closer relationship between [the United States and Germany] is forged." Villard was to set aside those Grand Rapids bonds immediately and arrange a meeting with "your American friends" at the American Social Science Association in Boston. The idea was to connect a US railroad corporation directly to German banks in Berlin, like the Berliner Bankverein or Deutsche Bank. They, in turn, would extend "a private mortgage" to the American company and resell it in the form of bonds on the Berlin Stock Exchange. After all, German banks knew their clients much better than Villard could ever hope to and, as Kapp put it, were ready to "move heaven and hell" to sell American securities to German investors. Most important, the potential payout was considerable. Instead of the paltry 1 percent commission typically granted to bond salesmen, he and Villard would stand to earn 8 to 10 percent on the entire issue—what Kapp described as the "customary profits" that accrued to the banks.[35]

It was a promising scheme, though in truth there was nothing novel about it: What Kapp was describing was the commonplace practice of a bank underwriting a corporate bond issue. Still, there was good reason to be excited. In Berlin, a relative newcomer on the European financial markets, the practice of underwriting foreign corporate bond issues was still uncommon, if not altogether unheard of.[36] Even in the early 1870s, the vast majority of US securities were underwritten by consortia of British and American bankers in places like Boston, New York, London, and Philadelphia. Most of the US securities that were sold on the continent, including in cities like Amsterdam and Frankfurt, arrived there via British bankers who had passed them on to friends and colleagues. Kapp's proposition, by contrast, was to circumvent the British middleman altogether and link German capital directly to an American corporation.[37]

Villard, meanwhile, seemed taken by the prospect of a tenfold increase in his commission. Before long, he had consented to the plan. By early 1872, he had made his rounds at the American Social Science Association in Boston and convinced financier Charles L. Colby to enter into direct negotiations with Berliner Bankverein. In the ensuing arrangement, Berliner Bankverein would advance $1 million to Colby's Wisconsin Central Railroad Company. Since an underwriting bank "earns its commission upfront," Kapp believed that profits were virtually guaranteed, so he and Villard "could care less" about what later happened to the bonds. "Personally," he concluded, "I find it easier to make money in Germany than in America."[38]

Villard couldn't agree more. Just a few years earlier, he was languishing as a paper-pusher at the American Social Science Association in Boston. Now, he was a rising star in an emerging transatlantic *haute finance*. That spring of 1872 he finally earned his first fortune: a $50,000 commission on the Wisconsin Central deal.³⁹

As it turned out, however, the anticipated triumph never became a reality. To begin with, much like the American Charles L. Colby before him, Friedrich Kapp soon discovered that working with Villard could be an agonizing experience. Not a letter came to pass in the 1870s in which Kapp did not feel compelled to repeat some instruction or to voice his frustrations over the fact that Villard had once more reneged on one of their gentleman agreements. He also admonished Villard about his ham-handed attempts to boost German emigration to their properties. "Why do you mention Maine, Georgia, Florida etc?," he demanded to know about one of their emigration brochures. "You will defeat the purpose of the brochure, if you gave it away for free. Set a cheap price for Germany, for example 5–6 pennies, that will move them best." He advised Villard to speak to Paul Lindau, a Berlin socialite, novelist, and playwright, who could help craft a narrative.⁴⁰

These irritations were just the beginning. Even more disconcerting was when, in November 1871, a group of Berlin bondholders circulated a devastating report about the financial prospects of one of the most ambitious American railroading enterprises of its time, the two thousand mile–long Northern Pacific Railway Company. The roots of this controversy extended back to May 1869, when the US financier Jay Cooke decided to enter the railroad business. Cooke, who had previously made a name for himself in the 1860s selling large amounts of US treasuries, wanted to make an entry worthy of his name and agreed to underwrite an extraordinary $100 million loan for the company, which he planned to split equally between the American and European markets. He then engaged US diplomat Aaron A. Sargent, as well as two Germans—Henry Villard and Friedrich Kapp—to place the European tranche of $50 million at exchanges in Amsterdam, Berlin, Frankfurt, and Vienna. Yet even when spread across different markets around the continent, the sum was still extraordinarily large by contemporary standards. Put off by the huge number, European investors grew suspicious and demanded more information on what exactly they were buying. In July 1871, bankers in Berlin dispatched two auditors, one of them a certain "Mr. Haas," to the United States to inspect the books and properties of the road and prepare a detailed report with recommendations to investors.⁴¹

The report prepared by Haas became a serious public relations disaster for Kapp and Villard. Its author did not equivocate in his assessment of whether to buy Northern Pacific bonds. "I consider [an investment] hazardous," Haas wrote. To be sure, it was not the first time that a European auditor raised doubts about an American railroad project. By the early 1870s, Europeans knew to expect sloppy bookkeeping, exuberant salesmanship, and even outright fraud as a normal part of doing business in the United States. What made Haas's report so devastating was that its recommendation against an investment in the Northern Pacific had little to do with any of these routine problems. The issue it raised was a more fundamental one: "So far as human calculations can at all forecast," America's population was simply not growing fast enough for the bond math of the Northern Pacific to add up. As Haas explained, "We must not forget that though a growth of the population in regions newly traversed by railways is certain, it is not sufficiently rapid to cover thinly inhabited regions within a few years.... Even the most favorable rate of increase of the population during the last ten years, namely, that of Minnesota, or about 150 per cent., would, extended over the whole region of the Northern Pacific Railway, during another ten years, only result in an aggregate population of 1,500,000." Formidable though such numbers were— 1,500,000 was equivalent to "one-third of the population of the state of New York"—Haas still found them to be woefully inadequate.[42]

Haas's calculations were alarming, and not only because they were so precise. Haas should have been an ally. He had been perfectly happy to admit that the American context deserved special consideration on account of the "well known fact that, contrary to what we see in Germany, where railways are the product of already cultivated and well-populated regions, the railways in America have hitherto drawn culture and population after them into uncultivated regions, and thereby drawn an income to themselves." But the Northern Pacific was too much even for Haas. He wrote that the "most superficial critic" would have to recognize that no amount of immigration would be sufficient for the company to earn an "income of $20,000,000 a year," which was the amount necessary to cover construction costs, maintenance, advertisement expenses, and, crucially, interest payments to bondholders. He recommended that German bankers not "rely so confidently and strongly upon the exertions and efforts in favor of an immigration, the results of which must be reserved for a future day."[43]

This was a troublesome verdict, and it left an immediate mark on the American securities business in Berlin and Frankfurt. Following the report's distribution (an abbreviated version was also published in the *New York Daily Tribune*), Cooke's Northern Pacific issue suffered a resounding rebuke, especially in German financial circles. Not a single German bank would accept the bonds, making it the first American railroad of the postwar period that failed to attract German investors. More worrisome still, the episode rattled the foundations of a myth that had enabled German investment in the United States since at least the early 1860s: that America's population growth alone made even the most daring speculation in the country a worthwhile investment. If that no longer held true for the Northern Pacific, why would it for any other road, let alone the United States as a whole?

Kapp had, to some degree, anticipated the trouble. During the previous summer, he wondered whether a loan worth tens of millions of dollars would be "a little too strong a dose" for German markets. Still, the issue had proceeded and the damage was done. In early 1872, Kapp informed Villard that Wisconsin paper no longer enjoyed "much traction" in Berlin; Berliner Bankverein projected write-offs of $20,000. "Nobody advances money on American paper anymore," he wrote. "I fear that the time for American bonds has passed. Years might pass until we can even think about introducing them again in Europe, and especially in Germany." He added that "should I kick the bucket make sure to drink a sixer or twelver in my memory." Villard, for his part, was in no position to write obituaries. In December 1872, the thirty-seven-year-old had just survived a major stroke.⁴⁴

There was a silver lining, however. It turned out that Haas had limited his calculations to a fixed thirty-year period, which, in the context of the grander story of America's progress, may as well have been a New York minute. Even Haas admitted as much. "The experience of the past in the United States has shown that, as a rule, after a number of years have passed... new settlements have been established in consequence of the railway." As a result, "though a period of several years following immediately upon the opening of a line may have few sales to show, yet in the long run all will be alright." Haas himself was arguing that in the long run his calculations ceased to matter, that if time horizons were sufficiently extended, then the company's optimistic projections made sense.⁴⁵

Desperate to stabilize the American securities market in Germany, Kapp exploited this logic to the fullest. As was so often the case, he relied on his gifts as a storyteller along with "my 20 years of practical experience in America." Dismissing concerns that the overall volume of German emigration would decline, especially in light of the unification of the German Empire (est. 1871), he reminded anyone who would listen that "what drives these people to America is the old Germanic character (*Germanischer Zug*)." As any German patriot would know, he explained to deputies at the Reichstag, the "Germanic hunger for land" was insatiable, ancient, and ever-lasting. If it "once drove our ancestors...across the entire continent of Europe," now "it leads them to America."[46]

In the long run, all will be alright. If Haas's dictum was true, then it made good sense to appeal to the nation's well-known proclivity for wandering—what Friedrich Schiller had once hailed as the "spirit of migration and plunder." It was in reference to this spirit that Kapp would go on to profess that emigration was quite simply a "fact" of German national life and, though it was a lamentable fact, there really was "nothing that government can do." On second thought, there were some things that Kapp believed government could do. For example, it could stop acting like one of those miserly princely states of the past and take seriously its role as the patron and protector of the German nation, which meant it might approach the issue of emigration with the magnanimity that was becoming of a government that claimed to speak for a nation in which the "freedom to emigrate" (*Auswanderungsfreiheit*) was but a "constitutional right." A good place to start would be the establishment of a new office or even ministry—Kapp proposed calling it the Reich Commissioner of Emigration—whose task it would be to monitor the movement, generate statistics, and prepare annual reports and policy recommendations on how to better support German emigration to North America where, he emphasized, "946.2 out of every 1,000 emigrants" were choosing to settle. A budget should also be set aside to enlarge and modernize the Reich's consular representation, especially in North America. New bilateral treaties should be negotiated between the United States and the German Empire to facilitate communication across the Atlantic and ease the administrative burdens associated with small cash transfers and long-distance property claims. New rules and regulations might be put in place to rein in conniving land agents as well as the notoriously exploitative maritime passenger industry.[47]

Not all of these proposals can be dismissed as mere cynical bluster aimed at the bondholding public. Large-scale emigration from Germany to America had indeed been a "fact" for some time; the abuses by emigration agents and shipping magnates were no mere figment of Kapp's imagination; and the "freedom to emigrate" really did enjoy the status of a constitutional right, at least insofar as such a right had been articulated by past governments that claimed to represent the German nation, like Wilhelm I of Württemberg in 1819 or the National Assembly in Frankfurt am Main during the Revolution of 1848. It was therefore not entirely out of the question that the highest legislative body of the newly established German Empire would at least acknowledge the issue, if not also provide some modicum of relief. Kapp, for his part, backed up his combative rhetoric with an ambitious legislative proposal titled "Law Regarding the Transportation of Emigrants to Non-German Countries," which was put before the Reichstag in 1877. The law was never adopted, but the fact that it was put up for debate points to the seriousness of its sponsor, who would have had to rally a minimum of support from his colleagues to get it to that stage.[48]

And yet, Kapp likely knew from the very beginning that the Reichstag was not going to act on his proposals. The last time a German national parliament had taken up legislative measures to protect emigrants, namely, in 1848 at the Paulskirche in Frankfurt, the effort had gone nowhere. While there had been universal support for the inclusion of a "freedom to emigrate" among the basic rights (*Grundrechte*) of the constitution then under consideration, very few of the Frankfurt parliamentarians had been interested in elaborating exactly what this might mean for actual policy. The issue raised thorny legal questions that could not so easily be set aside. If a government was responsible for ensuring the well-being and safety of those who chose to venture beyond its borders, where did its responsibilities end? It could hardly be regarded as in the interest of a nation to encourage its citizens to leave for foreign lands, but as critics at the time were swift to note, that would be the de facto consequence of any policy aimed at reducing the risks and financial burdens, not to mention the stigma, associated with emigration. Once abroad, emigrants stopped paying taxes and serving in the military. So why should they be allowed to continue placing demands on the state for attention and resources? And if the government did intervene on their behalf, say, to enforce property rights or to protect from physical harm, would this not mean that it would be interfering in the domestic affairs of another state? It would, and then the government would have to choose between honoring international law and defending the rights of its citizens. Either way, it would end up compromising its own legitimacy—a scenario that no parliamentarian in Frankfurt, no matter his political colors, had been willing to entertain.[49]

Kapp himself had been privy to these debates, having witnessed them firsthand from the gallery seats of the Paulskirche. There, he had watched as a row of speakers who asked for more clarity on paragraph 136, the part of the proposed constitution that guaranteed the "freedom to emigrate," were heckled by colleagues who insisted that they either move on to other topics or take their seats. Granted, some thirty years had passed since those raucous sessions at the Frankfurt Parliament. But there was little reason to believe that the politics on this particular issue had changed in the interim. If anything, it was even less likely now that legislation regarding emigration would be taken up.

The Frankfurters of '48 had at least been compelled to pay their tributes to the emigrant; the National Assembly's authority had been far from secure at the time, so by inscribing the "freedom to emigrate" into their constitution the parliamentarians had hoped to lend their proceedings a veneer of German national legitimacy. As one of them warned at the time, the Frankfurt parliamentarians would rue the day on which it was decided to elevate a liberty so fraught with "difficulties" simply because "it made for a rather good toast."[50] The Reichstag of the 1870s, by contrast, had no need for such pageantry, and the reaction to Kapp's legislative proposal from 1878 was correspondingly subdued. Save for some rumblings in Conservative Junker circles and among the Social Democratic Party (the former complaining about the loss of cheap peasant labor and the latter insisting that more should be done to tackle the problem of emigration at its root, which was to say, to improve living conditions in Germany), there was little response from the audience, whether in support or in opposition. Most of those assembled seemed to share Chancellor Otto von Bismarck's well-known attitude toward emigrants: good riddance.[51]

This was, of course, a tolerable outcome for Friedrich Kapp, inasmuch as he was ultimately only interested in how Berlin's bondholding public viewed the issue. That the Reichstag was contending with his legislative proposal at all was more than sufficient to lend credence to his argument about emigration from Germany to North America: that it was a "fact" of national life, that it remained so even after the nation had been formally unified, and that the population math proposed by the Northern Pacific and other such US ventures added up. Far more disconcerting than any grumbling Junker or hotheaded Social Democrat was Kapp's own party, the National Liberal Party. Some members took seriously his assertions about emigration being a fact and, in a move that directly contradicted Kapp's interests in US railroads, began lobbying for the establishment of new settler colonies in Africa, South America, and the Pacific to direct German emigrants toward. "I believe that German emigration, which was already a great historical fact in the past, must continue and will continue," observed Johannes Franz von Miquel, a leading figure in the National Liberal Party and one of the founders of the German Colonial Society (est. 1882), as he made his case for new German protectorates in Africa and the Pacific. Like so many others in this younger generation of colonial enthusiasts, Miquel was only tangentially interested in bringing settlers to the new colonies. But he recognized the political potency of emigration, the way its mere mention could silence critics and knock opponents off balance. Emigration is a "fact . . . so obvious to anyone who is familiar with

German history," Miquel reminded detractors of the new African protectorates, "that it really is not necessary to even discuss it."[52]

Kapp initially failed to recognize the threat that arguments like these posed to his interests, if only because he struggled to take seriously the idea of a German settler colony in Africa or anywhere else in the world. Emigrants, he always argued, and seemed to genuinely believe, would never choose a destination other than America, which offered "everything and more of what they leave behind," and which on account of its culture and liberties and myriads of other advantages would always be preferable to any "colonial cuckoo land in Africa."[53] Although these predictions proved correct—as the 1880s and 1890s would show, very few emigrants settled in the new protectorates that were acquired in Africa, the Pacific, and elsewhere—this was not why the colonial lobby was trouble for Kapp's stock jobbing efforts. The problem had more to do with the uncertainty that was introduced into the story about German emigration and, with that, about the long-term trajectory of economic growth in the United States. Undergirding the idea that one could establish new settler colonies in places where Germans had never ventured before, from Southwest Africa to the islands of Samoa in the Pacific, was the assumption that, given the right incentives, support, and encouragement, emigrants could actually be "re-directed" toward wherever the government saw fit. Even though initial efforts to settle Germans in Africa had fallen short of expectations, there was at least the possibility that future attempts—more money, better infrastructure, smarter advertisement—might succeed. Emigration may well have been a fact of German national life, something which Kapp had always argued, but it remained subject to the whims of politics, which he had tried to deny.[54]

The problem eventually did dawn on Kapp, judging by his increasingly alarmist rhetoric about any colonial project undertaken outside North America. Especially after it became clear, in the fall of 1883, that Bismarck supported protectorates in Africa, reversing the government's long-standing position, Kapp embarked on a dubious campaign to snuff out the new colonialism on humanitarian grounds. Thus, he warned of harsh climates and disease-infested environments for which the "northern German" was entirely unsuited. He pointed to the fact that, in places like Brazil, Venezuela, East Africa, or the Sandwich Islands of the Pacific, the Germans would find themselves toiling in conditions resembling slavery and that by working alongside "Chinese, Malayans, Hungarians, or whoever" they risked being "morally degraded" and "shed[ding] their national distinctiveness if they do not dissolve altogether into the lower developed race." Such cultural chauvinism was not unusual for the period, but Kapp knew better. Indeed, he had long distinguished himself by his sensitivity to the complexities of different colonial settings and to historical context more generally. He knew full well that the climate in many parts of North America could be just as unforgiving, that in the United States Germans would be living and working alongside diverse immigrants from around the world, that there was a difference between wage labor and slavery, and that the financial incentives offered to settlers in the new colonies had nothing to do with the "trade in human beings" of another period.[55]

None of that mattered now, however, because, short of falling back on purely essentialist arguments about the Germans' eternal and never-abating interest in North America—arguments that Kapp, for all his bombast, never dared to make—there was nothing left for him to do other than put the region on a pedestal. If hypocrisy was the charge that awaited him, then he was unmoved. He had given up on dogma, sometime between the disappointments of his youth during the Revolution of 1848, his subsequent struggles to make it in American business and politics, and finally his spectacular rise into the upper echelons of an Atlantic *haute finance*. And so, there was nothing to wrangle with when, after a long and exhausting day of hurling invectives at the colonial lobby from the speaker's podium at the Reichstag, Kapp strolled back to his apartments in Berlin Mitte, sat down at his desk, and wrote letters to New York updating his associate Henry Villard on the events of the day. US rails were doing well again, he told his friend. Had Villard "heard about the notorious persecution of Jews in Russia"? It was a potential "gold mine" for the Northern Pacific Railway Company, which they both knew was in desperate need of settlers. He wrote, "Already more than 60,000 have been driven out of Russia or have emigrated; that is just the beginning: 100,000, yes, millions will follow. And strangely enough these Jews, who all have their sights set on America, they don't want [to go] peddling, they want to become farmers. A whole new vein in the emigrant stream has opened up. In my view, which is not by any means sanguine, the United States could pick up 2–3 million souls from this stream." Kapp's instructions were as follows:

> You must set your levers in New York. Reach out to Seligmann...and offer immediate, tangible profits, cheap transportation [and] free passage from Duluth...so that you can attract the whole stream to yourself. In other words, you must orchestrate the scheme in New York, later you can build on it further by hiring agents here [in Berlin]. At that point I will provide you with the right addresses of the embarkations. Do not forget that over the course of the year we are dealing with

millions of new settlers, that makes so and so many millions of dollars. Next spring the whole thing will really get going but you must attract the pioneers right away. [London bankers] expect to put together at least 100,000 pounds right away so get on with it (*also druff*)!⁵⁶

Handsome returns were guaranteed so long as the scheme was executed as outlined. In the meantime, Villard needed to keep everything strictly confidential, to ensure that "my name is not mentioned in any way" in any promotional materials. There was a chance that he, Kapp, might lose his Reichstag seat and, even worse, his "credibility as an expert" on America and on German emigration, a matter on which "I have always assumed a purely objective stance."⁵⁷

On March 15, 1875, Paul Schulze, head of the land department of the Oregon & California Railroad Company, sat down at his desk in Portland, Oregon, to write a letter to Henry Villard, his associate in New York. Schulze felt irritated. The most recent batch of German-language immigration brochures had just arrived from New York, and they were full of mistakes and false descriptions of conditions on the ground. "There are no prairie chickens in Oregon," he began, and last year Oregon produced only "4,150,000 bushels of wheat," not 44,550,000, as was claimed in the brochures. As the railroad's land agent on-site, Schulze was in no mood to deal with disappointed and angry immigrants. Villard should recognize, moreover, that word of these falsities might spread to Germany and discourage more emigrants from coming to Oregon.⁵⁸

Villard, for his part, cared little about whether the details cited in the brochures were in order. As a railroad financier, his main interest regarded the price of Oregon & California's bonds, and to that end even a factually inaccurate immigration brochure would do the job. Ultimately, all that such a brochure needed to accomplish was to inspire confidence among investors, not emigrants, and to that end an engaging description complete with prairie chickens was par for the course. The more colorful, the better. Bankers in Berlin or Frankfurt am Main were steeped in such romantic imagery about the American West. It was a given that few of them had ever tilled a field and that even fewer had ever been to Oregon.

Villard also knew that they did not care. What immigrant brochures proved to German bondholders was that people were migrating across the Atlantic and that the state of Oregon was among their destinations. The fact that his promotional literature overpromised was neither here nor there. To the contrary, the fiction of it all was only appropriate because Villard and Kapp were storytellers, and the story they told was of the Germanic spirit of migration and the growth of the United States population that this world-historical force would secure in the long run.[59]

The Migrant's Spirit: How Industrial Modernity Came to the German Lands. Benjamin P. Hein, Oxford University Press. © Oxford University Press 2025. DOI: 10.1093/9780197831052.003.0008

8

Reckoning with the Migrant's Spirit

FRIEDRICH AUGUST KLUSEMANN, the son of a pastor in Löderburg near Magdeburg, was a man who had come far in the business of machine building. He began his career as a journeyman working at various tool-making workshops in Aachen, Düsseldorf, Magdeburg, and Berlin, including under the auspices of the brilliant locomotive engineer and entrepreneur August Borsig. From Borsig Klusemann learned a great deal about advanced machinery designs, and by the time he completed his apprenticeship he had already invented a pathbreaking machine of his own, a *"Kohlenwaschmaschine,"* a machine that could cut and wash sugar beets and prepare them for processing in a sugar refinery. After filing patents on his invention with Prussian authorities in 1849, Klusemann opened his own "machine-factory" in the village of Sudenburg near Magdeburg with the name Klusemann & Woltersdorf.[1]

His timing proved auspicious. The sugar industry in the Saxon-Anhalt region was expanding in these years, especially during the 1860s, generating brisk demand for Klusemann's sugar beet–washing machines. By the time the German Empire was established in 1871, the company furnished no fewer than fifty sugar-processing companies across the country with machinery, tools, and repair services. Annual net profits regularly reached into the tens of thousands of talers, particularly during the banner year of 1872, when Klusemann reported a stunning profit of 76,212 talers—nearly as much as the value of the entire establishment, which including inventory was pegged at 108,386 talers. By this time, Klusemann's operations had long attracted the attention of the financial community in Magdeburg, which in August 1872 sent an agent, Julius Levy of the Magdeburger Wechsler- und Discontobank. Levy made Klusemann an attractive offer: 600,000 talers for the business, patents included, with an immediate cash payment of 10 percent. The rest would be paid in the form of stock and stock options in a soon-to-be established joint-stock corporation (*Aktiengesellschaft*), the Sudenburger Machine Factory and Iron Foundry, Incorporated, which would henceforth manage the business. As a stockholder and member of the new company's administrative board, Klusemann would be entitled to future dividends, which Levy and his associates estimated at 10 percent, eventually rising to 15 percent. Finally, to sweeten the deal for the craftsman tinkerer, the bankers allowed Klusemann to keep any "tools and utensils" he might require for "private use."

While it is impossible to determine what exactly went through Klusemann's head that August, it seems safe to say that when he accepted Levy's offer just a few weeks later, he did not anticipate that just over a year later he would find himself at the center of a high-profile criminal trial in which he and six co-conspirators stood accused of engaging in a brazen scheme to defraud investors. The Royal Appeals Court of Magdeburg eventually rendered a guilty verdict on all those indicted, with Klusemann sentenced to three months in prison and a fine of 1,500 marks for falsifying financial statements and lying in an investor prospectus about the health of his business, which had declined markedly amid a deep economic recession in the mid-1870s. Although Klusemann emerged from the affair a financially independent man, the experience clearly wore on him. Just a few years later, in 1878, he died at age fifty-six.[2]

Klusemann's trial, along with that of a handful of other criminal trials referred by contemporary observers as the "founder trials" (*Gründerprozesse*) that followed in the wake of the global financial crisis of 1873, is a bit of a historical curiosity. By no means was the German Empire harder hit by fraudulent activity in 1873 than other parts of the world; arguably, the financial mischief was far more spectacular in Vienna, capital of the Austro-Hungarian Empire, and perhaps also on Wall Street in New York. Yet nowhere else in Europe, and certainly not in the United States, did anyone attempt to drag bankers and entrepreneurs like Klusemann before a criminal court. "England managed to overcome its bubbles, France the mischief on the Rue Quincampoix, and Holland its tulip fraud," remarked one stunned observer. And they all had done so "without the help of the state prosecutor!"[3]

What, then, was different in the German Empire? It can be tempting to see these founder trials as the manifestation of a peculiar German affinity for and trust in the state. There is some truth to that interpretation, but the story is also more complicated. To begin with, the hysteria surrounding the crisis of 1873 was in large part a reflection of deeply entrenched assumptions about what commerce in Germany ought to look like and how it should be conducted. When it came to money, work, and business, the Germans were different from the English, French, Dutch, Austrians, or Americans—so at least the argument of many a German patriot. Speculation and financial skullduggery were supposedly alien to German culture, certainly less pronounced than in those ostensibly less principled and more money-oriented national traditions. The Germans also thought about and approached their work and businesses not just as a means for securing a material livelihood but also in a corporate sense, that is, as a source of pride, meaning, dignity, and personhood. Stories like Klusemann's, in which worthy craftsmen hawked off their businesses in pursuit of windfall profits at the stock market, flew in the face of these assumptions about German morality governing work and commerce (*Sittengesetz*). They also turned the question on its head. For most contemporaries, the puzzle of 1873 was not why the dynamics in Germany differed from those in other nations: It was why they were so similar.[4]

Because of the striking similarity to dynamics associated with other national cultures, and because it seemed rather unlikely that the German people should have simply forgotten who they were—it became quite easy to suspect that the country had fallen under the sway of foreign value systems linked to the French, the English, the Americans, or "the Jews"—in the 1870s, each of them at one point or another stood accused of ensnaring unsuspecting Germans like Klusemann into their devious schemes. Criminal trials were in this sense not just an attempt to bring accountability to homegrown financial miscreants. Rather, they were part and parcel of a much broader campaign to extricate the nation from the deleterious sway of foreign culture and values, to shore up a Sittengesetz that had proven unexpectedly fragile in the face of what some were beginning to call the "capitalist spirit": a new and socially corrosive set of norms, assumptions, and ethical maxims that some argued belonged to the Jews or, as the influential economist Werner Sombart contended some years later, originated in the "colonial economies" of the Americas.[5]

Nevertheless, by the end of 1876, the founder trials had, for all intents and purposes, run their course, with observers chafing at the prosecutions of supposed fraud, because many cases had indeed been built on rather shaky evidence and dubious argumentation. This did not mean, however, that the struggle between a capitalist spirit of foreign import and the guardians of Sittengesetz had come to an end—far from it. Attacks on "Jewish" hucksterism, French "laissez-faire, laissez aller" dogma, English Manchester-dom, and American gangsterism continued unabated in various corners of the press and in politics, and were also pursued with increasing zeal and venom. Similarly, calls for the state to restore order and to "revitalize" the nation's traditional "ethics of social responsibility" did not go away and continued to be taken seriously by German governments. From the culture wars of the 1870s (*Kulturkampf*) to the wholesale ban of the Social Democratic Party in the 1880s, to a dizzying array of laws aimed at the more "purposeful regulation of the individual," the state in this period continuously expanded its activities within the national economy, ushering in what has since become known as the German "interventionist" state.[6]

New strategies also emerged after approximately 1876—strategies that were much less defensive in their posture and more creative and forward-looking. As the years went by and the crisis of 1873 receded into memory, it was becoming increasingly obvious that the capitalist spirit was not going anywhere, that in fact it might have already changed the nation's moral sensibilities in a lasting way. This realization became the starting point for a daring and quite innovative attempt at legal engineering, in which reformers sought to better align German commercial law with what was understood to be an entirely new "people's psychology" (*Völkerpsychologie*), constituted in equal parts of the capitalist spirit and the nation's traditional moral predilections. As was true of the defensive posture that gave rise to the so-called interventionist state in Germany, this effort yielded policies and institutions that would shape the nation's economic life for years to come.[7]

Crises in the world of commerce were nothing new to Wilhelm Oechelhäuser, one of nineteenth-century Germany's most influential industrialists and a well-regarded liberal statesman. The first time Oechelhäuser witnessed one firsthand was amid the great political upheavals of 1848, when his father had been forced to shut down the family's paper manufactory in Siegen in the Prussian province of Westphalia. The second time came less than a decade later, not long after Oechelhäuser became the managing director of the Deutsche Continental-Gas-Gesellschaft in Dessau, in the Duchy of Anhalt, a pioneering natural gas producer founded in 1855 by the energetic Hans Victor von Unruh, an engineer, entrepreneur, and fellow national-liberal politician. The world financial crisis of 1857, as it came to be known, had very nearly put an end to the business by interrupting its access to capital in the middle of an aggressive period of expansion that involved the construction of no less than eleven new natural gas utilities in cities as far away as Hagen in the Westphalian Sauerland and Warsaw in the Russian Empire. This time, disaster was averted. Thanks to Oechelhäuser's vigorous management, not to mention the sheer force of his optimism about the future of natural gas, investors remained patient and the company survived long enough to reap the rewards of the boom that followed in the 1860s, when it began yielding impressive dividends of twelve percent per annum. What the natural gas magnate took away from these experiences was that crises, even major ones, were transient events; though challenging in the moment, they represented aberrations to the norm, which tended toward steady growth.[8]

But the financial crisis of 1873 was an altogether different phenomenon. In Oechelhäuser's view, it was not just its scale that set this financial calamity apart, although the stock market volatility and cascading bankruptcies in every imaginable branch of industry were unlike anything he had seen before. Nor was it the corruption, mismanagement, and fraud that had been brought to light and that aroused such ire in the public. What was different about this crisis was that it lingered for so long. Although the financial markets stabilized in due time, commerce and industry never seemed to regain their former vitality. Businesses continued to collapse long after the crisis, and prices continued to fall well into the 1880s and 1890s. Dividends rarely reached into the double digits anymore, and returns on stocks declined from an average of 8.64 percent to a comparatively slender 5.03 percent. While Oechelhäuser remained hopeful, refusing to submit to the belief that "the entire economic system should have fallen apart," he could not help but regard the events of 1873 as a genuine watershed. "The character which this crisis has assumed is best described as a general paralysis of economic forces," he wrote in a reflection from 1877. "It is a chronic sickness, not a... crisis," and it could "only be explained in subjective, psychological terms": a kind of "fortune fever" (*Reichtumsfieber*).[9]

In the years leading up to the crisis, this fortune fever had "penetrated deep into all classes of society." Hence, the problem was not just a few brazen stock jobbers and railroad barons, be they Jewish, American, French, or otherwise, and their nefarious stock market schemes. Equally culpable and certainly complicit was a shockingly spendthrift German middle class that had quite frankly "allow[ed] itself to be pulled into the speculation." Ordinary working men, although not directly implicated in the speculative debauchery at the stock market, had nevertheless contributed their share to the broader economic malaise with their own greed and envy. Large wage hikes granted during the economic expansion of the 1860s turned out to have had profoundly "demoralizing consequences" on these workers who, as Oechelhäuser understood it, had no experience in coping with such a "sudden change in their entire social condition." A "new world of illusions suddenly opened up to [them]," and before long they had lost their "yearning to excel at their job"—a yearning "which used to define the German worker." Strikes and other workplace mayhem followed on an ever-growing scale. No less than a thousand work stoppages were recorded in the German Empire between 1869 and 1874, some of them encompassing tens of thousands of workers, with no end in sight. No wonder industry had struggled to regain its footing. Pampered by wage hikes, "an entire worker-generation is ruined" and refuses to "submit [itself] to any control." No business, much less a national economy, could sustain itself for long in this kind of environment.[10]

Even this, however, was just the beginning. Arguably the most destructive and repulsive symptom of fortune fever, at least as far as Oechelhäuser was concerned, was the newly fashionable practice of "converting" ordinary proprietorships into publicly tradable joint-stock corporations. Made possible by the liberalizing reforms of prior years, above all the Free Incorporation Act of 1870, which had made the corporation available to almost any entrepreneur who so desired it, this rather simple legal maneuver offered proprietors and their bankers a one-time shot at an enormous financial windfall—the so-called founder reward (*Gründeragio*). Oechelhäuser knew full well that there was nothing illegal about the Gründeragio, that it merely reflected the risks assumed by an underwriter in the pricing of new stock. But this did not prevent him from joining the chorus of critics who regarded it as deeply problematic from a societal perspective. The Gründeragio was to Oechelhäuser yet another example of the demoralizing consequences of sudden riches: The human mind was not hardwired to deal with them.[11]

Apart from the Gründeragio, another important issue related to the conversion of rather ordinary proprietorships into joint-stock corporations was that, in Oechelhäuser's opinion, such a legal recategorization rarely made much sense from a business point of view. For the same reason that a manufacturer of, say, screws or umbrellas or lamps would have avoided a corporate legal form designed for enterprises engaged in mining and mineral extraction (the so-called *Gewerkschaft*), he would do well to steer clear of a joint-stock corporation conceived solely for the purpose of solving problems so "odd and risky" that they fell entirely "outside the sphere of normal business": insurance, for example, or central banks, railways, or telegraphy, along with any other application "where public use, not profit," was the primary concern, like zoos, botanical gardens, and museums. Of course, it was true, and Oechelhäuser conceded as much, that the joint-stock corporation boasted features that were potentially attractive to many kinds of entrepreneurs, like limited liability protections and the ability to quickly raise large amounts of capital. Yet contrary to popular belief, he warned, these legal features were no "economic panacea," and in certain respects they threatened significant drawbacks to aspiring businesses.[12]

To understand why, Oechelhäuser proceeded to explain, one needed to look no further than human "psychology," the key to "all matters concerning the economy." It was an "empirically proven fact" that people "work less, and less intensively" if they were not personally liable for, and invested in, their enterprise, and indeed "at many joint stock corporations there prevails an atmosphere of jovial recklessness, laziness, and profligacy...from the director all the way to the lowest employee. [M]oney is handled less economically, the value of each thaler is pondered less before it is spent." None of this should come as a surprise: "After all it lies deep within human nature, and it has been irrefutably proven through experience in all countries and historical epochs, that on average human beings accomplish more in the material sphere if their work is tied to their inner existence, their interests, their honor."[13]

Other problems lurked. Citing his twenty years of experience in business, during which he had sat on the boards of numerous joint-stock corporations, Oechelhäuser found that the capital raised from investors who possessed little notion of what a business actually did often far exceeded its needs, leading managers to waste resources on unnecessarily "luxurious accommodations" and to embark on ill-conceived business expansions designed less with "profitability" in mind than with an eye to the "willingness of the stock market to buy [its] stock." In all these ways, the joint-stock corporation might well be regarded as a "step backwards economically." Certainly, "whenever the highest individual performance is required, the use of a joint-stock corporation is, quite naturally, out of the question."[14]

At least it should have been. The fact that this had not been the case—nearly a fifth of the approximately 1.3 billion talers in capital invested in joint-stock corporations between 1870 and 1873 flowed to "converted" businesses—went a long way toward explaining the protracted economic doldrums in which the German Empire now found itself. The undue fascination with joint-stock corporations had not just ruined many an otherwise sound business's bottom line but had also shaken competitors in the same markets. Buoyed by speculative capital, inefficient joint-stock corporations nevertheless managed to eschew the disciplining forces of the market and survive for years, thereby haunting the national economy in zombie-like fashion. No wonder the contagion had spread even to healthy enterprises that, despite all the temptations, had stuck to "the right economic path" and declined to convert into joint-stock corporations.[15]

The situation called for bold intervention, including on the part of the state, which he argued needed to seriously consider putting in place new legal "safeguards" against the improper uses of this popular legal form. It was a radical proposition for someone like Wilhelm Oechelhäuser. Although, like most German liberals in this period, he was under no illusion that government had an important role to play in the economy, and he rarely missed an opportunity to articulate his contempt for French laissez-faire dogma, it was also true that "for a long time" he had failed to see the harm in efforts to reduce bureaucratic oversight. The Free Incorporation Act of 1870 had gone quite far in this respect, arguably too far, but at the time of its passage Oechelhäuser had not been concerned. He had trusted people's judgment in choosing the proper legal "tool" for their business, especially in light of the (alleged) fact that "the profits of a joint stock corporation are...on average lower than those of a privately-owned business in the same sector."[16]

Needless to say, he wrote in 1877, "My view today is the opposite." He still believed that the reforms of 1870 had been "right in principle." The joint-stock corporation undoubtedly had a place in the construction of modern civilization, for which the profit motive would never suffice, and so it made little sense to return to the older, much more restrictive system, let alone to abolish the institution altogether, as some critics demanded. But the cracks exposed by the events of 1873 in the moral foundation of the nation were large and growing. Oechelhäuser, who was an engineer in both heart and mind, was already contemplating how best to reinforce the structure.[17]

On October 9, 1878, Chancellor Otto von Bismarck took to the podium at the Reichstag in Berlin and began musing about the nation's character. "In essence, the German has a strong tendency toward unhappiness," he opined. "I do not know anyone among us who knows a happy compatriot." Chuckles echoed through the main chamber at Leipziger Strasse 4. It was conceivable that at least some of the "unhappiness" the chancellor was referring to was of his own making, a consequence of his botched struggle against "Reich enemy" number one: political Catholicism.[18] But Bismarck was only half joking, since he was not interested in talking about Catholics that day. After briefly pausing for the audience to quiet down, he went on:

> I know very many Frenchmen who are completely satisfied with their abilities, and their experiences. When they pick up a craft, their goal is to save a certain amount of money by the time they are 45 or 50 years old; and as soon as they have it, their sole ambition is to live as a rentier for the remainder of their lives. Compare this with the German; his ambition, by nature, is not limited to the pursuit of a modest retirement

at the age of 50—indeed, his ambition knows no bounds. The baker… does not just want to become the richest in his village, no, he wants to become a homeowner, a rentier, and ultimately he wants to become his great Berlin idol, a banker, a millionaire.[19]

It was a clever rhetorical ploy. Bismarck knew that the image of bakers aspiring to be millionaires would nudge a good portion of Reichstag delegates toward the edges of their seats, which was exactly where he needed them to be for his impending maneuver against Reich enemy number two: social democracy. In 1878, the Reichstag was a chamber filled with wealthy businessmen, industrialists, railroad tycoons, and landowning nobility, all of whom owed their fortunes in large part to a pliant working class and all of whom knew full well the dangers that lurked when bakers aspired to be something they were not. The reference to "Frenchmen" was no coincidence. Most remembered the horrific violence that had transpired during the recent Paris Commune in 1871. Ambition, Bismarck continued, "is a characteristic that has its good sides, for it is the German industriousness [*Strebsamkeit*]." At the same time, too much ambition bred unhappiness and envy, and soon "the German contracts the disease of socialism."[20]

Ten days later, on October 19, 1878, the Reichstag approved Bismarck's consequential Anti-Socialist Law, which outright banned any political parties of said character, by a comfortable margin of 221 to 149. Among those voting in favor was the freshman delegate from the Duchy of Anhalt, Wilhelm Oechelhäuser. Although he did not always agree with the iron chancellor, Oechelhäuser very much shared his enmity toward "the social democratic agitation." He, too, deemed the proverbial baker-who-wants-to-be-a-millionaire a threat to social peace.[21] For years, these parvenus had subverted moral norms and good business sense by recklessly converting their workshops into joint-stock corporations. And, if Bismarck solved the problem by preventing an "ambitious" but "unhappy" German populace from sending Social Democrats to the Reichstag, then Oechelhäuser would do the same with regard to the joint-stock corporation; he would try to make it "as difficult as possible" to engage in such "speculative company founding."[22]

The idea was simple in theory, less so in practice. "It is very difficult to find places to set the levers of reform without violating the principles of economic freedom, to cut away the infected without touching the healthy." He vehemently opposed any policy that "places shackles on a solid entrepreneurial spirit" because that would run counter to liberal principles; at the same time, he reminded himself that "it is the duty of the state to clearly identify the economic significance of every form of corporation, in terms of its absolute and its relative value, in its specific advantages and disadvantages." How, then, could one prevent impudent bakers from founding joint-stock corporations without also intervening in the "freedom of economic choice to utilize one's money and ability?"[23]

As he sought to navigate these challenges, Oechelhäuser returned to his bottom line: The joint-stock corporation should "really appertain to the wealthy, not the 'little man.'" Stopping short of a Bismarckian approach of simply banning joint-stock corporations altogether, he would pursue any policy that prevented, nay "protect[ed]," the "little man" from straying too far beyond his natural habitat. A legal minimum value for individual stocks of "10,000 marks, at the very least 5,000 marks," would prevent those of "no means" (*Unbemittelte*) from investing their savings in stocks. Next, the practice of using securities as collateral for loans was to end, and a new rule requiring that the minimum initial cash paid into a joint-stock corporation be raised from the current 10 percent to 25 percent would thin the ranks of potential little men capable of putting up the necessary cash. Special public agencies were to be created to review every new joint-stock corporation to ensure that the type of business to be pursued matched this category of corporation. Bonuses for managers and founders were to be subjected to hard caps to dampen the speculative incentives of a joint-stock corporation. A slew of other regulations regarding the corporate governance of joint-stock corporations would dramatically expand stockholder rights, manager accountability, and overall company transparency, all of which would reduce the likelihood of what Oechelhäuser deemed "fraudulent" start-ups.[24]

These restrictions of the joint-stock corporate form were striking in several respects. Squaring them with the principle of "commercial freedom" (*Handelsfreiheit*) was not impossible, but it was a bit like threading a rather small needle.[25] In a defense of his ideas before the Reichstag in February 1880, Oechelhäuser drew immediate ridicule from the ranks of conservative delegates like the Prussian Junker Otto von Helldorff-Bedra. "I was not able to follow the highly interesting remarks of the gentleman speaker completely in all their specifics," observed von Helldorff-Bedra. He could agree, however, that the decision to free the joint-stock corporation from governmental oversight back in 1870 had been, as the Conservative Party had long been insisting, a "serious political mistake." Oechelhäuser's support for strict limitations on that freedom was a welcome development, and von Helldorff-Bedra was pleased to learn that the matter had finally stopped being a "partisan issue." Another leading member of the conservative delegation, the Lower Silesian noble Wilhelm Carl Friedrich August Hellmuth Ludwig von Kardorff followed up von Helldorf's speech with more direct words. "With this great opening speech of Mr. Oechelhäuser I had expected that he would offer us some positive suggestions, something we have not already read in the papers." Since that "did not happen," von Kardorff wanted to take the opportunity to propose a different, more straightforward plan. Why not just ban all joint-stock corporations and revive the time-honored concession system, leaving it to the government to decide who should and should not be allowed to operate a joint-stock corporation?[26]

To be sure, such taunts were never directed at Oechelhäuser alone. They targeted the entire liberal establishment, both within and outside the Reichstag. While there had always been differences of opinion, in situations like these German liberals generally preferred to do nothing, citing "legal uncertainties" that would be "worse" than any legal void. If new regulations were indeed necessary for maintaining public order, as the chamber of commerce in Berlin argued, then lawmakers were to proceed with the "utmost care and prudence." Everyone agreed with Oechelhäuser's call for better protections for the "reputable quarters of the business world." This was no departure from liberal orthodoxy; it was merely an attempt at protecting the honest by keeping the scoundrels at bay.[27]

Still, the matter would not go away easily, and the negotiations over the precise form of the corporate reform bill wound up dragging on for more than a dozen years, from 1873 all the way to 1884. Throughout those years, progress on implementing the reforms was continuously paralyzed by an endless debate over who exactly counted as a member of this "reputable quarter of the business world"—who, in essence, should be entitled to the privileges of a joint-stock corporation. The question of a new minimum value for individual stocks was a case in point. Everyone agreed that it should be raised from the current 300 marks to prevent the little man from buying in, but what exactly was to be the minimum threshold? Did the "reputable" business community start at 500 marks a share, or perhaps 1,000, or 2,000, or 5,000, or, as Oechelhäuser proposed, 10,000 marks? This was no minor detail: The question of who would be entitled to contribute to, let alone found, joint-stock corporations stood at the heart of all the other questions to be addressed by any future legislation.[28]

The law that ultimately emerged did not heed all of Oechelhäuser's wishes, though it came close. An abundance of new public disclosure stipulations, including new standards governing prospectuses, balance sheets, and a company's initial stock distribution, all aimed to improve the transparency of joint-stock corporations. Noncompliance was punished more harshly, in some cases even criminalized; stockholder rights, responsibilities, and liabilities were broadened and streamlined; and a formal division of labor was established between a company's supervisory board (*Aufsichtsrat*) and the board of directors (*Vorstand*). These changes went a long way toward improving the transparency of joint-stock corporations. Even more important, from Oechelhäuser's perspective, was that they restricted access to this corporate form. The amount of paperwork and the number of attorneys required for establishing (and operating) a new joint-stock corporation were effectively multiplied, making these types of corporations vastly more expensive and complex. Hefty legal fees accomplished what formal and more politically controversial measures, like the new minimum stock value, could not: They helped achieve consensus after it became clear that a minimum of 1,000 marks was all that would be politically feasible, given opposition from the banking lobby, which complained that excluding "small investors" constituted an unacceptable infringement on its business. One thousand marks was well below the 10,000-mark-threshold originally envisioned by Oechelhäuser and his allies, but in the grand scheme of things, the minimum stock value was no longer a sticking point. Founding a joint-stock corporation had become so complex and tedious that the legal form became "nearly unusable for practical purposes."[29]

Oechelhäuser praised the bill as "one of the best legislative documents ever put before the Reichstag." Notwithstanding various minor adjustments he still "would have liked to see," the so-called Joint Stock Corporation Act of 1884 delivered all he had asked for; namely, it guaranteed that "henceforth a careful, conscientious man can fulfill the duties that come with managing foreign property without risking injury to his honor and his interests."[30]

When Albrecht "Al" Groth boarded the Hamburg steamer *Wieland* in May 1888 to travel to New York City, he was barely twenty years old.[31] Despite the extraordinary journey to be made at such a young age, it was not an unusual choice for a craftsman's son such as Groth. His apprenticeship in horticulture, a business he had entered into only because it happened to be his father's métier, was headed nowhere. Had this been the 1860s or even the 1870s, things may have been different. Back then, Groth might have followed in his father's footsteps and opened his own flower and gardening shop in Deutsch-Rixdorf (today Berlin-Neukölln), his hometown just south of Berlin. In 1888, with the rise of the city's sprawling department stores, such a business seemed to have little future. Granted, Groth had explored other prospects. He had tried to earn his *Abitur*, for example, which would have enabled him to go to university. But failure to pass the difficult examinations left him languishing in a craft with few good prospects.

It was likely at this point that North America began to loom large in Groth's mind, and he began trying to convince two fellow apprentices to join him in emigrating to America and setting up a small horticulture shop there instead. In the United States, Groth knew, "the worker is as good as the millionaire. Everyone is treated equally, nobody is looked at askance." He also believed that "there is money to be earned for anyone who is independent. And you don't even need a very big capital to start, $1,500 is plenty."[32] He already had a plan worked out. He and his companions would head for the booming metropolis of Chicago, which, according to rumors he had heard, was "famous in North America" for its "rose cultivation." Once they had learned a little more about the trade and acquired a basic command of English, they would move on to "nearby" Milwaukee, "where I would like to open my own business." A small loan from his father, to which all young apprentices were customarily entitled, would provide the necessary start-up funds.[33]

Emigrants like Al Groth were precisely the kind of people that Wilhelm Oechelhäuser had begun growing nervous about in the early 1880s. To be sure, for the past few years, things had been looking up. The get-rich-quick mentality of '73 seemed to have subsided somewhat. It appeared that the Reichstag's anti-Socialist law had borne fruit and that a certain sense of diligence, hard work, and purpose had been restored among the working classes. But then, around 1880, the pendulum had swung back hard. Fortune fever had returned with a vengeance, although this time it manifested itself not in a stock market crash but, rather, in a migration event to North America of unprecedented scale. Between 1880 and 1884, close to a million German workers, peasants, and craftsmen arrived on American shores, which was nearly as many people as the entire population of Berlin, then the German Empire's largest metropolis. In 1882 alone, the number of emigrants was estimated to have exceeded a quarter million.[34] Germany had a long history of emigration bouts, yet at no time in the past had the numbers reached such astonishing magnitude.

In light of this worrisome exodus, Oechelhäuser decided to weigh in again on the Reichstag debate over reforming joint-stock corporations. He began by recounting another disconcerting development he had been registering over the past few years: the rather common formation of extraordinarily small joint-stock corporations constituted by no more than three or four individuals. This was a cause for concern because the capital raised in these enterprises could amount to almost laughable sums; he had heard of cases in which just "four people" registered a joint-stock corporation "with a combined capital of 400 taler." Furthermore, there seemed to be "nothing" in the current law proposal that could prevent such entities from establishing themselves "at a moment's notice." They could simply enter themselves into the public registry and forgo the sale of their stock on a public exchange, which meant that, for all intents and purposes, the "law no longer needs to concern them in the least bit." All the new rules under consideration, including stricter provisions on annual balance sheets, public disclosure of information, and the establishment of new oversight bodies within corporations, were for naught because "where there is no litigator, there is no judge either."

This sort of "abuse" of the joint-stock corporate form was hardly the end of the story. "In considering the question," Oechelhäuser explained,

> Gentlemen, be advised how German capital migrates overseas on an ever growing scale, so that we have perhaps one to two billion invested in foreign securities. Furthermore, take into account that annually 100,000, often 200,000 or more persons are emigrating. Now, even though the latter emigration question may be, in part, a fundamentally separate issue, it will surely be worth all the effort to counteract this emigration of capital and people through the opening of new channels for associating people and capital. We would encourage such persons to associate themselves productively here [in Germany] rather than overseas, and instead of emigrating themselves, they would export the material products of their associations to foreign countries.

As he went on to explain, in light of the exodus of capital and people from Germany, the mere imposition of stricter rules governing joint-stock corporations—the overarching purpose of the current law proposal—would not suffice to bring to an end the above-mentioned abuses. Clever parvenus would always find a way to establish a joint-stock corporation. If, for example, the Reichstag banned such "miniature" joint-stock corporations by "stipulating a minimum capital requirement," as some had proposed, clever people would likely head overseas instead and establish their businesses there, exacerbating an already extraordinary flight of people and capital from the German Empire.[35]

The answer, Oechelhäuser concluded, was to think beyond new rules and regulations for the joint-stock corporation itself. Perhaps "it is time to examine all the existing legal forms of incorporation" and to consider "whether they are sufficient to meet all the business purposes that may arise from the association of capital." It seemed to him that one of the main reasons for the routine formation of miniature joint-stock corporations was that they offered limited liability protections for shareholders—a privilege that at the time was offered by no other legal form of incorporation. Many of these small businesses, though legally incorporated as joint-stock corporations, were still operated as if they were ordinary partnerships: their stockholders still ran the business themselves or, as Oechelhäuser put it, they still "personally fertilized" their own capital rather than outsourcing that responsibility to others.[36]

This, in turn, begged the question of whether it still made sense to continue to limit the broader public's access to limited liability, which the migration exodus suggested had become an increasingly popular principle in "our entire modern business life." Why not instead direct this fashionable "trend" into more appropriate channels, perhaps by establishing a new form of incorporation beside the joint-stock corporation? "Imagine a type of company that is organized on the principles of our current ordinary partnership, except that its liability is limited to a designated amount of capital," Oechelhäuser mused. Such a "simple type of company" would essentially "bring together all the advantages of an ordinary partnership with those of a joint stock corporation," even while it would eliminate the "disadvantages and dangers" of either form of incorporation. On the one hand, associates in such a corporation would enjoy limited liability protections, which is to say, they would not be asked to risk anything beyond their original investment, like their "honor, their capital, their entire existence." On the other hand, as privately held partnerships, they would not be able to trade their shares on a public exchange, which would remove the "speculative" incentives that turned a joint-stock corporation into such a dangerous legal instrument in the hands of uncouth people. Oechelhäuser was sure that such a new type of corporation could "serve an extraordinary number of business purposes," especially those of individuals with little to no capital to speak of. Lawmakers might call it a "Gesellschaft mit beschränkter Haftbarkeit," or a "GmbH" for short.[37]

This proposal for a hybrid kind of limited liability partnership was decidedly short on details, yet even at this early stage, Oechelhäuser's vision was nothing short of remarkable. Not only was it a novel concept for the period, but also it constituted a clear departure from Oechelhäuser's own longstanding thinking on joint-stock corporations.[38] Had he not, for the past half a dozen years or so, emphasized the incommensurable "economic differences" between various forms of incorporation? Had he not decried so-called conversions as a dangerous and economically regressive subversion of the natural order? Had he not done everything in his power to raise barriers around joint-stock corporations, barriers that would shield them from abuse by society's get-rich schemers and little men?[39] Now, he seemed to suggest, it was not just possible but also desirable to attempt to "organically merge" an ordinary partnership and a joint-stock corporation. The GmbH would secure the joint-stock corporation not by raising barriers around it, but by creating alternative "channels of associating capital and people." A "supplementation" of German corporate law is what he would call it: "I am fully convinced," he concluded, "that the country which offers the safest, simplest and most manifold legal forms for associating capital and people will have an economic advantage over other nations who will otherwise fall behind."[40]

With so much at stake, one might have expected a lively discussion to follow Oechelhäuser's speech that Monday of March 24, 1884. Yet nothing of the sort transpired. Official transcripts of the proceedings that day record "applause," but it must have been of the tepid kind because, when the presiding speaker of the chamber solicited responses, not a single Reichstag delegate volunteered. Granted, by the time Oechelhäuser spoke it was nearly 4:00 p.m. and business in the chamber was winding down. He tried once more to make his case, at the final debate on the corporate reform bill in June, but to no avail. What exactly explains the muted response is unclear. Perhaps the idea was just too novel, too much at odds with contemporary thinking on corporations. Or perhaps the rationale he had offered, about the need to stem the outflow of emigrants and capital, was too much of a non sequitur. As Oechelhäuser himself had put it, emigration "may be, in part, a fundamentally separate issue." What is clear is that, for the time being, the plan to assemble a new corporate form that would stave off emigration and capital flight was, for all intents and purposes, dead on arrival.[41]

Two years later, on April 30, 1886, leading officials of the 12,500-member strong German Colonial Society (*Deutscher Kolonialverein*) gathered in Karlsruhe near Stuttgart for their annual summit.[42] The mood was buoyant. Over the four years since the society's founding in 1882, colonial "business" had assumed "ever larger dimensions," with "expansive swaths of land"

acquired over the past three years along the west coast of Africa. Just a few weeks earlier, news had broken of the government's approval of protectorate status for several new territories in the "hinterland of Angra Pequena" (present-day coastal Namibia). The agenda was packed, covering such hot-button issues as emigration (how it might be "redirected" from America to Africa), a new "overseas bank" (to finance colonial business endeavors), and the African "liquor and weapons trade" (exceedingly lucrative).[43]

Item seven, just after emigration and before the liquor and weapons issues, concerned the recently enacted Joint Stock Corporation Act of 1884. The law had proven an enormous headache for colonial enthusiasts and businessmen who were active overseas. Joint-stock corporations, which the act was to render more transparent and less prone to speculative abuse, were also the primary legal vehicle for doing business abroad. They offered limited liability protections to investors, a legal feature widely believed to be indispensable for colonial businesses because no investor, not even the most patriotic of them, was willing to risk "his whole luck and well-being on a pretty unfamiliar project." The problem with the Joint Stock Corporation Act of 1884, so the argument went, was that it levied a dizzying array of new regulations that, though perhaps appropriate for stamping out the "excesses of stock market gambling" (*Börsenspiel*) back in Germany, also prevented the effective exploitation of the nation's new colonial territories.[44]

Of particular concern was the new law's provision to improve transparency in all joint-stock corporations. Nobody would deny the need for more transparency, but in the real world this turned out to be a "delicate issue." On the one hand, it was "never pleasant" to have to submit to public scrutiny, not "even for the most honorable businessman." Proving that one had acted like a "conscientious businessman" seemed especially burdensome when the business was done in a colonial context like Africa.[45] On the other hand, the law's demand for biannual balance sheets apparently produced a maddening logistical dilemma for colonial entrepreneurs. It was argued that communication between a company's newly empowered supervisory board (*Aufsichtsrat*), which sat in Europe, and its managers (*Vorstand*), stationed in Africa, could well stretch over weeks, often months—making a mockery of the close monitoring that had been stipulated. "How on earth," a skeptic wondered, "can a person in Germany be expected to put together a balance sheet about objects that are thousands of oceanic miles away [and] hundreds of miles inland from the coast?"[46]

The most vexing problem created by the Joint Stock Corporation Act of 1884 was that it created a public relations disaster for joint-stock corporations.

In targeting this corporate form as part of a campaign to rein in fraud and excess, the law had effectively discredited the joint-stock corporation as a trustworthy form of incorporation. Given the profoundly speculative character of colonial enterprises, many of which had nothing to show for themselves but pieces of paper asserting title to territory nobody had ever heard of, let alone visited, it went without saying that any further erosion of trust was "not exactly conducive to the kind of business we intend to do." The mere word *founder* (*Gründer*) had already proven to be a serious liability when establishing colonial businesses. In one instance involving a project in Angra Pequena in Southwest Africa, for example, "patriotic investors" had put up hundreds of thousands of marks for a new venture, and yet "not a single one of them" had dared to accept the "honor" of being called a founder of that enterprise.[47]

Intentionally or not, the Joint Stock Corporation Act of 1884 had placed "far-reaching" shackles on the joint-stock corporation model, such that it became entirely unsuited for the purposes of exploiting economic opportunities in overseas colonies.[48] It was proposed that solutions be found outside the legal framework of a joint-stock corporation. "The colonial society is convinced…that in light of the above-mentioned facts, the presently existing…legal forms of incorporation are inappropriate for the purpose of promoting German colonial endeavors, and that meeting this purpose will require new legal forms of incorporation, which will allow…the establishment of companies with limited liability alongside the joint stock corporation."[49] Leading the charge toward a "new corporate legal form" that would be better equipped to handle the business of colonialism was the cofounder of the colonial society and national liberal Reichstag delegate Friedrich Hammacher. Hammacher had already solicited legal advice from the nation's leading legal minds, including jurist and corporate law expert Levin Goldschmidt, Cologne attorney Robert Esser, and University of Breslau professor Karl von Stengel. Given just how critical the matter had become for the "development of our colonial endeavors," Hammacher promised to put the issue before the Reichstag as soon as possible.[50]

It is not known what Oechelhäuser's initial reactions were to the colonial lobby's inquiry into a new corporate form to facilitate business in Africa. On the one hand, it seemed like a promising opportunity to revive the moribund GmbH concept. Friedrich Hammacher was one of the most influential and well-connected men in German national politics. A founding member of the

National Liberal Party (est. 1867), he had served as its deputy chairman and organized countless legislative initiatives. A corporate lawyer who for years advised on mergers and acquisitions of mining enterprises in the Ruhr valley, and who had built up a sprawling portfolio of mines of his own, he also enjoyed personal relations with some of the biggest industrial tycoons in the country. If there was a figure whose support might move the needle on the GmbH, it was Hammacher.[51]

There were, however, good reasons to be wary about collaborating with this Ruhr mining magnate. Though he was powerful and well-connected, Hammacher was also a divisive figure. He insisted that Germany's economic and social ills, which had been ongoing through the 1870s and which Hammacher argued were caused by "overproduction" and "overpopulation," could only be solved through the establishment of African colonies, which would open new markets for German industry and offer new homesteads to disgruntled German workers who might otherwise flock to the Social Democratic Party. "We are stuck in overproduction across the board," he worried, referring to the sagging prices of coal, salt, and other minerals produced by his mines. "We must vent off by going overseas. If we don't then we will never get back on top."[52]

Such politics were not without controversy in the late 1870s. Indeed, they stood at the center of a historic falling out between the right and left wings of the National Liberal Party in the early 1880s. Oechelhäuser's sympathies lay more with those on the left; he believed that African colonialism was a distraction and a waste of resources and that the rationales offered in support of it, especially the idea of "overpopulation," were but "the hobbyhorse of economic dilettantes. It is based on the Malthusian hypothesis, itself made up out of thin air, whereby the Lord-Almighty has made a mathematical blunder by allowing… mankind to reproduce more quickly than the earth can feed it. From these murky ideas a dogma has crept into the minds of many, the notion that emigration from Germany is a necessity, a blessing, as if… the problem of so-called overproduction could only be balanced out and put back into equilibrium with demand via emigration."[53] Had any of the colonial firebrands noticed, Oechelhäuser wondered, that the vast majority of emigrants hailed from the "most thinly populated regions" of the German Empire? The issue was really more about distribution within the nation; it behooved the government to "turn our attention toward balancing out the temporary oversupply of manpower *between the different regions of the fatherland itself.*" In general, he continued, the solutions to economic and social stagnation should be sought in domestic policy, not in some perfunctory and grandiose proposal to conquer remote corners of the world. Hence, whereas the natural gas magnate from Dessau imagined a "supplementation" (*Ergänzung*) of the menu of available corporate forms, the coal magnate from the Ruhr valley always insisted on "expanding" (*Erweiterung*) existing corporations' sphere of activity. Hammacher wanted their legal capacities to be expanded in lockstep with territorial expansion overseas, to enable it to "make use of the gold discoveries in our protectorates."[54]

But the devil lay in the details. Oechelhäuser was a person of practical mind, and since the same was reportedly true of Hammacher, about whom it was often said that nobody else had figured out how to "blend" political idealism with personal interests in so seamless a manner, he spotted his opportunity.[55] Thus, in the fall of 1886—the same year he published his scathing critique of Malthusian economics—Oechelhäuser suddenly began to warm up to the African colonial project. When, in December, Bismarck solicited deep-pocketed investors to prop up the German East Africa Company, a poorly managed enterprise that stood to be gobbled up by the English unless it was infused with fresh cash, Oechelhäuser did not hesitate to step in.[56] He knew he was throwing good money after bad, but it was just the kind of high-profile project that would attract attention in colonialist circles. Next, he adjusted his GmbH pitch by replacing the word *Ergänzung* (supplementation) with Hammacher's preferred language: German corporate law, he now explained, "urgently requires supplementation, that is to say, expansion."[57] Finally, he dropped all references to the migration problem first alluded to in 1884 and instead began touting the GmbH as a potential facilitator of small-scale colonial exploitation. "It would be a mistake to think that we can pursue our colonial endeavors only in the form of large-scale ventures," he proclaimed before the Reichstag in 1888. "No, gentlemen, a large portion, numerically the larger part, of our colonial endeavors in the spheres of trade, plantations, etc can also be accomplished with small, at times with very small, capital. I am therefore convinced that it is of urgent necessity that we create new space in this sphere for the association of capital and labor."[58]

The response from Hammacher was immediate and was characterized by the kind of sentiment that Oechelhäuser had been angling for. Thus, on February 4, 1888, Hammacher returned the favor by using a Reichstag debate on the "legal environment in German protectorates" to put the original GmbH proposal back on the agenda. "First of all, based on my own experiences I can only confirm that in the sphere of colonial endeavors nothing obstructs and holds back economic activity in our colonial protectorates more than the ... inadequate options for incorporation offered by German law." He briefly peddled his own ideas for a retrofitted mining corporation (*Gewerkschaft*), but then continued: "I must go further: not just in the sphere of colonial endeavors but also with respect to the development of our economic life in the German Empire we have sensed this regrettable gap."[59] Later that month, he appointed himself and Oechelhäuser to head a special investigative committee to solicit opinions from key government ministries as well as important stakeholders in business and industry.[60]

It was Oechelhäuser's turn to move. Not long thereafter, he began to subtly pivot back toward his original designs of a GmbH that would prop up the joint-stock corporation by offering an outlet to "small" businesses—a preference made clear by his return to the language of "supplementation" rather than "expansion." He also reinserted the specter of continued "mass emigration of capital and people," warning that inaction at home, in the German Empire, would only exacerbate this disconcerting exodus.[61] This time, his proposal caught the attention of lawmakers and the business community. In May 1888, the business-friendly daily *Kölnische Zeitung* reported that Oechelhäuser's designs, in particular, had garnered "special interest" within the business world.[62] A survey of eighty-one chambers of commerce showed strong support for Oechelhäuser's version of the GmbH: some forty-nine of the eighty-one (61 percent) endorsed his model, while only three were convinced by Hammacher's idea of a new mining corporation redesigned for colonial exploitation.[63] "In our opinion," noted Berlin's chamber of commerce, "the needs of colonial enterprises do not justify...the creation of a new, *collectivist* form of incorporation."[64] It voted in favor of the proposal for a limited liability partnership.

Oechelhäuser had won the day. To be sure, it would take another three years for government ministries and legal experts to craft the new law and for the kaiser to add his blessing. But within months of the bill's passage in the spring of 1892, usage of the GmbH model grew at a brisk pace.[65] Some 1,028 GmbHs would be registered in the next three years, a significant number when compared to the 4,749 joint-stock corporations that had been created since as far back as the 1850s (by 1905, the total number of GmbHs reportedly surpassed 8,000). Crucially, the growth of registered GmbHs would outpace that of joint-stock corporations for the remainder of the century.[66] Nor did the new corporate form's popularity stop at German borders. By the early 1900s, the concept had already found imitators across the European continent. Austria-Hungary became the first to follow suit, adopting the German GmbH framework almost wholesale in 1906; Britain's Parliament enacted a similar structure under the Companies Act of 1907, which offered entrepreneurs the option of incorporating as "private limited" companies; and in 1925, the French used the GmbH as a blueprint on which to construct their own société à responsabilité limitée, which, incidentally, experienced an even more impressive growth rate than the one previously recorded in Prussia. Over the course of the twentieth century, versions of these "limited liability partnerships" were adopted around the globe, particularly in East Asia and Latin America.[67]

What explains the soaring and near-universal popularity of the GmbH at the moment of its creation? One way to understand its growth is through the lens of its utility for businesses. Unlike other limited liability corporations, the GmbH form granted company owners an unprecedented degree of autonomy and a simple path to incorporation. All that was required was entry into the commercial registry and a minimum capital of 20,000 marks (the *Stammkapital*, or core stock of capital), split into at least two nontradable "shares" (*Anteile*) of unspecified size.[68] Another advantage derived from the GmbH's private character: Because it did not raise its capital on a public stock exchange, it was not required to furnish annual reports or, for that matter, any other form of information. This sort of nontransparency lent it an enormous advantage over the joint-stock corporation model, whose public reporting requirements meant that it was forced to "grant competitors insight into every step the industry...takes and—what is especially alarming—open its books to foreign competition."[69]

Another way to understand the GmbH's appeal is to consider it in the context of contemporary politics. For years, deeper social and demographic shifts like urbanization and the expansion of the nation's industrial workforce at the expense of rural, agrarian labor had raised the electoral fortunes of budding mass parties like the Social Democratic Party and the Catholic Center Party, as well as the parties of minority nationalities like Poles and Danes. In 1890, for example, the combined popular vote of Socialists, Catholics, and national minorities amounted to 45 percent of the total; by 1893, it had grown to 48.1 percent and in 1898 it topped 52 percent. The fact that the German Empire offered universal male suffrage (to those over the age of twenty-five) made these trends even more alarming than elsewhere in Europe, including in Britain, where access to the vote remained far more restricted.[70]

In light of the increasing democratization of national politics, many liberals welcomed the GmbH as an institutional bulwark that might at least slow or even prevent a parallel democratization of the economy, a central element of the social democratic platform. At its annual meeting in 1888, the Deutsche Handelstag, a powerful business lobby, endorsed the GmbH legal form for just this reason, warning that with the joint-stock corporation model "it is scarcely possible, in the long run, to keep shares from running astray and into unknown hands." The GmbH, whose shares were not publicly tradable, would ensure the "socially desirable retention of such investments in the possession of the families...who founded the business." Indeed, almost from its inception, the GmbH served as the corporate form of choice for family trust funds, protecting what observers described as a natural "inequality of fate" in society. If they could not keep the state from becoming usurped by Social Democrats, at least they would keep capital from becoming socialized.[71]

More important than keeping capital in the right hands was that the GmbH offered an institutional vehicle with which to hide from public view one of the more objectionable aspects of modern industrial society, namely, its gaping inequalities. Hailed as an everyman's corporation that would finally make limited liability protections available to all, the GmbH in practice also extended the privilege of privacy to some of the largest and wealthiest corporations in the country—without, at the same time, denying them the privilege of limited liability. According to one tally from 1898, just 6.5 percent

Table 8.1 The GmbH by Size of Founding Capital, 1892–98

Founding Capital (marks)	Number of GmbH	Share of Total Capital Raised by GmbHs (%)
0–20,000	182 (10%)	0.3
20,001–50,000	342 (19%)	1.8
50,001–100,000	350 (19%)	4.1
101,000–200,000	295 (16%)	6.8
201,000–500,000	364 (20%)	19.7
501,000–1,000,000	186 (10%)	21.5
1,000,001–2,000,000	71 (4%)	16.4
2,000,001–3,000,000	24 (1%)	9.3
3,000,001–5,000,000	17 (<1%)	10.5
5,000,001–10,000,000	7 (<1%)	8.1
Over 10,000,000	1 (<1%)	1.5

Source: Calculated by the author based on data in Ernst Neukamp, "Die deutschen Gesellschaften mit beschränkter Haftung: Eine neue Gesellschaftsform," in *Zeitschrift für Volkswirtschaft, Socialpolitik, und Verwaltung. Organ der Gesellschaft Österreichischer Volkswirte*, edited by Eugen von Böhm-Bawerk, Karl Theodor von Inama-Sternegg, and Ernst von Plener (Vienna: Wilhelm Braumüller, 1899), 344–45. Percentages do not add up because of rounding error.

of the registered companies accounted for 41 percent of the capital invested, while another half made up just 6 percent of the total. Prior to the introduction of the GmbH, these inequities were made glaringly obvious and were institutionally echoed by a strictly enforced hierarchy of corporate forms. Now there was just one corporate form for all, and while this appeared to be in the spirit of the democratizing 1890s, it did not combat social and economic inequities but rather concealed them behind a cryptic four-letter acronym.[72]

That the GmbH should emerge as a bulwark of the liberal order is perhaps not surprising. What is surprising is how it had originally come about. The main lesson that Wilhelm Oechelhäuser had drawn from the crisis of 1873 was that the German Empire suffered from what he called "entrepreneurial promiscuity," especially the noxious practice of "converting" ordinary businesses into joint-stock corporations. He had spent the better part of the subsequent decade trying to create new legal and institutional mechanisms that would better safeguard the existing hierarchy of corporate forms. One of those mechanisms was the Joint Stock Corporation Act of 1884, which raised formidable new barriers to the joint-stock form and made it all but impossible for the little man to lay his hands on limited liability privileges again.

The other was the GmbH, which was supposed to expand or complement the existing menu of corporate forms to ensure that the little man did not run off to America in pursuit of limited liability privileges. Once it became a legal reality, however, the GmbH quickly took on a life of its own. More than that, it came to embody entrepreneurial promiscuity. "The variety of unique types and classes of GmbHs is extraordinarily large," the press opined, so large "that one marvels without reservation at the protean nature of this form of incorporation, which has found use in all areas of material and immaterial, business, spiritual, artistic, literary, public and private life." One could only "shake [one's] head over" it. And yet, to everyone's surprise, it did the job. As one member of the press concluded, the "hopes which the business world had placed in this new form of incorporation in general seem to have materialized."[73]

Epilogue

FORGETTING AMERICA

THE WORLD NEEDED to forget America, and fast. This thought preoccupied Max Weber as he returned to his hotel room at McFarland's Hotel and Café in Muskogee, a modest but rapidly growing settlement in what was at the time Indian Territory in eastern Oklahoma. Weber spent the day, September 28, 1904, touring the town and its vicinity, including the "utterly wild" forest and grasslands around the nearby Arkansas River, and he had the opportunity to speak at length about the region's history with local notables like Clarence B. Douglas, the editor of the *Muskogee Phoenix*, as well as two Native Americans, J. Blair Schoenfelt and J. George Wright, among others. What he learned was disturbing, but not altogether unexpected.

> The virgin forest's hour has struck even here. [O]ne does occasionally see groups of genuine old log cabins—those of the Indians recognizable by the colorful shawls and laundry hung out to dry—but also next to them quite modern wood-frame houses and cottages from the factory on stone foundations, from $500 and up, and next to them a large clearing planted with corn and cotton. Then there are large stretches of prairie, partly grazing land, partly again fields of cotton and corn. And suddenly it begins to smell like petroleum: one sees the tall Eiffel Tower–like structure of the drilling holes, right in the middle of the forest, and comes to a "town."... Tent camps of the workers, especially section hands for the numerous railroads under construction; "streets" in a natural state, usually doused with petroleum twice each summer to prevent dust, and smelling accordingly; wooden churches of at least 4–5 denominations (Muskogee had 4,000 inhabitants four years ago and now has 12,000, most of whom are Methodists).¹

It was really "too bad," Weber lamented. "In a year this place will look like Oklahoma [City], that is, like any other American city," and with "lightning speed everything that stands in the way [will be] crushed." Frederick Jackson

Turner, the Wisconsin historian who in 1893 described the "closing" of the American frontier, had been right. With the last "areas of free land...in the world vanishing," Weber opined, an exceptional era of "free and great development" had come to an end, and there would likely not be another "as long as the history of mankind shall last."[2]

This was bad news indeed. Weber knew just how important the frontier was to industrial modernity, or what he called the "modern economy."[3] At stake was not just the region's breathtaking natural beauty and mysticism or the apparent finitude of North America's natural resources and raw materials. The most worrisome part about the disappearing frontier, as Weber saw it, was how it had come to underwrite the social contract. In a world in which landed independence was widely considered the end of all toil and striving, the reward for accepting extraordinary sacrifice and change, land for settlement was foundational. It was what stood between order and chaos.[4]

The situation was particularly concerning for Weber's countrymen, the Germans. One of the reasons North America had long loomed large in the German imagination was that it was—allegedly—the only place in the world that was not already claimed and inhabited by other peoples. (One of the first observations Weber made as he rode the night train into Muskogee was that the area seemed all but "empty, with the exception of a single Indian fishing boat that I saw." Of course, the next day's events had him standing corrected.)[5] That the land was empty and that one could therefore "take possession of it peacefully," as historian Ernst Ludwig Brauns once put it, was crucial for the Germans, who, in contrast to the English or the French, lacked the pride and wherewithal to assert themselves forcefully over an Other. Compounding the problem, so Weber believed, was that the Germans abided by rather high standards of domesticity, not to mention a naive sense of idealism, which meant that they stood little chance of competing with others in the modern economy, least of all against less cultured peoples who were not so encumbered by "demands (*Ansprüche*) in living, both in a material and idealistic regard." All this narrowed their choice of frontiers, with only the American West remaining as a plausible destination for the proverbial German Völkerwanderer.[6]

To be sure, Weber had once been skeptical about these sorts of arguments. The first time he encountered them was in the early 1880s, when he was still a teenager, while sitting at the dinner table across from Friedrich Kapp.[7] A close confidante of Weber's father—the two men served together in the Reichstag—Kapp was then a frequent guest at the Weber home in Berlin, along with other friends and associates like Deutsche Bank director Georg Siemens and railroad financier Henry Villard. Much of the conversation at that time had revolved around US railroads, the West, and more generally America's exceptional place in German national life. This was a point that Kapp never failed to make, but in the 1880s he had been especially adamant about it because of growing public interest in the acquisition of new settler colonies in Africa, South America, and elsewhere in the world.[8] In his usual "fresh" and "rude" way, Kapp had excoriated the idea. No self-respecting emigrant would ever want to build a homestead in a tropical and disease-infested environment so at odds with "northern European" sensibilities. Even if colonies could be found in more agreeable climates (proposals were floated to colonize Hawaii or the Sandwich Islands), there was always the problem that the Germans would find themselves living and working alongside inferior peoples, with the inevitable result that "German labor is demeaned." In the Sandwich Islands, Kapp had explained in one of his speeches at the Reichstag, the Germans would likely work alongside Chinese immigrants. To succeed, they would have to shed their distinctive character, which "elevates them above the Chinese and the Blacks," if they did not "dissolve into the lesser developed race altogether."[9]

Weber, who had listened intently to Kapp's broadsides against non-American colonial spaces, later remembered not quite knowing what to make of them. Having come of age in 1870s and 1880s Berlin, the capital of a recently unified German Empire, he had absorbed a healthy dose of national pride at a young age and in some ways shared the German American's chauvinism. At the same time, he had found the contempt for the nation's colonial undertakings in Africa off-putting and "one-sided." Colonies were markers of national greatness—why should the German Empire be denied its own? And what exactly made North America so unique that the Germans could not find happiness anywhere else? As Weber put it to a friend in November 1884, shortly after Kapp passed away,

> [Kapp's] opinions—which were so arresting at the time that I would not have dared to disagree with him, even if I had been permitted to do so at my young age—often stirred objection within me. Usually they were of such wide-ranging import that they preoccupied my thoughts for some time, until I would conclude that there was a certain one-sidedness to the argument, which happened frequently. I think that he considered this kind of conversation to be a very stimulating provocation for younger people; in my case, anyway, my disagreement... prompted me to look up additional information.[10]

Weber had meant what he had said about finding more information. He would devote the next decade or so to studying the many outrageous claims that were so blithely tossed around at his father's dinner parties, starting with the economic history of corporations and, in his postdoctoral thesis (*Habitilation*), the agrarian origins of private property and law. Both had been subjects of heated debate at the Weber home in light of the constant controversies surrounding Henry Villard's brief stint as the president of the Northern Pacific Railway Company, one of America's largest corporations and a key purveyor of homesteads and private property in the West.[11] Weber's subsequent decision in 1893 to join the Pan-German League, an organization of middle-class intellectuals, businesspeople, and politicians who were committed to protecting the interests of "Germandom everywhere on earth," suggested that he remained wary of American exceptionalism. Tellingly, the Pan-Germans aimed to advance German interests and hegemony in eastern Europe as an alternative to a heretofore futile settler colonial project in Africa and elsewhere overseas.[12]

Equally telling was the fact that, in 1897, Weber quit the Pan-German League again. The reasons for changing his mind were many and complicated, but a key one was that he had developed doubts that the European "East" could ever replace the American West as a site of German power and settlement.[13] During the 1890s, he had had the opportunity to study up close the social and economic conditions in Prussia's easternmost provinces, and what he had found there had given him pause. While German farmers appeared to be leaving the region en masse, mostly for industrial centers like Breslau (Wrocław), Danzig (Gdańsk), and Berlin, and of course America, Polish day laborers and smallholders were arriving in even greater numbers to take their place. This, Weber had thought, was disturbing. It was also not surprising to him, probably the inevitable outcome of economic competition between two "races" in vastly different states of cultural development. Now echoing Kapp's chauvinist remarks with respect to Black people and the Chinese, Weber explained that the Poles were "displacing" the Germans "not despite of but because of [their] lower physiognomic and spiritual habitus." "The Polish smallholder gains ground because he feeds directly, as it were, on the grass of his pasture," he told an audience of colleagues and students at the University of Freiburg in 1895. The Germans, meanwhile, were gripped by a "dim, half-conscious urge to emigrate to distant lands," mostly America, which was regrettable but understandable. He regarded it a "mass-psychological" phenomenon peculiar to the Germans, adding that "whoever questions" the Pomeranian peasant's decision to head for America "does not understand the magic of freedom."[14]

Kapp, then, had been right all along about America's exceptionalism (or so Weber concluded), which was disastrous for Germany given that America—if Turner and other frontier pessimists were correct—ceased to be what it once was. The trip to Muskogee, Oklahoma, in 1904 confirmed Weber's worst fears, but by that time he was already contemplating alternative solutions. The Germans needed to forget America—not just the place itself but, more important, the underlying idea. If landed independence continued to be regarded as the end to all toil in the world, then Germany was almost certainly doomed. But what if something else could offer people meaning and purpose, something that did not require access to endless free and empty land? What seemed to be catching Weber's attention in this regard was the Protestant Reformation of the sixteenth century, a time when, as he saw it, people had wrestled at length with the meaning and purpose of their toil on earth. Leading reformers of church doctrine like the Calvinists had reminded fellow Christians that God had put man on earth to work, not to seek escape into leisure and idleness. What mattered was not the fruits of labor, but labor itself: Work, rather than the means to an end, was reimagined as a calling (*Beruf*).[15]

This idea, which Weber would associate with a "Protestant ethic," became a source of great fascination and speculation for him. In his first magnum opus, *The Protestant Ethic and the Spirit of Capitalism* (1905), he described it as nothing less than the ideological bedrock of "modern capitalism."[16] In contrast to previous iterations of capitalism, which Weber conceded had been around "for three millennia" and could be found everywhere in the world, "from China, India, Babylon, Greece, Rome, Florence, into the present," this modern capitalism did not depend on the desire for emancipation from work through the accumulation of wealth and power, and in particular through the "arrival in the safe harbor of the landed estate (*Fideikommißbesitz*)." It depended, rather, on the "restless striving" for the sake of striving itself: Work, and nothing else, was the purpose of life, the source of satisfaction and contentment, the path to self-actualization.[17]

Modern capitalism was a godsend for at least two reasons. On the one hand, it could preserve the "capitalist form of organization" for generations to come, regardless of the fate of the frontier, and therefore prevent a catastrophic war and revolution. On the other hand, Germany seemed to be a most fertile ground for modern capitalism, given that the historic roots of the Protestant ethic lay in Reformation Germany. Forgetting America might be easier for the Germans than one would be inclined to think. All they had to do was remember their past.

As it happened, the Germans struggled mightily to forget America. In the years that followed the publication of *The Protestant Ethic*, America—both as an actual place and as an idea—remained an inescapable facet of everyday life in the German Empire. A constant stream of cultural and political commentary in newspapers, feuilletons, parlor magazines, and novels kept the magic and mysticism alive, with Karl May's wildly popular Wild West dime novels leading the way. Correspondence with émigrés and emigrants in the United States also continued unabated and arguably grew more voluminous still in light of the continued improvements made to transatlantic travel and communication. The telegraph and the telephone, though still novel technologies at the time, were beginning to offer still more avenues for staying in touch. Entrepreneurs, industrialists, academics, activists, adventurers, and tourists shuttled back and forth across the Atlantic as never before. By this time, the German Empire and the United States had become so intimately connected, economically, socially, culturally, intellectually, and in manifold other ways, that any effort to disentangle them within the span of a few years seemed all but impossible and certainly would have defied all historical precedent. And indeed, not even two catastrophic world wars, in which they were cast as bitter enemies, could sever the ties between these two budding nations. Throughout the twentieth century, and arguably into the next, America continued to fascinate. It was an "irresistible empire" to some and an evil one to others, yet for all Germans it was a place to think with in their dealings with the challenges and opportunities presented by successive modernities.[18]

Some things did change, of course. For one, the United States ceased to be an all-consuming destination for German emigrants (though it retained its attraction to German capital).[19] Already in 1895, just two years after Turner announced his frontier thesis in Chicago, the number of German immigrants registered by US authorities had dwindled to a fraction of what it had been just a decade earlier. Never again would emigration from German states to America attain the great heights it had in the nineteenth century.[20]

For another, the German Empire of the early twentieth century was a very different place compared with a generation before. Years of record-setting growth had turned it into one of the largest and technologically most advanced industrialized economies in the world. By 1900, Germany had long passed the stage of simply catching up, having instead begun to blaze its own trail by leading the world in the so-called Second Industrial Revolution, a new phase in development that saw steel, chemicals, and electricity displace iron and textiles as the most dynamic sectors of the world economy. Cities like Berlin, Hamburg, and Munich were emerging as megametropolises in their own right, boasting all the dazzling and disturbing features that distinguished the modern urban space of this period and spearheading a new era of progressive urban planning and avant-garde culture and entertainment. As a case study of contemporary industrial modernity, moreover, the sprawling metallurgical complex of the Ruhr valley was arguably second to none. It was not just the built environment that so resembled contemporary Pittsburgh or Lowell, Massachusetts, but also, more important, the people who lived and worked there. America had long been a source of insight because its people were so extraordinarily diverse, but the workforce that toiled in the Ruhr valley's mines and furnaces easily rivaled that of any American city or mining camp in its social, cultural, and linguistic heterogeneity. In general, while the United States continued to hold the title of the world's leading destination for immigrants, the German Empire was no longer so far behind. It had emerged as an immigrant country in its own right, with hundreds of thousands from across central Europe searching for opportunities in its cities, factories, and mines. Amid these developments, America gradually shed its former function as a window into the future. It no doubt continued to inspire, mesmerize, and frighten, but the implications were growing less existential as time went on, because modernity had arrived in Germany. Advice on how to carry oneself and succeed in this new environment was no longer so necessary.[21]

Even with respect to the question of the meaning and purpose underwriting industrial modernity, the idea of America—landed independence as a reward for a life of toil—eventually lost its salience and began giving way to something resembling Weber's idea of the calling: work for work's sake. In this case, however, the change was anything but gradual. Well into the twentieth century, Weber's modern capitalism was ridiculed as wishful thinking, even utopianism.[22] Critics from across the political spectrum lambasted it as bourgeois hypocrisy and arrogance, as if the back-breaking labor forced on the masses by the industrial economy could ever be anything other than a source of hardship and suffering. The Nazis understood how to exploit the widespread indignation over the idea, placing the cynical slogan "Work sets you free" (*Arbeit macht frei*) above the gates of some of their concentration camps, like Auschwitz-Birkenau, where countless men and women and children were worked to death. The message was clear: Empire was not coincidental to modern industrialism, as someone like Weber, a self-declared "pure bourgeois," liked to argue. As the Nazis saw it, the quest for "living space" (*Lebensraum*) was merely an honest piece of industrial policy, even when—and perhaps especially when—it was pursued with genocidal ferocity.[23]

Ultimately, it was Nazi Germany's total defeat and the catastrophic destruction that was wrought on the country during the war that paved the way for a Weberian ethic. Amid the search for normalcy and the grinding labors of reconstruction, a nation of perpetrators sought salvation. Work was how Germans—at least those living in the West—believed they could assume their place among the civilized once again. "I never paid any attention to politics...I never belonged to a party...always worked, never skipped work," West Germans remembered about life in the Federal Republic in the 1940s and 1950s. "Live respectably, quietly, hard-working, modestly." And "Always saving. Not going to bars very much, or not at all. At the beginning we didn't allow ourselves any vacation." Drawing on such testimony, historians have concluded that in West Germany, "more than in any other developed country, life values marched hand-in-hand with the demands of a capitalist economy."[24]

As it turned out, this happy union of values and economic growth did not last. Already in the sixties the West German government began entering agreements with Italy, Greece, and Turkey to bring foreign "guestworkers" to the country who would do the kind of difficult work that West Germans no longer wished to do. Yet the dream of landed independence, the central tenet of what "America" had long been, did not re-emerge. What exactly came after Weber's modern capitalism is difficult to say. What is clear is that it is a different story, the story of yet another iteration of industrial modernity, that of the twentieth and twenty-first centuries. The migrant's spirit as it existed in the preceding period ceased to hold sway. America remained a place to think and wrestle with, but it had long ceded its privileged place at the heart of the German imaginary.

While writing this book, I often wrestled with the question of whether to end on a note about Max Weber. There seemed to be a risk that by invoking this larger-than-life intellectual in a concluding chapter, I would leave readers with the impression that the history recounted here matters for no other reason than the fact that it inspired Max Weber. That is decidedly not the case. *The Migrant's Spirit* is not a story about Weber and his ideas. Rather, it is a story about the millions of men and women in Germany who, like Weber, turned to a place called America to think through the implications of an emerging industrial modernity—and the unexpected historical trajectory that their emerging nation was put on as a consequence. Weber's fraught relationship with a figure like Friedrich Kapp, the proverbial "citizen of two worlds,"

whom Weber both looked up to and fervently disagreed with, exemplifies the complicated dynamics of transatlantic cultural exchange that the preceding pages have been concerned with.

Still, I would be remiss if I did not admit that this book owes a little more to Max Weber than a compelling allegory. In key respects, *The Migrant's Spirit* also thinks with Weber. One of Weber's many insights, and in my view a major reason why his works continue to resonate, is that he took seriously people's desire to always do the right thing—by themselves and by others. Although he acknowledged the importance to history of other human preoccupations, like greed, he believed that nothing exceeded the power of the human yearning to be good and do good. This was why modern capitalism could feel like such an all-powerful and inescapable "cosmos." Unlike previous iterations of capitalism, the modern variety was rooted in humanity's strength of character, in its abiding commitment to an ethical way of life—not in its weaknesses and moral failures.

I have found this insight to be quite useful for understanding the history explored in this book. To begin with, it helps us to appreciate the profound hesitation and skepticism that prevented so many contemporaries in Germany from fully embracing the industrial regime of production that modernizers had been championing for years. As historians continue to remind us, this hesitation had little to do with the material realities of the new economy. Genuine Luddites were few and far between in the nineteenth century, as were those who sought to simply freeze time in place. Most contemporaries were just as mesmerized by the pathbreaking ideas, ingenious institutions, and awesome technologies of the day as the champions of progress, and despite the fact that the links between these novelties and the growing miseries and inequities wrought by them were all too plain to see. Having resigned themselves to the idea that change was inevitable and wishing nothing more than to play their part in this great drama of human progress, these contemporaries merely wondered how they should go about it.

The question was not just a practical or logistical one (although that was an issue as well). It was, above all, a matter concerning morality. Longstanding norms and principles had to be either adjusted or set aside. Once again, the issue was not *whether* this should be done, but *how*. As I have tried to show in each chapter of this book, much of this new economy required contemporaries to not just tweak the existing system of values but also demolish it altogether—to act and think in ways that were diametrically at odds with what they once knew to be true and virtuous. As the poet Heinrich Heine put it,

> It's a topsy-turvy world indeed:
> Upon our heads we walk!
> Hunters by the score are shot
> By woodcocks that they stalk.
>
> The calves are roasting cooks today;
> The horses ride the men;
> The Catholic Owl comes out for light
> And a free school regimen.
>
> Let us not swim against the stream,
> My brothers—a fruitless thing!
> Let's climb the hill above Tempelhof
> And cry "Long live the king!"[25]

What makes these lines such a perceptive commentary on the zeitgeist is their levity and the absurdity that is implied by this. Heine understood that the challenge of modernity went far beyond a world turned upside down. Real trouble arose from the pretense that long-standing truths and values could somehow be dispensed with on a whim, as though they carried no weight at all. Even those who welcomed the changes in question often found this to be a heavy lift. Like Albert Krause, the emigrant who touted freedom at every turn, yet was repulsed, at the same time, by his own impudent behavior, they struggled mightily to pretend that right should now be wrong without the nagging feeling that they might lose their moral compass somewhere along the way.

The idiom of progress, which was so often proffered as a palliative to such concerns, never quite succeeded in delivering on that promise. Progress justified change by casting it as the individual's triumph over past falsehoods and ignorance.[26] But in asking people to condescend to the past, the idiom of progress made it difficult, if not altogether impossible, to access what was still a vital source of meaning and belonging. Becoming modern under the aegis of progress required forgetting a good portion of who one was and where one came from—a profoundly alienating and disorienting experience, as was captured so brilliantly in Caspar David Friedrich's iconic painting *Wanderer Above the Sea of Fog*. Such feelings of alienation were made all the worse by the fact that so much about the emerging industrial modernity of this period had its roots abroad, among rival peoples like the English or the French. Local proponents of modernization tried but largely failed to scrub institutions like the joint-stock corporation, the freedom of labor and enterprise (*Gewerbefreiheit*), or the breadwinner–homemaker household of these foreign associations.

Embracing progress in Germany consequently implied not just leaving behind a version of oneself but also associating more closely with French or English culture.

These shortcomings of the progress idiom are important for understanding why contemporaries' intensifying engagement with America after midcentury—what I have taken to calling the migrant's spirit—might have proven so consequential in comparison. For one, through the experiences of the diaspora in North America, contemporaries were able to rediscover many of the foundational institutions of an emergent industrial modernity, from the idea of free labor to that of the home, in a way that appeared distinct from English or French culture: As the Prussian consul J. J. Sturz put it in 1875, "[it] helped us become young again."[27] For another, listening to advice from America, and adopting what might be regarded as "American" ideas and practices, implied far less of a break, and much more continuity, with whatever had come before. America's identification in this period with a specifically German-national past, present, and future meant that in becoming American, as so many emigrants were embarrassed to admit, one did not necessarily stop being German. This continuity, however imaginary or specious it might have been, could provide a powerful form of assurance to those who were willing and eager to partake in the transformations of the day but worried about losing themselves in the process.

When I first began researching the great migrations of German peoples across the Atlantic, I was convinced that I would end up with a story about the cosmopolitan and transnational aspects of German history. Evidently, the exact opposite was the case. There was, it seems to me, very little that was genuinely cosmopolitan or transnational about Germany's encounter with America, which owed so much of its scale and intensity to the idea that those who went there never actually stepped beyond the pale of the nation.[28] The unhappy lesson here is that exchange across cultures is most meaningful and consequential when it is not actually understood as such. Simply put, people do not trust strangers, least of all when it comes to questions of right and wrong. They prefer the familiarity of kin.

The good news is that kinship is not a fixed category.[29] By most measures, emigrants in America were strangers to the families, friends, and communities they left behind in Europe, especially with the passage of time. That it was nevertheless plausible to pretend they were not may be read as encouraging. One wonders about other dialogues that may be in the offing.

The Migrant's Spirit: How Industrial Modernity Came to the German Lands. Benjamin P. Hein, Oxford University Press. © Oxford University Press 2025. DOI: 10.1093/9780197831052.003.0010

Endnotes

INTRODUCTION

1. As Karl Marx and Friedrich Engels observed in *The German Ideology* (1845–46), "hitherto men have constantly made up for themselves false conceptions about themselves, about what they are and what they ought to be.... The phantoms of their brains have got out of their hands." Nowhere was this more true than in Germany, they argued, where people lived "in the realm of the 'pure spirit.'" In proposing a new, materialist conception of history, the authors promised to "liberate [the Germans] from the chimeras, the ideas, dogmas, imaginary beings under the yoke of which they are pining away." C. J. Arthur, ed., *Karl Marx and Friedrich Engels: The German Ideology, Part One* (New York: International Publishers, 1970), 37, 60.
2. The Schlendrian was a shorthand for traditionalism, backwardness, indolence, or self-satisfied contentment (*Behaglichkeit*). For example, Max Weber referred to the "traditionalist *Schlendrian*" to describe a premodern, "precapitalist" mindset. Max Weber, *Die Protestantische Ethik und der Geist des Kapitalismus*, 3rd ed., ed. Dirk Kaesler (Munich: C.H. Beck, 2010), esp. 84–87. For an introduction to the period of rapid economic growth that began in the 1850s and 1860s, see Frank B. Tipton, *A History of Modern Germany Since 1815* (Berkeley: University of California Press, 2003), 90–99; and Cornelius Torp, "The Great Transformation: German Economy and Society, 1850–1914," in *The Oxford Handbook of Modern German History*, ed. Helmut Walser Smith (Oxford: Oxford University Press, 2011).
3. Germany's industrial revolution is one of the best studied in Europe. Still, as Richard Tilly and Michael Kopsidis observe in a recent assessment of the literature, important puzzles remain. For example, while there is general agreement about the crucial importance of Germany's comparatively large and skilled labor force as a driver of economic growth, scholars continue to debate how exactly this labor force was extracted from its original artisan milieu and mobilized for the emerging

industrial regime of production. Richard H. Tilly and Michael Kopsidis, *From Old Regime to Industrial State: A History of German Industrialization from the Eighteenth Century to World War I* (Chicago: University of Chicago Press, 2020), esp. 1–10, 137–49.

4. Recent years have seen a significant growth in scholarship on this topic. For an introduction, see Sebastian Conrad and Jürgen Osterhammel, eds., *An Emerging Modern World, 1750–1870* (Cambridge, MA: Belknap Press of Harvard University Press, 2018); Adam McKeown, "Global Migration, 1846–1940," *Journal of World History* 15, no. 2 (2004), 155–189; and Jürgen Osterhammel, *The Transformation of the World: A Global History of the Nineteenth Century* (Princeton: Princeton University Press, 2014), 117–66. On "classic" emigrant nations in Europe, see James Belich, *Replenishing the Earth: The Settler Revolution and the Rise of the Angloworld* (Oxford: Oxford University Press, 2009); David Blackbourn, *Germany in the World: A Global History, 1500–2000* (New York: Liveright, 2023); Mark Choate, *Emigrant Nation: The Making of Italy Abroad* (Cambridge, MA: Harvard University Press, 2008); H. Glenn Penny, *German History Unbound: From 1750 to the Present* (Cambridge: Cambridge University Press, 2022); Nancy L. Green and François Weil, eds., *Citizenship and Those Who Leave: The Politics of Emigration and Expatriation* (Urbana: University of Illinois Press, 2007); and Tara Zahra, *The Great Departure: Mass Migration from Eastern Europe and the Making of the Free World* (New York: W. W. Norton, 2016). Similar dynamics have been observed outside Europe; see, for example, Sunil S. Amrith, *Crossing the Bay of Bengal: The Furies of Nature and the Fortunes of Migrants* (Cambridge, MA: Harvard University Press, 2013). On diaspora as an analytical concept, see the discussion in Dirk Hoerder, "The German-Language Diasporas: A Survey, Critique, Interpretation," *Diaspora* 11, no. 1 (2002), 7–44; and Pieter Judson, "When Is a Diaspora Not a Diaspora? Rethinking Nation-Centered Narratives About Germans in Habsburg East Central Europe," in *The Heimat Abroad: The Boundaries of Germanness*, ed. Krista O'Donnell et al. (Ann Arbor: University of Michigan Press, 2005).

5. The English historian Arnold Toynbee is widely credited with popularizing the term *Industrial Revolution* in the 1880s. The concept's analytical value continues to be questioned. Maxine Berg and Pat Hudson, "Rehabilitating the Industrial Revolution," *The Economic History Review* 45, no. 1 (1992), 24–50; Toni Pierenkemper, *Umstrittene Revolutionen: Industrialisierung im 19. Jahrhundert* (Frankfurt am Main: Fischer Verlag, 1996).

6. How and why people suddenly changed their minds in this moment remains a subject of debate to this day. Some scholars contend that it was simply a matter of time before outdated norms, values, and perspectives would give way to new ones; the shift in the 1850s and 1860s was in this sense the culmination of decades of efforts at persuasion, as well as a necessary response to structural pressures at the regional, continental, and global levels. Another line of argumentation posits that the nationalization of politics in the wake of the Revolution of 1848, as well as the

subsequent unification of the German Empire in this period, was interpreted by contemporaries as a break with the past and a point of departure that required rethinking old norms and traditions. I tend to agree with the claim about the importance of nationalism as a vehicle and driver of the observed cultural shift. For an overview of the extensive literature on this topic, see Tilly and Kopsidis, *Old Regime*; and Ulrich Pfister and Nikolaus Wolf, eds., *An Economic History of the First German Unification: State Formation and Economic Development in a European Perspective* (London: Routledge, 2023), 1–16. See also the discussion in Yair Mintzker, *The Defortification of the German City: 1689–1866* (Cambridge: Cambridge University Press, 2012), 226–29, 235–55.

7. To be sure, not everyone found these concepts useful. Another commonplace approach was to assign historical agency to progress itself. Mintzker, *Defortification*, 244–51.

8. As Albert Hirschman puts it, contemporaries were confronted with an "endogenous process" and not an "independently conceived, insurgent ideology," as some observers, most famously Karl Marx, supposed. Consequently, it was often quite difficult to distinguish the old from the new, an issue that was compounded by the fact that the process of industrialization did not unfold uniformly across the region. As was true elsewhere in Europe, some areas experienced rapid transformations in a short period of time while others saw only gradual changes or even none at all. Still one of the best accounts of this regional aspect of industrialization is Sidney Pollard, *Peaceful Conquest: The Industrialization of Europe, 1760–1970* (Oxford: Oxford University Press, 1981). Albert O. Hirschman, *The Passions and the Interests: Political Arguments for Capitalism Before Its Triumph*, ed. Jeremy Adelman (Princeton: Princeton University Press, 2013), 4. More recently, see Mintzker, *Defortification*, 255.

9. Werner Sombart, *Die Genesis des Kapitalismus*, Vol. 1, Der moderne Kapitalismus (Leipzig: Duncker & Humblot, 1902), 378–90, here 388. Max Weber would make a similar observation in his own exegesis of capitalism. See Weber, *Die Protestantische Ethik*, 77–78, 88–90.

10. To be sure, this did not mean that the decision was a straightforward one. To the contrary, the implications of embracing factory work or investing in novel industries always extended beyond the material realm, raising various cultural, moral, and political concerns. Established norms and social taboos had to be tweaked or tossed out altogether, and quite often vices had to be turned into virtues (and vice versa). It would therefore be difficult to understand the mobilization of German society, whether it was labor or capital, through market forces alone. Hirschman, *Passions*; Klaus Tenfelde, "Konflikt und Organisation in einigen deutschen Bergbaugebieten 1867–1872," *Geschichte und Gesellschaft* 3, no. 2 (1977), 212–35; Toni Pierenkemper, "Historische Arbeitsmarkforschung: Vorüberlegungen zu einem Forschungsprogramm," in *Historische Arbeitsmarkforschung: Entstehung, Entwicklung und Probleme der Vermarktung von Arbeitskraft*, ed. Toni Pierenkemper

and Richard Tilly (Göttingen: Vandenhoeck & Ruprecht, 1982), esp. 23–29. More recently, see Richard Biernacki, *The Fabrication of Labour: Germany and Britain, 1640–1914* (Berkeley: University of California Press, 1995); and Jan de Vries, *The Industrious Revolution: Consumer Behavior and the Household Economy, 1650 to the Present* (Cambridge: Cambridge University Press, 2008).

11. The rise of the United States as the single most important destination for German emigrants marked an end to a previous geographical pattern of migration that had seen people from the region depart for destinations as wide-ranging as the Habsburg Balkans, the Volga basin in Russia, or New World colonies in Australia and South America. Detailed statistics can be found in Farley Ward Grubb, *German Immigration and Servitude in America, 1709–1920* (London: Routledge, 2013), esp. 17–43; Dirk Hoerder, *Cultures in Contact: World Migrations in the Second Millennium* (Durham, NC: Duke University Press, 2002), 221–27; and Marianne Wokeck, "The Flow and Composition of German Immigration to Philadelphia 1772–1775," *Pennsylvania Magazine of History and Biography* 105, no. 3 (1981): 249–78. On the nineteenth century, see the overview in Jochen Oltmer, *Migration im 19. und 20. Jahrhundert* (Munich: R. Oldenbourg Verlag, 2010), 1–15. On the uncle-in-America trope, see Franz Schnabel, *Erfahrungswissenschaften und Technik*, vol. 3, Deutsche Geschichte im neunzehnten Jahrhundert (Freiburg: Herder, 1954), 361.

12. Peasant literacy—and the consequent ability of broad segments of the population to communicate with emigrants abroad—is perhaps the most important distinguishing factor between Germany and other migration-prone regions in Europe, such as Ireland, Italy, and many Habsburg and Russian territories in eastern Europe. According to one estimate, male illiteracy in Germany (excluding Austria) was estimated to be as low as 2 percent in 1875, in contrast to Austria (42 percent), Italy (52 percent), Spain (63 percent), and Russia (63 percent). Other regions, such as Sweden or Switzerland, boasted rates comparable to those in Germany (1 percent and 6 percent, respectively). Eric J. Hobsbawm, *The Age of Capital, 1848–1875* (New York: Vintage Books, 1975), 43.

13. On the volume of German migrant correspondence in this period, see the introductory remarks in Wolfgang J. Helbich et al., eds., *Briefe aus Amerika: Deutsche Auswanderer schreiben aus der Neuen Welt, 1830–1930* (Munich: C. H. Beck, 1988), 31–32; Jürgen Macha et al., eds., *Wir verlangen nicht mehr nach Deutschland: Auswandererbriefe und Dokumente der Sammlung Joseph Scheben (1825–1938)*, Sprachgeschichte des Deutschen in Nordamerika: Quellen und Studien (Frankfurt am Main: Peter Lang, 2003); and Roland Paul, *"Hier hat man ein viel besseres Leben wie in Deutschland": Briefe pfälzischer Auswanderer aus Nordamerika (1733–1899)* (Kaiserslautern: Institut für Pfälzische Geschichte und Volkskunde, 2008). More recently, see Penny, *Unbound*, 97–140. On similar correspondence in other periods and national contexts, see Charlotte Erickson, *Leaving England: Essays on British Emigration in the Nineteenth Century* (Ithaca, NY: Cornell

University Press, 1994); David Fitzpatrick, "Irish Emigration and the Art of the Letter-Writing," in *Letters Across Borders: The Epistolary Practices of International Migrants*, ed. Bruce S. Elliott et al. (New York: Palgrave Macmillan, 2006); Bruce S. Elliott et al., eds., *Letters Across Borders: The Epistolary Practices of International Migrants* (New York: Palgrave Macmillan, 2006); and Karl-Peter Krauss, *Quellen zu den Lebenswelten deutscher Migranten im Königreich Ungarn im 18. und frühen 19. Jahrhundert*, Schriftenreihe des Instituts für Donauschwäbische Geschichte und Landeskunde (Stuttgart: Franz Steiner Verlag, 2015). The comparative statistics for Britain cited here are from Heinrich von Stephan, *Geschichte der Preußischen Post von ihren Ursprüngen bis auf die Gegenwart* (Berlin: Königlich Geheime Oberhofbuchdruckerei, 1859), 653.

14. The phrase is from Alexander Schmidt, *Reisen in die Moderne: Der Amerika-Diskurs des deutschen Bürgertums vor dem ersten Weltkrieg im europäischen Vergleich* (Berlin: Akademie Verlag, 1997). See also Jens-Uwe Guettel, *German Expansionism, Imperial Liberalism and the United States, 1776–1945* (Cambridge: Cambridge University Press, 2012); Christof Hamann et al., eds, *Amerika und die deutschsprachige Literatur nach 1848, Migration—kultureller Austausch—frühe Globalisierung* (Bielefeld: transcript Verlag, 2009); Wolfgang Johannes Helbich, "Land der unbegrenzten Möglichkeiten? Das Amerika-Bild der deutschen Auswanderer im 19. Jahrhundert," in *Deutschland und der Westen im 19. und 20. Jahrhundert*, ed. Jürgen Elvert and Michael Salewski (Stuttgart: Franz Steiner Verlag, 1997); and Andrew Zimmerman, *Alabama in Africa: Booker T. Washington, the German Empire, and the Globalization of the New South* (Princeton: Princeton University Press, 2010). It is worth noting that cultural exchange also went in the other direction: see Daniel T. Rodgers, *Atlantic Crossings: Social Politics in a Progressive Age* (Cambridge, MA: Belknap Press of Harvard University Press, 1998).

15. The negative perceptions of North America and emigrants are discussed in Chapter 1. As Bernard Bailyn puts it in his study of North Atlantic commerce in the seventeenth century, "colonial merchants were [regarded] inferior to Britishers" and "important only insofar as they contributed to...England's welfare." Daniel Rodgers and Victoria De Grazia find that such attitudes continued to prevail well into the nineteenth century and even the twentieth. Bernard Bailyn, *The New England Merchants in the Seventeenth Century* (Cambridge, MA: Harvard University Press, 1979), 166; Victoria De Grazia, *Irresistible Empire: America's Advance Through Twentieth-Century Europe* (Cambridge, MA: Belknap Press of Harvard University Press, 2005); Rodgers, *Atlantic Crossings*.

16. For example, see Oscar Handlin, *The Uprooted: The Epic Story of the Great Migrations That Made the American People* (Boston: Little, Brown, 1951); and Philip A. M. Taylor, *The Distant Magnet: European Emigration to the U.S.A* (London: Eyre & Spottiswoode, 1971).

17. It goes without saying that this founding ethos was a gift to many advocates of settler colonial projects, especially in the Americas. And indeed, if settler colonialism

is a structure more than an event, as Patrick Wolfe argues, then the myth-history of the people's migrations as it was conceived in this period can be understood as the ideological scaffolding of said structure. Patrick Wolfe, "Settler Colonialism and the Elimination of the Native," *Journal of Genocide Research* 8, no. 4 (2006), 387–409. "Spirit of migration..." and "prepared the stage" in Friedrich Schiller, "Ueber Völkerwanderung, Kreuzzüge, und Mittelalter," in *Kleinere prosaische Schriften: Aus mehrern Zeitschriften, vom Verfasser selbst gesammelt und verbessert. Erster Theil* (Leipzig: Siegfried Lebrecht Crusius, 1792), 387, 394.

18. On Germany's internalization of the emigrant in America in this period, see Guettel, *German Expansionism*; Bradley Naranch, "Inventing the Auslandsdeutsche," in *Germany's Colonial Pasts*, ed. Eric Ames et al. (Lincoln: University of Nebraska Press, 2005), 21–40; and Susanne Zantop, *Colonial Fantasies: Conquest, Family, and Nation in Precolonial Germany* (Durham, NC: Duke University Press, 1997). Citing the global dispersion of people of German linguistic and cultural background, H. Glenn Penny has argued for a wholesale reimagining of the boundaries of German history. Penny, *Unbound*.

19. "Dark art" in Immanuel Kant, *Anthropologie in pragmatischer Hinsicht*, ed. Wolfgang Becker (Stuttgart: Reclam, 2017), 269.

20. In a little-known pamphlet from 1875, Prussian consul and diplomat J. J. Sturz reflected on the positive influences on Germany of the diaspora in the Americas. "Had there not been an emigration," he wrote, "and had there not been a consequent backflow of technical experiences and practices, indeed of economic and *political* concepts, then truly we would not be where we are today... in this respect the emigration was the greatest blessing for Germany: it helped us become young again" (emphasis in the original). What Sturz seemed to be suggesting here is that experiences abroad helped the German people rediscover old concepts and institutions that they had long dismissed—in other words, to "[help] us become young again." Geheimes Staatsarchiv Preußischer Kulturbesitz, I HA, Rep 120, C XIII 20, Nr. 1, Bd. 9, "Die deutsche und die chinesische Aus- und Rückwanderung in ihrer Bedeutung für das Deutsche Reich," 1875.

21. Friedrich List is a good example of the kind of cultural exchange related to industrial modernity that this book is concerned with, but his story has already been recounted in detail elsewhere. This book pays attention to lesser-known figures whose efforts to introduce American insights to Germany were arguably even more consequential. "Higher perspective..." in Friedrich List, *Grundlinien einer politischen Ökonomie und andere Beiträge der Amerikanischen Zeit, 1825-1832*, vol. 2, ed. Wilhelm Notz, Friedrich List: Schriften, Reden, Briefe (Berlin: Reimar Hobbing, 1931), 41. Still one of the best biographies of List is Paul Gehring, *Friedrich List: Jugend- und Reifejahre, 1789–1825* (Tübingen: J. C. B. Mohr [Paul Siebeck], 1964).

22. Blackbourn, *Germany in the World*, esp. parts 1 and 2; Lars Maischak, *German Merchants in the Nineteenth Century Atlantic* (Washington, DC: German

Historical Institute, 2013); Ulrich Pfister, "Germany's Transition from a Post-Malthusian to a Modern Growth Regime, 1860s to 1880s," in *An Economic History of the First German Unification: State Formation and Economic Development in a European Perspective*, ed. Ulrich Pfister and Nikolaus Wolf (New York: Routledge, 2023); Steven Press, *Blood and Diamonds: Germany's Imperial Ambitions in Africa* (Cambridge, MA: Harvard University Press, 2021); Cornelius Torp, *Die Herausforderung der Globalisierung: Wirtschaft und Politik in Deutschland 1860–1914* (Göttingen: Vandenhoeck & Ruprecht, 2005); and Jutta Wimmler and Klaus Weber, eds., *Globalized Peripheries: Central Europe and the Atlantic World, 1680–1860* (Woodbridge, Suffolk: Boydell Press, 2020). See also the case studies by Hartmut Berghoff, *Zwischen Kleinstadt und Weltmarkt: Hohner und die Harmonika 1857–1961: Unternehmensgeschichte als Gesellschaftsgeschichte* (Paderborn: Ferdinand Schöningh, 1997); and Ralf Richter and Jochen Streb, "Catching-Up and Falling Behind: Knowledge Spillover from American to German Machine Toolmakers," *The Journal of Economic History* 71, no. 4 (2011), 1006–31.

23. For example, see Patrick O'Brien, "Agriculture and the Industrial Revolution," *The Economic History Review* 30, no. 1 (1977), 166–81. More recently, see Pfister, "Transition," 77–95; and Tilly and Kopsidis, *Old Regime*, 59–67. Echoing nineteenth-century critics of imperialism, like Rosa Luxembourg, Patrick Wolfe writes that "the Industrial Revolution, misleadingly figuring in popular consciousness as an autochthonous metropolitan phenomenon, required colonial land and labour to produce its raw materials just as centrally as it required metropolitan factories and an industrial proletariat to process them, whereupon the colonies were again required as a market." Wolfe, "Settler Colonialism," 394.

24. Charles Maier describes an "agrarian regime" that became hegemonic between 1770 and 1890, providing many of the intellectual impulses for modernization. The quote is from Manuel Belgrano's *Correo de Comercio de Buenos Aires* (1810–11) and is originally cited in Charles S. Maier, *Once Within Borders. Territories of Power, Wealth, and Belonging* (Cambridge, MA: Belknap Press of Harvard University Press, 2016), 139.

25. It is worth noting that this was not just a colonial or frontier mentality. Many continental thinkers on political economy, from Johann Heinrich von Thünen to Friedrich List, Max Weber, and Karl Marx, began their careers as agrarian theorists and economists. On the expansionist implications of Lockean liberalism, see Barbara Arneil, *John Locke and America: The Defence of English Colonialism* (Oxford: Oxford University Press, 1996); Jennifer Pitts, *A Turn to Empire: The Rise of Imperial Liberalism in Britain and France* (Princeton: Princeton University Press, 2005); and Ariel Ron, *Grassroots Leviathan: Agricultural Reform and the Rural North in the Slaveholding Republic* (Baltimore: Johns Hopkins University Press, 2020).

26. Eric Foner, *Free Soil, Free Labor, Free Men: The Ideology of the Republican Party Before the Civil War* (New York: Oxford University Press, 1995); Richard White,

The Republic for Which It Stands: The United States During Reconstruction and the Gilded Age, 1865–1896 (New York: Oxford University Press, 2017), 136–171. More recently, see Emily Pawley, *The Nature of the Future: Agriculture, Science, and Capitalism in the Antebellum North* (Chicago: University of Chicago Press, 2020); and Ron, *Grassroots*. For Germany, see David Ciarlo, *Advertising Empire Race and Visual Culture in Imperial Germany* (Cambridge, MA: Harvard University Press, 2011); and Bradley Naranch and Geoff Eley, eds., *German Colonialism in a Global Age* (Durham, NC: Duke University Press, 2014). Similarly, for Britain, see Frank Trentmann, *Free Trade Nation: Commerce, Consumption, and Civil Society in Modern Britain* (New York: Oxford University Press, 2008).

27. The wars with Indigenous peoples, together with the struggles over the institution of slavery, left little doubt that the ideological bedrock of these societies was land. Europeans who visited and studied the United States at length, including Alexis de Tocqueville, Friedrich List, and Max Weber, all recognized the connection in their works, while Werner Sombart argued the point in a study revealingly titled *Warum gibt es in den Vereinigten Staaten keinen Sozialismus* (*Why Is There No Socialism in the United States?*) (1906). On the debate over the agrarian and industrial state, see Hartmut Harnisch, "Agrarstaat oder Industriestaat: Die Debatte um die Bedeutung der Landwirtschaft in Wirtschaft und Gesellschaft Deutschlands an der Wende vom 19. zum 20. Jahrhundert," in *Ostelbische Agrargesellschaft im Kaiserreich und der Weimarer Republik*, ed. Hanz Reif (Berlin: Akademie Verlag, 1994); and Hans-Ulrich Wehler, *Von der 'Deutschen Doppelrevolution' bis zum Beginn des Ersten Weltkrieges 1849–1914*, vol. 3, Deutsche Gesellschaftsgeschichte, (Munich: C. H. Beck, 1995), esp. 619–20.

28. As contemporary historian F. C. Huber put it, "the ordinary German citizen (*deutscher Kleinbürger*)—including the tradesman—is drawn first and foremost to the ideal of a small plot of land and to the quiet life of a farmer." Alison Frank Johnson makes a similar observation about the strong interest of workers in Austria-Hungary's oil-rich province of Galicia to return to their rural ways of life. Sidney Pollard finds that the French peasantry tended to stick to its land "even if wages in the towns were higher" and that it "remained so inaccessible to...industrialism that even in the mid-twentieth century, industrial firms settling in their midst had to recruit labour from outside, since the local agrarian surplus labour was disinterested." Jacques Rancière, in a most perceptive account of working people's dreams in nineteenth-century France, contends that the French simply desired to be free from any and all work, though it is worth noting that in this period idleness of this sort tended to be associated with landed property. Alison Fleig Frank, *Oil Empire: Visions of Prosperity in Austrian Galicia* (Cambridge, MA: Harvard University Press, 2005), esp. 109–39; Jacques Rancière, *Proletarian Nights: The Workers' Dream in Nineteenth-Century France*, trans. John Drury (London: Verso Books, 2012); Pollard, *Peaceful Conquest*, 52–53. The quote by Huber can be found in F. C. Huber, "Auswanderung und Auswanderungspolitik im Königreich Württemberg," in *Auswanderung und Auswanderungspolitik in Deutschland: Berichte*

über die Entwicklung und den gegenwärtigen Zustand des Auswanderungswesens in den Einzelstaaten und um Reich, ed. Eugen von Philippovich (Leipzig: Duncker & Humblot, 1892), 254.

29. On Boston's so-called brahmins, see Noam Maggor, *Brahmin Capitalism: Frontiers of Wealth and Populism in America's First Gilded Age* (Cambridge, MA: Harvard University Press, 2017). The proximity of German capital to the American West is discussed in Benjamin Hein, "Old Regime in a New World: Frankfurt's Financial Market in the Nineteenth Century," *The Journal of Modern History* 92, no. 4 (2020), 735–73; Christopher Kobrak, *Banking on Global Markets: Deutsche Bank and the United States, 1870 to the Present* (Cambridge: Cambridge University Press, 2007); and David K. Thompson, "Reorienting Atlantic World Financial Capitalism: America and the German States," in *Globalized Peripheries: Central Europe and the Atlantic World, 1680–1860*, ed. Jutta Wimmler and Klaus Weber (Woodbridge, Suffolk: Boydell Press, 2020).

30. The term capitalism is deliberately not used here to describe the events and dynamics under consideration. In my view, capitalism is an imprecise term that tends to collapse the agrarian and industrial spheres into a single, continuous world. Arguably, that was its intended purpose for contemporary observers like Weber and Sombart, who had been witnessing in real time just this kind of collapsing of two formerly more distinct spheres. Other historians seem to share this concern about the analytical usefulness of the term capitalism. Sven Beckert, for example, recently coined the term *war capitalism* to distinguish the dynamics in the agrarian sphere from those characterizing the urban space, which he associates with *industrial capitalism*. Sven Beckert, *Empire of Cotton: A Global History* (New York: Penguin Vintage Books, 2014), 29–82. For a more general discussion of the analytical uses of the term capitalism, see Jürgen Kocka, "Writing the History of Capitalism," *Bulletin of the GHI* 47 (2010): 7–24; Kocka and von der Linden, *Capitalism*; Seth Rockman, Sven Beckert, and Christine Desan, eds., *American Capitalism New Histories* (New York: Columbia University Press, 2018). On the blending of urban spaces and their surroundings in this period, see Mintzker, *Defortification*, 251–55.

31. Hans Ratjen, *"Deutsche die nicht Deutsche sind": Der Kampf um die Reichsangehörigkeit* (Hamburg: Lucas Gräfe & Sillem, 1908), 50.

32. Needless to say, this love affair with the pagan, migratory past did not end with Weber's publication. See here Felix Wiedemann, *Am Anfang war Migration: Wanderungsnarrative in den Wissenschaften vom Alten Orient im 19. und frühen 20. Jahrhundert* (Tübingen: Mohr Siebeck, 2020), esp. 328–36.

CHAPTER 1

1. Ingrid Schöberl and Günter Moltmann, eds., *Aufbruch nach Amerika: Friedrich List und die Auswanderung aus Baden und Württemberg 1816/17: Dokumentation einer sozialen Bewegung* (Tübingen: Wunderlich, 1979), 144–45. For an account of

the circumstances that led to List's interviews of the emigrants, see Paul Gehring, *Friedrich List: Jugend- und Reifejahre, 1789–1825* (Tübingen: J. C. B. Mohr [Paul Siebeck], 1964), esp. 145–56.
2. All quotes in Schöberl and Moltmann, *Aufbruch*, 144–45.
3. Ibid., 145.
4. The year 1816, also known as the "year without a summer," saw temperatures dropping below freezing in the middle of the summer. The event has been linked to the 1815 eruption of Mount Tambora in modern-day Indonesia, one of the largest in recorded history, and one coinciding with plummeting temperatures around the globe. On the effects in Württemberg and its environs, see Daniel Krämer, *"Menschen grasten nun mit dem Vieh": die letzte große Hungerkrise der Schweiz 1816/17: mit einer theoretischen und methodischen Einführung in die historische Hungerforschung* (Basel: Schwabe Verlag, 2015). An exhaustive list of the causes of emigration from southern Germany in this period can be found in Wolfgang von Hippel, *Auswanderung aus Südwestdeutschland: Studien zur württembergischen Auswanderung und Auswanderungspolitik im 18. und 19. Jahrhundert* (Stuttgart: Klett-Cotta, 1984), 148–80.
5. Wilhelm I made several gestures at the beginning of his reign that suggested that he wished to rule by consensus rather than by decree. Ibid., 115. The quote is originally cited in Karl-Johannes Grauer, *Wilhelm I König von Württemberg: Ein Bild seines Lebens und seiner Zeit* (Stuttgart: Schwabenverlag, 1960), 138. "Unknown" in Schöberl and Moltmann, *Aufbruch*, 134.
6. List emphasizes in his report that he warned the emigrants about conditions in America. Schöberl and Moltmann, *Aufbruch*, 149.
7. Ibid., 145.
8. Cameralist thinker Johann Heinrich Gottlob von Justi once likened emigration to an act of suicide. See Andreas Brinkmann, *Die deutsche Auswanderungswelle in die britischen Kolonien Nordamerikas um die Mitte des 18. Jahrhunderts* (Stuttgart: Franz Steiner Verlag, 1993), 166; Georg Fertig, "'Man müßte es sich schier fremd vorkommen lassen': Auswanderungspolitik am Oberrhein im 18. Jahrhundert," in *Migration nach Ost- und Südosteuropa vom 18. bis zum Beginn des 19. Jahrhunderts*, ed. Mathias Beer and Dittmar Dahlmann (Stuttgart: Jan Thorbecke Verlag, 1999), 77–88; Harald Kleinschmidt, *People on the Move: Attitude Toward and Perceptions of Migration in Medieval and Modern Europe* (Westport, CT: Praeger, 2003); and Rudolf Möhlenbruch, "Freier Zug, Ius Emigrandi, Auswanderungsfreiheit. Eine verfassungsgeschichtliche Studie" (PhD diss., Rheinische Friedrich-Wilhelms-Universität, 1977), esp. 102–28. See also the comparative perspectives in Nicholas B. Miller, "Cameralism and the Politics of Populationism: Comparative Perspectives," in *Cameralism and the Enlightenment: Happiness, Governance and Reform in Transnational Perspective*, ed. Ere Nokkala and Nicholas B. Miller (New York: Routledge, 2020); and Jane McAdam, "An Intellectual History of Freedom of Movement in International Law: The Right to Leave as a Personal Liberty," *Melbourne Journal of International Law* 12, no. 1 (2011), 27–56.

9. In his eventual report, List settled on foul play as the only plausible explanation, although such claims were refuted by local officials, who reported that "there is no evidence that people who make a business out of persuading [others] to emigrate" were active in the region. All quotes in Schöberl and Moltmann, *Aufbruch*, 94, 133–34, 145, 149. The socioeconomic profile of the emigrants in this period is discussed in detail in Hippel, *Auswanderung*, 211–50.
10. As E. P. Thompson argues, understanding how people respond to socioeconomic hardship and crisis requires a consideration of the local moral economies and how they render certain solutions more meaningful than others. More recently, Sunil Amrith writes that "only where migration was thinkable and feasible…did episodic crises provoke large-scale movement." E. P. Thompson, "The Moral Economy of the English Crowd in the Eighteenth Century," *Past & Present* 50, no. 1 (1971), 76–136; Sunil S. Amrith, *Crossing the Bay of Bengal: The Furies of Nature and the Fortunes of Migrants* (Cambridge, MA: Harvard University Press, 2013), 267.
11. The last known emigration event in Württemberg took place in 1804, when the charismatic pietist Johann Georg Rapp took seven hundred of his most devoted followers to settle with him in Pennsylvania. Karl J. Arndt, "George Rapp's Harmony Society," in *America's Communal Utopias*, ed. Donald E. Pitzer (Chapel Hill: University of North Carolina Press, 1997). On the scale of the movement, see Hippel, *Auswanderung*, 137–47; figures cited here are from table 13.
12. Cited and translated in Hubert Cole, *First Gentleman of the Bedchamber: The Life of Louis-François-Armand, Maréchal Duc de Richelieu* (London: Heinemann, 1965), 226–27.
13. Christine van den Heuvel, "Justus Möser und die Englisch-Hannoversche Reichspolitik zwischen Siebenjährigem Krieg und Fürstenbund," *Zeitschrift für Historische Forschung* 29, no. 3 (2002): 393–94. My account of Möser also draws on Klaus Epstein, *The Genesis of German Conservatism* (Princeton: Princeton University Press, 1966), 297–341.
14. "Totally new" cited in Paul Göttsching, "Justus Mösers Staats- und Geschichtsdenken: Der Nationsgedanke des aufgeklärten Ständetums," *Der Staat* 22, no. 1 (1983): 38. On Osnabrück's constitutional history, see van den Heuvel, "Möser," esp. 390–404.
15. "Quite lovely theory" cited in Göttsching, "Staats- und Geschichtsdenken," 38. Möser published his theory in a lengthy compendium titled *Osnabrücksche Geschichte* (1768). My reading here draws on Christopher B. Krebs, *A Most Dangerous Book: Tacitus's Germania from the Roman Empire to the Third Reich* (New York: W. W. Norton, 2011), 164–71.
16. All quotations in Cornelius P. Tacitus, *Agricola Germania*, trans. Harold Mattingly (London: Penguin Books, 2010), 40–42.
17. On Möser's diplomacy in England and Hanover, see van den Heuvel, "Möser," 402–4. On Montesquieu's claim regarding magna carta, see Charles Louis de Secondat, Baron de Montesquieu, *The Spirit of the Laws*, trans. Thomas Nugent, 2nd ed., vol. 1 (London: J. Nourse and P. Vaillant), 11.6 and 18.30, 28.2, and 31.4. References are to book and chapter.

18. It should be noted that, while Möser's account would have given George III certain assurances, the king was also much less interested in German affairs than his father. Preoccupied with the war in North America, he happily left Osnabrück in Möser's hands. Van den Heuvel, "Justus Möser," 401–4.
19. For eighteenth-century national thinkers, individual enlightenment was a prerequisite of political, or national, consciousness. My account here is based on James J. Sheehan, *German History, 1770–1866* (Oxford: Clarendon Press, 1989), 144–206. The quotes by Herder are originally cited in Benjamin W. Redekop, *Enlightenment and Community: Lessing, Abbt, Herder, and the Quest for a German Public* (Montreal: McGill-Queen's University Press, 2014), 184, 185.
20. Historian and Hessian statesman Hans Christoph Ernst von Gagern shared the sentiment when he declared in his *National History of the Germans* (1813) that German history no longer turned on "the sad negotiations at Münster and Osnabrück," by which he meant the Treaty of Westphalia of 1648. Hans Christoph Ernst von Gagern, *Von der uralten Zeit bis zu dem Gotenreich unter Hermanrich*, vol. 1, Die Nationalgeschichte der Deutschen (Vienna: Anton Strauß, 1813), viii. See also the discussion in Krebs, *Dangerous Book*, 157–81. The first quote is by Joachim Winckelmann and the second is by the legal scholar Karl Friedrich Eichhorn; both are originally cited and translated in Sheehan, *German History*, 172, 548. "Where does…" in Heinrich Heine, *Über Ludwig Börne* (Hamburg: Hoffmann und Campe, 1840), 227–28.
21. Justus Möser, *Osnabrückische Geschichte* (Osnabrück: Schmidische Buchhandlung, 1768), 2. On Möser's national politics, see Göttsching, "Staats- und Geschichtsdenken," 35–36. Herder cited in ibid., 35.
22. Originally cited in Peter-André Alt, *Schiller. Leben—Werk—Zeit. Eine Biographie. Erster Band, 1759–1791*, (Munich: C. H. Beck, 2000), 590.
23. The position at Jena was in part arranged by Goethe, who wielded considerable influence at the university and who was likewise impressed by Schiller's historical writings. Ibid., 592–93.
24. Ibid., 593–94.
25. Friedrich Schiller, *Kleinere prosaische Schriften: Aus mehrern Zeitschriften, vom Verfasser selbst gesammelt und verbessert. Erster Theil* (Leipzig: Siegfried Lebrecht Crusius, 1792), 55–56.
26. "Fertile and expansive field" in ibid., 55. The other quotes are originally cited in Alt, *Schiller*, 595.
27. To be sure, Sieyès's view of the past was much more nuanced than this. Thus, he hastened to add that the "blood of the Franks (none the better for being pure) now mingles with the blood of the Gauls." As recent scholarship on the revolution in France has emphasized, interest in history and historical philosophy during the radical period from 1789 to mid-1794 remained far more widespread than previously believed. Joseph Zizek, "'New History': The Radical Pasts of the French Revolution, 1789–1794," in *Rethinking the Age of Revolutions: France and the Birth*

of the Modern World, ed. David A. Bell and Yair Mintzker (New York: Oxford University Press, 2018). All quotes originally cited and translated in François Furet, *Revolutionary France, 1770–1880*, trans. Antonia Nevill (Oxford: Wiley–Blackwell, 1995), 48, 49; and Oliver W. Lembcke and Florian Weber, *Emmanuel Joseph Sieyès: The Essential Political Writings* (Leiden: Brill, 2014), 48–49.

28. On race in German nationalist writing, see Jens-Uwe Guettel, *German Expansionism, Imperial Liberalism and the United States, 1776–1945* (Cambridge: Cambridge University Press, 2012), esp. 43–59; and Brian E. Vick, "The Origins of the German Volk: Cultural Purity and National Identity in Nineteenth-Century Germany," *German Studies Review* 26, no. 2 (2003), 241–56. Herder is originally cited and translated in Susanne Zantop, *Colonial Fantasies: Conquest, Family, and Nation in Precolonial Germany* (Durham, NC: Duke University Press, 1997), 95.

29. Schiller, *Schriften*, 1, 389–90. On the Romantics' stance on the revolution, see Sheehan, *German History*, 358–88; and Vick, "Origins," 242–46.

30. All quotes in Schiller, *Schriften*, 1, 387–93, 396. Emphases in the original.

31. Ibid., 97. The idea of a singular Völkerwanderung had been around for several decades but, according to Klaus Rosen, it only came into widespread use as a historical concept thanks to Schiller. Klaus Rosen, *Die Völkerwanderung*, 5th ed. (Munich: C. H. Beck, 2020), 29–35.

32. For example, Forschungsbibliothek Gotha, Deutsche Auswandererbriefsammlung (DABS), Kaper/Meinecke-Hayssen Series, *Sophie Meinecke*, 2 April 1859.

33. To be sure, the essay on the Völkerwanderung was not Schiller's best-known work. He did restate some of its ideas in a later, much more popular essay titled *Ueber die ästhetische Erziehung des Menschen* (1794), which can be found in Friedrich Schiller, *Schillers Sämmtliche Werke, Vierter Band* (Stuttgart: J. G. Cotta, 1879). See also Josef Chytry, *The Aesthetic State: A Quest in Modern German Thought* (Berkeley: University of California Press, 1989), 70–106.

34. Friedrich Ludwig Jahn, a leading figure in the national youth movement, wrote that "ancient is the German's urge to wander; presumably it led him from the Orient to settle by the six rivers of Germany and made him see the glory of Rome beyond the Alps." Friedrich Ludwig Jahn, *Deutsches Volksthum* (Lübeck: Niemann, 1810), 443–44; Heinrich Luden, *Einige Worte über das Studium der vaterländischen Geschichte: Vier öffentliche Vorlesungen* (Jena: Akademische Buchhandlung, 1810), 52, 59.

35. Immanuel Kant, *Anthropologie in pragmatischer Hinsicht*, ed. Wolfgang Becker (Stuttgart: Reclam, 2017), 273–74.

36. Ibid., 29, 269. On Kant and the French Revolution, see Ferenc Fehér, "Practical Reason in the Revolution: Kant's Dialogue with the French Revolution," *Social Research* 56, no. 1 (1989), 161–85; Christian Hillgruber, "Humanitäre Intervention, Grossmachtpolitik und Völkerrecht," *Der Staat* 40, no. 2 (2001): esp. 165–69; Reidar Maliks, "Revolutionary Epigones: Kant and His Radical Followers," *History of Political Thought* 33, no. 4 (2012), 647–71; and Christopher Meckstroth,

"Hospitality, or Kant's Critique of Cosmopolitanism and Human Rights," *Political Theory* 46, no. 4 (2018), 537–559.

37. Kant, *Anthropologie*, 268–75. The English were indeed quite interested in German colonists in the seventeenth and eighteenth centuries; see James Belich, *Replenishing the Earth: The Settler Revolution and the Rise of the Angloworld* (Oxford: Oxford University Press, 2009), 62–67; and Renate Vollmer, "Assisted Emigration From Northern Germany to South Australia in the Nineteenth Century," *Australian Journal of Politics and History* 44, no. 1 (1998), 33–47.

38. Kant, *Anthropologie*, 269. This is not to say that German work lacked world-historical significance. Like other thinkers of the eighteenth-century enlightenment, including the French philosophe Montesquieu (who in turn drew inspiration from the seventeenth-century historian Henri de Boulainvilliers), Kant believed that German tilling of the soil explained some of the most advanced systems of government invented by humankind. Matthew D'Auria, *The Shaping of French National Identity: Narrating the Nation's Past, 1715–1830* (Cambridge: Cambridge University Press, 2020); Harold A. Ellis, *Boulainvilliers and the French Monarchy: Aristocratic Politics in Early Eighteenth-Century France* (Ithaca, NY: Cornell University Press, 1988); Krebs, *Dangerous Book*, esp. 157–64.

39. Von Gagern, *Nationalgeschichte*, 1, 3, 7. Note that von Gagern distinguished between nomadic hunters and pastoral peoples like the Germans who "arrive in masses." Historically, the latter "outweighs" the former because pastoral people "want to move onward and know where they are going." Such statements serve as a reminder that the romanticization of ancient German history differed from the Romantics' interest in the pedagogical and spiritual functions of individual mobility and "wandering." Andrew Cusack, *The Wanderer in Nineteenth-Century German Literature: Intellectual History and Cultural Criticism* (Rochester, NY: Camden House, 2008).

40. Ernst Ludwig Brauns, *Amerika und die moderne Völkerwanderung: Nebst einer Darstellung der gegenwärtig zu Ökonomie—Economy—am Ohio angesiedelten Harmonie-Gesellschaft, und einem Kupfer: Georg Rapp, Leiter der Harmoniegesellschaft, vorstellend* (Potsdam: H. Vogler'sche Buchhandlung, 1833), v–vi, 127–29. Brauns was not alone in describing the settlement of North America as unfolding in a more peaceful manner than similar colonial projects elsewhere. Writers from Christoph Meiners to Gottfried Duden, Gustav Koerner, and Traugott Bromme argued along similar lines, as did the French statesman and renowned cultural critic of the United States Alexis de Tocqueville. Guettel, *Expansionism*, 43–78; H. Glenn Penny, *Kindred by Choice: Germans and American Indians Since 1800* (Chapel Hill: University of North Carolina Press, 2013); Zantop, *Fantasies*, 102–20.

41. All quotes in Schöberl and Moltmann, *Aufbruch*, 132–34.

42. Of course, the nation was not incompatible with local or other identities. Celia Applegate, *A Nation of Provincials: The German Idea of Heimat* (Berkeley: University of California Press, 1990); Alon Confino, *The Nation as a Local*

Metaphor: Württemberg, Imperial Germany, and National Memory, 1871–1918 (Chapel Hill: University of North Carolina Press, 1997). More recently, see Helmut Walser Smith, *Germany: A Nation in Its Time: Before, During, and After Nationalism, 1500–2000* (New York: Liveright, 2020).

43. Grauer, *Wilhelm I*, 92–95. Another good biography is Paul Sauer, *Reformer auf dem Königsthron: Wilhelm I. von Württemberg* (Stuttgart: Deutsche Verlags-Anstalt, 1997).

44. The phrase "kaiser of the Germans" is by Heinrich von Treitschke, originally cited in Grauer, *Wilhelm I*, 94–95. All other quotes in Friedrich Georg Ludwig Lindner, *Manuscript aus Süd-Deutschland*, ed. George Erichson (London: James Griphi, 1820), 6, 12–13.

45. On Friedrich I, see Paul Sauer, *Der schwäbische Zar. Friedrich, Württembergs erster König* (Stuttgart: Deutsche Verlags-Anstalt, 1984).

46. My account of Württemberg's constitutional crisis between 1815 and 1817 is based primarily on Gehring, *List*, 52–55, 94–96, 114–16, 144–45, 156–58; Grauer, *Wilhelm I*, 124–74; and Eugen Schneider, *Württembergische Geschichte* (Stuttgart: J. B. Metzler, 1896), 479–87. On the proliferation of constitutions in German states in this period, see Sheehan, *German History*, 411–25.

47. The quote is from the Berlin law professor Theodor Schmalz, originally cited in Sheehan, *German History*, 421.

48. Bayrische Staatsbibliothek, "Rede, Gehalten von Seiner Königlichen Majestät in dem Saale der Stände-Versammlung bei Wiedereröffnung Derselben," in *Königlich-Württembergisches Staats- und Regierungs-Blatt*, no. 14 (Stuttgart: Gottlieb Hasselbrink, 1817), 105–9. "Resolute defender…" in Lindner, *Manuscript*, 170.

49. When Altrechtler referred to Württemberg's old constitution, they meant the Tübinger Vertrag of 1514, which was an agreement struck between Duke Ulrich of Württemberg and the estates in the wake of a major peasant revolt.

50. Wilhelm would expound on this argument some years later; see Lindner, *Manuscript*. It should be noted that another reason for Wilhelm to embrace the nation was that it enabled him to bridge the confessional divide, and especially to reach Catholics in the recently acquired Swabian territories.

51. Contemporary observers noted that the Altrechtler struggled to mount a response. Tellingly, their counterproposal that spring dwelled on the authority and independence of "servants of the state" (*Staatsdiener*), the function and role of the estates in government, and the form and membership of representative bodies like the Landtag. Carl Victor Fricker and Theodor von Geßler, *Geschichte der Verfassung Württemberg's: Zur Feier des fünfzigjährigen Bestehens der Verfassungs-Urkunde vom 25. September 1819* (Stuttgart: J. B. Metzler, 1869), 209.

52. Apart from the harvest failures associated with 1816, the so-called year without a summer, Württembergers in the 1810s struggled with an economic slump in industry and manufacturing, the result of reduced state demand as well as growing competition from abroad (especially England) following the end of the Napoleonic

Wars. See Richard H. Tilly and Michael Kopsidis, *From Old Regime to Industrial State: A History of German Industrialization from the Eighteenth Century to World War I* (Chicago: University of Chicago Press, 2020), 51–58.

53. Although most governments in this period—Württemberg included—were committed to securing individuals' mobility and right to leave, they also sought to discourage the practice by stigmatizing emigrants and erecting various administrative hurdles. An overview of the different types of chicanery can be found in Möhlenbruch, "Freier Zug," 102–8. On migrants claiming capital from afar, see Karl-Peter Krauss, *Quellen zu den Lebenswelten deutscher Migranten im Königreich Ungarn im 18. und frühen 19. Jahrhundert*, Schriftenreihe des Instituts für Donauschwäbische Geschichte und Landeskunde (Stuttgart: Franz Steiner Verlag, 2015), esp. 30–37, 61–90.

54. "Power of comprehensible speech" in William H. Sewell Jr., *Work and Revolution in France: The Language of Labor from the Old Regime to 1848* (Cambridge: Cambridge University Press, 1980), 200. On paternal theater and its politics, see the classic study by E. P. Thompson, *Customs in Common* (New York: New Press, 1993). More recently, see T. C. W. Blanning, *The Culture of Power and the Power of Culture: Old Regime Europe 1660–1789* (Oxford: Oxford University Press, 2002); Caroline Castiglione, *Patrons and Adversaries: Nobles and Villagers in Italian Politics, 1640–1760* (New York: Oxford University Press, 2005); and James C. Scott, *Domination and the Arts of Resistance: Hidden Transcripts* (New Haven, CT: Yale University Press, 2008). On the territories of the Holy Roman Empire specifically, see Hubertus Büschel, *Untertanenliebe: Der Kult um deutsche Monarchen 1770–1830* (Göttingen: Vandenhoeck & Ruprecht, 2006); Stefan Brakensiek, "Akzeptanzoriente Herrschaft: Überlegungen zur politischen Kultur der Frühen Neuzeit," in *Die Frühe Neuzeit als Epoche*, ed. Helmut Neuhaus, Historische Zeitschrift (Munich: R. Oldenbourg Verlag, 2009); and Helmut Gabel, *Widerstand und Kooperation: Studien zur politischen Kultur rheinischer und maasländischer Kleinterritorien (1648–1794)* (Tübingen: Bibliotheca Academica, 1995).

55. It is worth noting that Friedrich List was no neutral observer and that he went to Heilbronn with an agenda. Still, there is little reason to doubt the veracity of his claim regarding the public nature of the event and the willingness of the emigrants to volunteer their testimony. "Wily maneuvering" in Castiglione, *Patrons*, 168. References to the public nature of the event in Schöberl and Moltmann, *Aufbruch*, 91–102, 110–15, 191–97. On List's politics and, more specifically, his agenda in Heilbronn, see Gehring, *List*, 150–54.

56. Note that List, too, reports the emigrants as having "shed bitter tears." Schöberl and Moltmann, *Aufbruch*, 134. Hübner was among the most successful genre painters of the period. Carmen Flum, *Armeleutemalerei: Darstellungen der Armut im deutschsprachigen Raum 1830–1914* (Merzhausen: ad picturam, 2013), esp. 135–39.

57. "Truly a spectacle..." and "Wish the wanderers..." in University of Texas Dolph Briscoe Center, Jacques Arnold Papers, Krüth, 13 February 1858.

58. To be sure, the royal authorities did attempt to dissuade the emigrants from following through with their plans. But such efforts tended to be orchestrated by surrogates; the king himself refrained from making public announcements on the subject. Friedrich List, for example, received his assignment to head to Heilbronn and to talk to the emigrants from Wilhelm's minister of the interior, Karl Friedrich von Kerner, one of the king's most trusted confidantes. Frederike Middlehoff, "R/Emigration Verhindern. 'Heimat' im Kontext der Auswanderung von 1816/17," *The Germanic Review* 96, no. 3 (2021), 256–75.

59. A 10 percent tax on an individual's net worth was common in this period. Möhlenbruch, "Freier Zug," 107–9. The announcement of the tax's abolition is reproduced in Schöberl and Moltmann, *Aufbruch*, 109. "I will give…" in Deutsche Digitale Bibliothek, *Schwäbischer Merkur, mit Schwäbischer Kronik und Handelszeitung*, 7 June 1817, p. 413. It may well have been the drama in Heilbronn that emboldened Wilhelm to embark on an even more confrontational course vis-à-vis the Landtag and to dissolve it outright just a few weeks later, on June 4, 1817. This step bore considerable political risks, leaving the king vulnerable to charges of despotism and possibly creating a pretext for foreign rivals like Austria or Prussia to intervene. It is unlikely that he would have accepted these risks had he not felt certain of the public's support.

60. Lindner, *Manuscript*, esp. 13–45. Starting in the 1820s, for example, Wilhelm I permitted the staging of an annual festival in honor of Friedrich Schiller, the great protagonist of the nation's Germanic heritage, in his palace gardens in the center of Stuttgart. Along the same lines, in 1828 he gifted a castle in Bad Mergentheim to his cousin, Duke Paul Wilhelm von Württemberg, a renowned explorer and natural historian of North America. The duke promptly turned the palace into a museum for his large collection of zoological, botanical, and ethnographic materials related to North America, thus demonstrating the ruling family's strong patronage of knowledge about the region. Kilian Klann, *Die Sammlung indianischer Ethnographica aus Nordamerika des Herzog Friedrich Paul Wilhelm von Württemberg* (Wyk auf Föhr: Verlag für Amerikanistik, 1999); Nikolaus Stolle, "Ein Leben für Forschung und Entdeckung," *Tribus: Jahrbuch des Linden-Museums Stuttgart* 71–72 (2023), 237–307; Lucie Prinz, *Schillerbilder: Die Schillerverehrung am Beispiel der Festreden des Stuttgarter Liederkranzes (1825–1992)* (Marburg: diagonal-Verlag, 1994); and Gustav Wais, *Die Schiller-Stadt Stuttgart: Eine Darstellung der Schiller-Stätten in Stuttgart* (Stuttgart: W. Kohlhammer Verlag, 1955), esp. 70–76.

61. The principle of free movement had a long history in the Holy Roman Empire; however, it was not until the nineteenth century that the term *Auswanderungsfreiheit* entered the popular vocabulary and began to appear in legal documents like constitutions. In fact, Württemberg's constitution of 1819 was among the very first to make explicit reference to it. The reluctance of other governments to follow suit is perhaps best illustrated by the case of revolutionary France, which despite its ideological commitment to an individual's mobility remained deeply suspicious of

emigrants and erected numerous practical and administrative hurdles to prevent Frenchmen from leaving their country. McAdam, "Movement"; Möhlenbruch, "Freier Zug," 13–19, 125–29, 131–34. On the subsequent debate in Germany about whether to guarantee citizens a "freedom to emigrate" (*Auswanderungsfreiheit*), see Dieter Gosewinkel, *Einbürgern und Ausschließen: Die Nationalisierung der Staatsangehörigkeit vom Deutschen Bund bis zur Bundesrepublik Deutschland* (Göttingen: Vandenhoeck & Ruprecht, 2001), 102–35, 278–327; and Michael Kuckhoff, "Die Auswanderungsdiskussion während der Revolution von 1848/49," in *Deutsche Amerikaauswanderung im 19. Jahrhundert*, ed. Günter Moltmann (Stuttgart: J. B. Metzler, 1976). On the contemporary debate over the freedom of emigration in Württemberg specifically, see Fricker and Geßler, *Geschichte der Verfassung*, 196–208.

62. Lindner, *Manuscript*, 5.
63. Casualties from the Russian campaign (1812) and the Battle of Leipzig (1813) alone have been estimated to have exceeded fifteen thousand. Bodie A. Ashton, *The Kingdom of Württemberg and the Making of Germany, 1815–1871* (London: Bloomsbury Academic, 2017), 27.
64. Alain Corbin, *Village Bells: Sound and Meaning in the 19th Century French Countryside* (New York: Columbia University Press, 1998); Sewell, *Work*, esp. 197–98.
65. On the appropriation of the national idiom in this period, see Sewell, *Work*, 194–218; and Marc H. Lerner, *A Laboratory of Liberty: The Transformation of Political Culture in Republican Switzerland, 1750–1848* (Leiden: Brill, 2012), 137–57. On the geographic and temporal patterns of emigration in this region, see Hippel, *Auswanderung*; Norman Laybourn, *L'Émigration des Alsaciens et de Lorrains du XVIII au XX Siècle: Essai d'histoire démographique*, 2 vols. (Strasbourg: Association des publications près les universités de Strasbourg, 1986); and Heiner Ritzmann-Blickenstorfer, *Alternative Neue Welt: die Ursachen der schweizerischen Überseeauswanderung im 19. und frühen 20. Jahrhundert* (Zurich: Chronos Verlag, 1997).
66. See Felix Wiedemann's comprehensive overview of the many national mythologies in Europe that were rooted in stories of migration. Felix Wiedemann, *Am Anfang war Migration: Wanderungsnarrative in den Wissenschaften vom Alten Orient im 19. und frühen 20. Jahrhundert* (Tübingen: Mohr Siebeck, 2020).
67. The Treaty of Augsburg of 1555, which introduced the principle of "cuius regio, eius religio" within the Holy Roman Empire, allowing princes to adopt the confession of their choice in their territories, provided for a sweeping right to migrate to territories corresponding to one's confession (*ius emigrandi*). Although it was not always honored in full, the concept did ensure that certain forms of emigration were more acceptable than others. On *ius emigrandi*, see Möhlenbruch, "Freier Zug," 56–79. On the role of confession in determining patterns of early modern migration, see Gabriele Emrich, *Die Emigration der Salzburger Protestanten 1731–1732: Reichsrechtliche und kofessionspolitische Aspekte*, Historia profana et ecclesiastica (Münster: LIT Verlag, 2018); Vollmer, "Assisted Emigration"; Heinz Schilling, "Confessional Migration as a Distinct Type of Old European Long Distance

Migration," in *Le migrazioni in Europa, secc. XIII–XVIII*, ed. Simonetta Cavaciocchi (Florence: Le Monnier, 1994); Alexander Schunka, "Konfession und Migrationsregime in der frühen Neuzeit (Migrants and the Early Modern Confessional State)," *Geschichte und Gesellschaft* 35, no. 1 (2009), 28–63; and Wulf Wäntig, *Grenzerfahrungen: Böhmische Exulanten im 17. Jahrhundert* (Konstanz: UVK Verlagsgesellschaft, 2007).

68. All quotes in Hans Christoph Ernst von Gagern, *Der Deutsche in Nord-Amerika* (Stuttgart: J. G. Cotta, 1818), 123–24.

CHAPTER 2

1. Walter D. Kamphoefner, *The Westfalians: From Germany to Missouri* (Princeton: Princeton University Press, 1987), 148–50. Similar ambitions have been found among Americans and English immigrants. Jonathan Levy, *Freaks of Fortune: The Emerging World of Capitalism and Risk in America* (Cambridge, MA: Harvard University Press, 2012), 150–90; Charlotte Erickson, *Invisible Immigrants: The Adaptation of English and Scottish Immigrants in Nineteenth-Century America* (Coral Gables: University of Florida Press, 1972), 13, 27–28.

2. Kamphoefner, *The Westfalians*, 150. "Advantages" and "too anxious" in Forschungsbibliothek Gotha, Deutsche Auswandererbriefsammlung (DABS), Bauer Series, 30 November 1856. "Godless" and the plans for Illinois in ibid., 2 September 1857 and 10 June 1855. Many of the letters contained in the collection cited here were previously transcribed using a typewriter as part of the *Bochumer Auswandererbriefsammlung* initiative (Bochum Emigrant Letter Collection) spearheaded by historians Wolfgang J. Helbich in the 1980s. While I was able to independently verify some of the transcriptions using originals, this was not always possible because in many cases the originals are no longer in the possession of the Forschungsbibliothek Gotha, which currently administers the collection (renamed more recently as *Deutsche Auswandererbriefsammlung*). I nevertheless judged these transcriptions to be reliable given that they were created under the supervision of a team of professional historians. The project is described in Wolfgang J. Helbich et al, eds., *Briefe aus Amerika: Deutsche Auswanderer scheiben aus der neuen Welt, 1830–1930* (Munich: C. H. Beck, 1988); Walter D. Kamphoefner and Wolfgang J. Helbich, eds., *Germans in the Civil War: The Letters They Wrote Home* (Chapel Hill: University of North Carolina Press, 2006). As noted in the opening pages of this book, all translations into English are my own unless otherwise indicated.

3. On the challenges of farming in the middle West in this period, see William Cronon, *Nature's Metropolis: Chicago and the Great West* (New York: W. W. Norton, 1991), 97–120; and John Mack Faragher, *Sugar Creek: Life on the Illinois Prairie* (New Haven, CT: Yale University Press, 1986).

4. Estimates from Ohio, Indiana, and Michigan called for $300 to $500 to pay for land, animals, farming tools, and construction materials. Further west, the figure could range from $750 to $1,500. One guidebook from the 1880s recommended budgeting

some $250 for housebuilding, $180 for team and harness, $22 for a breaking plow, $10 for a harrow, $30 for a cow, and $323 for seed. B. C. Keeler, *Where to Go to Become Rich: Farmers', Miners' and Tourists' Guide to Kansas, New Mexico, Arizona and Colorado* (Chicago: Belford, Clarke & Co., 1880), 43, cited in Levy, *Freaks*, 157–58; Richard White, *"It's Your Misfortune and None of My Own": A History of the American West* (Norman: University of Oklahoma Press, 1991), 185. On the wage estimate for German immigrants, see Kamphoefner, *The Westfalians*, 50.

5. FG, DABS, Bauer Series, 10 June 1855; FG, DABS, Hambloch/Hambloch Series, 3 June 1855.

6. On purchasing land in the West, see White, *"It's Your Misfortune,"* 140–45; and Faragher, *Sugar Creek*, 39–78, 181–99. On mortgage markets, see Levy, *Freaks*, 150–90.

7. Kathleen Neils Conzen, *Immigrant Milwaukee, 1836–1860: Accommodation and Community in a Frontier City* (Cambridge, MA: Harvard University Press, 1976), 44–46, 50–59; Erickson, *Invisible Immigrants*, 40–63; Kamphoefner, *The Westfalians*, 135–69; James M. Bergquist, "German Communities in American Cities: An Interpretation of the Nineteenth-Century Experience," *Journal of American Ethnic History* 4, no. 1 (1984), 9–30; White, *"It's Your Misfortune,"* 194–99.

8. FG, DABS, Bauer Series, 2 September 1857.

9. FG, DABS, Bauer Series, 9 February 1868, 14 November 1871, 3 November 1872, and 1 February 1877. On financial interests as a motivating factor behind migrant correspondence, see Karl-Peter Krauss, *Quellen zu den Lebenswelten deutscher Migranten im Königreich Ungarn im 18. und frühen 19. Jahrhundert* (Stuttgart: Franz Steiner Verlag, 2015), 22–29; and Marionela Wolf, "Aus dem württembergischen Haberschlacht nach Königsgnad im Banat: Briefe südwestdeutscher Auswanderer in ihre alte Heimat," in *Österreichisch-Siebenbürgische Kulturbeiträge: Ein Sammelband der Österreich-Bibliothek Cluj-Napoca/Klausenburg/Kolosvár*, edited by Rudolf Gräf et al. (Cluj-Napoca: Presa Universitară Clujeană, 2005), 47–92.

10. Kamphoefner, *The Westfalians*, 47, 52.

11. Others not only dreaded running into family in the United States but also sought to absolve themselves of all Germans, period. "The Germans here are really obnoxious, at least the ones I have met so far," one Georg Schwarting explained. "As soon as he has earned a little money [the German emigrant] thinks he owns the whole world." Bergquist, "German Communities"; Stanley Nadel, *Little Germany: Ethnicity, Religion, and Class in New York City, 1845–80* (Chicago: University of Illinois Press, 1990). All quotes in FG, DABS, Neidhöfer/Scharting Series, 27 September 1859; and FG, DABS, Bauer Series, 10 June 1855 and 3 November 1871.

12. Helbich et al., *Briefe*, 31–2. Alfred Koch, "Deutsche Schiffs- und Seeposten sowie mögliche Briefbeförderungsgelegenheiten nach Übersee," *Archiv für deutsche Postgeschichte* 22, no. 1 (1964), 2–46. On the American side, see Cameron Blevins, *Paper Trails: The US Post and the Making of the American West* (New York: Oxford University Press, 2021); and George E. Harfest, *History of Letter Communication*

Between the United States and Europe, 1845–1875 (Washington, DC: Quartermann, 1971), 16, 111, 199–224.

13. On European consuls and other diplomatic representation in this period, see Eva Susanne Fiebig, "The Consular Service of the Hansa Towns Lübeck, Bremen and Hamburg in the 19th Century," in *Consuls et services consulaires au XIXe siecle = Die Welt der Konsulate im 19. Jahrhundert = Consulship in the 19th Century*, ed. Jörg Ulbert and Lukian Prijac (Hamburg: Dokumentation & Buch, 2010); Ferry de Goey, *Consuls and the Institutions of Global Capitalism, 1783–1914* (London: Pickering & Chatto, 2014); and Simeon Andonov Simeonov, "Empire of Consuls: Consulship, Sovereignty, and Empire in the Revolutionary Atlantic (1778–1848)" (PhD diss., Brown University, 2021).

14. On *Sprechsucht*, see James J. Sheehan, *German History, 1770–1866* (Oxford: Clarendon Press, 1989), 678–79. On the Frankfurt Parliament and the particularities of the revolution in Germany, see Jonathan Sperber, *The European Revolutions, 1848–1851* (Cambridge: Cambridge University Press, 2005), 208–57; and Brian E. Vick, *Defining Germany: The 1848 Frankfurt Parliamentarians and National Identity* (Cambridge, MA: Harvard University Press, 2002).

15. Alison Clark Efford, *German Immigrants, Race, and Citizenship in the Civil War Era* (Washington, DC: German Historical Institute, 2013); Mischa Honeck, *We Are The Revolutionists: German-Speaking Immigrants and American Abolitionists After 1848* (Athens, GA: University of Georgia Press, 2011), 13–37; Bruce C. Levine, *The Spirit of 1848: German Immigrants, Labor Conflict, and the Coming of the Civil War* (Urbana: University of Illinois Press, 1992). From the US perspective, see Matthew Frye Jacobson, *Whiteness of a Different Color: European Immigrants and the Alchemy of Race* (Cambridge, MA: Harvard University Press, 1998), 39–90.

16. Many forty-eighters shared Kapp's sentiment, enough to compel Walt Whitman to write a poem in their name titled "To a Foil'd European Revolutionaire" (1855). On Friedrich Kapp, see Hans-Ulrich Wehler's remarks in Friedrich Kapp et al., *Vom radikalen Frühsozialisten des Vormärz zum liberalen Parteipolitiker des Bismarckreichs: Briefe 1843–1884* (Frankfurt am Main: Insel-Verlag, 1969). All quotes in Wolfgang Hinners, *Exil und Rückkehr: Friedrich Kapp in Amerika und Deutschland, 1824–1884* (Stuttgart: Akademischer Verlag, 1987), 51, 75, 77.

17. Friedrich Kapp, *Aus und über Amerika: Tatsachen und Erlebnisse* (Berlin: Julius Springer, 1876), 17, 74, 312–13. As the contemporary historian Ernest Bruncken wrote, "Within a few years after their arrival nearly all of them had found some work to do, some occupation, business or profession which gave them a standing in the community and saved them from the make-belief activities of the early days." Ernest Bruncken, *German Political Refugees in the United States During the Period from 1815–1860* (Chicago: R. and E. Research Associates, 1904), 32.

18. Hinners, *Exil*, 44; Hermann Eduard von Holst, "Friedrich Kapp," *Preussische Jahrbücher* 55, no. 3 (1885): 253–68.

19. Henry Villard, *Lebenserinnerungen von Heinrich Hilgard-Villard: Ein Bürger zweier Welten, 1835–1900* (Berlin: G. Reimer, 1906), 160. To be sure, most historians in the

early twenty-first century agree that German immigrants were rarely as disoriented as this quote suggests.
20. The records of Kapp's firm did not survive; most information about it comes from the memoirs of Friedrich Fröbel. Hinners, *Exil*, 44–46.
21. Cited in ibid. Fröbel later regretted lending his name to the enterprise. Julius Fröbel, *Ein Lebenslauf: Aufzeichnungen, Erinnerungen, und Bekenntnisse* (Stuttgart: J. G. Cotta, 1890), 33, 390.
22. Friedrich Kapp, *Immigration, and the Commissioners of Emigration of the State of New York* (New York: Nation Press, 1870), 143.
23. Kamphoefner, *The Westfalians*, 45–52. See also examples in the University of California Berkeley Bancroft Library, MSS P-B 220, Box 17, Fred. Kammholz to Paul Schulze, 6 April 1879; Heinrich Müller to Paul Schulze, 2 April 1879; and Wilhelm Hartmann to Paul Schulze, 27 January 1879.
24. FG, DABS, Adams/Scheuermann Series, 27 October 1872 and 14 August 1873. Similarly, FG, DABS, Hambloch/Hambloch Series, 17 April 1859. On the customs and laws of inheritance in this period, see Johannes Bracht, *Geldlose Zeiten und überfüllte Kassen: Sparen, Leihen und Vererben in der ländlichen Gesellschaft Westfalens, 1830–1866* (Stuttgart: Lucius & Lucius, 2013), esp. 101–43.
25. FG, DABS, Betke Series, 3 December 1860, 13 December 1860, and 7 February 1867. For context, see Bracht, *Geldlose Zeiten*, 311–62.
26. "Immigrant promotion business" in Library of Congress, Friedrich Kapp Papers, 22 February 1853. "Live independent" in Kate Asaphine Everest, *How Wisconsin Came by Its Large German Element* (Madison: State Historical Society of Wisconsin, 1892), 24–26. It is worth noting that while transfers of capital among migrants were not entirely new, they had previously been the exception rather than the rule. See the discussion in Krauss, *Quellen*, 22–27, 30–37. For the estimate on average farm prices in this period, see Charlotte Erickson, *Leaving England: Essays on British Emigration in the Nineteenth Century* (Ithaca, NY: Cornell University Press, 1994), 68.
27. Cited in Honeck, *Revolutionists*, 57.
28. Nadel, *Little Germany*, 1–46, 104–21; Anita Rapone, *The Guardian Life Insurance Company, 1860–1920. A History of a German-American Enterprise* (New York: New York University Press, 1987), 11–14; Reinhard R. Doerries, "Making It in Banking: The German Savings Bank in the City of New York as a Test Case of Ethnic Enterprise in Nineteenth Century America," in *Liberalitas: Festschrift für Erich Angermann zum 65. Geburtstag*, ed. Norbert Finzsch and Hermann Wellenreuther (Stuttgart: Steiner Verlag, 1992); Agnes Bretting and Hartmut Bickelmann, *Auswanderungsagenturen und Auswanderungsvereine im 19. und 20. Jahrhundert* (Stuttgart: Franz Steiner Verlag, 1991).
29. The number of consulates that emigrants might have approached grew sharply in the early nineteenth century. Prussia alone established 342 new consulates between 1818 and 1867. Lübeck had 202 consulates by 1867, Bremen 217, and Hamburg 286. Goey, *Consuls*, 104–5.

30. Ibid., 27–28; Helbich et al., *Briefe*, 41. Reports of fraud and embezzlement on the part of some consuls in the 1860s, including those in New York and Milwaukee, may have further discouraged contemporaries from using them. Bundesarchiv Lichterfelde, R 4701/15057, *Bericht an den Staats-Minister für auswärtige Angelegenheiten Otto von Bismarck*, Berlin, November 25, 1864; Geheimes Staatsarchiv Preussischer Kulturbesitz, III. HA, Abt. II, Nr. 578, "Sach-Darstellung und Rechtsgutachten betreffend die von dem (verstorbenen) königl: Konsul Spangenberg in Milwaukee unterschlagenen Geldbeträge," no date. Still, on occasion emigrants did communicate directly with authorities in Germany, which suggests that some faith in officials remained, for example, Hauptstaatsarchiv Baden-Württemberg, E40/76 Bü 431, Conrad Schutter to Schultheiss, 13 August 1864.
31. For examples of inquiries on the whereabouts and estates of German immigrants, see BL, MSS P-B 220, Box 16, Adolph Rosenthal to Paul Schulze, 2 August 1877, 4 July 1877, 10 April 1878, 12 April 1878, 7 October 1878, 4 January 1880, 15 July 1880, 30 September 1880, 11 August 1882, and 2 June 1883. For requests to collect outstanding debts, see ibid., 24 June 1876, 1 August 1877, 15 August 1877, 10 May 1882, and 11 August 1882.
32. BL, MSS P-B 220, Box 17, Gebrüder Sulzbach to Paul Schulze, 4 July 1878; H. D. Meyling to Paul Schulze, 20 January 1879; Otto F. Lehmann to Paul Schulze, 21 April 1879; Fred Kammholz to Paul Schulze, 6 April 1879; Heinrich Müller Bank- Und Kommissionsgeschäft to Paul Schulze, 2 April 1879; Hans Sievers to Paul Schulze, 29 May 1879; Charles H. Miller to Paul Schulze, 2 June 1879; Chas Lorenz to Paul Schulze, no date; Simon Gottstein to Paul Schulze, 31 March 1879. A similar business run by the German American Francis A. Hoffmann in Illinois reveals that such lawyers possessed close relationships with banks and attorneys' offices in Basel, Berlin, Bremen, Cologne, Cronach, Frankfurt am Main, Heilbronn, Altenburg, Braunschweig, Breslau, Bückeburg, Eisenach, Freiburg, Gera, Glogau, Luxemburg, Mühlhausen, Osnabrück, Paris, Strassburg, Trier, Hamburg, Hannover, Leipzig, Nuremberg, Stuttgart, Stettin, and Ulm. Institut für Stadtgeschichte Frankfurt am Main, W 1/9:5 Nr. 94, P.P. by Hoffmann & Gelpcke, 1 January 1859.
33. References to the size of Schulze's commission can be found in BL, MSS P-B 220, Box 17, Office of the North German Lloyd to Paul Schulze, 15 February 1879 and 24 February 1879. Schulze's other business interests, which included investments in local transportation businesses like the Yakima Sunnyside Canal and a new streetcar system in Tacoma, are described in his obituary in the *San Francisco Call*. LoC, *San Francisco Call*, "Tragedy at Tacoma," 13 April 1895. Kapp's business and financial engagements will be considered in detail in Chapters 5, 6, and 7.
34. Jürgen Osterhammel, *The Transformation of the World: A Global History of the Nineteenth Century* (Princeton: Princeton University Press, 2014), 708.
35. See here the discussion in Chapter 1. On the shifting social and geographic profile of German emigrants in the nineteenth century, see Klaus J. Bade, *Migration in European History* (Cambridge, MA: Blackwell, 2003), 81–120; Günter Moltmann,

"The Pattern of German Emigration to the United States in the Nineteenth Century," in *America and the Germans: An Assessment of a Three-Hundred-Year History*, ed. Frank Trommler and Joseph McVeigh (Philadelphia: University of Pennsylvania Press, 1985); and Jochen Oltmer, *Migration im 19. und 20. Jahrhundert* (Munich: R. Oldenbourg Verlag, 2010), 9–32.

36. All quotes in Wilhelm G. Bek, *The German Settlement Society* of Philadelphia, and Its Colony, Hermann, Missouri (Philadelphia: Americana Germanica Press, 1907), esp. 83–105; similarly, Hugo Münsterberg, *Aus Deutsch-Amerika* (Berlin: Ernst Siegfried und Sohn, Königliche Hofbuchhandlung, 1909), v–vi. On the fate of these emigrant societies, see Karl J. R. Arndt, *George Rapp's Harmony Society* (Chapel Hill: University of North Carolina Press, 2010); Michael Kuckhoff, "Die Auswanderungsdiskussion während der Revolution von 1848/49," in *Deutsche Amerikaauswanderung im 19. Jahrhundert*, ed. Günter Moltmann (Stuttgart: J. B. Metzler, 1976), 102–11; and Mack Walker, *Germany and the Emigration, 1816–1885* (Cambridge, MA: Harvard University Press, 1964). See also the poignant account of the Westphalia settlement in Missouri in Adolf E. Schroeder and Carla Schulz-Geisberg, eds., *Hold Dear, as Always: Jette, a German Immigrant Life in Letters* (Columbia: University of Missouri Press, 1988). So spectacular were the failures of emigration societies in the 1850s that they became the subject of extensive cultural commentary. See, for example, Ferdinand Kürnberger, *Der Amerika-Müde: Amerikanisches Kulturbild* (Frankfurt am Main: Meidinger Sohn & Cie, 1855); and Balduin Möllhausen, *Die Hyänen des Kapitals*, vol. 4, Illustrierte Romane (Leipzig: Verlagsbuchhandlung von Paul List, 1912, 1876).

37. "Wordy" and "formulaic" in Helbich et al., *Briefe*, 49. On the identity- and community-building functions of migrant correspondence, see Bruce S. Elliott et al., eds., *Letters Across Borders: The Epistolary Practices of International Migrants* (New York: Palgrave Macmillan, 2006); David Fitzpatrick, *Oceans of Consolation: Personal Accounts of Irish Migration to Australia* (Ithaca, NY: Cornell University Press, 1994); David A. Gerber, *Authors of Their Lives: The Personal Correspondence of British Immigrants to North America in the Nineteenth Century* (New York: New York University Press, 2006); and Walter D. Kamphoefner, "Immigrant Epistolary and Epistemology: On the Motivators and Mentality of Nineteenth-Century German Immigrants," *Journal of American Ethnic History* 28, no. 3 (2009), 34–54. On the financial motives in migrant correspondence, see the introductory discussion in Krauss, *Quellen*, 21–35.

38. FG, DABS, Grimm/Kessel & Rückels Series, 27 January 1862 and 14 November 1863.

39. Ibid., 14 November 1863.

40. FG, DABS, Bauer Series, 9 October 1862. Other examples of long-lasting, sustained dialogue include FG, DABS, Kaper/Meinecke-Hayssen Series (six years); Fleig/Frick Series (twelve years); Krause/Krause Series (sixteen years); Grimm/Kessel & Rückels Series (seventeen years); Johann Schipper Series (twenty-four

years); Krooß-Krooß Series (twenty-seven years), and Bauer Series (thirty-seven years). Likewise, see University of Texas Dolph Briscoe Center for American History, Henry Baumberger Papers (nine years); Jacques Arnold Papers (eleven years); and Anton Pfeiffer Papers (twenty-five years). Sophienburg Museum & Archives in New Braunfels, Peter Wilhelm Fenske Papers (twelve years) and Schlameus Family Papers (nineteen years). Similar patterns have been found in English and Irish migrant correspondence later in the century. Gerber, *Authors*; David Fitzpatrick, "Irish Emigration and the Art of the Letter-Writing," in *Letters Across Borders: The Epistolary Practices of International Migrants*, ed. Bruce S. Elliott et al. (New York: Palgrave Macmillan, 2006).
41. FG, DABS, Bauer Series, 17 November 1871 and 8 February 1880.
42. All quotes in Frederick Law Olmsted, *A Journey Through Texas: Or, A Saddle-Trip on the Southwestern Frontier with a Statistical Appendix* (New York: Dix, Edwards, 1857), vii, xvi–xvii.
43. Olmsted was a well-known Germanophile; interestingly enough, he and Friedrich Kapp knew each other and would become good friends. Honeck, *Revolutionists*, 43–56. On the "free labor" movement in the United States in this period, see Eric Foner, *Free Soil, Free Labor, Free Men: The Ideology of the Republican Party Before the Civil War* (New York: Oxford University Press, 1995); and William E. Gienapp, *The Origins of the Republican Party, 1852–1856* (New York: Oxford University Press, 1987).
44. Olmsted, *Journey*, 139.
45. For example, ibid., 142–45, 149–50.
46. Ibid., 149.
47. Ibid.
48. What Olmsted failed to note is that the construction material and building design used by "Mexicans" made good sense in the arid climate of west Texas. Ibid., 427.
49. Ibid., 184.
50. Ibid., 111, 281. To be sure, it would be impossible to determine what exactly accounted for the success of the two men Olmsted claims to have observed in San Marcos. Hard work undoubtedly played a role. But it is unlikely to have been a coincidence that, as Olmsted observed, the two individuals' progress had been uncommonly fast "within the last two years," in other words, since 1853 or 1854—around the time that forty-eighters like Friedrich Kapp began establishing their businesses all across the country. Olmsted may in fact have been aware of the services offered by German forty-eighter émigrés, given his well-documented personal friendships with Adolf Douai, Eduard Degener, August Siemering, and, of course, Friedrich Kapp himself. On Olmsted's relations to the forty-eighter community, see Honeck, *Revolutionists*, 43–46.
51. All quotes in Olmsted, *Journey*, 281–82, 431.
52. To be sure, economic concerns were also at play: As Willis A. Gorman, governor of the Territory of Minnesota, put it, "sound political economy has taught us that

population is the basis of wealth and greatness." However, it should be emphasized that in antebellum America the definitions of "population" and "wealth and greatness" were highly contested and usually turned on the question of slavery. Gorman cited in Livia Appel and Theodore C. Blegen, "Official Encouragement of Immigration to Minnesota During the Territorial Period," *Minnesota History Bulletin* 5, no. 3 (1923): 173.

53. "To stand shoulder to shoulder…" cited in Ingrid Schöberl, *Amerikanische Einwandererwerbung in Deutschland 1845–1914* (Stuttgart: Franz Steiner Verlag, 1990), 74. On state-by-state recruitment efforts, see ibid., 34–38. More recently, see Leonard Dinnerstein and David M. Reimers, *Ethnic Americans: A History of Immigration* (New York: Columbia University Press, 1999), esp. 27–28. On the varying ideological and political motivations for intensifying immigrant recruitment, see Bruce E. Baker and Brian Kelly, *After Slavery: Race, Labor, and Citizenship in the Reconstruction South* (Gainesville: University Press of Florida, 2013); Eric Foner, *Reconstruction: America's Unfinished Revolution, 1863–1877* (New York: Harper & Row, 1989), 124–75; Moon-Ho Jung, *Coolies and Cane: Race, Labor, and Sugar in the Age of Emancipation* (Baltimore: Johns Hopkins University Press, 2006); Leslie A. Schwalm, *Emancipation's Diaspora: Race and Reconstruction in the Upper Midwest* (Chapel Hill: University of North Carolina Press, 2009); and Richard White, *The Republic for Which It Stands: The United States During Reconstruction and the Gilded Age, 1865–1896* (New York: Oxford University Press, 2017), 425–39.

54. "Class of…" in Richard Cleghorn Overton, *Burlington West: A Colonization History of the Burlington Railroad* (Cambridge, MA: Harvard University Press, 1941), 160. The federal government's "Act to Encourage Immigration" (1864) was designed to address war-induced labor shortages in manufacturing via recruitment from England, Scotland, and Wales. Schöberl, *Einwandererwerbung*, 39–46, 138–39; Charlotte Erickson, *American Industry and the European Immigrant, 1860–1885* (Cambridge, MA: Harvard University Press, 2014), 2–32. See also the comparative perspective across nineteenth-century colonial frontiers in James Belich, *Replenishing the Earth: The Settler Revolution and the Rise of the Angloworld* (Oxford: Oxford University Press, 2009), 58–65, 177–218.

55. Systematic efforts to recruit German immigrants to frontier states date to the 1840s at least. However, much of this recruitment targeted immigrants after their arrival in eastern ports. The exception seems to have been the Illinois Central Railroad Company, which dispatched an agent to Europe as early as 1854. Maurice G. Baxter, "Encouragement of Immigration to the Middle West During the Era of the Civil War," *Indiana Magazine of History* 46, no. 1 (1950): 29; Paul Wallace Gates, *The Illinois Central Railroad and Its Colonization Work, by Paul Wallace Gates* (Cambridge, MA: Harvard University Press, 1934), 188–224; Marcus Lee Hansen, "Official Encouragement of Immigration to Iowa," *The Iowa Journal of History and Politics* XIX, no. 2 (1921): 159–95; Schöberl, *Einwandererwerbung*, 22–23, 33; and

John F. Stover, *History of the Illinois Central Railroad* (New York: Macmillan, 1975), 113–19.
56. Harris cited in Overton, *Burlington West*, 303.
57. "Bring with them…" cited in Appel and Blegen, "Official Encouragement," 173. All other quotes can be found in Schöberl, *Einwandererwerbung*, 73, 169–71.
58. Jung, *Coolies*, esp. 39–106. On the patterns of European immigrant settlement within the United States in this period, see Elliott Robert Barkan, *From All Points: America's Immigrant West, 1870s–1952* (Bloomington: Indiana University Press, 2007), 35–94; and White, *"It's Your Misfortune,"* 186–211.
59. Jacobson, *Whiteness*, 39–90. More recently, see Belich, *Replenishing*, 58–67, esp. 63.
60. Herbert Quick, *The Fairview Idea: A Story of the New Rural Life* (Indianapolis, IN: Bobbs-Merrill, 1919), 12. As the contemporary historian A. B. Faust put it, German immigrants were among the "most successful farmers in America" because they were often "paying cash" for the "best farm land" available. This, Faust argued, enabled German immigrants to "displac[e] even the native element." Albert Bernhardt Faust, *The German Element in the United States: With Special Reference to Its Political, Moral, Social, and Educational Influence*, vol. 2. (Boston: Houghton Mifflin, 1909), 28–34. A more sober account of the achievements, contributions, and importance of German immigrants in US agriculture can be found in Kathleen Neils Conzen, *Making Their Own America: Assimilation Theory and the German Peasant Pioneer, with Comments by Mack Walker and Jörg Nagler* (New York: Berg, 1990), 3–5; and Kathleen Neils Conzen, "Die deutsche Amerikaeinwanderung im ländlichen Kontext: Problemfelder und Forschungsergebnisse," in *Auswanderer—Wanderarbeiter—Gastarbeiter: Bevölkerung, Arbeitsmarkt und Wanderung in Deutschland seit der Mitte des 19. Jahrhunderts*, ed. Klaus J. Bade (Ostfildern: Scripta Mercaturae, 1984).

CHAPTER 3

1. The term Gewerbefreiheit is often translated as "freedom of enterprise." In the nineteenth century, the concept usually referred to commercial reforms aimed at curtailing the power of guilds and similar corporate institutions. Another referent is the contemporary American concept of free labor, according to which an individual should have the liberty to dispose of their own labor as they wish in an open marketplace (although, unlike free labor, Gewerbefreiheit was not explicitly defined in opposition to slavery). For an introduction, see the discussions in Eric Foner, *Free Soil, Free Labor, Free Men: The Ideology of the Republican Party Before the Civil War* (Oxford: Oxford University Press, 1995); Daniel T. Rodgers, *The Work Ethic in Industrial America: 1850–1920* (Chicago: University of Chicago Press, 2014); Andrew Schupanitz, "Revolutionary Competition: Coalitions, Labor, and the Birth of French Antitrust, 1791–1864" (PhD diss., Stanford University,

2020); William H. Sewell Jr., *Work and Revolution in France: The Language of Labor from the Old Regime to 1848* (Cambridge: Cambridge University Press, 1980); Barbara Vogel, *Allgemeine Gewerbefreiheit: Die Reformpolitik des preußischen Staatskanzlers Hardenberg (1810–1820)* (Göttingen: Vandenhoeck & Ruprecht, 1983); and Mack Walker, *German Home Towns: Community, State, and General Estate, 1648–1871* (Ithaca, NY: Cornell University Press, 1971). The quotes can be found in Johann C. Leuchs, *Realrechte und Gewerbs-Privilegien beseitigt und versöhnt mit der Freiheit der Gewerbe und der Ansässigung* (Nürnberg: C. Leuchs, 1860), 5, 13. Leuchs also wrote on patent law, science, technology, and agriculture. His other publications include, among others, Johann C. Leuchs, *Deutscher Haus- und Fabrikschatz: Zweiter Band* (Nürnberg: C. Leuchs, 1860); Johann C. Leuchs, *Einführungs-Schutz. Entwurf und Begründung eines Gesezes zum Schuze der Erfindungen für die deutschen Staaten* (Nürnberg: C. Leuchs, 1862); Johann C. Leuchs, *Gewerbefreiheit für Nürnberg* (Nürnberg: C. Leuchs, 1839); Johann C. Leuchs, *Zweihundert und fünfzig Entdeckungen und Verbesserungen in der Färberei und Druckerei, gemacht in den Jahren 1828 bis 1839* (Nürnberg: C. Leuchs, 1839). A biographical overview of Leuchs can be found in Gerhard Hirschmann, "Leuchs, Johann Carl," *Neue Deutsche Biographie* 14 (1985): 366.

2. To be sure, not all contemporaries who embraced liberal principles supported an immediate end to the institution of the guild, citing the potential for social unrest. James J. Sheehan, *German Liberalism in the Nineteenth Century* (Chicago: University of Chicago Press, 1978), 19–34, 85–87. All quotes in Leuchs, *Realrechte*, 2, 5–7, 13.

3. Leuchs, *Realrechte*, 2, 9. A similar emphasis on stupidity (*Dummheit*) can be found in the writings of another notable champion of economic modernization, Friedrich List. See Friedrich List, *Das nationale System der politischen Ökonomie* (Stuttgart: J. G. Cotta, 1841), 208.

4. Mack Walker, *Home Towns*, 390–91. Jonathan Sperber observes a similar "clerical–conservative symbiosis" between church and state. Jonathan Sperber, *Popular Catholicism in Nineteenth Century Germany* (Princeton: Princeton University Press, 1984), 124.

5. The long-standing notion that the 1850s constituted a period of reaction has been largely refuted. States did support conservative policies on the local level but, in most cases, continued to pursue a liberal agenda at the state level by backing the construction of railroads, banks, and the like. James M. Brophy, *Capitalism, Politics, and Railroads in Prussia, 1830–1870* (Columbus: Ohio State University Press, 1998); Christopher Clark, *Iron Kingdom: The Rise and Downfall of Prussia, 1600–1947* (Cambridge, MA: Belknap Press of Harvard University Press, 2006), 500–509.

6. In 1860, for example, the Duchy of Nassau and the city state of Bremen introduced laws guaranteeing Gewerbefreiheit; the kingdom of Württemberg in the south followed in 1861, and its smaller neighbor, Baden, did so in 1862. Hessen-Darmstadt

instated its reforms in 1866 and Bavaria adopted them in 1868. Prussia followed in 1869. For a chronology of similar reforms across the German lands in this period, see Adolf Braun, *Die Arbeiterschutzgesetze der Europäischen Staaten: Mit Exkursen über Gewerbeverfassung, Industriestatistik, Entwicklung, und Durchführung der Arbeiterschutzgesetzgebung*, vol. 1, Deutsches Reich (Tübingen: H. Laupp, 1890), 2–49. On the New Era more generally, see Thomas Nipperdey, *Deutsche Geschichte 1800–1866: Bürgerwelt und starker Staat* (Munich: C. H. Beck, 2013), 34–55; Gerhard Deter, ed., *Zwischen Gilde und Gewerbefreiheit: Rechtsgeschichte des selbständigen Handwerks im Westfalen des 19. Jahrhunderts (1810–1869)*, vol. 1, *Vierteljahrschrift für Sozial- und Wirtschaftsgeschichte—Beihefte* (Stuttgart: Franz Steiner Verlag, 2015); and James Brophy, "The End of the Economic Old Order: The Great Transition, 1750–1860," in *The Oxford Handbook of Modern German History*, ed. Helmut Walser Smith (Oxford: Oxford University Press, 2011).

7. Citing the writings of reformers and modernizers themselves, Gerhard Deter sees an all but unstoppable "advance of liberal thought," thanks to liberals' persistent penmanship. Jürgen Kocka argues that the modern German working-class movement had been "conditioned" by interactions with bourgeois employers. Klaus Tenfelde refers to a "learning process" and a loss of "traditional values" (*überkommene Wertorientierungen*) that took place amid rapid urbanization and industrialization. David Blackbourn emphasizes structural shifts in contemporary parliamentary politics, especially in Prussia, where the regency of Wilhelm I forced the retreat of the Conservative Party and paved the way for a new political liberalism. Henning Albrecht, "Preußen, ein 'Judenstaat': Antisemitismus als konservative Strategie gegen die 'Neue Ära' - Zur Krisentheorie der Moderne," *Geschichte und Gesellschaft* 37, no. 4 (2011), 455–81; David Blackbourn, *History of Germany 1780–1918: The Long Nineteenth Century* (Malden, MA: Blackwell, 2003), 233; Deter, *Zwischen Gilde*, 9–39; Karl Heinrich Kaufhold, "Gewerbefreiheit im 19. Jahrhundert," in *Wirtschaftliches Geschehen und ökonomisches Denken: Ausgewählte Schriften von Karl Heinrich Kaufhold herausgegeben aus Anlass seines 75. Geburtstages*, ed. Markus A. Denzel and Hans-Jürgen Gerhard (Stuttgart: Franz Steiner Verlag, 2007), 139; Jürgen Kocka, "Arbeiterbewegung in der Bürgergesellschaft: Überlegungen zum deutschen Fall," *Geschichte und Gesellschaft* 20, no. 4 (1994): 491; Jürgen Kocka, *Industrial Culture and Bourgeois Society: Business, Labor, and Bureaucracy in Modern Germany* (New York: Berghahn Books, 1999), 208–31; and Klaus Tenfelde, "Konflikt und Organisation in einigen deutschen Bergbaugebieten 1867–1872," *Geschichte und Gesellschaft* 3, no. 2 (1977): 212–35, here 233.

8. "The pendulum..." in Walker, *Home Towns*, 390–91. "[It] would be superfluous..." in Leuchs, *Realrechte*, 2, 13.

9. To be sure, this was no peculiarly German understanding of labor. Similar ideas could be found throughout the European continent and in North America as well. It was perhaps best articulated by Henri Bergson, who, in an influential publication

titled *Creative Evolution* (1907), spoke of "homo faber," defining man by his labor. Henri Bergson, *Creative Evolution*, trans. by Arthur Mitchell (New York: Henry Holt, 1911. 1907). "Key to the entire…" in Thomas Welskopp, "The Vision(s) of Work in the Nineteenth-Century German Labour Movement," in *Work in a Modern Society: The German Historical Experience in Comparative Perspective*, ed. Jürgen Kocka (New York: Berghahn Books, 2010), 57. "It is not success…" in Wilhelm Heinrich Riehl, *Die deutsche Arbeit* (Stuttgart: J. G. Cotta, 1862), 159–60. "Prime masculine virtue" in Welskopp, "Vision(s)," 57, 60. On the gendered character of work in this period, see Karin Hausen, "Work in Gender, Gender in Work: The German Case in Comparative Perspective," ibid., 73–92.

10. "Grasp the full scope…" in Georg Herold, *Keine Gewerbefreiheit: Eine bürgerliche Antwort auf die vom gesetzgebenden Körper am 16. Jan. I. J. angeregte Frage* (Frankfurt am Main: Carl Horstmann, 1860), 7. "Political-moral" in J. C. Bluntschli and R. Brater, eds., *Deutsches Staats-Wörterbuch*, vol. 4 (Stuttgart: Expedition des Staats-Wörterbuchs, 1859), 326. "Mischief" in Helmut Bernert, ed., *Handwerk zischen Zunft und Gewerbefreiheit: Edikte und Ausschreiben aus dem Königreich Westphalen, dem Kurfürstenthum Hessen, dem Herzogthum Nassau, dem Fürstenthum Waldeck, der freien Stadt Frankfurt sowie Entwürfe zum Handwerks- und Gewerberecht aus dem Jahre 1848* (Kassel: euregio verlag, 1998), 166. "Undermine [our] moral and physical power…" in *Gegen Gewerbefreiheit: Eine Rede* (Lübeck: Friedrich Aschenfeldt, 1862), 13.

11. A version of the argument is still being made in the early twenty-first century. Joel Mokyr writes that the reforms of the 1860s "cleared away" the "institutional debris" left over from "centuries of predatory rule and rent-seeking." Joel Mokyr, *The Enlightened Economy: Britain and the Industrial Revolution 1700–1850* (London: Penguin Books, 2009), 11. Marx cited in Welskopp, "Vision(s)," 56.

12. *Gegen Gewerbefreiheit*, 5. See also similar arguments cited in Florian Tennstedt, *Vom Proleten zum Industriearbeiter: Arbeiterbewegung und Sozialpolitik in Deutschland, 1800 bis 1914* (Cologne: Bund-Verlag, 1983), 174–75.

13. According to James Sheehan, "the educated elites who spoke for [liberal reforms] were separated from the masses of the German people by a social distance great enough to impede an understanding of workingmen and effective interaction with them." James J. Sheehan, *German History, 1770–1866* (Oxford: Clarendon Press, 1989), 598; Helmut Walser Smith, "Authoritarian State, Dynamic Society, Failed Imperialist Power, 1878–1914," in *The Oxford Handbook of Modern German History*, ed. Helmut Walser Smith (Oxford: Oxford University Press, 2015), 318. Similarly, see David Blackbourn, "The Mittelstand in German Society and Politics, 1871–1914," *Social History* 2, no. 4 (1977): 417.

14. Forschungsbibliothek Gotha, Deutsche Auswandererbriefsammlung (DABS), Krause/Krause Series, 27 July 1861. There is some uncertainty about the name of the village. At one point, he refers to an address in Goreyzykowo, which to my

knowledge does not exist. One possibility is the town Borzykowo, especially in light of references to "nearby" Bromberg (Bydgoszcz). The reference to Goreyzykowo is in FG, DABS, Krause/Krause Series, 1 December 1864. Another biographical sketch of Albert Krause can be found in Walter D. Kamphoefner and Wolfgang Johannes Helbich, *Germans in the Civil War: The Letters They Wrote Home* (Chapel Hill: University of North Carolina Press, 2006), 195–218.

15. There is evidence that suggests collective reading by the family since Albert often addressed different members of the family directly by their names. The fact that most of his siblings were too young to read at the time of his departure suggests that his letters were read out loud. In a letter dated March 2, 1864, moreover, Krause comments on the family's traditional "evening conversations." FG, DABS, Krause/Krause Series, 2 January 1864 and 2 March 1864. Similar scenes of excitement surrounding stories from abroad have been described in other contexts. "It was the greatest source of joy for me when Ernst told stories of Brazil, describing the people and their doings, the orange trees with the gorgeous fruit, and the wild Botokude peoples," recalls a man named Theodor Bromme about a boarder in his childhood home who had previously spent years living in South America. "I could not hear enough and never grew tired [of his stories]." Cited in Barbara Beuys, *Familienleben in Deutschland: Neue Bilder aus der deutschen Vergangenheit* (Reinbeck: Rowohlt, 1980), 380–81.

16. All quotes from FG, DABS, Krause/Krause Series, 27 July 1861.

17. Little is known about the Krause family's financial affairs. Comparable *Instfamilien* in this period were unlikely to be able to afford even a modest library of their own. On incomes in the province of Posen, see Max Weber, *Die Verhältnisse der Landarbeiter in Deutschland*, vol. 3, *Schriften des Vereins für Sozialpolitik* (Leipzig: Duncker & Humblot, 1892), 415–38. See also the discussion in Kamphoefner and Helbich, *Germans in the Civil War*, 195–218.

18. Schooling appears to have been widely accessible at the time. Christian Meyer, *Geschichte der Provinz Posen* (Breslau: F. A. Perthes, 1891), 221; Weber, *Verhältnisse*, 3, 408, 415.

19. Albert Krause could be verbose in his correspondence. One letter dating from February 27, 1863, contained approximately 8,300 words. FG, DABS, Krause/Krause Series, 27 February 1863.

20. FG, DABS, Krause/Krause Series, 19/22 August 1863.

21. The letters sent to Albert Krause from Germany did not survive. However, it is possible to reconstruct their contents on the basis of Albert's own letters, in part because he often repeated his family's questions and concerns before answering them—a common practice among letter writers in this period because of frequent delays and occasional losses of correspondence. FG, DABS, Krause/Krause Series, 9 October 1862.

22. Weber, *Verhältnisse*, 3, 276.

23. In his first letter from July 27, 1861, Albert described his plans to acquire a farm and bring the remainder of his family to America. That said, little is known about

the exact situation of his family in Prussia. Contemporary accounts reveal that artisans and part-time cottagers in the region had been facing increasing competition from the machine and tool industry in Saxony. In addition, estate owners had begun to hire more Polish migrant laborers rather than employ German farmhands year-round. Kamphoefner and Helbich, *Germans in the Civil War*, 195–96.

24. The vow to his family is in FG, DABS, Krause/Krause Series, 10 October 1863. "Living aimlessly" in FG, DABS, Krause/Krause Series, 9 October 1862.
25. In his letter from October 9, 1862, Albert explained that for the time being he could not afford to purchase a farm.
26. Ibid.
27. Ibid. Similarly, FG, DABS, Kuhn/Wagner-Kuhn Series, 5 May 1867.
28. FG, DABS, Krause/Krause Series, 9 October 1862.
29. Ibid. Similar requests for paternal blessing in FG, DABS, Johann Schipper Series, 9 November 1868. Still, not all emigrant writers were willing to have this conversation. "I can't write you much about my doings because everything changes all the time and here one's fortune quickly turns in good and bad ways." FG, DABS, Hackenberg/Jürgens Series, 15 March 1867.
30. Correspondents often expressed open contempt toward proponents of liberal politics. In a letter from October 12, 1869, a certain Nikolaus Pack, formerly of Schiffweiler in the Saar region, now residing in Mount Oliver, Pennsylvania, blamed the US Civil War on "those dear 48ers, the heroes of freedom, who have broken with God and their respective monarchs." Jürgen Macha et al., eds., *Wir verlangen nicht mehr nach Deutschland: Auswandererbriefe und Dokumente der Sammlung Joseph Scheben (1825–1938)* (Frankfurt am Main: Peter Lang, 2003), 514.
31. Mobility is a near-universal theme in migrant letters from this period. That it was a controversial topic is evident from the occasional use of anti-Jewish tropes that compare mobility to "Jewish" wandering, disloyalty, and inconstancy. For example, FG, DABS, Treutlein/Treutlein Series, 16 November 1872; Bauer/Löwen Series, 20 May 1877; Hackenberg/Jürgens, 12 January 1870; Johannes Köster Series, 11 July 1862; Grimm/Kessel & Rückels Series, 27 November 1859; Ruess, Meister & Zeller Series, 11 September 1870; and Werner/Dieffenbach Series, 20 August 1853.
32. FG, DABS, Krause/Krause Series, 31 December 1865. Similar instances of hedging in FG, DABS, Kuhn/Wagner-Kuhn, 20 November 1868; and Groth/Groth Series, 10 March 1901; as well as in Hauptstaatsarchiv Baden-Württemberg, E40/76 Bü 430, Johann Jacob Beck, Memphis, Tennessee, 20 April 1864. On migrants as cultural interlocutors, see Dirk Hoerder, "Losing National Identity or Gaining Transcultural Competence: Changing Approaches in Migration History," in Heinz-Gerhard Haupt and Jürgen Kocka, eds., *Comparative and Transnational History: Central European Approaches and New Perspectives* (New York: Berghahn Books, 2009).

33. All quotes in FG, DABS, Krause/Krause Series, 27 August 1865.
34. All quotes in FG, DABS, Krause/Krause Series, 31 December 1865.
35. There were variations on the term. Albrecht Groth reported having "become very different, I move forward ruthlessly [*rücksichtslos*]." Barbara Meister admitted that she had become "quite wild [*ganz wild*] because otherwise you don't make it here." A contemporary dictionary lists "audacity" first and "impudence" second on the entry for Dreistigkeit. Jacob Grimm and Wilhelm Grimm, *Deutsches Wörterbuch. Zweiter Band* (Leipzig: Verlag von S. Hirzel 1860), 1395–96. All quotes in FG, DABS, Groth/Groth Series, 27 November 1890; and FG, DABS, Ruess, Meister & Zeller Series, 11 September 1870.
36. As Riehl put it, "the simple work-more [*Arbeitssitte*] of the German people, as it was, is, and hopefully will remain, puts to shame the modern presumption of a kind of work that claims to be able to do everything except acknowledge its own shortcomings." Riehl, *Arbeit*, 170–71.
37. All quotes from FG, DABS, Krause/Krause Series, 31 December 1865.
38. FG, DABS, Krause/Krause Series, 31 December 1865. Similar reasoning in FG, DABS, Treutlein/Treutlein Series, 16 November 1872; Groth/Groth Series, 27 November 1890; and Ruess, Meister & Zeller Series, 13 December 1869. See also Daughters of the Republic of Texas Library at the Alamo, San Antonio, Henry Baumberger Papers, Doc. 5171, f. 6, 28 August 1867.
39. FG, DABS, Krause/Krause Series, 27 August 1865. As another emigrant put it, "[Americans] do not steal, but in scamming they have no equal... whoever earns money with the most ordinary frauds remains, despite this, an honest and respected man... anyone who deceives a good amount is honored as a '*smart man*.'" FG, DABS, Johann Schipper Series, October 17, 1865. Similar accounts of the "smart Yankee" in FG, DABS, Neidhöfer/Schwarting Series, July 1864, 15 August 1864. On mobility as a survival strategy, see Foner, *Free Soil*, xxii–xxiv.
40. FG, DABS, Krause/Krause Series, 27 August 1865. Echoes on the apparent struggle to act in uncouth ways in FG, DABS, Treutlein/Treutlein Series, 16 November 1872.
41. FG, DABS, Krause/Krause Series, 31 December 1865. Similar observations in FG, DABS, Breimaier-Carstens/Hummel Series, 15 July 1860; Johann Schipper Series, 12 February 1867; Bauer Series, 11 April 1868; and Kaper/Meinecke-Hayssen, 4 March 1864. It is worth juxtaposing Albert Krause's reflections on the freedom of enterprise to those of another letter writer in Germany, Carl Beckmann of Rulle, a small town near Osnabrück. "The world stands on its head," Beckmann complained. "Everyone here is at war with each other... we used to have good times when every person who wanted to was able to earn money.... But the best times are in the past over here; with Gewerbefreiheit anything goes, and now everybody wants to trade. It used to be 2 in Rulle, now it's 7, way too many in Rulle." DRTL, Beckmann Family Papers, Box 1, f. 1, 30 December 1870.

42. As Allyson Hobbs puts it, "the Civil War... was America's first experiment in creating a "postracial" society.... These heady times—when the prospect of being both black and a citizen existed—were nothing short of revolutionary." She goes on to argue that "the bright promises of Reconstruction affirm that the American racial order was neither fixed nor timeless, but rather fluid and unpredictable." Allyson Hobbs, *A Chosen Exile: A History of Racial Passing in American Life* (Cambridge, MA: Harvard University Press, 2014), 74; and Matthew Frye Jacobson, *Whiteness of a Different Color: European Immigrants and the Alchemy of Race* (Cambridge, MA: Harvard University Press, 1998), 15–38. An extended discussion of the so-called second founding can be found in Eric Foner, *The Second Founding: How the Civil War and Reconstruction Remade the Constitution* (New York: W. W. Norton, 2019).
43. This was not just true in theory; nativists in the 1840s and 1850s routinely singled out the inclusiveness of the Naturalization Act of 1790. Jacobson, *Whiteness*.
44. All quotes in FG, DABS, Kuhn/Wagner Series, 20 November 1868. On the shift in German immigrant strategies in these years, see Alison Clark Efford, *German Immigrants, Race, and Citizenship in the Civil War Era* (Washington, DC: German Historical Institute, 2013). Interestingly, there are parallels in the history of "racial passing." Allyson Hobbs finds that Black Americans were much less likely to attempt to pass as white during Reconstruction. Hobbs, *A Chosen Exile*, esp. 74–85.
45. FG, DABS, Kuhn/Wagner Series, 20 November 1868. Like most German emigrants, Kuhn supported the emancipation of enslaved Black people. But this did not keep him from feeling unease, as one of his compatriots put it, about being put "on equal political and social footing with the negroes just extracted from the mire of slavery." Cited in Andrea Mehrländer, *The Germans of Charleston, Richmond and New Orleans During the Civil War Period, 1850–1870: A Study and Research Compendium* (Berlin: De Gruyter, 2011), 274. On German American politics vis-à-vis slavery and emancipation, see Efford, *German Immigrants*; and Mischa Honeck, *We Are the Revolutionists: German-Speaking Immigrants and American Abolitionists After 1848* (Athens, GA: University of Georgia Press, 2011).
46. All quotes in FG, DABS, Kuhn/Wagner Series, 20 November 1868. On the theme of "subservience," see also FG, DABS, Breimaier-Carstens/Hummel Series, 25 December 1850. It is worth noting that native-born Americans often experienced similar internal struggles. See, for instance, Brian Roberts, *American Alchemy: The California Gold Rush and Middle-Class Culture* (Chapel Hill: University of North Carolina Press, 2000); and Rodgers, *The Work Ethic*.
47. FG, DABS, Kuhn/Wagner Series, 20 November 1868.
48. FG, DABS, Kuhn/Wagner Series, 5 May 1867, 27 November 1867, 20 November 1868, and 9 March 1870. By 1870, Kuhn was commenting on the increasingly positive reputation that the Germans enjoyed among Americans.
49. Albert's father died on December 8, 1862. Albert did not learn of his death until the following summer. FG, DABS, Krause/Krause Series, 19/22 August 1863.

On the relationship between *Sitte* and God, see Köstlin Julius, "Studien über das Sittengesetz," *Jahrbücher für deutsche Theologie* 13 (1868), 383–461. On values related to work, see Riehl, *Arbeit*, 151–52, 160.

50. FG, DABS, Krause/Krause Series, 19 August 1863. Aurelius's age comes through in FG, DABS, Krause/Krause Series, 19/22 August 1863. In 1892, Max Weber completed a detailed study of tenant farmers in the Vistula valley. He found that it was quite common for children to work alongside their parents. Aurelius, in other words, likely possessed a rudimentary knowledge of farming. Weber, *Verhältnisse*, 3, 408.
51. "An opportunity" and "see the world" in the letters from October 9, 1862, and August 19, 1863. Similar advice directed at siblings in FG, DABS, Kuhn/Wagner-Kuhn Series, 27 November 1867.
52. FG, DABS, Krause/Krause Series, 19 August 1863.
53. The original letter from Albert's mother does not exist. I have reconstructed her arguments based on Albert's responses. Ibid.
54. Ibid. In a subsequent letter from August 22, 1863, directed at Aurelius, Albert asked his brother to read through his mother's letter.
55. Ibid.
56. Ibid.
57. Ibid.
58. FG, DABS, Krause/Krause Series, 19 August 1863 and 22 August 1863.
59. Aurelius came to visit Albert for the first time in the early 1880s. FG, DABS, Krause/Krause Series, 20 July 1882.
60. Weber, *Verhältnisse*, 3, 278.
61. FG, DABS, Krause/Krause Series, 19 August 1863.
62. Ibid.
63. Hessisches Hauptstaatsarchiv Wiesbaden, 1199/130.3, "Lebenslauf," January 1879, 1–35, here 33.
64. Caesar admits only to have wished to visit the city of Hamburg, about which "so much praise was sung." The timing, as well as the fact that he witnessed emigrants on their way to America all around him, suggests that there may have been more to the story. Ibid., 17–37, here 16.
65. It was not until years later, in 1862, that a rail connection operated by the Royal Hanoverian State Railways was completed between Bremen and Bremerhaven.
66. To be sure, he notes, he did still make it to "the great port" of Hamburg. But the visit was brief, no more than a few days. Ibid., 32–37, here 34–35.
67. Carl Dittmann was known as a snake-oil salesman who peddled miracle drugs for deafness and who claimed various labor-saving inventions for the tanning industry, none of which seemed to have come to fruition. This may help explain why he accepted Caesar as an apprentice: Neither man seems to have been especially interested in the work of tanning. Ibid., 39–43. On the state of the tanning industry in

this period, see Werner Sombart, *Die Genesis des Kapitalismus, vol. 1*, Der moderne Kapitalismus (Leipzig: Duncker & Humblot, 1902), 452–58.

68. Following his apprenticeship with Carl Dittmann, Caesar did find work with another master in Koblenz, but his stay there was brief. HHStW, 1199/130.3, "Lebenslauf," January 1879, 43–49, 66.

69. It is possible that his name was in fact Julius Caesar. The first name—Julius—was not uncommon in this period, and he mentions a cousin in Hachenburg whose last name was also Caesar. Ibid., 17.

70. Ibid., 12, 24, 29–31, 33, 66.

CHAPTER 4

1. On the idea of a "pastor's gravitas," see the description in Wilhelm Heinrich Riehl, *Die Familie* (Stuttgart: J. G. Cotta, 1861), 354. For a more recent discussion, see Margaret Hunt, *Women in Eighteenth Century Europe* (London: Routledge, 2010), 49–89. On Germany in particular, see Heide Wunder, *Er ist die Sonn', sie ist der Mond: Frauen in der Frühen Neuzeit* (Munich: C. H. Beck, 1992).

2. My account here draws on Ute Frevert, *Frauen-Geschichte Zwischen Bürgerlicher Verbesserung und Neuer Weiblichkeit* (Frankfurt am Main: Suhrkamp Verlag, 1986), 15–32; and Hunt, *Women*, esp. 168–208. Contrary to common belief, women enjoyed more expansive rights to property and divorce in the absolutist states of the eighteenth century than in many of the republics that emerged during the revolutionary era. Karen Hagemann, "Nation, Krieg und Geschlechterordnung: Zum kulturellen und politischen Diskurs in der Zeit der antinapoleonischen Erhebung Preußens 1806–1815," *Geschichte und Gesellschaft* 22, no. 4 (1996), 562–91; Reinhart Koselleck, "Die Auflösung des Hauses als ständischer Herrschaftseinheit: Anmerkungen zum Rechtswandel von Haus, Familie und Gesinde in Preußen zwischen der Französischen Revolution und 1848," in *Familie zwischen Tradition und Moderne: Studien zur Geschichte der Familie in Deutschland und Frankreich vom 16. bis zum 20. Jahrhundert*, ed. Neithard Bulst et al. (Göttingen: Vandenhoeck & Ruprecht, 1981); Diemut Majer, *Frauen—Revolution—Recht: die grossen europäischen Revolutionen in Frankreich, Deutschland und Österreich 1789 bis 1918 und die Rechtsstellung der Frauen: unter Einbezug von England, Russland, der USA und der Schweiz* (Zurich: Nomos, 2008), 157; Mary Beth Norton, "The Evolution of White Women's Experience in Early America," *The American Historical Review* 89, no. 3 (1984): 605–6; and Wunder, *Er ist die Sonn'*, 257, 262–68. The quote by Goethe is cited and translated in Sarah Josephina Hale, *Woman's Record; or, Sketches of All Distinguished Women, from "The Beginning" till A.D. 1850: Arranged in Four Eras with Selections from Female Writers of Every Age* (New York: Harper & Brothers, 1853), viii.

Notes to Pages 94–97   257

3. To be sure, there were also ideological impulses, in that the nuclear family was believed to play an important function in republican forms of government. This political-ideological dimension was especially key in revolutionary societies like France and the United States. See Nancy F. Cott, *The Bonds of Womanhood: "Woman's Sphere" in New England, 1780–1835* (New Haven, CT: Yale University Press, 2021); and Lynn Hunt, *The Family Romance of the French Revolution* (Berkeley: University of California Press, 1992). On Germany, see Karen Hagemann and Jean H. Quataert, eds., *Gendering Modern German History: Rewriting Historiography* (New York: Berghahn Books, 2007); Isabel V. Hull, *Sexuality, State, and Civil Society in Germany, 1700–1815* (Ithaca, NY: Cornell University Press, 1996); and Koselleck, "Auflösung."

4. For simplicity's sake, I will use the term *reformer* to describe the (mostly *bürgerliche*) proponents of a new ideal of domesticity and femininity. On their social profile, see Frevert, *Frauen-Geschichte*, 33–79; Hagemann, "Nation"; and James J. Sheehan, *German History, 1770–1866* (Oxford: Clarendon Press, 1989), 535–42. Notable reformers included the nationalist activist Friedrich Jahn, the painter Ludwig Richter, the economist Lorenz von Stein, the poet Leopold Schefer, the novelists Franz Grillparzer and Adalbert Stifter, and the philosopher Georg Friedrich Wilhelm Hegel.

5. "Doing service..." in Fernand Braudel, *The Structures of Everyday Life*, vol. 1, Civilization and Capitalism, 15th–18th Century (New York: Harper & Row, 1982), 283. Another useful description of the material conditions of peasant homes can be found in Anne-Charlott Trepp, *Sanfte Männlichkeit und selbständige Weiblichkeit: Frauen und Männer im Hamburger Bürgertum zwischen 1770 und 1840* (Göttingen: Vandenhoeck & Ruprecht, 1996), 184–210; and Rudolf Weinhold, ed., *Volksleben zwischen Zunft und Fabrik: Studien zu Kultur und Lebensweise werktätiger Klassen und Schichten während des Übergangs vom Feudalismus zum Kapitalismus* (Berlin: Akademie-Verlag, 1982), esp. 142–49, 251–80.

6. The dynamics described here are generally associated with the "protoindustrial" household. Because they specialized in mobilizing all marginal resources and labor, Jan de Vries refers to these households as "industrious households." Jan de Vries, *The Industrious Revolution: Consumer Behavior and the Household Economy, 1650 to the Present* (Cambridge: Cambridge University Press, 2008).

7. Frevert, *Frauen-Geschichte*, 63–72; Sheehan, *German History*, 535–42.

8. Originally cited in Friedrich Sengle, *Biedermeierzeit: Deutsche Literatur im Spannungsfeld zwischen Restauration und Revolution, 1815–1848*, 3 vols. (Stuttgart: J. B. Metzler, 1971–80), 61; Sheehan, *German History*, 537.

9. Examples of this kind of argumentation include the works of Johann Ludwig Tieck, Fanny Lewald, Adalbert Stifter, Franz Grillparzer, Friedrich Hebbel, Jeremias Gotthelf, and Ida von Hahn-Hahn. Eda Sagarra and Elka Schloendorn,

"'Echo und Antwort': Die Darstellung der Frau in der deutschen Erzählprosa 1815–1848," *Geschichte und Gesellschaft* 7, no. 3/4 (1981): 395–96. That the argument was limited to married mothers did not change the underlying challenge to the image of Eve because it suggested, at the very least, a wide range of feminine affects. This was in fact the beginning of a long debate over the nature of women's rights (i.e., whether they derived from women's difference or sameness to men) that would carry on well into the twentieth century. For an introduction, see Richard J. Evans, *The Pursuit of Power: Europe 1815–1914* (New York: Penguin Books, 2016), 499–509, 537–48. On the German case, see Frevert, *Frauen-Geschichte*, 72–80, 92–145.

10. The breadwinner–homemaker division of labor did not win widespread acceptance until the second half of the nineteenth century, both in Germany and in other parts of the continent. The exception was the United States, for reasons I will consider in some detail below. De Vries, *Industrious*, 232–37; Frevert, *Frauen-Geschichte*, esp. 33–40, 63–80.

11. As the eighteenth-century physician and lexicographer Johann Georg Krünitz noted, there were significant concerns about whether there could ever be "two… equal rulers in a single government." In his study of the German family, which he began working on in the 1850s, Wilhelm Heinrich Riehl warned that "out of the reconstruction of the home a new society…inevitably emerges." Krünitz cited in Frevert, *Frauen-Geschichte*, 27; Riehl, *Die Familie*, 155–6. On the French Revolution as a source of anxiety about women, see Hagemann, "Nation."

12. A succinct discussion of the fiscal concern can be found in Koselleck, "Auflösung."

13. To be sure, some scholars have argued that a reduction in a woman's income did not necessarily lead to diminished influence or increased vulnerability. Jan de Vries suggests that, to the contrary, women's "bargaining power" may have been enhanced by adopting a breadwinner–homemaker model. De Vries, *Industrious*, 210–37.

14. If the blockbuster novels of other *Vormärz* writers like Johann Ludwig Tieck, Jeremias Gotthelf, and Henriette Hanke are any guide, many men appeared to agree. For Tieck and Gotthelf especially, an attractive woman was still the one who was most able to perform hard physical labor, bear many healthy children, and, above all, take initiative and responsibility for herself. "I am earning…" in Ludwig Geiger, *Therese Huber, 1764 bis 1829: Leben und Briefe einer deutschen Frau* (Stuttgart: J. G. Cotta, 1901), 343. "True German womanhood" and "small woman" in Sagarra and Schloendorn, "Echo," 400, 409.

15. Similar parodies can be found in the works of some of the leading novelists of the *Vormärz* period, including Johann Heinrich Tieck and Johanna Schopenhauer, the mother of the philosopher by the same name. "There are times…" originally cited in Sagarra and Schloendorn, "Echo," 410. On Heinrich Hoffmann, see the discussion in Sheehan, *German History*, 539–42.

16. In Germany, the rise of the breadwinner–homemaker model of domesticity is generally dated to the middle decades of the nineteenth century. It is evidenced by

a notable rise in this period of household expenditures on furniture, lighting, kitchenware, and decoration, as well as various items related to personal health and hygiene. Other indicators often cited include decreased spending on alcohol, falling rates of illegitimacy, and declining use of *Gesinde*. See Walther G. Hoffmann, *Das Wachstum der deutschen Wirtschaft seit der Mitte des 19. Jahrhunderts*, ed. W. Kunkel et al., *Enzyklopädie der Rechts- und Staatswissenschaft* (Berlin: Springer-Verlag, 1965), 116–17. On alcohol consumption, see James S. Roberts, "Der Alkoholkonsum deutscher Arbeiter im 19. Jahrhundert," *Geschichte und Gesellschaft* 6, no. 2 (1980): 227. Jonathan Sperber argues that child legitimacy was increasing sharply in the early 1860s. Jonathan Sperber, *Popular Catholicism in Nineteenth Century Germany* (Princeton: Princeton University Press, 1984), 39–98.

17. According to Jan de Vries, "a division of labor within the household was the only feasible route to enter the realm of this consumption cluster for families of modest income. What people wanted to consume was not what the industrializing economy made available; in the face of this reality the household remained—or, rather, it once again became—an important site of production in urbanizing and industrializing societies." De Vries, *Industrious*, 205.
18. All quotes in Riehl, *Familie*, 196–99, 203.
19. Forschungsbibliothek Gotha, Deutsche Auswandererbriefsammlung (DABS), Kaper/Meinecke-Hayssen Series, 2 March 1859.
20. Ibid., 2 March 1859 and 2 April 1859.
21. Ibid., 2 March 1859, 2 April 1859, and 3 December 1859. Another emigrant, Barbara Meister, justified her new domestic life in the United States by noting that "I have already received more clothes here than I would have in Germany in half a year," including "white pants," a "white apron," and "beautiful leather boots, as they wear them in big cities [in Germany]." Needless to say, the color of this wardrobe reflected the fact that Meister was "not permitted to work much" and spent much of her time "helping with cooking." Like Meinecke, she chose to emphasize the positive sides. In just a few days, she wrote, "I have learned more about a kitchen than I did in Augsburg in an entire year." FG, DABS, Ruess/Meister/Zeller Series, 21 June 1868.
22. Jürgen Macha et al., eds., *Wir verlangen nicht mehr nach Deutschland: Auswandererbriefe und Dokumente der Sammlung Joseph Scheben (1825–1938)* (Frankfurt am Main: Peter Lang, 2003), 328–31, 529. Similarly, FG, DABS, Ruess/Meister/Zeller Series, 21 June 1868.
23. Similar sentiments prevailed in the United States. Harriet Beecher Stowe, writing in the 1840s and 1850s, went to great lengths to emphasize that housework constituted difficult and hard labor. The key, according to Stowe, was to keep this fact secret so as not to embarrass men. "She shall scrub floors, wash, wring, bake, brew, and yet her hands shall be small and white; she shall have no perceptible income, yet always be handsomely dressed; she shall have not a servant in her home, with

a dairy to manage, hired man to feed, a boarder or two to care for, unheard-of pickling and preserving to do,—and yet you commonly see her every afternoon sitting at her shady parlor-window behind the lilacs, cool and easy, hemming muslin cap-strings, or reading the last new book." Daniel T. Rodgers, *The Work Ethic in Industrial America: 1850–1920* (Chicago: University of Chicago Press, 2014), 182–209, here 185.

24. FG, DABS, Kaper/Meinecke-Hayssen Series, *Sophie Meinecke*, 2 April 1863; Macha et al., *Wir verlangen*, 529. For examples of Meinecke's epistolary focus on domestic labor, see also the letters dated 18 December 1858, 2 March 1859, 2 April 1859, 7 June 1861, and 26 April 1862.

25. The quote is in FG, DABS, Hackenberg/Jürgens Series, 15 March 1867.

26. Reproduced in Wolfgang J. Helbich et al., eds., *Briefe aus Amerika: Deutsche Auswanderer schreiben aus der Neuen Welt, 1830–1930* (Munich: C. H. Beck, 1988), 506–8.

27. Reproduced in ibid., 507–8.

28. For example, Anna Maria Schano, 22 December 1856 and 16 August 1857, following a letter with similar contents by Franz Schano, 14 August 1857. Reproduced in ibid., 506, 520–21.

29. Meinecke could communicate disapproval in subtle ways, for example, by dropping cues that could arouse suspicion about men's conduct. "Fritz's tours are always unpleasant business tours," she once wrote. "Several times during the week he also drives to [Stockton, CA] for the papers and to run errands," which is when "I feel very lonely and weird right away." However, she maintained, Fritz usually "is very reluctant to be away," and he took his trips to Stockton in the mornings and afternoon only. "Evenings he is never out," she insisted, in an attempt to dispel suspicions that Fritz was neglecting her. FG, DABS, Kaper/Meinecke-Hayssen Series, 2 March 1859, 7 June 1861, 26 April 1862, and 2 April 1863.

30. FG, DABS, Kaper/Meinecke-Hayssen Series, 3 December 1859.

31. According to Wilhelm Heinrich Riehl, speculation was not only "the most thoughtless game of chance" but also closely associated with the devil. Riehl provides a useful summary of the moral economy of speculation and gambling in this period. Wilhelm Heinrich Riehl, *Die deutsche Arbeit* (Stuttgart: J. G. Cotta, 1862), 159–60.

32. FG, DABS, Kaper/Meinecke-Hayssen Series, 15 October 1861.

33. Ibid., 7 June 1861.

34. Ibid., 15 October 1861.

35. Ibid., 2 April 1863. It is telling that she concluded the letter with a story about an unfaithful wife who abandoned her husband, who was also Fritz's intended business partner in their San Joaquin endeavor.

36. On October 12, 1864, Meinecke apologized for an interruption in their correspondence. She had not been able to write because of illness, and Fritz, "who could

have informed you about my illness," did not write home because "he thought you would be worried if he wrote to you and not I." Ibid., 12 October 1864. On the outcome of the San Joaquin speculation, see Sophie Meinecke's brother Wilhelm Hayssen's letter from August 17, 1864.
37. Some scholars, including Jan de Vries, argue that a lack of income did not necessarily deprive women of influence vis-à-vis their husbands. To the contrary, de Vries suggests that women's "bargaining power" may have been enhanced by adopting a breadwinner–homemaker model. De Vries, *Industrious*, 210–37.
38. There is an extensive literature on the idea of the home in nineteenth-century America. For an introduction, see Nicole Martin, "In the Name of the Home: The Politics of Gender, Race, and Reconstruction in Nineteenth-Century America" (PhD diss., Stanford University, 2018); and Richard White, *The Republic for Which It Stands: The United States during Reconstruction and the Gilded Age, 1865-1896* (New York: Oxford University Press, 2017), 136–71.
39. Cott, *Bonds*; Glenna Matthews, *"Just a Housewife": The Rise and Fall of Domesticity in America* (New York: Oxford University Press, 1987). The quote by Ruess is in FG, DABS, Ruess/Meister/Zeller Series, 20 September 1869.
40. I am especially grateful to Nicole Martin for bringing to my attention the concept of manifest domesticity. Martin, "Home," esp. 1–15, 20–24. See also Amy Kaplan, "Manifest Domesticity," *American Literature* 70, no. 3 (1998), 581–606; Anders Stephanson, *Manifest Destiny: American Expansionism and the Empire of Right* (New York: Hill & Wang, 1995); and White, "Home." "Horse and mule fashion" cited in Silvia Federici, *Caliban and the Witch: Women, the Body and Primitive Accumulation* (New York: Autonomedia, 2004), 111. "Little Domestick affair" cited in Matthews, *Housewife*, 4. "If the American women…" cited in Martin, "Home," 30.
41. Martin, "Home," 49–61; Rodgers, *The Work Ethic*, 182–209.
42. The quote dates from 1861 and is by a minister in Georgia. Cited in Martin, "Home," 71.
43. As the Louisiana planter Antoine-Simon Le Page du Pratz put it in the 1750s, a "father and his wife are great enemies to their posterity when they give their children [to a Black wet nurse]. For the milk being the purest blood of the woman, one must be a step-mother indeed to give her child to a negro." Cited and translated in Shannon Lee Dawdy, "Proper Caresses and Prudent Distance: A How-To Manual from Colonial Louisiana," in *Haunted by Empire: Geographies of Intimacy in North American History*, ed. Ann Laura Stoler (Durham, NC: Duke University Press, 2006), 149. On the home idea in the South, see Thavolia Glymph, *Out of the House of Bondage: The Transformation of the Plantation Household* (New York: Cambridge University Press, 2008); and Bruce Levine, *The Fall of the House of Dixie: The Civil War and the Social Revolution That Transformed the South* (New York: Random House, 2013).

44. Martin, "Home"; Amy Dru Stanley, "Home Life and the Morality of the Marketplace: Slavery and Freedom, Women and Men," in *The Market Revolution in America*, ed. Melvyn Stokes and Stephen Conway (Charlottesville: University of Virginia Press, 1996).
45. "The wild lands…" in Roy P. Basler, ed., *The Collected Works of Abraham Lincoln*: Volume 7, 1863–1864 (New Brunswick, NJ: Rutgers University Press, 1953), 16. All other quotes can be found in Martin, "Home," 71–72.
46. Reproduced in Macha et al., *Wir verlangen*, 60–61.
47. All quotes in ibid. On the endurance of the household as a contractual and economic unit in the early nineteenth century, see Koselleck, "Auflösung."
48. All quotes in Macha et al., *Wir verlangen*, 60–61.
49. All quotes in ibid.
50. All quotes are in Daughters of the Republic of Texas Library at the Alamo, San Antonio, Henry Baumberger Papers, doc5171, f. 6, 23 January 1861. Other emigrants were less forgiving: Valentin Ruess of St. Joseph, Michigan, complained bitterly that "American women want to be paid for their work, that is how it is, because they are terribly lazy." Ruess spoke similarly ill of a relative in America, Barbara Meister, whom he believed had fallen prey to the American interpretation of femininity and therefore no longer worked very hard. FG, DABS, Ruess/Meister/Zeller Series, 10 April, no year given (likely late 1860s). See also the letters in the same series by Karl Zeller (no date, likely April 1868) and J. G. Zeller (21 May 1869). Barbara Meister's indignant replies to these allegations date from December 13, 1869, and September 11, 1870.
51. Ibid.
52. Macha et al., *Wir verlangen*, 330–31, 528–29.
53. Johann Joseph Thie to Bernhard Anton Joseph Thie, 23 February 1849, reproduced in ibid., 465–66.
54. University of Texas Dolph Briscoe Center for American History, Johann Baethge Family Papers, 2.325/B97, Heinrich Pape, 2 March 1856.
55. Macha et al., *Wir verlangen*, 465–66.
56. DBC, Johann Baethge Family Papers, 2.325/B97, Heinrich Pape, 14 June 1855.
57. As another emigrant put it, "Because you are in a new and almost uncharted land, you have enough material to fill the paper of an entire book, every plant every tree and bush that we don't have its description is interesting to us." FG, DABS, Hambloch/Hambloch Series, 17 March 1861. All in-text quotes are in DBC, Johann Baethge Family Papers, 2.325/B97, Heinrich Pape, 14 June 1855; and FG, DABS, Kaper/Meinecke-Hayssen Series, 2 April 1859. In another letter from April 2, 1859, Meinecke promises that "I will tell you very exactly how I have arranged my home."
58. In this respect, Sophie Meinecke had good reason to tell her parents that she ran "a household that has quite a few resemblances to yours." FG, DABS, Kaper/Meinecke-Hayssen Series, 3 April 1860.

CHAPTER 5

1. For comparison, the steel-casting firm of Friedrich Krupp at this time struggled to raise anything close to the sums cited by Marshall & Co. It took the Krupps years before finally securing a 12,000-taler investment from a relative in the mid-1830s, which valued the firm at approximately 36,000 talers, or less than 5 percent of Marshall's Temple investment. Harold James, *Krupp: A History of the Legendary German Firm* (Princeton: Princeton University Press, 2012), 29–30. Mevissen's visit to England is recounted in Joseph Hansen, *Gustav von Mevissen: Ein rheinisches Lebensbild, 1815–1899*, vol. 1 (Berlin: Georg Reimer, 1906), 161–63. His observation regarding child labor can be found in a letter Mevissen sent during a second trip to the industrial establishments around Leeds in 1846, reproduced in ibid., 465n1.
2. All quotes in Walter Bagehot, *Lombard Street: A Description of the Money Market*, 3rd ed. (London: Henry S. King, 1873), 4–5. On the question of industrial finance in Germany, see Richard H. Tilly, *Kapital, Staat und sozialer Protest in der deutschen Industrialisierung: Gesammelte Aufsätze* (Vandenhoeck & Ruprecht, 1980), 65–91. See also the more recent overview in Richard H. Tilly and Michael Kopsidis, *From Old Regime to Industrial State: A History of German Industrialization from the Eighteenth Century to World War I* (Chicago: University of Chicago Press, 2020), 194–204.
3. My account here is based on Hansen, *Mevissen*, 1, 618–20. "Material progress" is from an essay by Gustav Mevissen titled *Über Wesen, Aufgabe und Rechtsverhältnis der Aktiengesellschaften* (1856) and reproduced in ibid., 532. "Petty philistinism" and "narrow subjectivity" in ibid., 159. I cite the English case as an alternative mechanism because England was the most common point of reference for contemporaries in this period, especially with respect to the financing of industry. Still useful as an introduction, see Tilly, *Kapital*, 197–206.
4. That, at least, is what his biographer Joseph Hansen argues. Mevissen already knew about the joint-stock form from observing its use in Ghent and Anderlecht in Belgium. Hansen, *Mevissen*, 1, 158–59, 618–19.
5. "Capital and spiritual powers" and "bright future" in Mevissen, *Über Wesen* (1856), reproduced in Joseph Hansen, *Gustav von Mevissen: Ein rheinisches Lebensbild, 1815–1899*, vol. 2 (Berlin: Georg Reimer, 1906), 532, 620.
6. All quotes in Mevissen, *Über Wesen* (1856), reproduced in ibid., 532–33. The concerns of the business community are detailed in Jürgen Kocka, *Unternehmer in der deutschen Industrialisierung* (Göttingen: Vandenhoeck & Ruprecht, 1975), 65–73. A useful comparative perspective can be found in Jeffrey R. Fear and Christopher Kobrak, "Diverging Paths: Accounting for Corporate Governance in America and Germany," *The Business History Review* 80, no. 1 (2006), 1–48.
7. "Ruins of a bygone era" in Mevissen, *Über Wesen* (1856), reproduced in Hansen, *Mevissen*, 2, 533.

8. The phrase "dirty crowd of little men" is by Walter Bagehot, who used it to mock the corporatist presumptions of the continental European business establishment. Bagehot, *Lombard Street*, 9.
9. Efforts to limit the rights of stockholders are described in Kocka, *Unternehmer*, 69–70. More recently, though with a focus on a later period, see Sibylle Hofer, "Das Aktiengesetz von 1884 - ein Lehrstück für prinzipielle Schutzkonzeptionen," in *Aktienrecht im Wandel*, ed. Walter Bayer and Mathias Habersack (Tübingen: Mohr Siebeck, 2007); and Felix Selgert, *Macht und Kontrolle im Unternehmen: Die politische Ökonomie des Aktionärsschutzes im Deutschen Reich, 1870–1945* (Göttingen: Vandenhoeck & Ruprecht, 2020). Others turned to altogether different institutions for raising capital, such as cooperatives, which were being championed by the Saxon progressive economist Hermann Schulze-Delitzsch. Timothy Guinnane, "Die Reiffeisen-Kreditgenossenschaften 1864: Die Expansion des genossenschaftlichen Kredits im 19. Jahrhundert," in *Schlüsselereignisse der deutschen Bankengeschichte*, ed. Carsten Burhop, Dieter Lindenlaub, and Joachim Scholtyseck (Stuttgart: Franz Steiner Verlag, 2014), 120-35; Institut für bankhistorische Forschung e. V., ed., *Die Geschichte der DZ Bank: das genossenschaftliche Zentralbankwesen in Deutschland vom 19. Jahrhundert bis heute* (Munich: C. H. Beck, 2013).
10. On efforts to reform the laws governing joint-stock corporations prior to 1870, see Christoph Bergfeld, "Aktienrechtliche Reformvorhaben vor dem ADHGB," in *Aktienrecht im Wandel*, ed. Walter Bayer and Mathias Habersack (Tübingen: Mohr Siebeck, 2007); Louis Pahlow, "Aktienrecht und Aktiengesellschaft zwischen Revolution und Reichsgründung: Das Allgemeine Deutsche Handelsgesetzbuch von 1861," in ibid. "Money-power" in Jan Lieder, "Die 1. Aktienrechtsnovelle vom 11. Juni 1870," in ibid., 324. All other quotes in Hansen, *Mevissen*, 2, 535.
11. Kocka, *Unternehmer*, 69–73; Lieder, "Die 1. Aktienrechtsnovelle."
12. "Daily progress," "ever-expanding circle," and "large merchants..." in Library of Congress, MSS Kapp, Friedrich Kapp to his father, 12 August 1856. "The small and ignorant..." in Leo Baeck Institute, MS 568, MSF 54, Friedrich Kapp to Eduard Cohen, 9 December 1865 and 26 June 1874.
13. Kapp never put words to this anxiety regarding his business. He was, however, well aware of the fact that to some degree he owed his livelihood in New York to the misfortunes of his countrymen, given that one of his partners, Julius Fröbel, left the firm because he thought it morally unconscionable to continue the work. In the same vein, Friedrich Engels once wrote to Marx in 1851, "You can see more and more that emigration is an institution that turns everyone [who gets involved with it] into a fool, a donkey or a mean scoundrel." On Fröbel's reservations, see Julius Fröbel, *Ein Lebenslauf: Aufzeichnungen, Erinnerungen, und Bekenntnisse* (Stuttgart: J. G. Cotta, 1890), 33, 390. Engels cited in Jürgen Kuczynski, *Darstellung der Lage der Arbeiter in Deutschland von 1849 bis 1870* (Berlin: Akademie Verlag, 1962), 59.

14. "For weeks..." in Bayrische Staatsbibliothek, Verhandlungen des deutschen Reichstags (VdR), Friedrich Kapp, 2 December 1881. Heine quoted in Gustav Karpeles, ed., *Heinrich Heine's Gesammelte Werke: Achter Band* (Berlin: G. Grote, 1909), 174. The figures cited for immigration to the United States can be found in Susan B. Carter, *Historical Statistics of the United States: Earliest Times to the Present* (New York: Cambridge University Press, 2006).
15. The biographies of Steuben and Kalb were not the only forays into German American history that Kapp undertook in these years. He also published monographs on German mercenaries in North America and on the so-called economic value of immigration to the United States. While some of this work was clearly intended as a rebuttal to nativist, anti-immigrant sentiment, it is worth noting that Kapp saw himself as primarily in dialogue with a German readership in Europe. He wanted to raise awareness in Germany about the magnitude of the losses that the country incurred day in and day out as a consequence of emigration. As such, his work can be seen as part of a general effort on the part of German Americans to create what has been described as the "German living abroad" (*Auslandsdeutsche*). Bradley Naranch, "Inventing the Auslandsdeutsche," in *Germany's Colonial Pasts*, ed. Eric Ames et al. (Lincoln: University of Nebraska Press, 2005), 21–40; and Glenn Penny and Stefan H. Rinke, "Germans Abroad: Respatializing Historical Narrative," *Geschichte und Gesellschaft* 41, no. 2 (2015), 173–96. For a complete list of Kapp's historical writings, see Wolfgang Hinners, *Exil und Rückkehr: Friedrich Kapp in Amerika und Deutschland, 1824–1884* (Stuttgart: Akademischer Verlag, 1987), 313–18.
16. This was why delegates at the National Assembly in Frankfurt in 1848–49 refused to consider specific policies on emigration, even as they acknowledged that it was a problem. Many were convinced that emigration would simply cease once the German nation-state had been created. Michael Kuckhoff, "Die Auswanderungsdiskussion während der Revolution von 1848–49," in *Deutsche Amerikaauswanderung im 19. Jahrhundert: Sozialgeschichtliche Beiträge*, ed. Günter Moltmann (Stuttgart: J. B. Metzler, 1976).
17. For an introduction to these settler colonial projects, see Agnes Bretting and Hartmut Bickelmann, *Auswanderungsagenturen und Auswanderungsvereine im 19. und 20. Jahrhundert* (Stuttgart: Franz Steiner Verlag, 1991); Kathleen Neils Conzen, *Making Their Own America: Assimilation Theory and the German Peasant Pioneer: With Comments by Mack Walker and Jörg Nagler* (New York: Berg, 1990); and Mack Walker, *Germany and the Emigration, 1816–1885* (Cambridge, MA: Harvard University Press, 1964). On Hermann specifically, see William G. Bek, *The German Settlement Society of Philadelphia, and Its Colony, Hermann, Missouri* (Philadelphia: Americana Germanica Press, 1907); and Adolf E. Schroeder and Carla Schulz-Geisberg, eds., *Hold Dear, as Always: Jette, a German Immigrant Life in Letters* (Columbia: University of Missouri Press, 1988).

18. On Schurz's primary election loss, see Jasper W. Cross Jr., "The Forty-Eighter and the Election of 1860," *The Historical Bulletin* 27, no. 4 (1949), 79–89. For an introduction to German American politics in this period, see Alison Clark Efford, *German Immigrants, Race, and Citizenship in the Civil War Era* (Washington, DC: German Historical Institute, 2013); Mischa Honeck, *We Are the Revolutionists: German-Speaking Immigrants and American Abolitionists After 1848* (Athens, GA: University of Georgia Press, 2011); and Naranch, "Inventing."
19. The argument can be found in Friedrich Kapp, "Zur Sklavenfrage in den Vereinigten Staaten," *Amerikanische Studien* 8 (1854): 119–20. On Kapp's position in American politics, see Hinners, *Exil*, 115–52; and Honeck, *Revolutionists*, 38–70.
20. "At the center" in Hermann Eduard von Holst, "Friedrich Kapp," *Preussische Jahrbücher* 55, no. 3 (1885): 237. "Role of money-making..." in Friedrich Kapp, *Aus und über Amerika: Tatsachen und Erlebnisse* (Berlin: Julius Springer, 1876), 17, 312–13. On the Germania Life Insurance Company, see Anita Rapone, *The Guardian Life Insurance Company, 1860–1920: A History of a German-American Enterprise* (New York: New York University Press, 1987); and Robert E. Wright and David Smith, *Mutually Beneficial: The Guardian and Life Insurance in America* (New York: New York University Press, 2004).
21. On the history of insurance in antebellum America, see Sharon Ann Murphy, *Investing in Life: Insurance in Antebellum America* (Baltimore: Johns Hopkins University Press, 2010); Jonathan Levy, *Freaks of Fortune: The Emerging World of Capitalism and Risk in America* (Cambridge, MA: Harvard University Press, 2012), esp. 60–103. On the German side, see Ludwig Arps, *Auf sicheren Pfeilern: Deutsche Versicherungswirtschaft vor 1914* (Göttingen: Vandenhoeck & Ruprecht, 1965); and Peter Borscheid, *Mit Sicherheit leben: die Geschichte der deutschen Lebensversicherungswirtschaft und der Provinzial-Lebensversicherungsanstalt von Westfalen*, 2 vols. (Münster: Westfälische Provinzial, 1993). On Wesendonck's background and social networks, see Elisabeth Engel, "Hugo Wesendonck," (2016), accessed October 31, 2024, http://www.immigrantentrepreneurship.org/entries/hugo-wesendonck/.
22. Mevissen detailed his views on life insurance in a pamphlet from 1851 titled "Germania, Lebensversicherungs- und Rentenbank für Deutschland," which is reproduced in Hansen, *Mevissen*, 2, 512–17. For similar contemporary perspectives, see Hessisches Wirtschaftsarchiv in Darmstadt, S 11185, "Die Lebensversicherung und ihre Bedeutung für alle Stände" (Hamburg, 1870), as well as Institute für Stadtgeschichte Frankfurt am Main, R 689, Bd. 1, "Zustand und Fortschritt der deutschen Versicherungsanstalten" (Gotha, 1868).
23. It is revealing of the difference in narratives that the Germania in New York would eventually rename itself the Guardian Life Insurance Company, while the Germania in Cologne changed its name to Concordia, Kölnische Lebensversicherungsgesellschaft und Rentenbank. Hansen, *Mevissen*, 2, 622–24; Rapone, *The Guardian*, 143–63.

24. While there were some disagreements in the early years of the republic over whether joint-stock corporations were the best means to achieve the shared objective of securing the nation's future economic prosperity, by the 1830s at the latest, most observers accepted that they had some role to play. The debate by this time revolved almost exclusively around the extent of the state's involvement, with Democrats typically favoring privatization through free incorporation and Whigs insisting on broadened government supervision and public ownership. Eric Foner, *Free Soil, Free Labor, Free Men: The Ideology of the Republican Party Before the Civil War* (Oxford: Oxford University Press, 1995), esp. 170–77; Robert E. Wright, "Capitalism and the Rise of the Corporation Nation," in *Capitalism Takes Command: The Social Transformation of Nineteenth-Century America*, ed. Gary J. Kornblith and Michael Zakim, 145–68 (Chicago: University of Chicago Press, 2011); Heather Cox Richardson, *The Greatest Nation of the Earth: Republican Economic Policies During the Civil War* (Cambridge: Harvard University Press, 1997); William G. Roy, *Socializing Capital: The Rise of the Large Industrial Corporation in America* (Princeton: Princeton University Press, 1997), 41–77.

25. "Combine...recklessness" in Richard White, *Railroaded: The Transcontinentals and the Making of Modern America* (New York: W. W. Norton, 2011), 23. On the West as a site in the struggle over slavery, see Stacey L. Smith, *Freedom's Frontier: California and the Struggle over Unfree Labor, Emancipation, and Reconstruction* (Chapel Hill: University of North Carolina Press, 2013); and Nicole Martin, "In the Name of the Home: The Politics of Gender, Race, and Reconstruction in Nineteenth-Century America" (PhD diss., Stanford University, 2018).

26. Rapone, *The Guardian*, esp. 31–49. The agency total cited here is for the year 1865; see M. Kesslinger, *Guardian of a Century, 1860–1960* (New York: Guardian Life Insurance Company of America, 1960), 28.

27. High premiums and low commission paid to agents—among the consequences of the company's costly expansion in the West—eventually hurt the Germania's business. When a major financial crisis in 1873 put a near halt to new immigration to the United States, the company was faced with an existential challenge and survived only because of extensive cost-cutting measures. Plans for new general agencies were either suspended or scrapped altogether, while some existing ones were consolidated. Premiums were raised for policyholders in remote places like the South and West. Stricter guidelines for health evaluations screened out risky customers. In the most glaring example of the company's retreat from its founding mission, directors even began weighing the idea of marketing to a non-German clientele. The step was avoided for the time being, but the writing was on the wall: The Germania was fast becoming something its founders had never really intended, namely, a life insurance company like any other. Rapone, *The Guardian*, 63–78. On the return to Germany of German Americans in this period, see Alfred Vagts, *Deutsch-Amerikanische Rüchwanderung: Probleme—Phänomene—Statistik—Soziologie—Biographie*

(Heidelberg: Carl Winter Universitätsverlag, 1960); and Klaus J. Bade, *Migration in European History* (Cambridge, MA: Blackwell, 2003), 81–128. The quote can be found in LBI, MS 568, MSF 54, Friedrich Kapp to Eduard Cohen, 9 December 1865.

28. The scene is described in Geheimes Staatsarchiv Preußischer Kulturbesitz, I HA Rep. 120, C VIII 4, Nr. 20, 29 March 1869. Bankers in Frankfurt had taken an interest in business opportunities since at least the early 1860s. Benjamin Hein, "Old Regime in a New World: Frankfurt's Financial Market in the Nineteenth Century," *The Journal of Modern History* 92, no. 4 (2020), 735–73; David K. Thompson, "Reorienting Atlantic World Financial Capitalism: America and the German States," in *Globalized Peripheries: Central Europe and the Atlantic World, 1680–1860*, ed. Jutta Wimmler and Klaus Weber (Woodbridge, Suffolk: Boydell Press, 2020).

29. August Osterieth, ed., *Geschichte der Frankfurter Zeitung 1856–1906* (Frankfurt am Main: Verlag der Frankfurter Zeitung, 1906), 177. On the frenzy to establish overseas trade banks in 1869, see the internal correspondence at the Frankfurt house Gebrüder Bethmann in ISG, W 1/9:5 Nr. 806, 11 June 1870, 13 June 1870, and 14 June 1870.

30. Marcuse served on the company's board of directors and led one of the standing committees, the Auditing Committee, during the Germania's founding in the summer of 1860. Rapone, *The Guardian*, 21. "Intelligence and business acumen" in GStAPK, I HA Rep. 120, C VIII 4, Nr. 20, 29 March 1869; "one of the leading…" in *The New York Times*, "Hermann Marcuse," 10 April 1900.

31. GStAPK, I HA Rep. 120, C VIII 4, Nr. 20, 20 April 1869 and 15 June 1869.

32. "Almost impossible" in GStAPK, I HA Rep. 120, C VIII 4, Nr. 20, 29 March 1869. Between 1857 and 1867, Prussia granted eighty-two charters to joint-stock corporations, none of them banks. See Pahlow, "Aktienrecht," 275; on Frankfurt's place in German politics during the nineteenth century, see Carl Ludwig Holtfrerich, *Finanzplatz Frankfurt: Von der mittelalterlichen Messestadt zum europäischen Bankenzentrum* (Munich: C. H. Beck, 1999).

33. On the different corporate legal forms available to entrepreneurs in this period, see Timothy W. Guinnane et al, "Putting the Corporation in Its Place," in *NBER Working Paper Series* (Cambridge, MA: National Bureau of Economic Research, 2007), 1–61; and Richard H. Tilly, *Financial Institutions and Industrialization in the Rhineland, 1815–1870* (Madison: University of Wisconsin Press, 1966), 115–17.

34. While Prussian bureaucrats enjoyed a reputation for honesty and incorruptibility, it was nonetheless true that they were physically and socially closer to their communities than to Berlin. Many had relatives and business interests in their jurisdiction and therefore had a personal stake in whether to allow a joint-stock corporation to be established. See Hans-Joachim Henning, *Die deutsche*

Beamtenschaft im 19. Jahrhundert: zwischen Stand und Beruf (Stuttgart: Franz Steiner Verlag, 1984); and James J. Sheehan, *German History, 1770–1866* (Oxford: Clarendon Press, 1989), 519–23. Examples of opposition from local stakeholders can be found in GStAPK, I HA Rep. 120, A XII 5, Nr. 7, 24 October 1863, 26 April 1865, 3 May 1865, and 19 May 1865.

35. GStAPK, I HA Rep. 120, A XII 5, Nr 8, 12 June 1855 and 19 March 1858. On von der Heydt and other reform-minded Prussian ministers, see James M. Brophy, "The Political Calculus of Capital: Banking and the Business Class in Prussia, 1848–1856," *Central European History* 25 (1992), 149–76; Christopher Clark, *Iron Kingdom: The Rise and Downfall of Prussia, 1600–1947* (Cambridge, MA: Belknap Press of Harvard University Press, 2006), 500–509; and Sheehan, *German History*, 509–20.

36. "Promot[ing] and facilitate[ing]..." in GStAPK, I HA Rep. 120, C VIII 4, Nr. 20, 15 June 1869. The Prussian law on incorporation from 1843 stipulated that joint-stock corporations were to serve the "common weal" (*Gemeinwohl*), an ambiguous term that was readily exploited by local stakeholders to extract concessions from new joint-stock enterprises. An ordinance from December 17, 1855, that was circulated among Prussian ministries further reinforced the legal grounds for such claims, stating explicitly that financial contributions toward the construction of schools and churches in local communities should be treated as a "general condition" for earning a joint-stock corporation concession in Prussia. August von der Heydt's ministerial correspondence is revealing of this transactional dynamic: More than once, the minister felt compelled to explain to his counterparts that the law's reference to Gemeinwohl was not to be confused with the interests of the communities (*Gemeindewohl*). GStAPK, I HA Rep. 120, A XII 5, Nr 8, 12 June 1855, 7 March 1857, 9 June 1857, 19 March 1858, 27 August 1858, and 1 October 1859. On the incorporation law of 1843, see Erik Kießling, "Das preussische Aktiengesetz von 1843," in *Aktienrecht im Wandel*, ed. Walter Bayer and Mathias Habersack (Tübingen: Mohr Siebeck, 2007), 193–236.

37. The Germania itself was not mentioned in the proposal. My argument here is only that the specter of loss as it had been articulated by the Germania in New York also informed the narrative that the Deutsch-Amerikanische presented to the Prussian government, and that this is probably not a coincidence. All quotes in GStAPK, I HA Rep. 120, C VIII 4, Nr. 20, 15 June 1869.

38. "Long thought about" in ibid., 29 March 1869.

39. Ibid., 29 March 1869, 11 April 1869, 20 April 1869, 25 April 1869, 2 May 1869, and 9 May 1869. On the Blücher family and Prussian politics, see Michael V. Leggiere, *Blücher: Scourge of Napoleon* (Norman: University of Oklahoma Press, 2014).

40. On the negotiations about bylaws, see GStAPK, I HA Rep. 120, C VIII 4, Nr 20, 30 June 1869, 25 April 1869, 2 May 1869, and 15 June 1869. The note citing the Ordinance of 1512 can be found in ibid., 8 October 1869.

41. Ibid., 25 October 1869.

42. Ibid., 26 January 1870.
43. Adelbert Delbrück, *Aufzeichnungen unseres Vaters Adelbert Delbrück: geb. 16. Januar 1822, gest. 26. Mai 1890: Für die Enkel und Urenkel gedruckt 1922* (Leipzig: J. A. Brockhaus, 1922); Gustav Dufresne, "Denkschrift über die Aufgaben und Ziele der neu zu errichtenden Deutschen Bank," in *Studies on Economic and Monetary Problems and on Banking History* (Neuwied: Hase & Koehler, 1988), 729–30, 738–39.
44. ISG, W 1/9:5 Nr. 806, 17 June 1870.
45. "Sole person suitable" in GStAPK, I HA Rep. 120, C VIII 4, Nr. 20, 20 April 1869.
46. On Bismarck's diplomatic maneuvers in these months, see Gordon A. Craig, *Germany, 1866–1945* (Oxford: Clarendon Press, 1978), 22–27.
47. On Bismarck's politics vis-á-vis France, see ibid.
48. "Hastily cobbled together" in Levin Goldschmidt, *Die Reform des Aktiengesellschaftsrechts* (Stuttgart: Verlag von Ferdinand von Enke, 1884), 69, 75. Similarly, Lieder, "Die 1. Aktienrechtsnovelle," 322–27, 338, 381–87.

CHAPTER 6

1. E. J. Carter, "Breaking the Bank: Gambling Casinos, Finance Capitalism, and German Unification," *Central European History* 39, no. 2 (2006), 191; Friedrich Otto, *Geschichte der Stadt Wiesbaden* (Wiesbaden: Franz Bossong, 1877), esp. 130–42.
2. Marcuse's reluctance is described in correspondence between two friends, Ludwig Bamberger and Friedrich Kapp. Library of Congress, MSS Kapp, Friedrich Kapp to Ludwig Bamberger, 18 September 1869.
3. Manfred Pohl, "Selected Documents on the History of the Deutsche Bank," in *Studies on Economic and Monetary Problems and on Banking History*, ed. Manfred Pohl (Mainz: v. Hase & Koehler, 1988), 777.
4. Gustav Dufresne, "Denkschrift über die Aufgaben und Ziele der neu zu errichtenden Deutschen Bank," in *Studies on Economic and Monetary Problems and on Banking History*, ed. Manfred Pohl(Neuwied: Hase & Koehler, 1988), 729–37.
5. Ibid.
6. They were Heinrich Hardt (47,000 taler via Hardt & Co.), Eduard von der Heydt (63,400 taler), Friedrich Kapp (board member only), Gustav Kutter (63,400 taler), Wilhelm O. Loeschigk (53,600 taler), Hermann Rose (9,400 talers), and Otto Wesendonck (64,200 taler). Note that these figures represent par values only. Pohl, "Selected Documents," 776–78.
7. "Archetypical" in Lothar Gall et al., *The Deutsche Bank, 1870–1995* (London: Weidenfeld & Nicolson, 1995), xiii, 18–19. The classic articulation of the argument—that Deutsche Bank's universal banking model was merely a response to the particular circumstances and needs of German industries—is Alexander Gerschenkron, *Economic Backwardness in Historical Perspective: A Book of Essays*

(Cambridge, MA: Belknap Press of Harvard University Press, 1962). Although the extent to which universal banks played the functions Gerschenkron described has since been refuted, most observers in the early twenty-first century agree that universal banking was uniquely suited to German development in this period. Carsten Burhop, "Did Banks Cause the German Industrialization?," *Explorations in Economic History* 43, no. 1 (2006), 39–63; Caroline Fohlin, *Finance Capitalism and Germany's Rise to Industrial Power* (New York: Cambridge University Press, 2007); Timothy W. Guinnane, "Delegated Monitors, Large and Small: Germany's Banking System, 1800–1914," *Journal of Economic Literature* 40, no. 1 (2002), 73–124. See also the overview in Richard H. Tilly and Michael Kopsidis, *From Old Regime to Industrial State: A History of German Industrialization from the Eighteenth Century to World War I* (Chicago: University of Chicago Press, 2020), 194–204.

8. A detailed account of the groups of investors that initially backed Deutsche Bank can be found in Fritz Seidenzahl, *100 Jahre Deutsche Bank, 1870–1970* (Frankfurt am Main: Deutsche Bank AG, 1970), 27–42.

9. "No profit…" in Guinnane, "Delegated Monitors," 98. All other quotes in Karl Helfferich, *Georg von Siemens: Ein Lebensbild aus Deutschlands großer Zeit*, vol. 1 (Berlin: Julius Springer, 1921), 210.

10. Cited in Benedikt Koehler, *Ludwig Bamberger: Revolutionär und Bankier* (Stuttgart: Deutsche Verlags-Anstalt, 1999), 142.

11. Karl Helfferich was the first to make this argument, but a similar explanation can be found in later accounts, for example, Gall et al., *The Deutsche Bank, 1870–1995*; Seidenzahl, *100 Jahre*. On managerial practices in German banking and finance in this period more generally, see the discussion in Morten Reitmayer, "Führungsstile und Unternehmensstrategien deutscher Großbanken vor 1914," *Zeitschrift für Unternehmensgeschichte/Journal of Business History* 46, no. 2 (2001), 160–81.

12. "Stupefying" cited in Koehler, *Bamberger*, 58. All other quotes in Ludwig Bamberger, *Erinnerungen von Ludwig Bamberger* (Berlin: Georg Reimer, 1899), 251.

13. Historisches Archiv Deutsche Bank, S4513, Georg Siemens to Kilian Steiner, 20 January 1876.

14. All quotes in Bundesarchiv Lichterfelde, N2008/103, Friedrich Kapp to Ludwig Bamberger, 9 November 1866 and 9 February 1869. See also Bamberger's own reflections on the matter in Bamberger, *Erinnerungen*, 505, 512.

15. All quotes in ibid., 221, 395. On the formative years of Kapp and Bamberger's friendship, see Koehler, *Bamberger*.

16. Max Weber once wrote of Kapp that he was always "fresh, outright juvenile in his expressions, rude in an American way, often so rude that he well-nigh stunned those who did not already know him. It always seemed as though he managed to throw those old men around him back into their student days." Marianne Weber, ed., *Max Weber: Jugendbriefe* (Tübingen: J. C. B. Mohr, 1936), 141. Bamberger, by

contrast, spoke out fervently against the chauvinism of his time, most notably during the so-called Berlin anti-Semitism dispute of 1879. See Marcel Stoetzler, *The State, the Nation, & the Jews: Liberalism and the Antisemitism Dispute in Bismarck's Germany* (Lincoln: University of Nebraska Press, 2008); Heinrich August Winkler, *Deutsche Geschichte vom Ende des Alten Reiches bis zum Untergang der Weimarer Republik*, vol. 1, Der lange Weg nach Westen (Munich: C.H. Beck, 2000), 235ff. Examples of the two men's affection for each other can be found in BArch, N2008/103, Friedrich Kapp to Ludwig Bamberger, 20 November 1860, 12 April 1862, 14 July 1865, 9 November 1866, 26 January 1867, 26 May 1868, and 9 February 1869.

17. For example, when Bamberger campaigned for a seat in the North German Confederation's parliament, Kapp confessed that, "while I have not written since February, this whole time I have lived together with you more than usual." BArch, N2008/103, Friedrich Kapp to Ludwig Bamberger, 26 May 1868.

18. Kapp had intended to return to Germany since at least 1862, but he consistently struggled to find remunerative employment. Wolfgang Hinners, *Exil und Rückkehr: Friedrich Kapp in Amerika und Deutschland, 1824–1884* (Stuttgart: Akademischer Verlag, 1987), 155–58, 177–84.

19. In his obituary, Bamberger went so far as to describe Kapp as "a true son of God, an eternal youth." A digital copy of the newspaper obituary has been preserved by the Leo Baeck Institute as part of the Fritz Victor Lenel Family Collection (AR 25424), pp. 316–17. "Original wit" and "ur-strong manliness" in Ludwig Bamberger, "Ein Vademecum für deutsche Unterthanen," *Deutsche Jahrbücher für Politik und Literatur* 13 (1864): 70.

20. BArch, N2008/103, Friedrich Kapp to Ludwig Bamberger, 9 November 1866 and 11 December 1866.

21. Ibid.; "le commencement..." originally cited in Koehler, *Bamberger*, 97.

22. Kapp had made the request for *Die Gartenlaube* back in May 1868; see BArch, N2008/103, Friedrich Kapp to Ludwig Bamberger, 26 May 1868. All quotes in ibid., 6 July 1869.

23. Ibid. The same letter indicates that Bamberger made this suggestion in a letter to Kapp from June 11, 1869.

24. See the detailed account of their meeting in Koehler, *Bamberger*, 129–46.

25. Years later, Bamberger claimed that he agreed to help Delbrück with his bank idea because "I was confident I had some knowledge" of the opportunities for a German bank to "expand into the transatlantic arena." Statements like these are often cited as evidence that Bamberger took on the project on his own account, out of sheer personal interest, which would imply that he was one of the creative forces behind Deutsche Bank. But the tortured phrasing—he was "confident of some knowledge"—could just as well constitute an admission that whatever Bamberger knew about the business came to him secondhand. Bamberger, *Erinnerungen*, 385.

26. Dufresne, "Denkschrift." Gustav Dufresne was a Dutch banker with experience in East Asian trade finance. He seemed to have been hired for the purposes of committing ideas to paper and adding statistical material for rhetorical effect. Apart from this work, Dufresne played no other role at Deutsche Bank, not even as an investor. Werner Plumpe et al., *Deutsche Bank: The Global Hausbank* (London: Bloomsbury, 2020), 10, esp. n31.
27. Dufresne, "Denkschrift," 735.
28. A similar critique can be found in the pamphlet by Prussian consul J. J. Sturz that was cited in the introduction to this study. Geheimes Staatsarchiv Preußischer Kulturbesitz, I HA, Rep 120, C XIII 20, Nr. 1, Bd. 9, "Die deutsche und die chinesische Aus- und Rückwanderung in ihrer Bedeutung für das Deutsche Reich," 1875.
29. BArch, N2008, Nr. 103, Friedrich Kapp to Ludwig Bamberger, 26 January 1867.
30. Friedrich Kapp, *Immigration, and the Commissioners of Emigration of the State of New York* (New York: Nation Press, 1870), 144–47.
31. Bamberger even documented his observations on Hessians in Paris in a short essay published in 1867. Ludwig Bamberger, "Hessische Straßenkehrer in Paris (1867)," in *Hessisches Auswandererbuch: Berichte, Chroniken und Dokmente zur Geschichte hessischer Einwanderer in den Vereinigten Staaten 1683–1983*, ed. Hans Herder (Frankfurt am Main: Insel Verlag, 1984), 415.
32. "Second to none" (*unübertrefflich*) in Bamberger, *Erinnerungen*, 403.
33. If Kapp's calculations about the resources that were being mobilized by the diaspora were correct, the idea was not all that far-fetched. A global, diaspora-centered strategy might have helped Deutsche Bank succeed where the domestic-oriented Crédit Mobilier failed.
34. Friedrich Kapp, *Der Soldatenhandel deutscher Fürsten nach Amerika (1775 bis 1783)* (Berlin: Franz Duncker, 1864).
35. Bamberger, "Vademecum."
36. Friedrich List, *Das nationale System der politischen Ökonomie* (Stuttgart: J. G. Cotta, 1841), 4–5, 16. See also List's essays titled *Outlines of American Political Economy* (1827), where he argued that "national wealth is increased and secured by national power, as national power is increased and secured by national wealth." Friedrich List, Thomas Jefferson, and James Madison, *Outlines of American Political Economy, in a series of letters addressed by Friedrich List to Charles J. Ingersoll. To which is added the celebrated letters of Mr. Jefferson to Benjamin Austin, and of Mr. Madison to the Editors of the Lynchburg Virginian* (Philadelphia: Samuel Parker, 1827), 10.
37. The memorandum was quite explicit about the fact that the Germans could do as much business with the world as they wanted, but unless they enjoyed the backing of a "powerful financial institution that was up to the task," they would always be settling their accounts in pounds or francs. Dufresne, "Denkschrift."
38. Ibid.
39. For Bamberger, Kapp quite literally embodied *Kraft*, which may be translated as strength, power, or vigor. Bamberger, "Vademecum," 70.

40. Koehler, *Bamberger*, 142.
41. A good portion of the original investors had sold their stakes in Deutsche Bank by this time. Others probably did not remember all the details from the original memorandum, which, after all, was already a year old. Plumpe et al., *Deutsche Bank*, 10–24.
42. This is indeed the role that Kapp would eventually assume. All quotes in LoC, MSS Kapp, Friedrich Kapp to Ludwig Bamberger, 18 September 1869.
43. "The man was..." cited in Helfferich, *Siemens*, I, 228. Bamberger and Delbrück also hired Hermann Wallich, a distant relative of Bamberger's, as a third manager, but Wallich was not able to start working at the bank until the following year. He also is not generally believed to have been the creative force behind Deutsche Bank. As a recent historian of the bank's early history puts it, "Georg Siemens had been the driving force behind the development of Deutsche Bank's various business segments." Plumpe et al., *Deutsche Bank*, 47.
44. Cited and translated in ibid., 23.
45. Cited in Seidenzahl, *100 Jahre*, 27.
46. BArch, N2008, Nr. 46, Adelbert Delbrück to Ludwig Bamberger, 14 June 1870. Delbrück was not the only one to express misgivings about Siemens. He was also maligned in the financial press, at least initially. Plumpe et al., *Deutsche Bank*, 20–21.
47. Gall et al, *The Deutsche Bank*, 49–77; Christopher Kobrak, *Banking on Global Markets: Deutsche Bank and the United States, 1870 to the Present* (Cambridge: Cambridge University Press, 2007), 24–35. See also the essays by Manfred Pohl and Ernst Klein in Manfred Pohl, ed., *Studies on Economic and Monetary Problems and on Banking History* (Neuwied: Hase & Koehler, 1988), 423–62, 471–86.
48. Manfred Pohl, "Glimpses of Deutsche Bank's Early Days—Through the Papers of Hermann Wallich," in *Studies on Economic and Monetary Problems and on Banking History*, ed. Manfred Pohl (Neuwied: Hase & Koehler, 1988), 384.
49. This proposal made good sense from a financial and business point of view. The interest rate was competitive for this class of investment, and because of the ongoing Franco-Prussian War, such securities were selling at a discount (even though the outcome of the hostilities had for all intents and purposes been decided at the Battle of Sedan in September, when the Prussians captured the French emperor, Napoleon III). Plumpe et al., *Deutsche Bank*, 25.
50. As Wallich put it in his memoirs, "Initially my work at the bank, though not unproductive, was a tremendous uphill struggle. The founders [of Deutsche Bank]...had not realized that the bank could not live on overseas business alone but, for some time to come, would have to make ends meet with bread-and-butter lines in the main. They did their best...to obstruct [my efforts] at every turn and particularly to curb the freedom of its managers, degrading them to the position of clerks whose job was merely to carry out whatever the

Administrative Board, or its executive committee, had ordained." Cited and translated in Pohl, "Glimpses," 383.
51. Ibid., 384.
52. Reproduced in Helfferich, *Siemens*, 1, 249–50. Because this proposal appears to be in Wallich's handwriting, the idea for a Germanische Transatlantische Bank has at times been attributed to Wallich, not Siemens. But there are reasons to suspect that the idea in fact originated with Siemens. First, Helfferich describes Wallich as being deeply reluctant about doing any business in the Americas, partially because he knew so little about the region. Second, correspondence between Siemens and Wallich suggests that the former often sought the latter's help in turning his meandering business ideas into more "carefully worked out" proposals that would pass muster with Deutsche Bank's board. And third, Wallich himself liked to credit Siemens with Deutsche Bank's more daring and innovative ideas: "Possibly, my younger colleague's fire was more useful than my own perhaps over-cautious, if not downright old-fashioned, style of management." All quotes cited and translated in ibid., 246–47; Pohl, "Glimpses," 383, 389; Manfred Pohl, "Deutsche Bank's East Asia Business (1870–1875)," in *Studies on Economic and Monetary Problems and on Banking History*, ed. Manfred Pohl (Neuwied: Hase & Koehler, 1988), 426.
53. HADB, A1343, Gustav Kutter to Georg Siemens, 12 July 1872; Hermann Wallich and Rudolph von Koch to Lichtenstein, 1 August 1872; Knoblauch to Georg Siemens, 6 August 1872. Not all these "branches" were wholly owned subsidiaries of Deutsche Bank because of local regulations governing the banking industry. In some jurisdictions, like London and New York, Deutsche Bank purchased large stakes in an already-registered domestic enterprise. Plumpe et al., *Deutsche Bank*, 28–29.
54. Cited and translated in Pohl, "Glimpses," 390.
55. For example, HADB, S4510, H. H. Meier to Deutsche Bank Berlin, 15 November 1875; HADB, S4510, A. W. Mencke to Deutsche Bank, 8 November 1875; and HADB, S4510, H. Sonnenberg to Deutsche Bank, 22 November 1875. On the Bremen challenge, see Seidenzahl, *100 Jahre*, 39–42. Hermann Wallich likewise argued that "the deals initiated by my gifted colleague rested, as it were, on spring-loaded foundations, engrossing our liquid resources and frequently cramping our freedom of movement in other directions." Cited and translated in Pohl, "Glimpses," 394.
56. Cited and translated in ibid., 393.
57. HADB, SG 18/8, Georg Siemens to Hermann Wallich, 23 September 1875.
58. On the losses incurred by the East Asian branches, see HADB, Geschäftsberichte 1870–1944, "Zweiter Geschäfts-Bericht der Direktion der Deutsche Bank," 31 Dezember 1871, 3–4. All quotes in HADB, S4510, Circular by Joh. Wilckens on behalf of Bremen stockholders, November 1875.
59. Max Steinthal, cited in Plumpe et al., *Deutsche Bank*, 45.

60. Ibid., 46–48.
61. Seidenzahl, *100 Jahre*, 51–54; HADB, S4516, Minutes of Board Meeting, Berliner Bankverein, 25 January 1876; HADB, S4513, Friedrich Kapp to Georg Siemens, 12 August 1876.
62. Gall et al, *The Deutsche Bank*, 18, 55–56; Pohl, "East Asia Business," 423–62.
63. LBI, MS 568, MSF 54, Friedrich Kapp to Eduard Cohen, 18 November 1877.
64. HADB, A1343, Hermann Marcuse to Hermann Wallich, 5 November 1877.
65. The quote is from Bamberger, "Vademecum," 70.
66. Starting in the mid-1870s, Siemens began arguing that the only way for Deutsche Bank to succeed abroad was to first develop its domestic business, in particular, the retail banking side. Plumpe et al., *Deutsche Bank*, 24–25, 48.
67. To be sure, I am not suggesting that capital export was not in Germany's economic interest—it was. The point is merely that any such benefits to the country as a whole were more likely to be an unintended consequence of the bank's business activities.
68. Under Siemens's auspices, Deutsche Bank's business in the United States grew so extensive that the bank organized an entire "America bureau." Kobrak, *Banking*.

CHAPTER 7

1. Hans Fürstenberg, *Carl Fürstenberg; die Lebensgeschichte eines deutschen Bankiers, 1870–1914* (Berlin: Ullstein Verlag, 1931), 526–28. The phrase "world's greatest debtor nation" is from Mira Wilkins, *The History of Foreign Investment in the United States to 1914* (Cambridge, MA: Harvard University Press, 1989).
2. "Hillbilly stage" by Albert Krause, whom we encountered in Chapters 3 and 4. Forschungsbibliothek Gotha, Deutsche Auswandererbriefsammlung (DABS), Krause/Krause Series, 28 January 1877. The comment on American farmers is by Friedrich Kapp; see Leo Baeck Institute, MS 568. MSF 54, Friedrich Kapp to Eduard Cohen, 9 December 1856.
3. John J. Madden, *British Investment in the United States, 1860–1880* (New York: Garland, 1985), 78–79, esp. table 14–15. See also Wilkins, *Investment*, 90–92, esp. table 4.1.
4. The figure reflects par values. In 1865, Prussia's debt stood at approximately $330 in contemporary dollars. On the emergence of Amsterdam, Frankfurt am Main, Stuttgart, and Geneva as key centers of transatlantic finance, see R. C. Michie, *The Global Securities Market: A History* (Oxford: Oxford University Press, 2006), 93–97, 115. All figures are in Wilkins, *Investment*, 109.
5. All quotes in ibid., 170, 227. On middle-class discourse about the United States in this period, see Jens-Uwe Guettel, *German Expansionism, Imperial Liberalism and the United States, 1776–1945* (Cambridge: Cambridge University Press, 2012); and Alexander Schmidt, *Reisen in die Moderne: Der Amerika-Diskurs des deutschen Bürgertums vor dem ersten Weltkrieg im europäischen Vergleich* (Berlin: Akademie Verlag, 1997).

6. As Otto Braunfels, a banker at Frankfurt's J. S. H. Stern bank, put it in 1876, even "the best railroads are allowed to be ruined by some scoundrel or idiot without the law having the capacity to protect the bondholders in retrospect." Harvard Baker Library, MSS 8993, V.719, Box 99, f.727, Otto Braunfels to Henry Villard, 1 November 1876. Dietrich Buss finds that British investors "considered western railroads in general too speculative, involving more risk than the eastern roads." Mira Wilkins observes that French investors backed away from American enterprises after incurring heavy losses in 1869 on an investment in the Memphis, El Paso and Pacific Railroad Corporation. Dietrich G. Buss, *Henry Villard: A Study of Transatlantic Investments and Interests, 1870–1895* (New York: Arno Press, 1978), 34; Wilkins, *Investment*, 116–17.

7. Stefan Link and Noam Maggor, "The United States as a Developing Nation: Revisiting the Peculiarities of American History," *Past & Present* 246, no. 1 (2020), 269–306. Elsewhere, I describe the institutional particularities of the Frankfurt stock exchange, which played an important role in facilitating German investments in the United States around midcentury. Benjamin Hein, "Old Regime in a New World: Frankfurt's Financial Market in the Nineteenth Century," *The Journal of Modern History* 92, no. 4 (2020), 735–73.

8. "Through their manifold…" in Thomas R. Kabisch, *Deutsches Kapital in den USA: von der Reichsgründung bis zur Sequestrierung (1917) und Freigabe* (Stuttgart: Klett-Cotta, 1982), 201. Wilkins observes a "dual function" in German financial institutions' US involvement: "Their first role was as foreign investors. Their second role was as communicators of U.S. investment opportunities to *their* clients, to the users of their services." Elsewhere she writes, "The German banks were international; they brought foreign issues to Germany and assisted German industry abroad." It is worth emphasizing that not every enterprise active in US markets relied on financial institutions to do so. Some firms, particularly smaller ones, relied on the information flows generated by migration itself, with relatives and acquaintances who had emigrated or settled abroad assuming the role of market researcher and, in some cases, local retailer. For example, see Hartmut Berghoff, *Zwischen Kleinstadt und Weltmarkt: Hohner und die Harmonika 1857–1961: Unternehmensgeschichte als Gesellschaftsgeschichte* (Paderborn: Ferdinand Schöningh, 1997), esp. 68–72. See also Wilkins, *Investment*, 269–75, 352–57, 389–400. The quotes can be found on pages 479 and 490.

9. "Motherland…" in Cornelius Torp, *Die Herausforderung der Globalisierung: Wirtschaft und Politik in Deutschland 1860–1914* (Göttingen: Vandenhoeck & Ruprecht, 2005), 325. The varieties of German foreign direct investment (FDI) in the United States are discussed in Wilkins, *Investment*, 386. Deutsche Bank's role in the Allgemeine Elektricitätsgesellschaft–Edison joint venture is described in detail in Christopher Kobrak, *Banking on Global Markets: Deutsche Bank and the United States, 1870 to the Present* (Cambridge: Cambridge University Press, 2007), 45–61, 126–43. The businesses cited here are discussed in Kabisch, *Kapital*, 243–49, 257–61, 262–79. On the importance of foreign direct investment for these

emerging industries in particular, see the discussion in Gerhard Kling et al., "FDI of German Companies During Globalization and Deglobalization," *Open Economies Review* 22, no. 2 (2011), 247–70.

10. The success of Germany's export economy in this period has inspired much commentary and study, from contemporaries and historians alike. Most explanations emphasize the relative abundance of human capital in Germany, the dynamism of its science-based industries, and a nuanced and place-specific approach to marketing. An overview can be found in Richard H. Tilly and Michael Kopsidis, *From Old Regime to Industrial State: A History of German Industrialization from the Eighteenth Century to World War I* (Chicago: University of Chicago Press, 2020), 207–12. On the importance of product differentiation and intraindustry trade to German exporters, see the discussion in Wolf-Fabian Hungerland and Markus Lampe, "Globalization and Foreign Trade," in *An Economic History of the First German Unification: State Formation and Economic Development in a European Perspective*, ed. Ulrich Pfister and Nikolaus Wolf (London: Routledge, 2023), 274–94; and Wolf-Fabian Hungerland and Nikolaus Wolf, "The Panopticon of Germany's Foreign Trade, 1880–1913: New Facts on the First Globalization," *European Review of Economic History* 26, no. 4 (2022): 479–507. The figures on German trade are cited in Torp, *Herausforderung*, 76–83.

11. Henry Villard was among the most controversial railroad tycoons in nineteenth-century America. Kobrak, *Banking*; Richard White, *Railroaded: The Transcontinentals and the Making of Modern America* (New York: W. W. Norton, 2011), esp. 193–96, 217–23, 389–97.

12. Originally cited in Matthew Simon, *Cyclical Fluctuations and the International Capital Movements of the United States, 1865–1897* (New York: Arno Press, 1979), 98.

13. My description is based on accounts by Richard Goerdeler, who briefly served as one of Villard's associates in Berlin. Bundesarchiv Lichterfelde, R901/30500, Richard Goerdeler to Otto von Bismarck, 11 November 1884.

14. Henry Villard, *Lebenserinnerungen von Heinrich Hilgard-Villard: Ein Bürger zweier Welten, 1835–1900* (Berlin: G. Reimer, 1906), 286, 409. What exactly Villard thought on the matter is unclear since his own letters did not survive. I have reconstructed his thinking based on letters sent to him by Charles Colby. HBL, MSS 8993, V719, box 11, f. 84, Charles Colby to Henry Villard, 19 January 1871, 19 March 1871, 14 March 1871, and 1 November 1871; HBL, MSS 8993, V719, box 11, f. 83, Charles Colby to Henry Villard, 10 October 1872; HBL, MSS 8993, V719, box 11, f. 82, Charles Colby to Henry Villard, 8 January 1871.

15. HBL, MSS 8993, V719, box 11, f. 83, Charles Colby to Henry Villard, 10 October 1872.

16. Richard White, *"It's Your Misfortune and None of My Own": A History of the American West* (Norman: University of Oklahoma Press, 1991), 55–85. "Mend the..." in Frederick Law Olmsted, *A Journey Through Texas: Or, A Saddle-Trip on*

the Southwestern Frontier with a Statistical Appendix (New York: Dix, Edwards, 1857), 281–82.

17. Note that the precise number of acres granted varied by state and territory. White, *Railroaded*, 24. Figures are in Edward Winslow Martin, *History of the Grange Movement; Or, The Farmer's War Against Monopolies: Being a Full Account of the Struggles of the American Farmers Against the Extortions of the Railroad Companies. With a History of the Rise and Progress of the Order of Patrons of Husbandry, Its Objects, Present Condition and Prospects. To Which Is Added Sketches of the Leading Grangers* (Philadelphia: National Publishing Company, 1874), 230–31. On the Northern Pacific in its early years, see M. John Lubetkin, *Jay Cooke's Gamble: The Northern Pacific Railroad, the Sioux, and the Panic of 1873* (Norman: University of Oklahoma Press, 2006).

18. This was a welcome repurposing because it simultaneously absolved railroad operators from the logistical nightmare of transferring settlers to remote territories and enforcing their claims in territories claimed and inhabited by Indigenous nations. White, *Railroaded*, 26–38; William G. Roy, *Socializing Capital: The Rise of the Large Industrial Corporation in America* (Princeton: Princeton University Press, 1997), 78–134.

19. "That *people* along..." (emphasis in the original) in *Burlington Weekly Hawkeye*, November 30, 1858, cited in Richard Cleghorn Overton, *Burlington West: A Colonization History of the Burlington Railroad* (Cambridge, MA: Harvard University Press, 1941), 110. All other quotes in R. M. Newport to Oakes, 18 October 1881, cited in James B. Hedges, "The Colonization Work of the Northern Pacific Railroad," *The Mississippi Valley Historical Review* 13, no. 3 (1926): 331. See also descriptions by the Northern Pacific's emigration agent in Berlin Richard Goerdeler in BArch, R901/30500, Richard Goerdeler to Otto von Bismarck, 11 November 1884.

20. Economic growth is at least partially a reflection of demographic growth (other sources are increases in labor productivity or technological advances that raise per capita output). Most of America's economic growth in the nineteenth century was due to the demographic variety. Figures are in Jürgen Osterhammel, *The Transformation of the World: A Global History of the Nineteenth Century* (Princeton: Princeton University Press, 2014), 155; and Sidney Pollard, *Peaceful Conquest: The Industrialization of Europe, 1760–1970* (Oxford: Oxford University Press, 1981), 148–49.

21. A catalog of this literature can be found in Christoph Strupp et al., eds., *German Americana, 1800–1955: A Comprehensive Bibliography of German, Austria, and Swiss Books and Dissertations on the United States* (Washington, DC: German Historical Institute).

22. Hoffmann added that in 1840, Chicago counted a mere "4479 souls." Less than ten years later, in 1848, there were more than 20,000. In 1859, Hoffmann marveled that Chicago had become "what it is today, *a city of 120,000* inhabitants" (emphasis

in the original). On Hoffmann, see Hartmut Keil and John B. Jentz, eds., *German Workers in Chicago: A Documentary History of Working-Class Culture from 1850 to World War I* (Urbana: University of Illinois Press, 1988), 16–20. "Probably no other…" and "national wealth" in Eduard Wiss, *Das Gesetz der Bevölkerung und die Eisenbahnen: Eine volkswirthschaftliche und statistische Untersuchung geführt auf dem Terrain der Vereinigten Staaten von Nordamerika und als Vorbild deutscher Verhältnisse volkswirthschaftliche verwerthet mit Berücksichtigung des besonderen Characters der Industrie and des Handels der einzelnen Staaten sowohl, wie der gesammten Union vom Jahre 1790–1860* (Berlin: Verlag von F. A. Herbig, 1867), 1–2. "Hopes for Chicago's…" in Institut für Stadtgeschichte, Frankfurt am Main, W 1/9:5 Nr. 94, 1 January 1859.

23. FG, DABS, Bauer Series, 18 August 1869, 3 November 1872, and 21 May 1876.
24. FG, DABS, Krause/Krause Series, 28 January 1877.
25. Osterhammel, *Transformation*, 122–23.
26. Personal writing was even more likely to assume the position of distant observer. "Aus dem Nordwesten Amerikas," *Westermann's Illustrirte Monatshefte: Ein Familienbuch für das gesamte geistige Leben der Gegenwart*, 32 (April 1872): 112. See also the discussion in Undine Janeck, *Zwischen Gartenlaube und Karl May: Deutsche Amerikarezeption in den Jahren 1871–1913* (Aachen: Shaker Verlag, 2003), 245–58.
27. The author did explain that the wagon-mounted pioneers he saw belonged to the "Anglo-Saxon and therefore the Germanic tribes." But this was less an acknowledgment of the integral role played by contemporary transatlantic migrants and more a nod to the early period of settlement during the seventeenth and eighteenth centuries. All quotes from *Westermann's Illustrirte Monatshefte*, "Aus dem Nordwesten Amerikas," 32 (April 1872): 112. See also the examples in "Neuestes aus der Ferne" (vol. 30, Apr–Sept. 1871); "Die Concurrenzlinien der Pacific Bahn" (vol. 30, Apr–Sept. 1871); "Auswanderung nach Amerika" (vol. 32, Aug. 1872); "Statistisches über die Einwanderung in Amerika" (vol. 33, Oct. 1872–Mar. 1873).
28. Some writers—including Eduard Wiss—argued against the notion that America's demographic transformation had anything to do with immigration. Wiss, *Gesetz*, esp. 455–56. All quotes in Paul Reinganum, *Bericht über die Verhältnisse der Oregon- und California-Eisenbahn* (Frankfurt am Main: Mühlau & Waldschmidt, 1873), 10–11, 34.
29. For an example of the state of knowledge about the movement in Europe at the time, see A. Lammers, "Handel und Zollwesen; Konsularwesen; Auswanderung; wirthschaftliche Gesetzgebung," *Jahrbuch für Gesetzgebung, Verwaltung und Rechtspflege des Deutschen Reiches* 2 (1873): 128–131.
30. According to the historian Ernest Benz, Malthus's ideas had "penetrated the consciousness of the elite all over Europe," especially following the Revolution of 1848. Ernest Benz, "Escaping Malthus: Population Explosion and Human Movement, 1760–1884," in *The Oxford Handbook of Modern German History*, ed. Helmut

Walser Smith (Oxford: Oxford University Press, 2011), 199; Robert Mayhew, *Malthus. The Life and Legacies of an Untimely Prophet* (Cambridge, MA: Belknap Press of Harvard University Press, 2014), 142.

31. Malthus never even used the word immigration in his main work on the subject: Thomas Robert Malthus, *An Essay on the Principle of Population; or, a View of Its Past and Present Effects on Human Happiness; with an Inquiry into Our Prospects Respecting the Future Removal or Mitigation of the Evils which it Occasions*, 6th ed., 2 vols. (London: John Murray, 1826).

32. Richard White describes the American Social Science Association as "perhaps the most important liberal institution of the Gilded Age," a place where "intellectuals, professionals, journalists, businessmen, and politicians [intended] to collect facts and apply the principles that would reveal 'the general laws that govern social relations.'" Richard White, *The Republic for Which It Stands: The United States During Reconstruction and the Gilded Age, 1865–1896* (New York: Oxford University Press, 2017), 176–77. Villard was married to Fanny Garrison, daughter of the esteemed abolitionist William Lloyd Garrison. All quotes are in Alexandra Villard de Borchgrave and John Cullen, *Villard: The Life and Times of an American Titan* (New York: Nan A. Talese/Doubleday, 2001), 279–82, here 280; Villard, *Lebenserinnerungen*, 406–7.

33. Besides rising to the boards of two new joint-stock banks, the Berliner Bankverein and Deutsche Bank, Kapp helped found lesser-known mining ventures and hotel chains in Berlin. Wolfgang Hinners, *Exil und Rückkehr: Friedrich Kapp in Amerika und Deutschland, 1824–1884* (Stuttgart: Akademischer Verlag, 1987), 261–67.

34. Harvard University Houghton Library, MS Am 1322, Friedrich Kapp to Henry Villard, 17 July 1871.

35. HBL, MSS 8993, V719, Box 11, f. 88, Henry Villard to William Lawson, 17 December 1873; HHL, MS Am 1322, Friedrich Kapp to Henry Villard, 17 July 1871 and 9 February 1872.

36. On the Berlin stock exchange, see Michie, *Global Securities*; Rainer Gömmel and Hans Pohl, eds., *Deutsche Börsengeschichte* (Frankfurt am Main: Knapp, 1992); and Hellmut Gebhard, *Die Berliner Börse von den Anfängen bis zum Jahre 1896* (Berlin: R. L. Prager, 1928).

37. Wilkins, *Investment*, 49–138, esp. 113–38.

38. HHL, MS Am 1322, Friedrich Kapp to Henry Villard, 17 July 1871, 7 December 1871, 12 December 1871, and 2 January 1872; "earns…" and "could care less" in the letter from July. "Personally…" originally cited in Hinners, *Exil*, 265. In 1873, Kapp's Berliner Bankverein would pay an 18 percent dividend. Historisches Archiv Deutsche Bank, S4516, 25 January 1876.

39. HHL, MS Am 1322, Friedrich Kapp to Henry Villard, 2 March 1872.

40. For examples of Kapp's exhortations toward Villard, see HHL, MS Am 1322, Friedrich Kapp to Henry Villard, 29 November 1871, 2 January 1872, 23 January 1872, 19 February 1872, 2 March 1872, 7 December 1871, 26 February 1872, 8 March

1882, and 22 April 1882. Some years later, in 1882, Kapp explained to Villard that "literary agitation in illustrated papers etc, magazines is also very much successful promotion. More than you now think over there." Paul Lindau spent years working on behalf of Henry Villard and his railroad interests; see HHL, MS Am 1322, Friedrich Kapp to Henry Villard, 17 July 1871, 9 February 1872, 2 March 1872, and 8 March 1882; HHL, MS Am 1322, Paul Lindau to Henry Villard, 20 November 1886, 6 December 1886, 3 January 1887, 1 October 1887, 10 November 1890, 1 July 1891, 11 November 1890, and 20 August 1891. On Lindau, Harald Tanzer, *Theodor Fontanes Berliner Doppelroman: "Die Poggenpuhls" und "Mathilde Möhring": Ein Erzählkunstwerk zwischen Tradition und Moderne* (Paderborn: Igel-Verlag, 1997), 53–55.

41. Wilkins, *Investment*, 115–17. On Cooke's railroading career, see Lubetkin, *Cooke's Gamble*.
42. Martin, *History*, 226–27, 231.
43. Ibid., 223–24, 226–27.
44. HHL, MS Am 1322, Friedrich Kapp to Henry Villard, 17 July 1871, 2 January 1872, 27 November 1872, and 13 June 1873. See also the account in Villard de Borchgrave and Cullen, *Villard*, 285.
45. Martin, *History*, 230–31.
46. Bayrische Staatsbibliothek, Verhandlungen des deutschen Reichstags (VdR), 6 May 1872, p. 274.
47. He also appealed to the "spirit of the modern, civilized state (*Kulturstaat*)" to argue for greater care and protection for emigrants in the United States. BSB, VdR, Friedrich Kapp, 2 December 1881, p. 155. "Fact" and "Nothing that the government…" in his speech from 6 May 1872, p. 274–75; "946.2 out of 1,000" in his speech from 5 February 1883, 1298. The policy proposals are discussed in speeches from 9 June 1873, 14 March 1874, 16 April 1874, 18 December 1875, 2 December 1881, and 8 May 1882. A version of the emigration-as-fact argument can also be found in Kapp's lecture to Berlin's craftsmen association in 1871, as well as in the justification addendum to his signature law proposal, the Reich emigration law in 1878. Friedrich Kapp, *Über Auswanderung: Ein Vortrag, gehalten am 2. Februar 1871 im Berliner Handwerker-Verein* (Berlin: Carl Habel, 1871), 11.
48. The law proposal underwent several "readings" in the Reichstag. BSB, VdR, *Antrag Nr. 44: Entwurf eines Gesetzes, betreffend die Beförderung von Auswanderern nach außerdeutschen Ländern* (25 February 1878).
49. Michael Kuckhoff, "Die Auswanderungsdiskussion während der Revolution von 1848–49," in *Deutsche Amerikaauswanderung im 19. Jahrhundert: Sozialgeschichtliche Beiträge*, ed. Günter Moltmann (Stuttgart: Metzler, 1976), 102–45. See also the discussion in Brian E. Vick, *Defining Germany: The 1848 Frankfurt Parliamentarians and National Identity* (Cambridge, MA: Harvard University Press, 2002), 110–38.

50. The comment is by the Bavarian parliamentarian and philologist Ernst von Lasaulx, cited in Kuckhoff, "Auswanderungsdiskussion," 125. Tellingly, the last time the Prussian government made a concession to Germans living abroad was in 1870, on the eve of unification, when it was still engaged in a public campaign to win over southern German states for a Prussian-led unification of the nation. Dieter Gosewinkel, *Einbürgern und Ausschließen: Die Nationalisierung der Staatsangehörigkeit vom Deutschen Bund bis zur Bundesrepublik Deutschland* (Göttingen: Vandenhoeck & Ruprecht, 2001), 136–76.

51. The summarizing phrase "good riddance" is borrowed from Mack Walker, *Germany and the Emigration, 1816–1885* (Cambridge, MA: Harvard University Press, 1964), 196. As the government's internal correspondence suggests, there was reluctance to do anything that might "make emigration more comfortable and in so doing promote it." BArch, R43/675, Franz Johannes von Rottenburg to Minister von Boetticher, 9 November 1881.

52. Miquel is cited in Richard Lesser, ed., *Deutsche Kolonialzeitung: Organ des Deutschen Kolonialvereins*, vol. 3 (Frankfurt am Main, Verlag des deutschen Kolonialvereins, 1886), 302. The political, economic, and cultural forces driving the "new colonialism" of the 1880s were more wide-ranging than my account might suggest. Bradley Naranch and Geoff Eley, eds., *German Colonialism in a Global Age* (Durham, NC: Duke University Press, 2014); Steven Press, *Rogue Empires: Contracts and Conmen in Europe's Scramble for Africa* (Cambridge, MA: Harvard University Press, 2017).

53. BSB, VdR, Friedrich Kapp, 2 December 1881, p. 154; and 5 February 1883, p. 1298. Kapp also made his case in published articles and opinion pieces in the *Deutsche Rundschau*, the *Historische Zeitung*, and the *Preussische Jahrbücher*. For an overview of his publications, see Hinners, *Exil*, 313–18.

54. The question of whether emigrants could be directed elsewhere continued to be debated for years to come, especially in the 1890s in the context of the alleged "closure" of the American frontier. Gosewinkel, *Einbürgern*, 278–94.

55. All quotes in BSB, VdR, Friedrich Kapp, 2 December 1881, p. 154; 5 February 1883, p. 1298–9; and 14 February 1883, p. 1497.

56. HHL, MS Am 1322, Friedrich Kapp to Henry Villard, 22 April 1882.

57. "My name..." and "Credibility..." in HHL, MS Am 1322, Friedrich Kapp to Henry Villard, 17 July 1871 and 22 April 1882.

58. HBL, MSS 8993, V719, Box 13, f. 100, Paul Schulze to Henry Villard, 11 December 1874, 15 March 1875, and 9 February 1876. False reports were particularly dangerous during periods when chain migration defined much of German transatlantic migration. Walter D. Kamphoefner, *The Westfalians: From Germany to Missouri* (Princeton: Princeton University Press, 1987), 3–11.

59. Schulze's letters suggest that Villard grew frustrated with Schulze's repeated demands to stick closer to the facts. HBL, MSS 8993, V719, Box 13, f. 100, Paul Schulze to Henry Villard, 15 March 1875.

CHAPTER 8

1. Justinus Moeller, *Gründerprocesse: Eine Criminalpolitische Studie* (Berlin: Julius Springer, 1876), 48.
2. My account draws primarily on ibid., 43–45, 48, 54–55, 76–77.
3. Ibid., 37n**. Critics also demanded that the government "dissolve" all joint-stock corporations founded between 1871 and 1873 and distribute the proceeds to injured investors. Geheimes Staatsarchiv Preußischer Kulturbesitz, I HA Rep. 120, A XII 5, Nr. 1, Bd. 9, Kataster-Secretair Dreyßen to Preußisches Staatsministerium, 6 January 1877. For a recent, comparative account of the global financial crisis of 1873, see Hannah Catherine Davies, *Transatlantic Speculations: Globalization and the Panics of 1873* (New York: Columbia University Press, 2018).
4. Gustav Mevissen, an influential voice on the events surrounding 1873, argued in September 1873 that the Germans had been "forced, against their nature, to embrace a new profligacy." Cited in Joseph Hansen, *Gustav von Mevissen: Ein rheinisches Lebensbild, 1815–1899*, vol. 2 (Berlin: Georg Reimer, 1906), 602n*. The idea of *Sittengesetz* survives in modern German commercial law in the form of *Verkehrssitte* (customary practice in commerce). For a contemporary definition of Sittengesetz, see Julius Köstlin, "Studien über das Sittengesetz," *Jahrbücher für deutsche Theologie* 13 (1868), 383–461; and Franz Vorländer, *Das Evangelium der Wahrheit und Freiheit, gegründet auf das Natur- und Sittengesetz: Für Gebildete* (Leipzig: Eduard Heinrich Mayer, 1865). Hegel considered Sittengesetz to be indispensable to the functioning of civil society; see Georg Wilhelm Friedrich Hegel, *Grundlinien der Philosophie des Rechts oder Naturrecht und Staatswissenschaft im Grundriss: Mit Hegels eigenhändigen Notizen und den mündlichen Zusätzen*, vol. 7 (Frankfurt am Main: Suhrkamp Verlag, 1970), esp. 292–307.
5. Sombart described the colonies as the "actual nursery of the capitalist spirit." Werner Sombart, *Die Genesis des Kapitalismus*, vol. 1, Der moderne Kapitalismus (Leipzig: Duncker & Humblot, 1902), 390. On the siege mentality and suspicions of corruption that defined the 1870s, see Sven Beckert, "American Danger: United States Empire, Eurafrica, and the Territorialization of Industrial Capitalism, 1870–1950," *The American Historical Review* 144, no. 4 (2017), 1137–70; Helmut Walser Smith, ed., *Protestants, Catholics, and Jews in Germany, 1800–1914* (Oxford: Berg, 2001), esp. 17–49; and Fritz Stern, "Money, Morals, and the Pillars of Bismarck's Society," *Central European History* 3, no. 1/2 (1970), 49–72. For a general overview about the period, see Heinrich August Winkler, *Deutsche Geschichte vom Ende des Alten Reiches bis zum Untergang der Weimarer Republik*, vol. 1, Der lange Weg nach Westen (Munich: C. H. Beck, 2000), 213–65.
6. All quotes in Michael Stolleis, *Konstitution und Intervention: Studien zur Geschichte des öffentlichen Rechts im 19. Jahrhundert* (Frankfurt am Main: Suhrkamp, 2001), 253–82. Similarly, see Gerhard A. Ritter, *Der Sozialstaat: Entstehung und*

Entwicklung im internationalen Vergleich (Munich: R. Oldenbourg, 1989). It is no coincidence that the term *capitalism* was coined in this same period, often in reference to alternatives of the interventionist state. Jürgen Kocka and Marcel van der Linden, *Capitalism: The Reemergence of a Historical Concept* (London: Bloomsbury Academic, 2016), 1.

7. "People's psychology" in Sombart, *Kapitalismus*, 1, xxi. Note that in this period the word *psychology* was more commonly used to describe a person's "moral" or "ethical" capacities. As the contemporary economist Gustav Schmoller put it, "the psychological element in the economy (*Volkswirtschaft*) is essentially ethics." Gustav Schmoller, " Offenes Sendschreiben an Herrn Professor Dr. Heinrich von Treitschke über einige Grundfragen des Rechts und der Volkswirthschaft," *Jahrbücher für Nationalökonomie und Statistik* 23, no. 2 (1874), 253n25.

8. Oechelhäuser's Deutsche Continental-Gas-Gesellschaft continues to operate under the name Contigas. On Oechelhäuser, see Wolfgang von Geldern, *Wilhelm Oechelhäuser als Unternehmer, Wirtschaftspolitiker und Sozialpolitiker* (Munich: F. Bruckmann, 1971), 14, 20.

9. He also used terms like *Spekulationsfieber* (speculation fever), *Spielwut* (gambling rage), and *Gründerfieber* (founding fever). All quotes in Wilhelm Oechelhäuser, *Die Nachtheile des Aktienwesens und die Reform der Aktiengesetzgebung* (Berlin: Julius Springer, 1878), iv–v, 18, 35; and Wilhelm Oechelhäuser, *Die Wirthschaftliche Krisis* (Berlin: Julius Springer, 1876), 22, 94. All figures in Bernd Baehring, *Börsen-Zeiten: Frankfurter Wertpapierbörse 1585–1985 Frankfurt in vier Jahrhunderten zwischen Antwerpen, Wien, New York und Berlin aus dem Nachlaß Gerhard Löwenthal* (Frankfurt am Main: Frankfurter Wertpapierbörse, 1985), 122.

10. All quotes from Oechelhäuser, *Nachtheile*, 30, 24–25, 35–36, 47; Oechelhäuser, *Krisis*, 276–77. Complaints about the "ever advancing demoralization of the worker" were legion among German industrialists in the 1870s. See Lothar Machtan, "'Im Vertrauen auf unsere gerechte Sache…' Streikbewegungen der Industriearbeiter in den 70er Jahren des 19. Jahrhunderts," in *Streik: Zur Geschichte des Arbeitskampfes in Deutschland während der Industrialisierung* (Munich: C. H. Beck, 1981), 55. On the proliferation of strikes in this period, see Klaus Tenfelde, "Konflikt und Organisation in einigen deutschen Bergbaugebieten 1867–1872," *Geschichte und Gesellschaft* 3, no. 2 (1977), 212–35.

11. Oechelhäuser, *Krisis*, 17–18. Oechelhäuser was not alone in singling out the joint-stock corporation, as well as the reform act of 1870, as a major culprit behind the crisis. See, for instance, Felix Hecht, *Das Börsen- und Actienwesen der Gegenwart und die Reform des Actien-Gesellschafts-Rechts* (Mannheim: Verlag von J. Schneider, 1874); H Löwenfeld, *Das Recht der Actien-Gesellschaften: Kritik und Reformvorschläge* (Berlin: DeGruyter, 2018, 1879); Adolph Wagner, "Das Actiengesellschaftswesen," *Jahrbücher für Nationalökonomie und Statistik* 21 (1873), 271–340; and Hugo Keyßner, *Die Aktiengesellschaften und die*

Kommanditgesellschaften auf Aktien unter dem Reichs-Gesetz vom 11. Juni 1870 (Berlin: Carl Heymann, 1873). For an overview of the discourse on the reform act in particular, see Sibylle Hofer, "Das Aktiengesetz von 1884 - ein Lehrstück für prinzipielle Schutzkonzeptionen," in *Aktienrecht im Wandel*, ed. Walter Bayer and Mathias Habersack (Tübingen: Mohr Siebeck, 2007), 390–94.

12. Oechelhäuser, *Nachtheile*, 9–13, 34.
13. Ibid., 4–5.
14. While such problems "by no means plague all joint stock corporations," Oechelhäuser argued that a majority were affected and claimed to know of directors "who treat the interests of stockholders completely like their own, but not all are this conscientious." Ibid., xii–xiii, 4–5, 15, 25.
15. Ibid., 3, 35, 37–39.
16. Ibid., 2, 5; Oechelhäuser, *Krisis*, 2–3.
17. Oechelhäuser, *Nachtheile*, 34; Oechelhäuser, *Krisis*, 31–32. Oechelhäuser's thinking here is emblematic of the rationale behind the New Era reforms of the sixties, which rested on the assumption that, even in a deregulated economy, individuals would adhere to the customs and practices of their particular estate. See especially paragraphs 1 and 279 in the Allgemeines Deutsches Handelsgesetzbuch (ADHGB) of 1869.
18. All quotes from Bayrische Staatsbibliothek, Verhandlungen des deutschen Reichstags (VdR), Otto von Bismarck, 9 October 1878, p. 127. With "botched campaign" I mean to refer to the *Kulturkampf* (culture war) of the early 1870s, which by this time was nearing its end. For an introduction to the Kulturkampf, see Margaret Lavinia Anderson, *Windthorst: A Political Biography* (Oxford: Clarendon Press, 1981); Helmut Walser Smith, *German Nationalism and Religious Conflict: Culture, Ideology, Politics, 1870–1914* (Princeton: Princeton University Press, 1995); and Jonathan Sperber, *Popular Catholicism in Nineteenth Century Germany* (Princeton: Princeton University Press, 1984).
19. BSB, VdR, Otto von Bismarck, 9 October 1878, p. 127. Bismarck's Frenchman would have been a recognizable figure at the moment because the French prided themselves on precisely this attitude. See, for example, Alexis de Tocqueville's assessment of French character, reproduced in and translated by Jennifer Pitts, ed., *Writings on Empire and Slavery* (Baltimore: Johns Hopkins University Press, 2001), 1–2. Similarly, Jacques Rancière emphasizes an overarching desire in French craftsmen of this period to be emancipated from the drudgery of work. Jacques Rancière, *Proletarian Nights: The Workers' Dream in Nineteenth-Century France* (London: Verso Books, 2012).
20. BSB, VdR, Otto von Bismarck, 9 October 1878, p. 127.
21. Oechelhäuser, *Nachtheile*, 36. On Oechelhäuser's politics, see Wolther von Kieseritzky, *Liberalismus und Sozialstaat: liberale Politik in Deutschland zwischen Machtstaat und Arbeiterbewegung (1878–1893)* (Cologne: Böhlau, 2002), 42, 48, 190–92, 262–65, 316–19, 362–68; and Geldern, *Oechelhäuser*, 48–63.

22. Oechelhäuser, *Nachtheile*, 41.
23. Ibid., viii, 17, 49.
24. All quotes in ibid., 46–47, 50, 53–54, 85–86.
25. In the 1870s, many German liberals were taking a more skeptical stance toward commercial freedom, particular during the contemporary debates over new tariffs. James J. Sheehan, *German Liberalism in the Nineteenth Century* (Chicago: University of Chicago Press, 1978), 29–34.
26. All quotes from BSB, VdR, Otto von Helldorff-Bedra, 24 February 1880, pp. 96–98. Similar attacks came from the conservative politician Franz Perrot, whose writings on the "founder's crash" (*Gründerkrach*) constituted one of the most virulent attacks on contemporary liberalism. See Franz Perrot, *Die moderne Wirthschafts-Gesetzgebung und die sogenannte 'soziale Frage'* (Munich: M. Huttler, 1874); Franz Perrot, *Der Bank-, Börsen- und Actienschwindel: eine Hauptursache der drohenden sozialen Gefahr: Beiträge zur Kritik der politischen Oeconomie*, 3 vols. (Rostock: Stiller, 1874). The other key critic of liberal economic policy in this period was Otto Glagau, who published in the *Gartenlaube*. Otto Glagau, *Der Börsen- und Gründungs-Schwindel in Berlin: Gesammelte und stark vermehrte Artikel der "Gartenlaube"* (Leipzig: P. Frohberg, 1876).
27. Calls for reform could range from demands for "draconian harshness" (a bureaucrat in the Prussian government) to a quest for "more time" to deliberate the matter (representatives of the *Deutscher Handelstag*). GStAPK, I HA Rep 120, A XII 5, Nr. 1, Bd. 9, Kataster-Secretair Dreyßen to Staatsministerium, 6 January 1877; GStAPK, I HA Rep 120, A XII 5, Nr. 1, Bd. 9, Delbrück and Annecke to Staatsminister Hofmann, 22 October 1877. For an overview of the debate in the legislature, see Hofer, "Das Aktiengesetz von 1884," 390–94. "Legal uncertainties..." in GStAPK, I HA Rep 120, A XII 5, Nr. 1, Bd. 9, Delbrück/Annecke to Staatsminister Hofmann, 22 October 1877. "Utmost care" and "reputable quarters" in GStAPK, I HA Rep 120, A XII 5, Nr. 1, Bd. 9, Die Aeltesten der Kaufmannschaft Berlin to Reichskanzleramt, 5 December 1876.
28. Part of the delay was probably due to other controversial issues taking center stage at the time, including a widening debate over trade, worker's insurance, and colonialism. Sybille Hofer argues that the reason for the delay was to be found in concerns of the government not to act too rashly amid an economic downturn. Ibid., 392–94, 406–7. The 500-mark figures can be found in Landesarchiv Berlin, A Rep 200-01, Nr. 932, Handelskammer Leipzig, "Bericht des Ausschusses für Handelsgesetzgebungs-Fragen," 28 December 1883.
29. According to the business-friendly Cologne daily *Kölnische Zeitung*, this was a "jumble of restrictions and precautionary measures...which would render the joint stock corporation practically unusable." Bundesarchiv Lichterfelde, R1501/107146, *Kölnische Zeitung*, "Zur Verbesserung des Gesellschaftsrechts," 31 May 1888.
30. BSB, VdR, Wilhelm Oechelhäuser, 24 March 1884, p. 220; and 28 June 1884, p. 1149.

31. Forschungsbibliothek Gotha, Deutsche Auswandererbriefsammlung (DABS), Groth/Groth Series, 7 June 1888, 26 June 1888, 25 January 1889, 5 March 1889, and 21 April 1890.
32. All quotes in FG, DABS, Groth/Groth Series, 26 June 1888. Groth frequently spoke of others who had "made it" from simple craftsman to affluent entrepreneur in the United States. For example, FG, DABS, Groth/Groth Series, 25 January 1889.
33. FG, DABS, Groth/Groth Series, 5 March 1889.
34. Figures calculated based on Susan B. Carter, *Historical Statistics of the United States: Earliest Times to the Present* (New York: Cambridge University Press, 2006). Similar figures in BSB, VdR, *Berichte d. Reichs-Kommissars zur Ueberwachung des Auswanderungswesens* (1880–1884).
35. All preceding quotations in BSB, VdR, Wilhelm Oechelhäuser, 24 March 1884, p. 221. "Miniature" cited in Verein zur Wahrung der wirthschaftlichen Interessen von Handel und Gewerbe, *Die Erweiterung des Handelsrechts durch Einfügung neuer Gesellschaftsformen* (Berlin: Norddeutsche Buchdruckerei und Verlagsanstalt, 1891), 105.
36. BSB, VdR, Wilhelm Oechelhäuser, 24 March 1884, p. 221.
37. Oechelhäuser did not make the connection explicitly, but the order in which he arranged his speech suggests that he was thinking about emigrants when discussing the surging popularity of the principle of limited liability. All quotes from BSB, VdR, *Oechelhäuser*, 24 March 1884, pp. 220–21.
38. There were potential predecessors in several US states, dating to the late 1870s. Stanley E. Howard, "The Limited Partnership Association in New Jersey," *The Journal of Business* 9 (1936), 258–79.
39. For example, see his speeches from 24 February 1880, 24 March 1884, 26 March 1884, and 28 June 1884. All reproduced in BSB, VdR.
40. BSB, VdR, Wilhelm Oechelhäuser, 24 March 1884, p. 221.
41. Ibid.
42. Richard Lesser, ed., *Deutsche Kolonialzeitung: Organ des Deutschen Kolonialvereins*, vol. 3 (Berlin: Verlag des Deutschen Kolonialvereins, 1886), 1, 290ff.
43. All quotes from ibid., 290–91.
44. Ibid., 305–8.
45. Ibid., 306–307.
46. BSB, VdR, Friedrich Hammacher, 4 February 1888, p. 711.
47. The business-friendly *Berliner Börsen-Courier* went so far as to inquire whether the joint-stock corporation reform law "puts in question the very existence of joint stock corporations." BArch, R1501/100005, *Berliner Börsen-Courier*, "Berathungen über die Actien-Novelle," 19 November 1883. Similar commentary in BSB, VdR, Friedrich Hammacher, 24 March 1884, p. 205, as well as in the summary report by members of the *Deutscher Handelstag* from 7 December 1888, reproduced in Verein zur Wahrung, *Die Erweiterung des Handelsrechts*, 101–2. All quotes in Lesser, *Kolonialzeitung*, 306–7.

48. BSB, VdR, Friedrich Hammacher, 4 February 1888, p. 711. The Berlin chamber of commerce made a similar argument. BArch, R1501/107146, Korporation der Kaufmannschaft zu Berlin an Minister für Handel und Gewerbe, 12 September 1888, bl. 29–30.
49. Lesser, *Kolonialzeitung*, 307.
50. Ibid.
51. In the 1850s, Hammacher served in the Prussian *Abgeordnetenhaus* (House of Commons). He later became a member of the Reichstag of the North German Confederation and, since 1871, of the imperial Reichstag. Alex Bein, *Friedrich Hammacher: Lebensbild eines Parlamentariers und Wirtschaftsfürers, 1824–1904* (Berlin: E. S. Mittler, 1932).
52. BArch, N2105/Nr. 21, Friedrich Hammacher to Hugo Haniel, 7 February 1882.
53. Wilhelm Oechelhäuser, *Die Arbeiterfrage: Ein Sociales Programm* (Berlin: Julius Springer, 1886), 62.
54. Emphasis in the original, ibid. See Hammacher's use of the concept of expansion in BSB, VdR, Friedrich Hammacher, 28 February 1888, p. 1158. On the difference between *Ergänzung* and *Erweiterung*, see also the discussion in BArch, R1501/107146, *National-Zeitung*, "Die Entwicklung des Gesellschaftsrechts," 4 June 1888.
55. "Blend" in BArch, N2105/Nr. 52, *Tägliche Rundschau*, 12 December 1904. As a member of the corn and iron alliance in 1879, Hammacher had been all too willing to abandon his party's free market orthodoxy in favor of temporary protective tariffs for agrarian products, and he was no doubt partially inspired to do so by the fact that he owned a potash mine in Staßfurt, Anhalt-Saxony, that supplied east Prussian Junker estates with fertilizer. BArch, N2105/Nr. 21, Friedrich Hammacher to Hugo Haniel, 9 February 1880 and 20 February 1879.
56. Aside from making a personal investment, Oechelhäuser managed to convince friends like the Berlin financier Adelbert Delbrück to commit to large sums of their own. Otto Pflanze, *The Period of Fortification, 1880–1898*, vol. 3, *Bismarck and the Development of Germany* (Princeton: Princeton University Press, 1990), 137. See also Oechelhäuser's own account of the agreement in Wilhelm Oechelhäuser, *Die Deutsche-Ostafrikanische Centralbahn: Mit einer Uebersichtskarte* (Berlin: Julius Springer, 1899), iii–iv. On Bismarck's backdoor dealings with German bankers and businessmen, see Steven Press, *Rogue Empires: Contracts and Conmen in Europe's Scramble for Africa* (Cambridge, MA: Harvard University Press, 2017), 166–218.
57. BArch, R1501/107146. Wilhelm Oechelhäuser, "An die preussischen Handelskammern und kaufmaennischen Korporationen!," 28 April 1888, bl. 46–48.
58. All quotes from BSB, VdR, Wilhelm Oechelhäuser, 28 February 1888, p. 1156.
59. All quotes from BSB, VdR, Friedrich Hammacher, 4 February 1888, p. 710.
60. Geldern, *Oechelhäuser*, 40.

61. BArch, R1501/107146, Wilhelm Oechelhäuser, "An die preussischen Handelskammern und kaufmaennischen Korporationen!," 28 April 1888, pp. 46–48.
62. BArch, R1501/107146, *Kölnische Zeitung*, "Zur Verbesserung des Gesellschaftsrechts," 31 May 1888.
63. The remaining twenty-nine chambers of commerce rejected the need for a new type of corporation. A second round of opinions, solicited later that year, improved the rate of support for Oechelhäuser's version to 80 percent. Geldern, *Oechelhäuser*, 39–40.
64. BArch, R1501/107146, Aeltesten der Kaufmannschaft zu Berlin to Minister für Handel und Gewerbe, 12 September 1888.
65. Geldern, *Oechelhäuser*, 34–35. Apart from a belated comment by the economist Jakob Riesser in 1889, no additional opinions or challenges to the GmbH concept were published in the interim period. Government correspondence among the responsible ministries reveals that subsequent iterations of the law recycled Oechelhäuser's original language. In 1891, for example, Leo von Caprivi described the GmbH as "a more simply structured form for association for capital and labor for a limited number of participants and without the creation of publicly tradable securities" and one that was supposed to exist "alongside the joint stock corporation." BArch, R1501/107147, Leo von Caprivi to Kaiser Wilhelm II, 14 April 1892.
66. In 1893, for example, 183 new GmbHs were established compared to just 95 new joint-stock corporations; in 1894, the ratio was reportedly 254 to 92; in 1895, 250 to 161; and in 1896, 376 to 182. By 1907, nearly a quarter of all new companies in Prussia were GmbHs, and by the eve of the First World War the figure had climbed to about a third. Calculated based on Ernst Neukamp, "Die deutschen Gesellschaften mit beschränkter Haftung: Eine neue Gesellschaftsform," in *Zeitschrift für Volkswirtschaft, Socialpolitik, und Verwaltung: Organ der Gesellschaft Österreichischer Volkswirte* 8 (Vienna: Wilhelm Braumüller, 1899), 346. BArch, R1501/107147, *Hannoverscher Courier*, "Vorschläge zur Einschränkung der Gesellschaften m. b. H.," 11 March 1905.
67. Timothy W. Guinnane et al, "Putting the Corporation in Its Place," in *NBER Working Paper Series* (Cambridge, MA: National Bureau of Economic Research, 2007), 1–61. Also BArch R1501/107147, *Wiener Zeitung*, "Gesetz vom 6 March 1906 über Gesellschaften mit beschränkter Haftung," 15 March 1906.
68. The German distinguishes between tradable "stocks" (*Aktien*) and nontradable "shares" (*Anteile*). See Henry P. de Vries and Friedrich Jünger, "Limited Liability Contract: The GmbH," *Columbia Law Review* 64 (1964), 866–86, originally cited in Guinnane et al., "Putting the Corporation," 16n16. Note that despite the provision that GmbH shares were nontradable, a secondary market in such shares seems nonetheless to have formed. C. Greulich, "Der Verkehr in Geschäftsanteilen von Gesellschaften mit beschränkter Haftung," *Die Bank: Monatshefte für Finanz- u. Bankwesen* 1, no. 1 (1908), 263–66.

69. Verein zur Wahrung, *Die Erweiterung des Handelsrechts*, 106. There is much to be said about the versatility of the GmbH. By 1900, the German Empire had grown into one of the most highly advanced, cutting-edge technology economies in the world. Its leading industries were not in textiles, coal, and steel, as was the case for early industrializers like Britain and France, but in advanced machinery, chemicals, and pharmaceuticals, as well as the new field of electricity. These industries thrived because of their technological edge, which meant that the broad public transparency demanded of the joint-stock corporation model posed a serious threat to their business model. See Jutta Limbach, *Theorie und Wirklichkeit der GmbH: die empirischen Normaltypen der Gesellschaft mit beschränkter Haftung und ihr Verhältnis zum Postulat von Herrschaft und Haftung* (Berlin: Duncker & Humblot, 1966).
70. Helmut Walser Smith, "Authoritarian State, Dynamic Society, Failed Imperialist Power, 1878–1914," in *The Oxford Handbook of Modern German History*, ed. Helmut Walser Smith (Oxford: Oxford University Press, 2015), 322.
71. Verein zur Wahrung, *Die Erweiterung des Handelsrechts*, 107. Some observers argued that the GmbH enabled owners of real estate, a form of capital that at this time was concentrated in the hands of the nobility and the propertied bourgeoisie, to underreport capital gains and thus dramatically reduce their tax bill. Ludwig Eschwege, "Grundbesitz und GmbH," *Die Bank: Monatshefte für Finanz- u. Bankwesen* 1, no. 1 (1908), 533–62.
72. As the *Berliner Tageblatt* put it, the GmbH did little but "encourage deception." BArch, R1501/107147, *Berliner Tageblatt*, "G.m.b.H.," 2 October 1894.
73. BArch, R1501/107147, *Hannoverscher Courier*, "Vorschläge zur Einschränkung der Gesellschaften m. b. H.," 11 March 1905.

EPILOGUE

1. Cited and translated in Lawrence A. Scaff, *Max Weber in America* (Princeton: Princeton University Press, 2011), 91.
2. Ibid., 65–66, 90–92.
3. Weber here echoed concerns expressed more broadly among German and indeed European economic and political elites since the 1870s. Sven Beckert, "American Danger: United States Empire, Eurafrica, and the Territorialization of Industrial Capitalism, 1870–1950," *The American Historical Review* 144, no. 4 (2017), 1137–70; Jens-Uwe Guettel, *German Expansionism, Imperial Liberalism and the United States, 1776–1945* (Cambridge: Cambridge University Press, 2012), 217–32; Benjamin Hein, "Old Regime in a New World: Frankfurt's Financial Market in the Nineteenth Century," *The Journal of Modern History* 92, no. 4 (2020), 756–68.
4. This is my own reading of Weber's reaction to his observations in America. It should be noted that Weber used the term *Fideikommißbesitz* to describe what I have called *landed independence*. Strictly speaking, the two are not the same. The

Fideikommiß was a clearly defined legal concept within contemporary inheritance law. Like many trust funds in the early twenty-first century, it described an estate that could not be divided or sold and that had to remain within the family. But even though in theory a *Fideikommiß* could consist of any kind of property, in practice it usually referred to real estate. The relevant passage is in Max Weber, *Die Protestantische Ethik und der Geist des Kapitalismus*, Third ed., ed. Dirk Kaesler (Munich: C.H. Beck, 2010), 91.

5. Scaff, *Weber*, 91.
6. Max Weber, *Nationalstaat und Volkswirtschaftspolitik: Akademische Antrittsrede* (Freiburg: J. C. B. Mohr [Paul Siebeck], 1895), 8.
7. Max Weber's close relationship with Kapp has not gone unnoticed. In my view, however, it takes on new significance in light of what this book has unearthed about Kapp and the wide-ranging role he played in facilitating a transatlantic cultural exchange between Germany and America—what I have called the migrant's spirit. See Guenther Roth, "The Young Max Weber: Anglo-American Religious Influences and Protestant Social Reform in Germany," *International Journal of Politics, Culture, and Society* 10, no. 4 (1997), 659–71; Scaff, *Weber*, 12, 74–75, 98–99, 164–69.
8. See, for example, Kapp's speech before the Congress of German Economists in Berlin in 1880. Reproduced in Hans Fenske, ed., *Im Bismarckschen Reich 1871–1890* (Darmstadt: Wissenschaftliche Buchgesellschaft, 1978), 258–59.
9. "Fresh" and "rude" in Marianne Weber, ed., *Max Weber: Jugendbriefe* (Tübingen: Verlag von J. C. B. Mohr [Paul Siebeck], 1936), 141. All other quotations in Bayrische Staatsbibliothek, Verhandlungen des Reichstags (VdR), Friedrich Kapp, 5 February 1883, p. 1298; 14 February 1883, pp. 1497–98.
10. Max Weber to Hermann Baumgarten, 8 November 1884. Reproduced in Marianne Weber, *Max Weber*, 140–41.
11. In the fall of 1883, Villard hosted his German friends and several German dignitaries, including Georg Siemens and Max Weber Sr., for the Northern Pacific's opening ceremony in Bismarck, North Dakota. In an embarrassing turn of events, however, he was forced to resign from his position just months later. Villard at the time managed to persuade the Germans that hostile American stock holders were to blame, along with loose regulations governing corporate finance in the United States. Christopher Kobrak, *Banking on Global Markets: Deutsche Bank and the United States, 1870 to the Present* (Cambridge: Cambridge University Press, 2007), 62–92; Richard White, *Railroaded: The Transcontinentals and the Making of Modern America* (New York: W. W. Norton, 2011), 216–23.
12. An introduction to the Pan-German League (*Alldeutscher Verband*) can be found in Roger Chickering, *We Men Who Feel Most German: A Cultural Study of the Pan-German League, 1886–1914* (Boston: Allen & Unwin, 1984), 49–50.
13. Biographical studies of Max Weber abound. My account here draws on Dirk Kaesler, *Max Weber: Preuße, Denker, Muttersohn* (Munich: C. H. Beck, 2014);

Wolfgang J. Mommsen, *Max Weber and German Politics, 1890–1920*, trans. Michael S. Steinberg (Chicago: University of Chicago Press, 1984); Fritz Ringer, *Max Weber: An Intellectual Biography* (Chicago: University of Chicago Press, 2004); and Roth, "Weber."

14. All quotes in Weber, *Nationalstaat*, 8–11. Note that Kapp, too, had referred to emigration as a "people-psychological" (*völker-psychologisch*es) phenomenon; see Friedrich Kapp, *Über Auswanderung: Ein Vortrag, gehalten am 2. Februar 1871 im Berliner Handwerker-Verein* (Berlin: Carl Habel, 1871), 4–5.

15. This is, of course, a simplified version of the argument Weber presented in the book, which also offered a nuanced account of the theological debates that took place among various Protestant denominations in Europe and North America over the course of three centuries.

16. To be sure, in *The Protestant Ethic* Weber presented "modern capitalism" as though it was an existing phenomenon, rather than something that might emerge in the future. Nevertheless, he emphasized that modern capitalism was an "ideal type" (*Idealtypus*), whereas mere capitalism was supposedly knowable through historical inquiry into the ancient human past. Weber, *Die Protestantische Ethik*, 91.

17. Ibid., 77, 91. Needless to say, the intellectual origins of Weber's *The Protestant Ethic* were more diverse and far-reaching than is implied here; see Peter Ghosh, *Max Weber and The Protestant Ethic: Twin Histories* (Oxford: Oxford University Press, 2014). On the intellectual concerns of the period more generally, see Suzanne L. Marchand, *German Orientalism in the Age of Empire: Religion, Race, and Scholarship* (Cambridge: Cambridge University Press, 2009).

18. The literature on German–US relations in the twentieth century is quite rich and nuanced. For an introduction to the field, see Victoria de Grazia, *Irresistible Empire: America's Advance Through Twentieth-Century Europe* (Cambridge, MA: Belknap Press of Harvard University Press, 2005); and Guettel, *Expansionism*, 217–32.

19. The rate of new capital export to the United States slowed as well, with German investors shifting their attention toward emerging markets in Austria-Hungary, Italy, Brazil, and Argentina. Nevertheless, the United States continued to benefit from German investment, including more recently in the twenty-first century, when German financial institutions were among the most enthusiastic foreign investors in US mortgage-backed securities. Richard H. Tilly and Michael Kopsidis, *From Old Regime to Industrial State: A History of German Industrialization from the Eighteenth Century to World War I* (Chicago: University of Chicago Press, 2020), 217–25. On recent investments in US mortgage-backed securities, see Adam Tooze, *Crashed: How a Decade of Financial Crises Changed the World* (New York: Viking, 2018), esp. 72–79.

20. In 1895, the number of German immigrants to the United States dropped to approximately 32,000. It had averaged nearly 150,000 per year during the 1880s. All statistics from Susan B. Carter, *Historical Statistics of the United States: Earliest Times to the Present* (New York: Cambridge University Press, 2006).

21. As is often observed, the German Empire in this period (the 1890s) transformed from a country of emigrants into one of immigrants. Klaus J. Bade, *Migration in European History* (Cambridge, MA: Blackwell, 2003); Dieter Gosewinkel, *Einbürgern und Ausschließen: Die Nationalisierung der Staatsangehörigkeit vom Deutschen Bund bis zur Bundesrepublik Deutschland* (Göttingen: Vandenhoeck & Ruprecht, 2001). It should be noted that Glenn Penny more recently placed the moment of transition in a later period, namely, the immediate aftermath of World War 2. H. Glenn Penny, *German History Unbound: From 1750 to the Present* (Cambridge: Cambridge University Press, 2022).
22. Weber himself predicted that this would be the case, emphasizing how modern capitalists found themselves engaged in a "difficult struggle against a world of hostile forces." Weber, *Die Protestantische Ethik*, 80.
23. "Pure bourgeois" cited and translated in Roth, "Weber," 666. To be sure, the Nazis did not engage with Weber explicitly. On the "Arbeit macht frei" motto in Nazi concentration camps, see Wolfgang Brückner, *"Arbeit macht frei": Herkunft und Hintergrund der KZ-Devise* (Opladen: Leske + Budrich Verlag, 1998).
24. All quotes from Lutz Niethammer, "'Normalization' in the West: Traces of Memory Leading Back into the 1950s," in *The Miracle Years. A Cultural History of West Germany, 1949–1968*, ed. Hanna Schissler (Princeton: Princeton University Press, 2001), 246–47, 260–61.
25. Reproduced here are only the second, third, and final stanzas of the poem. Cited and translated in Hal Draper, *The Complete Poems of Heinrich Heine: A Modern English Version* (Oxford: Oxford University Press, 1982), 406.
26. On this point, see Yair Mintzker's illuminating discussion of the progress idiom and its place in the related context of the modernization of German cities. Yair Mintzker, *The Defortification of the German City, 1689–1866* (Cambridge: Cambridge University Press, 2013), 244–55, esp. 250.
27. Geheimes Staatsarchiv Preußischer Kulturbesitz, I HA, Rep 120, C XIII 20, Nr. 1, Bd. 9, "Die deutsche und die chinesische Aus- und Rückwanderung in ihrer Bedeutung für das Deutsche Reich," 1875.
28. This is not to say that German history was entirely lacking in cosmopolitan or transnational dimension. David Blackbourn, *Germany in the World: A Global History, 1500-2000* (New York: Liveright, 2023); Penny, *German History Unbound*; Helmut Walser Smith, *Germany: A Nation in Its Time. Before, During, and After Nationalism, 1500–2000* (New York: Liveright, 2020).
29. See the discussion in H. Glenn Penny, *Kindred by Choice: Germans and American Indians Since 1800* (Chapel Hill: University of North Carolina Press, 2013).

Bibliography

ARCHIVE ABBREVIATIONS

BArch	Bundesarchiv, Berlin-Lichterfelde
BL	Bancroft Library, University of California Berkeley, Berkeley, California
BSB	Bayrische Staatsbibliothek, Munich
DBC	University of Texas Dolph Briscoe Center, Austin, Texas
DDB	Deutsche Digitale Bibliothek, Berlin
DRTL	Daughters of the Republic of Texas Library at the Alamo, San Antonio, Texas
FG	Forschungsbibliothek Gotha, Gotha
GStAPK	Geheimes Staatsarchiv Preußischer Kulturbesitz, Berlin-Lichterfelde
HADB	Historisches Archiv Deutsche Bank, Frankfurt am Main
HBL	Harvard University Baker Library, Cambridge, Massachusetts
HHL	Harvard University Houghton Library, Cambridge, Massachusetts
HHStW	Hessisches Hauptstaatsarchiv, Wiesbaden
HStABW	Hauptstaatsarchiv Baden-Württemberg, Stuttgart
HWA	Hessisches Wirtschaftsarchiv, Darmstadt
ISG	Institut für Stadtgeschichte, Frankfurt am Main
LAB	Landesarchiv Berlin, Berlin
LBI	Leo Baeck Institute, New York, New York
LoC	Library of Congress, Washington, DC
SMA	The Sophienburg Museum and Archives, New Braunfels, Texas

PUBLISHED SOURCES

Bagehot, Walter. *Lombard Street: A Description of the Money Market*. London: Henry S. King, 1873.

Bamberger, Ludwig. *Erinnerungen von Ludwig Bamberger*. Berlin: Georg Reimer, 1899.

Bamberger, Ludwig. "Ein Vademecum für deutsche Unterthanen." *Deutsche Jahrbücher für Politik und Literatur* 13 (1864): 54–70.

Bergson, Henri. *Creative Evolution*. Translated by Arthur Mitchell. New York: Henry Holt, 1911. Originally published in 1907.

Bluntschli, J. C., and R. Brater, eds. *Deutsches Staats-Wörterbuch. Vierter Band*. Stuttgart: Expedition des Staats-Wörterbuchs, 1859.

Braun, Adolf. *Die Arbeiterschutzgesetze der Europäischen Staaten: Mit Exkursen über Gewerbeverfassung, Industriestatistik, Entwicklung, und Durchführung der Arbeiterschutzgesetzgebung*. Deutsches Reich. Vol. 1, Tübingen: Verlag der H. Laupp'schen Buchhandlung, 1890.

Brauns, Ernst Ludwig. *Amerika und die moderne Völkerwanderung: Nebst einer Darstellung der gegenwärtig zu Ökonomie—Economy—am Ohio angesiedelten Harmonie-Gesellschaft, und einem Kupfer: Georg Rapp, Leiter der Harmonie-gesellschaft, vorstellend*. Potsdam: H. Vogler'sche Buchhandlung, 1833.

Bruncken, Ernest. *German Political Refugees in the United States During the Period from 1815–1860*. Chicago: R. and E. Research Associates, 1904.

Delbrück, Adelbert. *Aufzeichnungen unseres Vaters Adelbert Delbrück: geb. 16. Januar 1822, gest. 26. Mai 1890: Für die Enkel und Urenkel gedruckt 1922*. Leipzig: J. A. Brockhaus, 1922.

Eschwege, Ludwig. "Grundbesitz und GmbH." *Die Bank: Monatshefte für Finanz- u Bankwesen* 1, no 1 (1908): 533–62.

Everest, Kate Asaphine. *How Wisconsin Came by Its Large German Element*. Madison: State Historical Society of Wisconsin, 1892.

Faust, Albert Bernhardt. *The German Element in the United States: With Special Reference to Its Political, Moral, Social, and Educational Influence*. Vol. 2, Boston: Houghton Mifflin, 1909.

Fricker, Carl Victor, and Theodor von Geßler. *Geschichte der Verfassung Württemberg's: Zur Feier des fünfzigjährigen Bestehens der Verfassungs-Urkunde vom 25. September 1819*. Stuttgart: J. B. Metzler, 1869.

Fröbel, Julius. *Ein Lebenslauf: Aufzeichnungen, Erinnerungen, und Bekenntnisse*. Stuttgart: J. G. Cotta, 1890.

Fürstenberg, Hans. *Carl Fürstenberg: die Lebensgeschichte eines deutschen Bankiers, 1870–1914*. Berlin: Ullstein Verlag, 1931.

Gagern, Hans Christoph Ernst von. *Von der uralten Zeit bis zu dem Gotenreich unter Hermanrich*. Die Nationalgeschichte der Deutschen. Vol. 1. Vienna: Anton Strauß, 1813.

Gagern, Hans Christoph Ernst von. *Der Deutsche in Nord-Amerika*. Stuttgart: J. G. Cotta, 1818.

Gegen Gewerbefreiheit: Eine Rede. Lübeck: Verlag von Friedrich Aschenfeldt, 1862.

Glagau, Otto. *Der Börsen- und Gründungs-Schwindel in Berlin: Gesammelte und stark vermehrte Artikel der "Gartenlaube."* Leipzig: P. Frohberg, 1876.

Goldschmidt, Levin. *Die Reform des Aktiengesellschaftsrechts*. Stuttgart: Verlag von Ferdinand von Enke, 1884.

Greulich, C. "Der Verkehr in Geschäftsanteilen von Gesellschaften mit beschränkter Haftung." *Die Bank: Monatshefte für Finanz- u. Bankwesen* 1, no. 1 (1908): 263–66.

Grimm, Jacob, and Wilhelm Grimm. *Deutsches Wörterbuch. Zweiter Band*. Leipzig: Verlag von S. Hirzel, 1860.

Hecht, Felix. *Das Börsen- und Actienwesen der Gegenwart und die Reform des Actien-Gesellschafts-Rechts*. Vol. 1, Mannheim: Verlag von J. Schneider, 1874.

Heine, Heinrich. *Über Ludwig Börne*. Hamburg: Hoffmann und Campe, 1840.

Hegel, Georg Wilhelm Friedrich. *Grundlinien der Philosophie des Rechts oder Naturrecht und Staatswissenschaft im Grundriss: Mit Hegels eigenhändigen Notizen und den mündlichen Zusätzen*. Vol. 7, Frankfurt am Main: Suhrkamp Verlag, 1970.

Helfferich, Karl. *Georg von Siemens: Ein Lebensbild aus Deutschlands großer Zeit*. Vol. 1. Berlin: Julius Springer, 1921.

Herold, Georg. *Keine Gewerbefreiheit: Eine bürgerliche Antwort auf die vom gesetzgebenden Körper am 16. Jan. i. J. angeregte Frage*. Frankfurt am Main: Carl Horstmann, 1860.

Holst, Hermann Eduard von. "Friedrich Kapp." *Preussische Jahrbücher* 55, no. 3 (1885): 253–68.

Jahn, Friedrich Ludwig. *Deutsches Volksthum*. Lübeck: Niemann, 1810.

Julius, Köstlin. "Studien über das Sittengesetz." *Jahrbücher für deutsche Theologie* 13 (1868): 383–461.

Kant, Immanuel. *Anthropologie in pragmatischer Hinsicht*. Edited by Wolfgang Becker. Stuttgart: Reclam, 2017. Originally published in 1798.

Kapp, Friedrich. *Aus und über Amerika: Tatsachen und Erlebnisse*. Berlin: Julius Springer, 1876.

Kapp, Friedrich. *Immigration, and the Commissioners of Emigration of the State of New York*. New York: Nation Press, 1870.

Kapp, Friedrich. *Der Soldatenhandel deutscher Fürsten nach Amerika (1775 bis 1783)*. Berlin: Franz Duncker, 1864.

Kapp, Friedrich. *Über Auswanderung: Ein Vortrag, gehalten am 2. Februar 1871 im Berliner Handwerker-Verein*. Berlin: Carl Habel, 1871.

Kapp, Friedrich. "Zur Sklavenfrage in den Vereinigten Staaten." *Amerikanische Studien* 8 (1854): 116–25.

Keyßner, Hugo. *Die Aktiengesellschaften und die Kommanditgesellschaften auf Aktien unter dem Reichs-Gesetz vom 11. Juni 1870*. Berlin: Carl Heymann, 1873.

Kürnberger, Ferdinand. *Der Amerika-Müde: Amerikanisches Kulturbild*. Frankfurt am Main: Meidinger Sohn & Cie, 1855.

Lammers, A. "Handel und Zollwesen; Konsularwesen; Auswanderung; wirthschaftliche Gesetzgebung." *Jahrbuch für Gesetzgebung, Verwaltung und Rechtspflege des Deutschen Reiches* 2 (1873): 124–40.

Lesser, Richard, ed. *Deutsche Kolonialzeitung: Organ des Deutschen Kolonialvereins.* Vol. 3. Berlin: Verlag des Deutschen Kolonialvereins, 1886.

Leuchs, Johann Carl. *Realrechte und Gewerbs-Privilegien beseitigt und versöhnt mit der Freiheit der Gewerbe und der Ansässigung.* 2nd ed. Nürnberg: C. Leuchs, 1860.

Leuchs, Johann Carl. *Deutscher Haus- und Fabrikschatz: Zweiter Band.* Nürnberg: C. Leuchs., 1860.

Leuchs, Johann Carl, ed. *Einführungs-Schutz. Entwurf und Begründung eines Gesezes zum Schuze der Erfindungen für die deutschen Staaten.* Nürnberg: C. Leuchs., 1862.

Leuchs, Johann Carl. *Gewerbefreiheit für Nürnberg.* Nürnberg: C. Leuchs., 1839.

Leuchs, Johann Carl. *Zweihundert und fünfzig Entdeckungen und Verbesserungen in der Färberei und Druckerei, gemacht in den Jahren 1828 bis 1839.* Nürnberg: C. Leuchs, 1839.

Lindner, Friedrich Georg Ludwig. *Manuscript aus Süd-Deutschland.* Edited by George Erichson. London: James Griphi, 1820.

List, Friedrich. *Das nationale System der politischen Ökonomie.* Stuttgart: J. G. Cotta, 1841.

List, Friedrich. *Grundlinien einer politischen Ökonomie und andere Beiträge der Amerikanischen Zeit, 1825–1832. Friedrich List: Schriften, Reden, Briefe.* Edited by Wilhelm Notz. Vol. 2, Berlin: Reimar Hobbing, 1931.

List, Friedrich, Thomas Jefferson, and James Madison. *Outlines of American Political Economy, in a series of letters addressed by Friedrich List to Charles J. Ingersoll. To which is added the celebrated letters of Mr. Jefferson to Benjamin Austin, and of Mr. Madison to the Editors of the Lynchburg Virginian.* Philadelphia: Samuel Parker, 1827.

Löwenfeld, Hermann. *Das Recht der Actien-Gesellschaften: Kritik und Reformvorschläge.* Berlin: DeGruyter, 2018. Originally published in 1879.

Luden, Heinrich. *Einige Worte über das Studium der vaterländischen Geschichte: Vier öffentliche Vorlesungen.* Jena: Akademische Buchhandlung, 1810.

Martin, Edward Winslow. *History of the Grange Movement; Or, The Farmer's War Against Monopolies: Being a Full Account of the Struggles of the American Farmers Against the Extortions of the Railroad Companies. With a History of the Rise and Progress of the Order of Patrons of Husbandry, Its Objects, Present Condition and Prospects. To Which Is Added Sketches of the Leading Grangers.* Philadelphia: National Publishing Company, 1874.

Malthus, Thomas Robert. *An Essay on the Principle of Population; or, a View of Its Past and Present Effects on Human Happiness; with an Inquiry into Our Prospects Respecting the Future Removal or Mitigation of the Evils which it Occasions.* 6th ed. 2 vols. London: John Murray, 1826.

Moeller, Justinus. *Gründerprocesse: Eine Criminalpolitische Studie.* Berlin: Julius Springer, 1876.

Montesquieu, Charles Louis de Secondat Baron de. *The Spirit of the Laws.* Translated by Thomas Nugent. 2nd ed. Vol. 1, London: J. Nourse and P. Vaillant, 1752.

Möllhausen, Balduin. *Die Hyänen des Kapitals. Illustrierte Romane.* Vol. 4, Leipzig: Verlagsbuchhandlung von Paul List, 1912. 1876.

Möser, Justus. *Osnabrücksche Geschichte.* Osnabrück: Schmidische Buchhandlung, 1768.

Münsterberg, Hugo. *Aus Deutsch-Amerika.* Berlin: Ernst Siegfried und Sohn, Königliche Hofbuchhandlung, 1909.

Neukamp, Ernst. "Die deutschen Gesellschaften mit beschränkter Haftung: Eine neue Gesellschaftsform." *Zeitschrift für Volkswirtschaft, Socialpolitik, und Verwaltung: Organ der Gesellschaft Österreichischer Volkswirte* 8 (Vienna: Wilhelm Braumüller, 1899): 337–64.

Oechelhäuser, Wilhelm. *Die Arbeiterfrage: Ein sociales Programm.* Berlin: Julius Springer, 1886.

Oechelhäuser, Wilhelm. *Die deutsche-Ostafrikanische Centralbahn: Mit einer Uebersichtskarte.* Berlin: Julius Springer, 1899.

Oechelhäuser, Wilhelm. *Die Nachtheile des Aktienwesens und die Reform der Aktiengesetzgebung.* Berlin: Julius Springer, 1878.

Oechelhäuser, Wilhelm. *Die wirthschaftliche Krisis.* Berlin: Julius Springer, 1876.

Olmsted, Frederick Law. *A Journey Through Texas: Or, A Saddle-Trip on the Southwestern Frontier with a Statistical Appendix.* New York: Dix, Edwards, 1857.

Osterieth, August, ed. *Geschichte der Frankfurter Zeitung 1856–1906.* Frankfurt am Main: Verlag der Frankfurter Zeitung, 1906.

Otto, Friedrich. *Geschichte der Stadt Wiesbaden.* Wiesbaden: Franz Bossong, 1877.

Perrot, Franz. *Der Bank-, Börsen- und Actienschwindel: eine Hauptursache der drohenden sozialen Gefahr: Beiträge zur Kritik der politischen Oeconomie.* 3 vols. Rostock: Stiller, 1874.

Perrot, Franz. *Die moderne Wirthschafts-Gesetzgebung und die sogenannte 'soziale Frage'.* Munich: M. Huttler, 1874.

Quick, Herbert. *The Fairview Idea: A Story of the New Rural Life.* Indianapolis, IN: Bobbs–Merrill, 1919.

Ratjen, Hans. *"Deutsche die nicht Deutsche sind": Der Kampf um die Reichsangehörigkeit.* Hamburg: Lucas Gräfe & Sillem, 1908.

Reinganum, Paul. *Bericht über die Verhältnisse der Oregon- und California-Eisenbahn.* Frankfurt am Main: Mühlau & Waldschmidt, 1873.

Riehl, Wilhelm Heinrich. *Die deutsche Arbeit.* Stuttgart: J. G. Cotta, 1862.

Riehl, Wilhelm Heinrich. *Die Familie.* Stuttgart: J. G. Cotta, 1861.

Schiller, Friedrich. *Kleinere prosaische Schriften: Aus mehrern Zeitschriften, vom Verfasser selbst gesammelt und verbessert, Erster Theil.* Leipzig: Siegfried Lebrecht Crusius, 1792.

Schiller, Friedrich. *Schillers Sämmtliche Werke, Vierter Band.* Stuttgart: J. G. Cotta, 1879.

Schmoller, Gustav. "Offenes Sendschreiben an Herrn Professor Dr. Heinrich von Treitschke über einige Grundfragen des Rechts und der Volkswirthschaft." *Jahrbücher für Nationalökonomie und Statistik* 23, no. 2 (1874): 225–349.

Schneider, Eugen. *Württembergische Geschichte.* Stuttgart: J. B. Metzler, 1896.

Sombart, Werner. *Die Genesis des Kapitalismus. Der moderne Kapitalismus.* Vol. 1, Leipzig: Duncker & Humblot, 1902.

Sombart, Werner. *Warum gibt es in den Vereinigten Staaten keinen Sozialismus?* Tübingen: J.C.B. Mohr [Paul Siebeck], 1906.

Stephan, Heinrich von. *Geschichte der Preußischen Post von ihren Ursprüngen bis auf die Gegenwart.* Berlin: Königlich Geheime Oberhofbuchdruckerei, 1859.

Tacitus, Cornelius P. *Agricola Germania.* Translated by Harold Mattingly. London: Penguin Books, 2010.

Tocqueville, Alexis de. *Democracy in America and Two Essays on America.* Translated by Gerald E. Bevan. London: Penguin Books, 2003. Originally published in 1835.

Verein zur Wahrung der wirthschaftlichen Interessen von Handel und Gewerbe. *Die Erweiterung des Handelsrechts durch Einfügung neuer Gesellschaftsformen.* Berlin: Norddeutsche Buchdruckerei und Verlagsanstalt, 1891.

Villard, Henry. *Lebenserinnerungen von Heinrich Hilgard-Villard: Ein Bürger zweier Welten, 1835–1900.* Berlin: G. Reimer, 1906.

Vorländer, Franz. *Das Evangelium der Wahrheit und Freiheit, gegründet auf das Natur- und Sittengesetz. Für Gebildete.* Leipzig: Eduard Heinrich Mayer, 1865.

Weber, Marianne, ed. *Max Weber: Jugendbriefe.* Tübingen: J. C. B. Mohr, 1936.

Weber, Max. *Nationalstaat und Volkswirtschaftspolitik: Akademische Antrittsrede.* Freiburg: J. C. B. Mohr (Paul Siebeck), 1895.

Weber, Max. *Die Protestantische Ethik und der Geist des Kapitalismus.* 3rd ed. Edited by Dirk Kaesler. Munich: C.H. Beck, 2010. Originally published in 1905.

Weber, Max. *Die Verhältnisse der Landarbeiter in Deutschland.* Schriften des Vereins für Sozialpolitik. Vol. 7, Leipzig: Duncker & Humblot, 1892.

Wiss, Eduard. *Das Gesetz der Bevölkerung und die Eisenbahnen: Eine volkswirthschaftliche und statistische Untersuchung geführt auf dem Terrain der Vereinigten Staaten von Nordamerika und als Vorbild deutscher Verhältnisse volkswirthschaftliche verwerthet mit Berücksichtigung des besonderen Characters der Industrie and des Handels der einzelnen Staaten sowohl, wie der gesammten Union vom Jahre 1790–1860.* Berlin: Verlag von F. A. Herbig, 1867.

SECONDARY LITERATURE

Albrecht, Henning. "Preußen, ein 'Judenstaat': Antisemitismus als konservative Strategie gegen die 'Neue Ära'—Zur Krisentheorie der Moderne." *Geschichte und Gesellschaft* 37, no. 4 (2011): 455–81.

Alt, Peter-André. *Schiller. Leben—Werk—Zeit. Eine Biographie. Erster Band,* 1759–1791. Munich: C. H. Beck, 2000.

Amrith, Sunil S. *Crossing the Bay of Bengal: The Furies of Nature and the Fortunes of Migrants.* Cambridge, MA: Harvard University Press, 2013.

Anderson, Margaret Lavinia. *Windthorst: A Political Biography.* Oxford: Clarendon Press, 1981.

Appel, Livia, and Theodore C. Blegen. "Official Encouragement of Immigration to Minnesota During the Territorial Period." *Minnesota History Bulletin* 5, no. 3 (1923): 167–203.

Applegate, Celia. *A Nation of Provincials: The German Idea of Heimat*. Berkeley: University of California Press, 1990.

Arndt, Karl J. R. *George Rapp's Harmony Society*. Chapel Hill: University of North Carolina Press, 2010.

Arndt, Karl J. "George Rapp's Harmony Society." In *America's Communal Utopias*, edited by Donald E. Pitzer, 68–93. Chapel Hill: University of North Carolina Press, 1997.

Arneil, Barbara. *John Locke and America: The Defence of English Colonialism*. Oxford: Oxford University Press, 1996.

Arps, Ludwig. *Auf sicheren Pfeilern: Deutsche Versicherungswirtschaft vor 1914*. Göttingen: Vandenhoeck & Ruprecht, 1965.

Arthur, C. J., ed. *Karl Marx and Friedrich Engels: The German Ideology, Part One*. New York: International Publishers, 1970.

Ashton, Bodie A. *The Kingdom of Württemberg and the Making of Germany, 1815–1871*. London: Bloomsbury Academic, 2017.

Bade, Klaus J. *Migration in European History*. Cambridge, MA: Blackwell, 2003.

Baehring, Bernd. *Börsen- Zeiten: Frankfurter Wertpapierbörse 1585–1985 Frankfurt in vier Jahrhunderten zwischen Antwerpen, Wien, New York und Berlin aus dem Nachlaß Gerhard Löwenthal*. Frankfurt am Main: Frankfurter Wertpapierbörse, 1985.

Bailyn, Bernard. *The New England Merchants in the Seventeenth Century*. Cambridge, MA: Harvard University Press, 1979.

Baker, Bruce E., and Brian Kelly. *After Slavery: Race, Labor, and Citizenship in the Reconstruction South*. Gainesville: University Press of Florida, 2013.

Barkan, Elliott Robert. *From All Points: America's Immigrant West, 1870s–1952*. Bloomington: Indiana University Press, 2007.

Basler, Roy P., ed. *The Collected Works of Abraham Lincoln*. Vol. 7, New Brunswick, NJ: Rutgers University Press, 1953.

Bayer, Walter, and Mathias Habersack, eds. *Aktienrecht im Wandel*. Tübingen: Mohr Siebeck, 2007.

Baxter, Maurice G. "Encouragement of Immigration to the Middle West During the Era of the Civil War." *Indiana Magazine of History* 46, no. 1 (1950): 25–38.

Beckert, Sven. "American Danger: United States Empire, Eurafrica, and the Territorialization of Industrial Capitalism, 1870–1950." *The American Historical Review* 144, no. 4 (2017): 1137–70.

Beckert, Sven. *Empire of Cotton: A Global History*. New York: Penguin Vintage Books, 2014.

Bein, Alex. *Friedrich Hammacher: Lebensbild eines Parlamentariers und Wirtschaftsführers, 1824–1904*. Berlin: E. S. Mittler, 1932.

Bek, William G. *The German Settlement Society of Philadelphia, and Its Colony, Hermann, Missouri*. Philadelphia: Americana Germanica Press, 1907.

Belich, James. *Replenishing the Earth: The Settler Revolution and the Rise of the Angloworld*. Oxford: Oxford University Press, 2009.

Benz, Ernest. "Escaping Malthus: Population Explosion and Human Movement, 1760–1884." In *The Oxford Handbook of Modern German History*, edited by Helmut Walser Smith, 195–210. Oxford: Oxford University Press, 2011.

Berg, Maxine, and Pat Hudson. "Rehabilitating the Industrial Revolution." *The Economic History Review* 45, no. 1 (1992): 24–50.

Berghoff, Hartmut. *Zwischen Kleinstadt und Weltmarkt: Hohner und die Harmonika 1857–1961: Unternehmensgeschichte als Gesellschaftsgeschichte*. Paderborn: Ferdinand Schöningh, 1997.

Bergquist, James M. "German Communities in American Cities: An Interpretation of the Nineteenth-Century Experience." *Journal of American Ethnic History* 4, no. 1 (1984): 9–30.

Bernert, Helmut, ed. *Handwerk zwischen Zunft und Gewerbefreiheit: Edikte und Ausschreiben aus dem Königreich Westphalen, dem Kurfürstenthum Hessen, dem Herzogthum Nassau, dem Fürstenthum Waldeck, der freien Stadt Frankfurt sowie Entwürfe zum Handwerks- und Gewerberecht aus dem Jahre 1848, Quellensammlung zum Handwerks- und Gewerberecht*. Kassel: euregio verlag, 1998.

Beuys, Barbara. *Familienleben in Deutschland: Neue Bilder aus der deutschen Vergangenheit*. Reinbeck: Rowohlt, 1980.

Biernacki, Richard. *The Fabrication of Labour: Germany and Britain, 1640–1914*. Berkeley: University of California Press, 1995.

Blackbourn, David. *Germany in the World: A Global History, 1500–2000*. New York: Liveright, 2023.

Blackbourn, David. *History of Germany 1780–1918: The Long Nineteenth Century*. Malden, MA: Blackwell, 2003.

Blackbourn, David. "The Mittelstand in German Society and Politics, 1871–1914." *Social History* 2, no. 4 (1977): 409–33.

Blanning, T. C. W. *The Culture of Power and the Power of Culture: Old Regime Europe 1660–1789*. Oxford: Oxford University Press, 2002.

Blevins, Cameron. *Paper Trails: The US Post and the Making of the American West*. New York: Oxford University Press, 2021.

Borscheid, Peter. *Mit Sicherheit leben: die Geschichte der deutschen Lebensversicherungswirtschaft und der Provinzial-Lebensversicherungsanstalt von Westfalen*. 2 vols. Münster: Westfälische Provinzial, 1993.

Bracht, Johannes. *Geldlose Zeiten und überfüllte Kassen: Sparen, Leihen und Vererben in der ländlichen Gesellschaft Westfalens, 1830–1866*. Stuttgart: Lucius & Lucius, 2013.

Brakensiek, Stefan. "Akzeptanzorientе Herrschaft: Überlegungen zur politischen Kultur der Frühen Neuzeit." In *Die Frühe Neuzeit als Epoche*, edited by Helmut

Neuhaus, 395–406. Historische Zeitschrift. Munich: R. Oldenbourg Verlag, 2009.

Braudel, Fernand. *The Structures of Everyday Life. Civilization and Capitalism, 15th-18th Century*. Vol. 1, New York: Harper & Row, 1982.

Bretting, Agnes, and Hartmut Bickelmann. *Auswanderungsagenturen und Auswanderungsvereine im 19. und 20. Jahrhundert*. Stuttgart: Franz Steiner Verlag, 1991.

Brinkmann, Andreas. *Die deutsche Auswanderungswelle in die britischen Kolonien Nordamerikas um die Mitte des 18. Jahrhunderts*. Stuttgart: Franz Steiner Verlag, 1993.

Brophy, James M. *Capitalism, Politics, and Railroads in Prussia, 1830–1870*. Columbus: Ohio State University Press, 1998.

Brophy, James M. "The End of the Economic Old Order: The Great Transition, 1750–1860." In *The Oxford Handbook of Modern German History*, edited by Helmut Walser Smith, 169–94. Oxford: Oxford University Press, 2011.

Brophy, James M. "The Political Calculus of Capital: Banking and the Business Class in Prussia, 1848–1856." *Central European History* 25 (1992): 149–76.

Brückner, Wolfgang. *"Arbeit macht frei": Herkunft und Hintergrund der KZ-Devise*. Opladen: Leske + Budrich Verlag, 1998.

Burhop, Carsten. "Did Banks Cause the German Industrialization?" *Explorations in Economic History* 43, no. 1 (2006): 39–63.

Büschel, Hubertus. *Untertanenliebe: Der Kult um deutsche Monarchen 1770–1830*. Göttingen: Vandenhoeck & Ruprecht, 2006.

Buss, Dietrich G. *Henry Villard: A Study of Transatlantic Investments and Interests, 1870–1895*. New York: Arno Press, 1978.

Carter, E. J. "Breaking the Bank: Gambling Casinos, Finance Capitalism, and German Unification." *Central European History* 39, no. 2 (2006): 185–213.

Carter, Susan B. *Historical Statistics of the United States: Earliest Times to the Present*. New York: Cambridge University Press, 2006.

Castiglione, Caroline. *Patrons and Adversaries: Nobles and Villagers in Italian Politics, 1640–1760*. New York: Oxford University Press, 2005.

Chickering, Roger. *We Men Who Feel Most German: A Cultural Study of the Pan-German League, 1886–1914*. Boston: Allen & Unwin, 1984.

Choate, Mark. *Emigrant Nation: The Making of Italy Abroad*. Cambridge, MA: Harvard University Press, 2008.

Chytry, Josef. *The Aesthetic State: A Quest in Modern German Thought*. Berkeley: University of California Press, 1989.

Ciarlo, David. *Advertising Empire Race and Visual Culture in Imperial Germany*. Cambridge, MA: Harvard University Press, 2011.

Clark, Christopher. *Iron Kingdom: The Rise and Downfall of Prussia, 1600–1947*. Cambridge, MA: Belknap Press of Harvard University Press, 2006.

Cole, Hubert. *First Gentleman of the Bedchamber: The Life of Louis-François-Armand, Maréchal Duc de Richelieu*. London: Heinemann, 1965.

Confino, Alon. *The Nation as a Local Metaphor: Württemberg, Imperial Germany, and National Memory, 1871–1918*. Chapel Hill: University of North Carolina Press, 1997.

Conrad, Sebastian, and Jürgen Osterhammel, eds. *An Emerging Modern World, 1750–1870*. Cambridge, MA: Belknap Press of Harvard University Press, 2018.

Conzen, Kathleen Neils. "Die deutsche Amerikaeinwanderung im ländlichen Kontext: Problemfelder und Forschungsergebnisse." In *Auswanderer—Wanderarbeiter—Gastarbeiter: Bevölkerung, Arbeitsmarkt und Wanderung in Deutschland seit der Mitte des 19. Jahrhunderts*, edited by Klaus J. Bade, 350–77. Ostfildern: Scripta Mercaturae, 1984.

Conzen, Kathleen Neils. *Immigrant Milwaukee, 1836–1860: Accommodation and Community in a Frontier City*. Cambridge, MA: Harvard University Press, 1976.

Conzen, Kathleen Neils. *Making Their Own America. Assimilation Theory and the German Peasant Pioneer: With Comments by Mack Walker and Jörg Nagler*. New York: Berg, 1990.

Corbin, Alain. *Village Bells: Sound and Meaning in the 19th Century French Countryside*. New York: Columbia University Press, 1998.

Cott, Nancy F. *The Bonds of Womanhood: "Woman's Sphere" in New England, 1780–1835*. New Haven, CT: Yale University Press, 2021.

Craig, Gordon Alexander. *Germany, 1866–1945*. Oxford: Clarendon Press, 1978.

Cronon, William. *Nature's Metropolis: Chicago and the Great West*. New York: W. W. Norton, 1991.

Cross, Jasper W., Jr. "The Forty-Eighter and the Election of 1860." *The Historical Bulletin* 27, no. 4 (1949): 79–89.

Cusack, Andrew. *The Wanderer in Nineteenth-Century German Literature: Intellectual History and Cultural Criticism*. Rochester, NY: Camden House, 2008.

D'Auria, Matthew. *The Shaping of French National Identity: Narrating the Nation's Past, 1715–1830*. Cambridge: Cambridge University Press, 2020.

Davies, Hannah Catherine. *Transatlantic Speculations: Globalization and the Panics of 1873*. New York: Columbia University Press, 2018.

Dawdy, Shannon Lee. "Proper Caresses and Prudent Distance: A How-To Manual from Colonial Louisiana." In *Haunted by Empire: Geographies of Intimacy in North American History*, edited by Ann Laura Stoler, 140–61. Durham, NC: Duke University Press, 2006.

De Grazia, Victoria. *Irresistible Empire: America's Advance Through Twentieth-Century Europe*. Cambridge, MA: Belknap Press of Harvard University Press, 2005.

De Vries, Henry P., and Friedrich Jünger. "Limited Liability Contract: The GmbH." *Columbia Law Review* 64 (1964): 866–86.

De Vries, Jan. *The Industrious Revolution: Consumer Behavior and the Household Economy, 1650 to the Present*. Cambridge: Cambridge University Press, 2008.

Deter, Gerhard, ed. *Zwischen Gilde und Gewerbefreiheit: Rechtsgeschichte des selbständigen Handwerks im Westfalen des 19. Jahrhunderts (1810–1869).* Edited by Günther Schulz, Jörg Baten, Markus A. Denzel, and Gerhard Fouquet. Vol. 1, *Vierteljahrschrift für Sozial- und Wirtschaftsgeschichte—Beihefte.* Stuttgart: Franz Steiner Verlag, 2015.

Deutsche Bank Board of Managing Directors, ed. *Studies on Economic and Monetary Problems and on Banking History.* Neuwied: Hase & Koehler, 1988.

Dinnerstein, Leonard, and David M. Reimers. *Ethnic Americans: A History of Immigration.* New York: Columbia University Press, 1999.

Doerries, Reinhard R. "Making It in Banking: The German Savings Bank in the City of New York as a Test Case of Ethnic Enterprise in Nineteenth Century America." In *Liberalitas: Festschrift für Erich Angermann zum 65. Geburtstag,* edited by Norbert Finzsch and Hermann Wellenreuther, 443–56. Stuttgart: Steiner Verlag, 1992.

Draper, Hal. *The Complete Poems of Heinrich Heine: A Modern English Version.* Oxford: Oxford University Press, 1982.

Dufresne, Gustav. "Denkschrift über die Aufgaben und Ziele der neu zu errichtenden Deutschen Bank." In *Studies on Economic and Monetary Problems and on Banking History,* edited by Deutsche Bank Board of Managing Directors, 729–37. Neuwied: Hase & Koehler, 1988.

Efford, Alison Clark. *German Immigrants, Race, and Citizenship in the Civil War Era.* Washington, DC: German Historical Institute, 2013.

Elliott, Bruce S., David A. Gerber, and Suzanne M. Sinke, eds. *Letters Across Borders: The Epistolary Practices of International Migrants.* New York: Palgrave Macmillan, 2006.

Ellis, Harold A. *Boulainvilliers and the French Monarchy: Aristocratic Politics in Early Eighteenth-Century France.* Ithaca, NY: Cornell University Press, 1988.

Emrich, Gabriele. *Die Emigration der Salzburger Protestanten 1731–1732: Reichsrechtliche und kofessionspolitische Aspekte.* Münster: LIT Verlag, 2018.

Engel, Elisabeth. "Hugo Wesendonck." (2016). Accessed October 31, 2024. http://www.immigrantentrepreneurship.org/entries/hugo-wesendonck/.

Epstein, Klaus. *The Genesis of German Conservatism.* Princeton: Princeton University Press, 1966.

Erickson, Charlotte. *American Industry and the European Immigrant, 1860–1885.* Cambridge, MA: Harvard University Press, 2014.

Erickson, Charlotte. *Invisible Immigrants: The Adaptation of English and Scottish Immigrants in Nineteenth-Century America.* Coral Gables: University of Florida Press, 1972.

Erickson, Charlotte. *Leaving England: Essays on British Emigration in the Nineteenth Century.* Ithaca, NY: Cornell University Press, 1994.

Evans, Richard J. *The Pursuit of Power: Europe 1815–1914.* New York: Penguin Books, 2016.

Faragher, John Mack. *Sugar Creek: Life on the Illinois Prairie*. New Haven, CT: Yale University Press, 1986.
Fear, Jeffrey R., and Christopher Kobrak. "Diverging Paths: Accounting for Corporate Governance in America and Germany." *The Business History Review* 80, no. 1 (Spring 2006): 1–48.
Federici, Silvia. *Caliban and the Witch: Women, the Body and Primitive Accumulation*. New York: Autonomedia, 2004.
Fehér, Ferenc. "Practical Reason in the Revolution: Kant's Dialogue with the French Revolution." *Social Research* 56, no. 1 (1989): 161–85.
Fenske, Hans, ed. *Im Bismarckschen Reich 1871–1890*. Darmstadt: Wissenschaftliche Buchgesellschaft, 1978.
Fertig, Georg. "'Man müßte es sich schier fremd vorkommen lassen': Auswanderungspolitik am Oberrhein im 18. Jahrhundert." In *Migration nach Ost- und Südosteuropa vom 18. bis zum Beginn des 19. Jahrhunderts*, edited by Mathias Beer and Dittmar Dahlmann, 71–88. Stuttgart: Jan Thorbecke Verlag, 1999.
Fiebig, Eva Susanne. "The Consular Service of the Hansa Towns Lübeck, Bremen and Hamburg in the 19th Century." In *Consuls et services consulaires au XIXe siecle = Die Welt der Konsulate im 19. Jahrhundert = Consulship in the 19th Century*, edited by Jörg Ulbert and Lukian Prijac, 248–60. Hamburg: Dokumentation & Buch, 2010.
Fitzpatrick, David. "Irish Emigration and the Art of the Letter-Writing." In *Letters Across Borders: The Epistolary Practices of International Migrants*, edited by Bruce S. Elliott, David A. Gerber, and Suzanne M. Sinke, 97–106. New York: Palgrave Macmillan, 2006.
Fitzpatrick, David. *Oceans of Consolation: Personal Accounts of Irish Migration to Australia*. Ithaca, NY: Cornell University Press, 1994.
Flum, Carmen. *Armeleutemalerei: Darstellungen der Armut im deutschsprachigen Raum 1830–1914*. Merzhausen: ad picturam, 2013.
Fohlin, Caroline. *Finance Capitalism and Germany's Rise to Industrial Power*. New York: Cambridge University Press, 2007.
Foner, Eric. *Free Soil, Free Labor, Free Men: The Ideology of the Republican Party Before the Civil War*. Oxford: Oxford University Press, 1995.
Foner, Eric. *Reconstruction: America's Unfinished Revolution, 1863–1877*. New York: Harper & Row, 1989.
Foner, Eric. *The Second Founding: How the Civil War and Reconstruction Remade the Constitution*. New York: W. W. Norton, 2019.
Frank, Alison Fleig. *Oil Empire: Visions of Prosperity in Austrian Galicia*. Cambridge, MA: Harvard University Press, 2005.
Frevert, Ute. *Frauen-Geschichte Zwischen Bürgerlicher Verbesserung und Neuer Weiblichkeit*. Frankfurt am Main: Suhrkamp Verlag, 1986.
Furet, François. *Revolutionary France, 1770–1880*. Translated by Antonia Nevill. Oxford: Wiley-Blackwell, 1995.

Gabel, Helmut. *Widerstand und Kooperation: Studien zur politischen Kultur rheinischer und maasländischer Kleinterritorien (1648–1794)*. Tübingen: Bibliotheca Academica, 1995.

Gall, Lothar, Gerald D. Feldman, Harold James, Carl-Ludwig Holtfrerich, and Hans E. Büschgen. *The Deutsche Bank, 1870–1995*. London: Weidenfeld & Nicolson, 1995.

Gates, Paul Wallace. *The Illinois Central Railroad and Its Colonization Work, by Paul Wallace Gates*. Cambridge, MA: Harvard University Press, 1934.

Gebhard, Hellmut. *Die Berliner Börse von den Anfängen bis zum Jahre 1896*. Berlin: R. L. Prager, 1928.

Gehring, Paul. *Friedrich List: Jugend- und Reifejahre, 1789–1825*. Tübingen: J. C. B. Mohr (Paul Siebeck), 1964.

Geiger, Ludwig. *Therese Huber, 1764 bis 1829: Leben und Briefe einer deutschen Frau*. Stuttgart: J. G. Cotta, 1901.

Geldern, Wolfgang von. *Wilhelm Oechelhäuser als Unternehmer, Wirtschaftspolitiker und Sozialpolitiker*. Munich: F. Bruckmann, 1971.

Gerber, David A. *Authors of Their Lives: The Personal Correspondence of British Immigrants to North America in the Nineteenth Century*. New York: New York University Press, 2006.

Gerschenkron, Alexander. *Economic Backwardness in Historical Perspective: A Book of Essays*. Cambridge, MA: Belknap Press of Harvard University Press, 1962.

Ghosh, Peter. *Max Weber and the Protestant Ethic: Twin Histories*. Oxford: Oxford University Press, 2014.

Gienapp, William E. *The Origins of the Republican Party, 1852–1856*. New York: Oxford University Press, 1987.

Glymph, Thavolia. *Out of the House of Bondage: The Transformation of the Plantation Household*. New York: Cambridge University Press, 2008.

Goey, Ferry de. *Consuls and the Institutions of Global Capitalism, 1783–1914*. London: Pickering & Chatto, 2014.

Gömmel, Rainer, and Hans Pohl, eds. *Deutsche Börsengeschichte*. Frankfurt am Main: Knapp, 1992.

Gosewinkel, Dieter. *Einbürgern und Ausschließen: Die Nationalisierung der Staatsangehörigkeit vom Deutschen Bund bis zur Bundesrepublik Deutschland*. Göttingen: Vandenhoeck & Ruprecht, 2001.

Göttsching, Paul. "Justus Mösers Staats- und Geschichtsdenken: Der Nationsgedanke des aufgeklärten Ständetums." *Der Staat* 22, no. 1 (1983): 33–61.

Grauer, Karl-Johannes. *Wilhelm I König von Württemberg: Ein Bild seines Lebens und seiner Zeit*. Stuttgart: Schwabenverlag, 1960.

Green, Nancy L., and François Weil, eds. *Citizenship and Those Who Leave: The Politics of Emigration and Expatriation*. Urbana: University of Illinois Press, 2007.

Grubb, Farley Ward. *German Immigration and Servitude in America, 1709–1920*. London: Routledge, 2013.

Guettel, Jens-Uwe. *German Expansionism, Imperial Liberalism and the United States, 1776–1945*. Cambridge: Cambridge University Press, 2012.

Guinnane, Timothy W. "Delegated Monitors, Large and Small: Germany's Banking System, 1800–1914." *Journal of Economic Literature* 40, no. 1 (2002): 73–124.

Guinnane, Timothy W. "Die Reiffeisen-Kreditgenossenschaften 1864: Die Expansion des genossenschaftlichen Kredits im 19. Jahrhundert." Translated by Claus Sprick. In *Schlüsselereignisse der deutschen Bankengeschichte*, edited by Carsten Burhop, *Dieter Lindenlaub and Joachim Scholtyseck*, 120–135. Stuttgart: Franz Steiner Verlag, 2014.

Guinnane, Timothy W., Ron Harris, Naomi R. Lamoreaux, and Jean-Laurent Rosenthal. "Putting the Corporation in Its Place." *NBER Working Paper Series* (Cambridge, MA: National Bureau of Economic Research, 2007): 1–61.

Hagemann, Karen. "Nation, Krieg und Geschlechterordnung: Zum kulturellen und politischen Diskurs in der Zeit der antinapoleonischen Erhebung Preußens 1806–1815." *Geschichte und Gesellschaft* 22, no. 4 (1996): 562–91.

Hagemann, Karen, and Jean H. Quataert, eds. *Gendering Modern German History: Rewriting Historiography*. New York: Berghahn Books, 2007.

Hale, Sarah Josephina. *Woman's Record; or, Sketches of All Distinguished Women, from "The Beginning" till A.D. 1850: Arranged in Four Eras with Selections from Female Writers of Every Age*. New York: Harper & Brothers, 1853.

Hamann, Christof, Ute Gerhard, and Walter Grünzweig, eds. *Amerika und die deutschsprachige Literatur nach 1848, Migration—kultureller Austausch—frühe Globalisierung*. Bielefeld: transcript Verlag, 2009.

Handlin, Oscar. *The Uprooted: The Epic Story of the Great Migrations That Made the American People*. Boston: Little, Brown, 1951.

Hansen, Joseph. *Gustav von Mevissen: Ein rheinisches Lebensbild, 1815–1899*. 2 vols., Berlin: Georg Reimer, 1906.

Hansen, Marcus Lee. "Official Encouragement of Immigration to Iowa." *The Iowa Journal of History and Politics* 19, no. 2 (1921), 159–95.

Harfest, George E. *History of Letter Communication Between the United States and Europe, 1845–1875*. Washington, DC: Quartermann, 1971.

Harnisch, Hartmut. "Agrarstaat oder Industriestaat: Die Debatte um die Bedeutung der Landwirtschaft in Wirtschaft und Gesellschaft Deutschlands an der Wende vom 19. zum 20. Jahrhundert." In *Ostelbische Agrargesellschaft im Kaiserreich und der Weimarer Republik*, edited by Hanz Reif, 33–50. Berlin: Akademie Verlag, 1994.

Haupt, Heinz-Gerhard, and Jürgen Kocka, eds. *Comparative and Transnational History: Central European History and New Perspectives*. New York, NY: Berghahn Books, 2009.

Hausen, Karin. "Work in Gender, Gender in Work. The German Case in Comparative Perspective." In *Work in a Modern Society: The German Historical Experience in Comparative Perspective*, edited by Jürgen Kocka, 73–92. New York: Berghahn Books, 2010.

Hedges, James B. "The Colonization Work of the Northern Pacific Railroad." *The Mississippi Valley Historical Review* 13, no. 3 (1926): 311–42.

Hein, Benjamin. "Old Regime in a New World: Frankfurt's Financial Market in the Nineteenth Century." *The Journal of Modern History* 92, no. 4 (2020): 735–73.

Helbich, Wolfgang Johannes. "Land der unbegrenzten Möglichkeiten? Das Amerika-Bild der deutschen Auswanderer im 19. Jahrhundert." In *Deutschland und der Westen im 19. und 20. Jahrhundert*, edited by Jürgen Elvert and Michael Salewski, 295–321. Stuttgart: Franz Steiner Verlag, 1997.

Helbich, Wolfgang Johannes, Walter D. Kamphoefner, and Ulrike Sommer, eds. *Briefe aus Amerika: Deutsche Auswanderer schreiben aus der Neuen Welt, 1830–1930*. Munich: C. H. Beck, 1988.

Henning, Hans-Joachim. *Die deutsche Beamtenschaft im 19. Jahrhundert: zwischen Stand und Beruf*. Stuttgart: Franz Steiner Verlag, 1984.

Herder, Hans, ed. *Hessisches Auswandererbuch: Berichte, Chroniken und Dokmente zur Geschichte hessischer Einwanderer in den Vereinigten Staaten 1683–1983*. Frankfurt am Main: Insel Verlag, 1984.

Hillgruber, Christian. "Humanitäre Intervention, Grossmachtpolitik und Völkerrecht." *Der Staat* 40, no. 2 (2001): 165–91.

Hinners, Wolfgang. *Exil und Rückkehr: Friedrich Kapp in Amerika und Deutschland, 1824–1884*. Stuttgart: Akademischer Verlag, 1987.

Hippel, Wolfgang von. *Auswanderung aus Südwestdeutschland: Studien zur württembergischen Auswanderung und Auswanderungspolitik im 18. und 19. Jahrhundert*. Stuttgart: Klett-Cotta, 1984.

Hirschman, Albert O. *The Passions and the Interests: Political Arguments for Capitalism Before Its Triumph*. Edited by Jeremy Adelman. Princeton: Princeton University Press, 2013.

Hirschmann, Gerhard. "Leuchs, Johann Carl." *Neue Deutsche Biographie* 14 (1985): 366.

Hobbs, Allyson. *A Chosen Exile: A History of Racial Passing in American Life*. Cambridge, MA: Harvard University Press, 2014.

Hobsbawm, Eric J. *The Age of Capital, 1848–1875*. New York: Vintage Books, 1975.

Hoerder, Dirk. *Cultures in Contact: World Migrations in the Second Millennium*. Durham, NC: Duke University Press, 2002.

Hoerder, Dirk. "The German-Language Diasporas: A Survey, Critique, Interpretation." *Diaspora* 11, no. 1 (2002): 7–44.

Hoffmann, Walther G. *Das Wachstum der deutschen Wirtschaft seit der Mitte des 19. Jahrhunderts*. Enzyklopädie der Rechts- und Staatswissenschaft. Edited by W. Kunkel, H. Peters, and E. Preiser. Berlin: Springer-Verlag, 1965.

Holtfrerich, Carl Ludwig. *Finanzplatz Frankfurt: Von der mittelalterlichen Messestadt zum europäischen Bankenzentrum*. Munich: C. H. Beck, 1999.

Honeck, Mischa. *We Are the Revolutionists: German-Speaking Immigrants and American Abolitionists After 1848*. Athens, GA: University of Georgia Press, 2011.

Howard, Stanley E. "The Limited Partnership Association in New Jersey." *The Journal of Business* 9 (1936): 258–79.

Huber, F. C. "Auswanderung und Auswanderungspolitik im Königreich Württemberg." In *Auswanderung und Auswanderungspolitik in Deutschland: Berichte über die Entwicklung und den gegenwärtigen Zustand des Auswanderungswesens in den Einzelstaaten und um Reich*, edited by Eugen von Philippovich, 233–84. Leipzig: Duncker & Humblot, 1892.

Hull, Isabel V. *Sexuality, State, and Civil Society in Germany, 1700–1815*. Ithaca, NY: Cornell University Press, 1996.

Hungerland, Wolf-Fabian, and Markus Lampe. "Globalization and Foreign Trade." In *An Economic History of the First German Unification: State Formation and Economic Development in a European Perspective*, edited by Ulrich Pfister and Nikolaus Wolf, 274–94. London: Routledge, 2023.

Hungerland, Wolf-Fabian, and Nikolaus Wolf. "The Panopticon of Germany's Foreign Trade, 1880–1913: New Facts on the First Globalization." *European Review of Economic History* 26, no. 4 (2022): 479–507.

Hunt, Lynn. *The Family Romance of the French Revolution*. Berkeley: University of California Press, 1992.

Hunt, Margaret. *Women in Eighteenth Century Europe*. London: Routledge, 2010.

Institut für bankhistorische Forschung e.V., ed. *Die Geschichte der DZ Bank: das genossenschaftliche Zentralbankwesen in Deutschland vom 19. Jahrhundert bis heute*. Munich: C. H. Beck, 2013.

Jacobson, Matthew Frye. *Whiteness of a Different Color: European Immigrants and the Alchemy of Race*. Cambridge, MA: Harvard University Press, 1998.

James, Harold. *Krupp: A History of the Legendary German Firm*. Princeton: Princeton University Press, 2012.

Janeck, Undine. *Zwischen Gartenlaube und Karl May: Deutsche Amerikarezeption in den Jahren 1871–1913*. Aachen: Shaker Verlag, 2003.

Judson, Pieter. "When Is a Diaspora Not a Diaspora? Rethinking Nation-Centered Narratives About Germans in Habsburg East Central Europe." In *The Heimat Abroad: The Boundaries of Germanness*, edited by Krista O'Donnell, Renate Bridenthal, and Nancy Reagin, 219–49. Ann Arbor: University of Michigan Press, 2005.

Jung, Moon-Ho. *Coolies and Cane: Race, Labor, and Sugar in the Age of Emancipation*. Baltimore: Johns Hopkins University Press, 2006.

Kabisch, Thomas R. *Deutsches Kapital in den USA: Von der Reichsgründung bis zur Sequestrierung (1917) und Freigabe*. Stuttgart: Klett-Cotta, 1982.

Kaesler, Dirk. *Max Weber: Preuße, Denker, Muttersohn*. Munich: C. H. Beck, 2014.

Kamphoefner, Walter D. "Immigrant Epistolary and Epistemology: On the Motivators and Mentality of Nineteenth-Century German Immigrants." *Journal of American Ethnic History* 28, no. 3 (2009): 34–54.

Kamphoefner, Walter D. *The Westfalians: From Germany to Missouri*. Princeton: Princeton University Press, 1987.
Kamphoefner, Walter D., and Wolfgang Johannes Helbich. *Germans in the Civil War: The Letters They Wrote Home*. Chapel Hill: University of North Carolina Press, 2006.
Kaplan, Amy. "Manifest Domesticity." *American Literature* 70, no. 3 (1998): 581–606.
Kapp, Friedrich, Otto von Bismarck, and Hans-Ulrich Wehler. *Vom radikalen Frühsozialisten des Vormärz zum liberalen Parteipolitiker des Bismarckreichs. Briefe 1843–1884*. Frankfurt am Main: Insel-Verlag, 1969.
Karpeles, Gustav, ed. *Heinrich Heine's Gesammelte Werke: Achter Band*. Berlin: G. Grote, 1909.
Kaufhold, Karl Heinrich. "Gewerbefreiheit im 19. Jahrhundert." In *Wirtschaftliches Geschehen und ökonomisches Denken: Ausgewählte Schriften von Karl Heinrich Kaufhold herausgegeben aus Anlass seines 75. Geburtstages*, edited by Markus A. Denzel and Hans-Jürgen Gerhard, 111–52. Stuttgart: Franz Steiner Verlag, 2007.
Keil, Hartmut, and John B. Jentz, eds. *German Workers in Chicago: A Documentary History of Working-Class Culture from 1850 to World War I*. Urbana: University of Illinois Press, 1988.
Kesslinger, M. *Guardian of a Century, 1860–1960*. New York: Guardian Life Insurance Company of America, 1960.
Kieseritzky, Wolther von. *Liberalismus und Sozialstaat: liberale Politik in Deutschland zwischen Machtstaat und Arbeiterbewegung (1878–1893)*. Cologne: Böhlau, 2002.
Klann, Kilian. *Die Sammlung indianischer Ethnographica aus Nordamerika des Herzog Friedrich Paul Wilhelm von Württemberg*. Wyk auf Föhr: Verlag für Amerikanistik, 1999.
Klein, Ernst. "The Deutsche Bank's South American Business Before the First World War." In *Studies on Economic and Monetary Problems and on Banking History*, edited by Manfred Pohl, 471–86. Mainz: v. Hase & Koehler, 1988.
Kleinschmidt, Harald. *People on the Move: Attitude Toward and Perceptions of Migration in Medieval and Modern Europe*. Westport, CT: Praeger, 2003.
Kling, Gerhard, Joerg Baten, and Kirsten Labuske. "FDI of German Companies During Globalization and Deglobalization." *Open Economies Review* 22, no. 2 (2011): 247–70.
Kobrak, Christopher. *Banking on Global Markets: Deutsche Bank and the United States, 1870 to the Present*. Cambridge: Cambridge University Press, 2007.
Koch, Alfred. "Deutsche Schiffs- und Seeposten sowie mögliche Briefbeförderungsgelegenheiten nach Übersee." *Archiv für deutsche Postgeschichte* 22, no. 1 (1964): 2–46.
Kocka, Jürgen. "Arbeiterbewegung in der Bürgergesellschaft. Überlegungen zum deutschen Fall." *Geschichte und Gesellschaft* 20, no. 4 (1994): 487–96.

Kocka, Jürgen, and Marcel van der Linden. *Capitalism: The Reemergence of a Historical Concept*. London: Bloomsbury Academic, 2016.
Kocka, Jürgen. *Industrial Culture and Bourgeois Society: Business, Labor, and Bureaucracy in Modern Germany*. New York: Berghahn Books, 1999.
Kocka, Jürgen. *Unternehmer in der deutschen Industrialisierung*. Göttingen: Vandenhoeck & Ruprecht, 1975.
Kocka, Jürgen. "Writing the History of Capitalism." *Bulletin of the GHI* 47 (2010): 7–24.
Koehler, Benedikt. *Ludwig Bamberger: Revolutionär und Bankier*. Stuttgart: Deutsche Verlags-Anstalt, 1999.
Koselleck, Reinhart. "Die Auflösung des Hauses als ständischer Herrschaftseinheit: Anmerkungen zum Rechtswandel von Haus, Familie und Gesinde in Preußen zwischen der Französischen Revolution und 1848." In *Familie zwischen Tradition und Moderne: Studien zur Geschichte der Familie in Deutschland und Frankreich vom 16. bis zum 20. Jahrhundert*, edited by Neithard Bulst, Joseph Goy, and Jochen Hoock, 109–23. Göttingen: Vandenhoeck & Ruprecht, 1981.
Krämer, Daniel. *"Menschen grasten nun mit dem Vieh": die letzte große Hungerkrise der Schweiz 1816/17: mit einer theoretischen und methodischen Einführung in die historische Hungerforschung*. Basel: Schwabe Verlag, 2015.
Krauss, Karl-Peter. *Quellen zu den Lebenswelten deutscher Migranten im Königreich Ungarn im 18. und frühen 19. Jahrhundert*. Stuttgart: Franz Steiner Verlag, 2015.
Krebs, Christopher B. *A Most Dangerous Book: Tacitus's Germania from the Roman Empire to the Third Reich*. New York: W. W. Norton, 2011.
Kuckhoff, Michael. "Die Auswanderungsdiskussion während der Revolution von 1848–49." In *Deutsche Amerikaauswanderung im 19. Jahrhundert: Sozialgeschichtliche Beiträge*, edited by Günter Moltmann, 102–45. Stuttgart: J. B. Metzler, 1976.
Kuczynski, Jürgen. *Darstellung der Lage der Arbeiter in Deutschland von 1849 bis 1870*. Berlin: Akademie Verlag, 1962.
Laybourn, Norman. *L'Émigration des Alsaciens et de Lorrains du XVIII au XX Siècle*. 2 vols. Strasbourg: Association des publications près les universités de Strasbourg, 1986.
Leggiere, Michael V. *Blücher: Scourge of Napoleon*. Norman: University of Oklahoma Press, 2014.
Lembcke, Oliver W., and Florian Weber. *Emmanuel Joseph Sieyès: The Essential Political Writings*. Leiden: Brill, 2014.
Lerner, Marc H. *A Laboratory of Liberty: The Transformation of Political Culture in Republican Switzerland, 1750–1848*. Leiden: Brill, 2012.
Levine, Bruce C. *The Fall of the House of Dixie: The Civil War and the Social Revolution That Transformed the South*. New York: Random House, 2013.
Levine, Bruce C. *The Spirit of 1848: German Immigrants, Labor Conflict, and the Coming of the Civil War*. Urbana: University of Illinois Press, 1992.
Levy, Jonathan. *Freaks of Fortune: The Emerging World of Capitalism and Risk in America*. Cambridge, MA: Harvard University Press, 2012.

Limbach, Jutta. *Theorie und Wirklichkeit der GmbH: die empirischen Normaltypen der Gesellschaft mit beschränkter Haftung und ihr Verhältnis zum Postulat von Herrschaft und Haftung*. Berlin: Duncker & Humblot, 1966.

Link, Stefan, and Noam Maggor. "The United States as a Developing Nation: Revisiting the Peculiarities of American History." *Past & Present* 246, no. 1 (2020): 269–306.

Lubetkin, M. John. *Jay Cooke's Gamble: The Northern Pacific Railroad, the Sioux, and the Panic of 1873*. Norman: University of Oklahoma Press, 2006.

Macha, Jürgen, Marlene Nikolay-Panter, and Wolfgang Herborn, eds. *Wir verlangen nicht mehr nach Deutschland: Auswandererbriefe und Dokumente der Sammlung Joseph Scheben (1825–1938)*. Frankfurt am Main: Peter Lang, 2003.

Machtan, Lothar. "'Im Vertrauen auf unsere gerechte Sache . . .' Streikbewegungen der Industriearbeiter in den 70er Jahren des 19. Jahrhunderts." In *Streik: Zur Geschichte des Arbeitskampfes in Deutschland während der Industrialisierung*, 52–73. Munich: C. H. Beck, 1981.

Madden, John J. *British Investment in the United States, 1860–1880*. New York: Garland, 1985.

Maggor, Noam. *Brahmin Capitalism: Frontiers of Wealth and Populism in America's First Gilded Age*. Cambridge, MA: Harvard University Press, 2017.

Maier, Charles S. *Once Within Borders. Territories of Power, Wealth, and Belonging*. Cambridge, MA: Belknap Press of Harvard University Press, 2016.

Maischak, Lars. *German Merchants in the Nineteenth Century Atlantic*. Washington, DC: German Historical Institute, 2013.

Majer, Diemut. *Frauen—Revolution—Recht: die grossen europäischen Revolutionen in Frankreich, Deutschland und Österreich 1789 bis 1918 und die Rechtsstellung der Frauen: unter Einbezug von England, Russland, der USA und der Schweiz*. Zurich: Nomos, 2008.

Maliks, Reidar. "Revolutionary Epigones: Kant and His Radical Followers." *History of Political Thought* 33, no. 4 (2012): 647–71.

Marchand, Suzanne L. *German Orientalism in the Age of Empire: Religion, Race, and Scholarship*. Cambridge: Cambridge University Press, 2009.

Martin, Nicole. "In the Name of the Home: The Politics of Gender, Race, and Reconstruction in Nineteenth-Century America." PhD diss., Stanford University, 2018.

Matthews, Glenna. *"Just a Housewife": The Rise and Fall of Domesticity in America*. New York: Oxford University Press, 1987.

Mayhew, Robert. *Malthus: The Life and Legacies of an Untimely Prophet*. Cambridge, MA: Belknap Press of Harvard University Press, 2014.

McAdam, Jane. "An Intellectual History of Freedom of Movement in International Law: The Right to Leave as a Personal Liberty." *Melbourne Journal of International Law* 12, no. 1 (2011): 27–56.

McKeown, Adam. "Global Migration, 1846–1940." *Journal of World History* 15, no. 2 (2004): 155–89.

Meckstroth, Christopher. "Hospitality, or Kant's Critique of Cosmopolitanism and Human Rights." *Political Theory* 46, no. 4 (2018): 537–59.

Mehrländer, Andrea. *The Germans of Charleston, Richmond and New Orleans During the Civil War Period, 1850–1870: A Study and Research Compendium*. Berlin: De Gruyter, 2011.

Meyer, Christian. *Geschichte der Provinz Posen*. Breslau: F. A. Perthes, 1891.

Michie, R. C. *The Global Securities Market: A History*. Oxford: Oxford University Press, 2006.

Middlehoff, Frederike. "R/Emigration Verhindern: 'Heimat' im Kontext der Auswanderung von 1816/17." *The Germanic Review* 96, no. 3 (2021): 256–75.

Miller, Nicholas B. "Cameralism and the Politics of Populationism: Comparative Perspectives." In *Cameralism and the Enlightenment: Happiness, Governance and Reform in Transnational Perspective*, edited by Ere Nokkala and Nicholas B. Miller, 127–47. New York: Routledge, 2020.

Mintzker, Yair. *The Defortification of the German City: 1689–1866*. Cambridge: Cambridge University Press, 2013.

Möhlenbruch, Rudolf. "Freier Zug, Ius Emigrandi, Auswanderungsfreiheit. Eine verfassungsgeschichtliche Studie" PhD diss., Rheinische Friedrich-Wilhelms-Universität, 1977.

Mokyr, Joel. *The Enlightened Economy: Britain and the Industrial Revolution 1700–1850*. London: Penguin Books, 2009.

Mommsen, Wolfgang J. *Max Weber and German Politics, 1890–1920*. Translated by Michael S. Steinberg. Chicago: University of Chicago Press, 1984.

Murphy, Sharon Ann. *Investing in Life: Insurance in Antebellum America*. Baltimore: Johns Hopkins University Press, 2010.

Nadel, Stanley. *Little Germany: Ethnicity, Religion, and Class in New York City, 1845–80*. Chicago: University of Illinois Press, 1990.

Naranch, Bradley. "Inventing the Auslandsdeutsche." In *Germany's Colonial Pasts*, edited by Eric Ames, Marcia Klotz, and Lora Wildenthal, 21–40. Lincoln: University of Nebraska Press, 2005.

Naranch, Bradley, and Geoff Eley, eds. *German Colonialism in a Global Age*. Durham, NC: Duke University Press, 2014.

Niethammer, Lutz. "'Normalization' in the West: Traces of Memory Leading Back into the 1950s." In *The Miracle Years: A Cultural History of West Germany, 1949–1968*, edited by Hanna Schissler, 237–65. Princeton: Princeton University Press, 2001.

Nipperdey, Thomas. *Deutsche Geschichte 1800–1866: Bürgerwelt und starker Staat*. Munich: C. H. Beck, 2013.

Norton, Mary Beth. "The Evolution of White Women's Experience in Early America." *The American Historical Review* 89, no. 3 (1984): 593–619.

O'Brien, Patrick. "Agriculture and the Industrial Revolution." *The Economic History Review* 30, no. 1 (1977): 166–81.

Oltmer, Jochen. *Migration im 19. und 20. Jahrhundert*. Munich: R. Oldenbourg Verlag, 2010.

Osterhammel, Jürgen. *The Transformation of the World: A Global History of the Nineteenth Century*. Princeton: Princeton University Press, 2014.

Overton, Richard Cleghorn. *Burlington West: A Colonization History of the Burlington Railroad*. Cambridge, MA: Harvard University Press, 1941.

Paul, Roland. *"Hier hat man ein viel besseres Leben wie in Deutschland": Briefe pfälzischer Auswanderer aus Nordamerika (1733–1899)*. Kaiserslautern: Institut für Pfälzische Geschichte und Volkskunde, 2008.

Pawley, Emily. *The Nature of the Future: Agriculture, Science, and Capitalism in the Antebellum North*. Chicago: University of Chicago Press, 2020.

Penny, H. Glenn. *German History Unbound: From 1750 to the Present*. Cambridge: Cambridge University Press, 2022.

Penny, H. Glenn. *Kindred by Choice: Germans and American Indians Since 1800*. Chapel Hill: University of North Carolina Press, 2013.

Penny, Glenn, and Stefan H. Rinke. "Germans Abroad: Respatializing Historical Narrative." *Geschichte und Gesellschaft* 41, no. 2 (2015): 173–96.

Pfister, Ulrich, and Nikolaus Wolf, eds. *An Economic History of the First German Unification: State Formation and Economic Development in a European Perspective*. London: Routledge, 2023.

Pflanze, Otto. *The Period of Fortification, 1880–1898*. Bismarck and the Development of Germany. Vol. 3, Princeton: Princeton University Press, 1990.

Pierenkemper, Toni. "Historische Arbeitsmarkforschung: Vorüberlegungen zu einem Forschungsprogramm." In *Historische Arbeitsmarkforschung: Entstehung, Entwicklung und Probleme der Vermarktung von Arbeitskraft*, edited by Toni Pierenkemper and Richard Tilly, 9–36. Göttingen: Vandenhoeck & Ruprecht, 1982.

Pierenkemper, Toni. *Umstrittene Revolutionen: Industrialisierung im 19. Jahrhundert*. Frankfurt am Main: Fischer Verlag, 1996.

Pitts, Jennifer. *A Turn to Empire: The Rise of Imperial Liberalism in Britain and France*. Princeton: Princeton University Press, 2005.

Pitts, Jennifer, ed. *Writings on Empire and Slavery*. Baltimore: Johns Hopkins University Press, 2001.

Plumpe, Werner, Alexander Nützenadel, and Catherine R. Schenk. *Deutsche Bank. The Global Hausbank*. London: Bloomsbury, 2020.

Pohl, Manfred. "Deutsche Bank's East Asia Business (1870–1875)." In *Studies on Economic and Monetary Problems and on Banking History*, edited by Deutsche Bank Board of Managing Directors, 423–51. Neuwied: Hase & Koehler, 1988.

Pohl, Manfred. "Glimpses of Deutsche Bank's Early Days—Through the Papers of Hermann Wallich." In *Studies on Economic and Monetary Problems and on Banking History*, edited by Deutsche Bank Board of Managing Directors, 381–95. Neuwied: Hase & Koehler, 1988.

Pohl, Manfred. "Selected Documents on the History of the Deutsche Bank." In *Studies on Economic and Monetary Problems and on Banking History*, edited by Manfred Pohl, 769–92. Mainz: Hase & Koehler, 1988.
Pollard, Sidney. *Peaceful Conquest: The Industrialization of Europe, 1760–1970*. Oxford: Oxford University Press, 1981.
Press, Steven. *Blood and Diamonds: Germany's Imperial Ambitions in Africa*. Cambridge, MA: Harvard University Press, 2021.
Press, Steven. *Rogue Empires: Contracts and Conmen in Europe's Scramble for Africa*. Cambridge, MA: Harvard University Press, 2017.
Prinz, Lucie. *Schillerbilder: Die Schillerverehrung am Beispiel der Festreden des Stuttgarter Liederkranzes (1825–1992)*. Marburg: diagonal-Verlag, 1994.
Rancière, Jacques. *Proletarian Nights: The Workers' Dream in Nineteenth-Century France*. London: Verso Books, 2012.
Rapone, Anita. *The Guardian Life Insurance Company, 1860–1920: A History of a German-American Enterprise*. New York: New York University Press, 1987.
Redekop, Benjamin W. *Enlightenment and Community: Lessing, Abbt, Herder, and the Quest for a German Public*. Montreal: McGill–Queen's University Press, 2014.
Reitmayer, Morten. "Führungsstile und Unternehmensstrategien deutscher Großbanken vor 1914." *Zeitschrift für Unternehmensgeschichte/Journal of Business History* 46, no. 2 (2001): 160–81.
Richardson, Heather Cox. *The Greatest Nation of the Earth: Republican Economic Policies During the Civil War*. Cambridge, MA: Harvard University Press, 1997.
Richter, Ralf, and Jochen Streb. "Catching-Up and Falling Behind: Knowledge Spillover from American to German Machine Toolmakers." *The Journal of Economic History* 71, no. 4 (2011): 1006–31.
Ringer, Fritz. *Max Weber: An Intellectual Biography*. Chicago: University of Chicago Press, 2004.
Ritter, Gerhard Albert. *Der Sozialstaat: Entstehung und Entwicklung im internationalen Vergleich*. Munich: R. Oldenbourg Verlag, 1989.
Ritzmann-Blickenstorfer, Heiner. *Alternative Neue Welt: die Ursachen der schweizerischen Überseeauswanderung im 19. und frühen 20. Jahrhundert*. Zurich: Chronos Verlag, 1997.
Roberts, Brian. *American Alchemy: The California Gold Rush and Middle-Class Culture*. Chapel Hill: University of North Carolina Press, 2000.
Roberts, James S. "Der Alkoholkonsum deutscher Arbeiter im 19. Jahrhundert." *Geschichte und Gesellschaft* 6, no. 2 (1980): 220–42.
Rockman, Seth, Sven Beckert, and Christine Desan, eds. *American Capitalism: New Histories*. New York: Columbia University Press, 2018.
Rodgers, Daniel T. *Atlantic Crossings: Social Politics in a Progressive Age*. Cambridge, MA: Belknap Press of Harvard University Press, 1998.
Rodgers, Daniel T. *The Work Ethic in Industrial America: 1850–1920*. Chicago: University of Chicago Press, 2014.

Ron, Ariel. *Grassroots Leviathan: Agricultural Reform and the Rural North in the Slaveholding Republic*. Baltimore: Johns Hopkins University Press, 2020.

Rosen, Klaus. *Die Völkerwanderung*. Munich: C. H. Beck, 2020.

Roth, Guenther. "The Young Max Weber: Anglo-American Religious Influences and Protestant Social Reform in Germany." *International Journal of Politics, Culture, and Society* 10, no. 4 (1997): 659–71.

Roy, William G. *Socializing Capital: The Rise of the Large Industrial Corporation in America*. Princeton: Princeton University Press, 1997.

Sagarra, Eda, and Elka Schloendorn. "'Echo und Antwort': Die Darstellung der Frau in der deutschen Erzählprosa 1815–1848." *Geschichte und Gesellschaft* 7, no. 3/4 (1981): 394–411.

Sauer, Paul. *Reformer auf dem Königsthron: Wilhelm I. von Württemberg*. Stuttgart: Deutsche Verlags-Anstalt, 1997.

Sauer, Paul. *Der schwäbische Zar. Friedrich, Württembergs erster König*. Stuttgart: Deutsche Verlags-Anstalt, 1984.

Scaff, Lawrence A. *Max Weber in America*. Princeton: Princeton University Press, 2011.

Schilling, Heinz. "Confessional Migration as a Distinct Type of Old European Long Distance Migration." In *Le migrazioni in Europa, secc. XIII–XVIII*, edited by Simonetta Cavaciocchi, 175–89. Florence: Le Monnier, 1994.

Schmidt, Alexander. *Reisen in die Moderne: Der Amerika-Diskurs des deutschen Bürgertums vor dem ersten Weltkrieg im europäischen Vergleich*. Berlin: Akademie Verlag, 1997.

Schnabel, Franz. *Erfahrungswissenschaften und Technik*. Deutsche Geschichte im neunzehnten Jahrhundert. Vol. 3, Freiburg: Herder, 1954.

Schöberl, Ingrid. *Amerikanische Einwandererwerbung in Deutschland 1845–1914*. Stuttgart: Franz Steiner Verlag, 1990.

Schöberl, Ingrid, and Günter Moltmann, eds. *Aufbruch nach Amerika: Friedrich List und die Auswanderung aus Baden und Württemberg 1816/17: Dokumentation einer sozialen Bewegung*. Tübingen: Wunderlich, 1979.

Schroeder, Adolf E., and Carla Schulz-Geisberg, eds. *Hold Dear, as Always: Jette, a German Immigrant Life in Letters*. Columbia: University of Missouri Press, 1988.

Schunka, Alexander. "Konfession und Migrationsregime in der frühen Neuzeit (Migrants and the Early Modern Confessional State)." *Geschichte und Gesellschaft* 35, no. 1 (2009): 28–63.

Schupanitz, Andrew. "Revolutionary Competition: Coalitions, Labor, and the Birth of French Antitrust, 1791–1864." PhD Diss., Stanford University, 2020.

Schwalm, Leslie A. *Emancipation's Diaspora: Race and Reconstruction in the Upper Midwest*. Chapel Hill: University of North Carolina Press, 2009.

Scott, James C. *Domination and the Arts of Resistance: Hidden Transcripts*. New Haven, CT: Yale University Press, 2008.

Seidenzahl, Fritz. *100 Jahre Deutsche Bank, 1870–1970*. Frankfurt am Main: Deutsche Bank AG, 1970.

Selgert, Felix. *Macht und Kontrolle im Unternehmen: Die politische Ökonomie des Aktionärsschutzes im Deutschen Reich, 1870–1945*. Göttingen: Vandenhoeck & Ruprecht, 2020.

Sengle, Friedrich. *Biedermeizerzeit: Deutsche Literatur im Spannungsfeld zwischen Restauration und Revolution, 1815–1848*. 3 vols. Stuttgart: J. B. Metzler, 1971–80.

Sewell, William H., Jr. *Work and Revolution in France: The Language of Labor from the Old Regime to 1848*. Cambridge: Cambridge University Press, 1980.

Sheehan, James J. *German History, 1770–1866*. Oxford: Clarendon Press, 1989.

Sheehan, James J. *German Liberalism in the Nineteenth Century*. Chicago: University of Chicago Press, 1978.

Simeonov, Simeon Andonov. "Empire of Consuls: Consulship, Sovereignty, and Empire in the Revolutionary Atlantic (1778–1848)." PhD Diss., Brown University, 2021.

Simon, Matthew. *Cyclical Fluctuations and the International Capital Movements of the United States, 1865–1897*. New York: Arno Press, 1979.

Smith, Helmut Walser. "Authoritarian State, Dynamic Society, Failed Imperialist Power, 1878–1914." In *The Oxford Handbook of Modern German History*, edited by Helmut Walser Smith, 307–36. Oxford: Oxford University Press, 2015.

Smith, Helmut Walser. *German Nationalism and Religious Conflict: Culture, Ideology, Politics, 1870–1914*. Princeton: Princeton University Press, 1995.

Smith, Helmut Walser. *Germany: A Nation in Its Time: Before, During, and After Nationalism, 1500–2000*. New York: Liveright, 2020.

Smith, Helmut Walser, ed. *Protestants, Catholics, and Jews in Germany, 1800–1914*. Oxford: Berg, 2001.

Smith, Stacey L. *Freedom's Frontier: California and the Struggle over Unfree Labor, Emancipation, and Reconstruction*. Chapel Hill: University of North Carolina Press, 2013.

Sperber, Jonathan. *The European Revolutions, 1848–1851*. Cambridge: Cambridge University Press, 2005.

Sperber, Jonathan. *Popular Catholicism in Nineteenth Century Germany*. Princeton: Princeton University Press, 1984.

Stanley, Amy Dru. "Home Life and the Morality of the Marketplace: Slavery and Freedom, Women and Men." In *The Market Revolution in America*, edited by Melvyn Stokes and Stephen Conway, 74–96. Charlottesville: University of Virginia Press, 1996.

Stephanson, Anders. *Manifest Destiny: American Expansionism and the Empire of Right*. New York: Hill & Wang, 1995.

Stern, Fritz. "Money, Morals, and the Pillars of Bismarck's Society." *Central European History* 3, no. 1/2 (1970): 49–72.

Stoetzler, Marcel. *The State, the Nation, & the Jews: Liberalism and the Antisemitism Dispute in Bismarck's Germany*. Lincoln: University of Nebraska Press, 2008.

Stolle, Nikolaus. "Ein Leben für Forschung und Entdeckung." *Tribus: Jahrbuch des Linden-Museums Stuttgart* 71–72 (2023): 237–307.

Stolleis, Michael. *Konstitution und Intervention: Studien zur Geschichte des öffentlichen Rechts im 19. Jahrhundert*. Frankfurt am Main: Suhrkamp, 2001.

Stover, John F. *History of the Illinois Central Railroad*. New York: Macmillan, 1975.

Strupp, Christoph, Birgit Zischke, and Kai Dreisbach, eds. *German Americana, 1800–1955: A Comprehensive Bibliography of German, Austria, and Swiss Books and Dissertations on the United States*. Washington, DC: German Historical Institute, 2007.

Tanzer, Harald. *Theodor Fontanes Berliner Doppelroman: "Die Poggenpuhls" und "Mathilde Möhring": Ein Erzählkunstwerk zwischen Tradition und Moderne*. Paderborn: Igel-Verlag, 1997.

Taylor, Philip A. M. *The Distant Magnet: European Emigration to the U.S.A.* London: Eyre & Spottiswoode, 1971.

Tenfelde, Klaus. "Konflikt und Organisation in einigen deutschen Bergbaugebieten 1867–1872." *Geschichte und Gesellschaft* 3, no. 2 (1977): 212–35.

Tennstedt, Florian. *Vom Proleten zum Industriearbeiter: Arbeiterbewegung und Sozialpolitik in Deutschland, 1800 bis 1914*. Cologne: Bund-Verlag, 1983.

Thompson, David K. "Reorienting Atlantic World Financial Capitalism: America and the German States." In *Globalized Peripheries: Central Europe and the Atlantic World, 1680–1860*, edited by Jutta Wimmler and Klaus Weber, 205–22. Woodbridge, Suffolk: Boydell Press, 2020.

Thompson, E. P. *Customs in Common*. New York: New Press, 1993.

Thompson, E. P. "The Moral Economy of the English Crowd in the Eighteenth Century." *Past & Present* 50, no. 1 (1971): 76–136.

Tilly, Richard H. *Financial Institutions and Industrialization in the Rhineland, 1815–1870*. Madison: University of Wisconsin Press, 1966.

Tilly, Richard H. *Kapital, Staat und sozialer Protest in der deutschen Industrialisierung: Gesammelte Aufsätze*. Göttingen: Vandenhoeck & Ruprecht, 1980.

Tilly, Richard H., and Michael Kopsidis. *From Old Regime to Industrial State. A History of German Industrialization from the Eighteenth Century to World War I*. Chicago: University of Chicago Press, 2020.

Tipton, Frank B. *A History of Modern Germany Since 1815*. Berkeley: University of California Press, 2003.

Tooze, Adam. *Crashed: How a Decade of Financial Crises Changed the World*. New York: Viking, 2018.

Torp, Cornelius. "The Great Transformation: German Economy and Society, 1850–1914." In *The Oxford Handbook of Modern German History*, edited by Helmut Walser Smith, 336–58. Oxford: Oxford University Press, 2011.

Torp, Cornelius. *Die Herausforderung der Globalisierung: Wirtschaft und Politik in Deutschland 1860–1914*. Göttingen: Vandenhoeck & Ruprecht, 2005.

Trentmann, Frank. *Free Trade Nation: Commerce, Consumption, and Civil Society in Modern Britain*. New York: Oxford University Press, 2008.

Trepp, Anne-Charlott. *Sanfte Männlichkeit und selbständige Weiblichkeit: Frauen und Männer im Hamburger Bürgertum zwischen 1770 und 1840*. Göttingen: Vandenhoeck & Ruprecht, 1996.
Trommler, Frank, and Joseph McVeigh, eds. *America and the Germans. An Assessment of a Three-Hundred-Year History*. Philadelphia: University of Pennsylvania Press, 1985.
Vagts, Alfred. *Deutsch-Amerikanische Rückwanderung: Probleme—Phänomene—Statistik—Soziologie—Biographie*. Heidelberg: Carl Winter Universitätsverlag, 1960.
Van den Heuvel, Christine. "Justus Möser und die Englisch-Hannoversche Reichspolitik zwischen Siebenjährigem Krieg und Fürstenbund." *Zeitschrift für Historische Forschung* 29, no. 3 (2002): 383–423.
Vick, Brian E. *Defining Germany: The 1848 Frankfurt Parliamentarians and National Identity*. Cambridge, MA: Harvard University Press, 2002.
Vick, Brian E. "The Origins of the German Volk: Cultural Purity and National Identity in Nineteenth-Century Germany." *German Studies Review* 26, no. 2 (2003): 241–56.
Villard de Borchgrave, Alexandra, and John Cullen. *Villard: The Life and Times of an American Titan*. New York: Nan A. Talese/Doubleday, 2001.
Vogel, Barbara. *Allgemeine Gewerbefreiheit: Die Reformpolitik des preußischen Staatskanzlers Hardenberg (1810–1820)*. Göttingen: Vandenhoeck & Ruprecht, 1983.
Vollmer, Renate. "Assisted Emigration from Northern Germany to South Australia in the Nineteenth Century." *Australian Journal of Politics and History* 44, no. 1 (1998): 33–47.
Wagner, Adolph. "Das Actiengesellschaftswesen." *Jahrbücher für Nationalökonomie und Statistik* 21 (1873): 271–340.
Wais, Gustav. *Die Schiller-Stadt Stuttgart: Eine Darstellung der Schiller-Stätten in Stuttgart*. Stuttgart: W. Kohlhammer Verlag, 1955.
Walker, Mack. *German Home Towns: Community, State, and General Estate, 1648–1871*. Ithaca, NY: Cornell University Press, 1971.
Walker, Mack. *Germany and the Emigration, 1816–1885*. Cambridge, MA: Harvard University Press, 1964.
Wäntig, Wulf. *Grenzerfahrungen: Böhmische Exulanten im 17. Jahrhundert*. Konstanz: UVK Verlagsgesellschaft, 2007.
Wehler, Hans-Ulrich. *Von der 'Deutschen Doppelrevolution' bis zum Beginn des Ersten Weltkrieges 1849–1914*. Deutsche Gesellschaftsgeschichte. Vol. 3, Munich: C. H. Beck, 1995.
Weinhold, Rudolf, ed. *Volksleben zwischen Zunft und Fabrik: Studien zu Kultur und Lebensweise werktätiger Klassen und Schichten während des Übergangs vom Feudalismus zum Kapitalismus*. Berlin: Akademie-Verlag, 1982.
Welskopp, Thomas. "The Vision(s) of Work in the Nineteenth-Century German Labour Movement." In *Work in a Modern Society: The German Historical Experience*

in Comparative Perspective, edited by Jürgen Kocka, 55–72. New York: Berghahn Books, 2010.

White, Richard. *"It's Your Misfortune and None of My Own": A History of the American West*. Norman: University of Oklahoma Press, 1991.

White, Richard. *Railroaded: The Transcontinentals and the Making of Modern America*. New York: W. W. Norton, 2011.

White, Richard. *The Republic for Which It Stands: The United States During Reconstruction and the Gilded Age, 1865–1896*. New York: Oxford University Press, 2017.

Wiedemann, Felix. *Am Anfang war Migration: Wanderungsnarrative in den Wissenschaften vom Alten Orient im 19. und frühen 20. Jahrhundert*. Tübingen: Mohr Siebeck, 2020.

Wilkins, Mira. *The History of Foreign Investment in the United States to 1914*. Cambridge, MA: Harvard University Press, 1989.

Wimmler, Jutta, and Klaus Weber, eds. *Globalized Peripheries: Central Europe and the Atlantic World, 1680–1860*. Woodbridge, Suffolk: Boydell Press, 2020.

Winkler, Heinrich August. *Deutsche Geschichte vom Ende des Alten Reiches bis zum Untergang der Weimarer Republik*. Der lange Weg nach Westen. Vol. 1, Munich: C.H. Beck, 2000.

Wokeck, Marianne. "The Flow and Composition of German Immigration to Philadelphia 1772–1775." *Pennsylvania Magazine of History and Biography* 105, no. 3 (1981): 249–78.

Wolf, Marionela. "Aus dem württembergischen Haberschlacht nach Königsgnad im Banat. Briefe südwestdeutscher Auswanderer in ihre alte Heimat." In *Österreichisch-Siebenbürgische Kulturbeiträge: Ein Sammelband der Österreich-Bibliothek Cluj-Napoca/Klausenburg/Kolosvár*, edited by Rudolf Gräf, Lenke Varga, and Lukas Marcel Vosicky, 47–92. Cluj-Napoca, Romania: Presa Universitară Clujeană, 2005.

Wolfe, Patrick. "Settler Colonialism and the Elimination of the Native." *Journal of Genocide Research* 8, no. 4 (2006): 387–409.

Wright, Robert E. "Capitalism and the Rise of the Corporation Nation." In *Capitalism Takes Command: The Social Transformation of Nineteenth-Century America*, edited by Gary J. Kornblith and Michael Zakim, 145–68. Chicago: University of Chicago Press, 2011.

Wright, Robert E., and David Smith. *Mutually Beneficial. The Guardian and Life Insurance in America*. New York: New York University Press, 2004.

Wunder, Heide. *Er ist die Sonn', sie ist der Mond: Frauen in der Frühen Neuzeit*. Munich: C. H. Beck, 1992.

Zahra, Tara. *The Great Departure: Mass Migration from Eastern Europe and the Making of the Free World*. New York: W. W. Norton, 2016.

Zantop, Susanne. *Colonial Fantasies: Conquest, Family, and Nation in Precolonial Germany*. Durham, NC: Duke University Press, 1997.

Zimmerman, Andrew. *Alabama in Africa: Booker T. Washington, the German Empire, and the Globalization of the New South*. Princeton: Princeton University Press, 2010.

Zizek, Joseph. "'New History': The Radical Pasts of the French Revolution, 1789–1794." In *Rethinking the Age of Revolutions. France and the Birth of the Modern World*, edited by David A. Bell and Yair Mintzker, 154–92. New York: Oxford University Press, 2018.

Index

For the benefit of digital users, indexed terms that span two pages (e.g., 52–53) may, on occasion, appear on only one of those pages.

abolitionists, 62, 65–6, 106–7
Africa, 1–2, 16, 180–2, 200–4, 210–12
agrarian ideal, 13–17, 23, 84, 209–11, 213
Aktiengesellschaft (joint-stock corporation) *See* joint-stock corporation model
alcoholism, 93–5
Alldeutscher Verband (Pan-German League), 212
Altrechtler (political coalition in Württemberg), 34–6, 40
America
    antebellum period, 51–2, 66, 82–3, 122, 126
    anti-immigrant sentiments in, 50–1, 64–5, 83
    assimilation into American culture, 11–12, 78, 82–3, 123–6
    breadwinner-homemaker model of domesticity, 11, 17, 94–5, 97–9, 104–6, 110, 218–19
    "closing" of the American frontier, 209–13
    demographic transformation of, 168–71
    encouraging immigration to, 66–8, 175
    gold discoveries in, 103, 165–6, 203–4
    growth of, 4–5, 168–72, 176–7
    the home as a cultural institution in, 106–8
    immigration by country of origin in mid-1800s, 121
    perceptions of, 7, 9, 20–1, 44–5, 47, 62, 68–9, 162–4
    slavery in, 50–1, 62–6, 68–9, 84, 106–8, 122, 126, 166, 181–2
    treatment of women in, 92, 103–6, 109–10
    Westward expansion in, 14, 16, 65–6, 105–8, 126–7, 161, 166–7, 210–12
    See also correspondence; German immigrants
American Dream, 172–3
American Revolution, 104–5, 120
American Social Science Association, 172–5
American West, 16, 65–6, 68–9, 83–4, 105–8, 126–7, 161, 166–8, 183, 210–12
Amerikabrief (letter from America), 4–5, 7, 74
Anneke, Mathilde Franziska, 50–2

antebellum America, 51–2, 66, 82–3, 122, 126
Anthropology from a Pragmatic Point of View (Kant), 29–32
anti-immigrant sentiment, 50–1, 64–5, 83
anti-slavery movement, 62, 65–6, 106–7, 122, 126–7
Anti-Socialist Law of 1878 (Imperial Germany), 193, 197
A. Schaaffhausen'scher Bankverein in Cologne, 130–1
Aufsichtsrat (supervisory board), 195–6, 201
Auswanderungsfreiheit (freedom to emigrate), 41, 178–80

Baden (grand duchy)
　as region of large-scale emigration, 21–2, 43
　Revolution of 1848 and, 51
Bamberger, Ludwig, 143–56, 159–60
banking and finance
　Deutsch-Amerikanische Handelsgesellschaft, 130–7, 141
　Deutsche Bank, 134–7, 140–3, 147–8, 150–61, 164, 173–4
　economic development and modernization, 126–7
　financial crisis of 1857, 116, 188–9
　financial crisis of 1873, 157–8, 164, 186, 189–90, 208
　Germania Life Insurance Company of New York, 124–8, 141
　joint-stock banks, 116–18, 128, 130–1, 133–6, 173, 195–6
　making money accessible to new generations of industry, 113–15, 142–3
　providing a national home through, 119–24, 137–8
　Société Générale de Crédit Mobilier, 11, 116–18, 129–30, 132–4, 142, 150–1

　supporting Germany's trade with the world, 140–1, 150–1, 163–5
　US railroads, 165–8, 171
　see also United States securities; joint-stock corporation model
Battle of Leipzig (1813), 33–5
Bauer, Johann, 46–9, 61–2, 64–5, 69, 169
Baumberger, Henry, 109–10
Beecher, Catharine, 105–7
Belgrano, Manuel, 12–14
Berlin, Germany, 12, 118–19, 129–38, 140–4, 146–9, 154, 156–7, 170, 173–7, 180–3, 192, 196–7, 210–12, 214–15
Berliner Bankverein, 158, 173–4, 177
Borzykowo, Prussia, 74–9, 84–5, 88–9
Boston, Massachusetts, 173–5
Brauns, Ernst Ludwig, 31–2, 210
Brautwagen in Niederwalgern (unknown artist), 59–61
breadwinner-homemaker model of domesticity, 11, 17, 94–5, 97–9, 104–6, 110, 218–19
Bremerhaven, Germany, 89–91
Buenos Aires, Argentina, 150, 156–9
Buffalo, New York, 78–9, 84–5

Caesar, Julius, 89–91
California, 99–100, 102–3, 120–2, 126–7, 165–6
capitalism
　modern, 3, 16, 213, 215–17
　previous iterations of, 213, 217
　triumph of, 3, 16
　work of Max Weber on, 16–17, 209–13, 215–17
　work of Werner Sombart on, 3–4, 187
capitalist spirit, 1–2, 16–17, 187–8
Castle Garden immigration facilities, New York, 52–3, 66–8, 119–20, 122–3, 149–50

Catholicism
  anti-Catholic sentiment in US, 50–1
  immigrants who identify with, 44–5,
    50–1, 108
  Kulturkampf (culture war), 192
Chicago, Illinois, 46–7, 58–9, 76, 129,
    169, 197
Colby, Charles L., 166–8, 174–5
Cologne, Germany, 50–1, 114–15, 124,
    129–30, 142
commerce
  financial crisis of 1873 and, 157–8, 164,
    186, 189–90, 208
  GmbH model and, 11–12, 17, 199–200,
    202–8
  ideas in Germany about, 70–3, 77–8,
    88–9, 186–8, 194–5
  overseas, 115–16, 128–9, 133–5, 137–8
  political upheaval of 1848 and, 4–5,
    49–52, 69, 71–2, 91, 119, 124, 144,
    178–9, 182, 188–9
  as a power-political contest between
    nations, 152–3
  protecting interests of, 131–5, 140
communication, 48. *See also*
    correspondence
concession system for joint-stock
    corporations, 116–19, 129–31, 135,
    139–40, 194–5
corporations
  Companies Act of 1907 (United
    Kingdom), 205–6
  Free Incorporation Act of 1870, 117–19,
    136–8, 190–2
  Gesellschaft mit beschränkter Haftung
    (limited liability partnership), 11–12,
    17, 199–200, 202–8
  Gewerkschaft (mining corporation),
    117–18, 204–5
  Kommanditgesellschaft auf Aktien
    (variety of joint-stock corporation),
    130–1
  legal forms of, 114–15, 199, 202, 205
  limited liability protections, 114,
    130–1, 190, 199–202, 205–8
  support of by US Congress, 126–7,
    166–7
  US railroad corporations, 57, 65–8,
    117–18, 126–7, 166–8, 171–4, 182,
    212
  Wilhelm Oechelhäuser's views on,
    193–4, 200, 203–4
  see also joint-stock corporation model
correspondence
  changing function of after ca. 1850,
    57–62
  sense of community maintained
    through, 59, 61, 84–5
  steam-powered mail services, 5–7,
    168–9
  women's role in, 101–2
cotton merchants, 129–30, 133–4, 154

Delbrück, Adelbert, 143, 147–8, 154–6,
    158
democracy
  1878 ban on Social Democratic Party
    (SPD) in Imperial Germany, 187–8,
    193
  introduction of the GmbH and, 206–8
  social democratic agitation for in
    Germany, 193
  Westward expansion as symbol of in
    US, 14
Deutsch-Amerikanische
    Handelsgesellschaft, 128–37, 139–41,
    147
Deutsch-Belgische La Plata Bank, 156–9
Deutsche Bank
  Deutsch-Amerikanische
    Handelsgesellschaft and, 135–7
  "economic-political"
    (*wirtschaftspolitische*) mission of,
    134–5, 142–3, 148–55

Deutsche Bank (Continued)
  Georg Siemens' involvement in, 143, 154–61, 210–11
  Germania Life Insurance Company of New York and, 124–8, 141
  official origin story of, 141–2
  universal banking model, 17, 141–2, 160
Deutscher Bund (German Confederation), 34
Deutscher Kolonialverein (German Colonial Society), 180–1, 200–2
Deutsche Union-Bank, 158, 173–4, 177
diaspora, 1. *See also* emigration
domesticity
  breadwinner-homemaker model of, 11, 17, 94–9, 104–6, 110, 218–19
  "horse and mule fashion of" in Indigenous nations, 31–2, 45, 65–6, 105–6
  manifest domesticity, 105–6
  new model of, 97–9, 111
  slaveholders' vision of, 106–7
dowries, 47–8, 54–5, 59–61, 149–50
Dreistigkeit (impudence), 78–82, 84–5, 92–3, 99

economic growth, 2, 70, 72–3, 132–3, 181, 216
economic liberalism, 11, 71–2, 118
emigration
  administrative and social hurdles to, 36–7, 40–1, 168–9, 178–9
  of capital, 198, 205
  encouraging to obtain workers, 67–8, 175
  Friedrich Kapp's views on, 36, 119–20, 178, 180–1
  Friedrich List's views on, 20
  German nationalism and, 12, 33–4, 120–2, 148–50
  magnitude of from Germany, 4–5, 58–9, 119–22, 197
  new cultural and political meaning of, 9–10, 21–2, 29, 36–40, 42–4, 58–9
  reluctance of emigrants to settle in Southern US, 68–9
  stigma of, 9–10, 13–14, 42–4, 179–80
  Thomas Malthus's views on, 172
  Wilhelm I's views on, 40–1, 178
  Wilhelm Oechelhäuser's views on, 200, 203–5
East India Company (English), 11, 115–16
Enlightenment, 9, 29–30
entrepreneurship
  financial crisis of 1857, 116, 188–9
  financial crisis of 1873, 157–8, 164, 186, 189–90, 208
  Free Incorporation Act of 1870, 117–19, 136–8, 190–2
  immigrant, 61–2, 102–3, 123–8, 196–7
  joint-stock corporations and, 114, 116–17, 190, 201

financial crisis of 1857, 116, 188–9
financial crisis of 1873, 157–8, 164, 186, 189–90, 208
financial institutions, 49, 115, 129–30, 132–3, 136, 140, 142–3, 163–4
financial markets, 129–31, 167, 174, 189
foreign trade banks, 134–5, 140, 147–8, 155–6, 160
forty-eighters, 50–2, 61–3, 66–8, 119, 122–4
Frankfurt Parliamentarians, 49–51, 128–36, 179–80
freedom
  of enslaved Black men and women, 82, 84
  of incorporation, 117–19, 136–8, 190–2
  of labor and enterprise (*Gewerbefreiheit*), 70–4, 77–8, 81, 88–9, 218–19
  of movement (*Freizügigkeit*), 41

to emigrate (*Auswanderungsfreiheit*), 41, 178–80
Free Incorporation Act of 1870, 117–19, 136–8, 190–2
French Revolution, 9–10, 26–9, 31, 93–4
Friedrich I (king of Württemberg), 20, 34–5
Fröbel, Julius, 53, 144
Fürstenberg, Carl, 162–5

Gänserupferinnen (Liebermann), 94–6
Gasthof zum Kranen in Heilbronn (Dörr), 37–8
Gemütlichkeit (comfort, community), 94–5, 98–9
Germania (Tacitus), 23, 25
Germania Life Insurance Company of New York, 124–7, 129, 132–3, 141
German immigrants
  anti-immigrant sentiment in the United States, 50–1, 64–5, 83
  assimilating into American society, 61–2, 104
  "capital value" of, 53, 149–50
  consulates and, 49, 56
  demographics of, 57–8, 120–2
  entrepreneurship, 61–2, 102–3, 123–8, 196–7
  expectation of financial support from home, 47–8
  experience of landing in New York City, 52–3, 66–8, 119–20, 122, 149–50
  female, 54, 99, 103–4, 108
  Naturalization Act of 1790, 82–3
  to non-US destinations, 7–9, 16, 44–5, 180–1, 210–11
  paternal institutions and policies, 10–11, 41, 46–7, 55–6, 178
  personalized legal and financial services for, 49, 54–7, 59–61
  recruitment efforts, 37–8, 65–8, 183–4
  slavery and, 62–3, 65–6
Germany
  ambiguous political geography, 146–9
  assets of emigrants from, 54–7
  capitalism and, 3, 16, 213, 215–17
  creating a unified nation-state in Europe, 32–4, 49–50, 58–9, 120–2, 128, 137–8, 141, 151
  industrialization of, 1–2, 11–14, 16–17, 113–15, 163–5
  industry, 12–13, 113–15, 117–18, 124–6, 141–3, 152–3, 163–4, 203, 214–15
  nationalization of emigrants in America, 11, 43–5
  patterns of emigration to North America, 58–9, 119–20, 178–81, 197–8
  participation in global trade, 11–13, 165
  perceptions of women in, 92–3, 103–6, 108
  Protestant Reformation and, 16–17, 213
  Revolution of 1848, 4–5, 49–52, 69, 71–2, 91, 119, 124, 144, 178–9, 182
  rise of modern interventionist state in, 187–8
Gesinde (domestic servants), 94–6, 98–9
Gewerbefreiheit (freedom of labor and enterprise), 70–4, 77–8, 81, 88–9, 218–19
Gewerkschaft (mining corporation), 190, 204–5
Gesellschaft mit beschränkter Haftung (limited liability partnership), 11–12, 17, 199–200, 202–8
Göttingen, Germany, 89–90, 98
Grand Rapids and Indiana Railroad Company, 172–3
Groth, Albrect "Al," 196–7
Gründerprozesse (founder trials), 186–8

Hammacher, Friedrich, 202–5
Heck, Angela, 100–2, 110
Heidelsheim, Germany, 46–8, 169

Heilbronn, Germany, 21, 32, 37–41
Heimat (cultural ideal in Germany), 41, 90
Heine, Heinrich, 25, 119–22, 217–18
Herder, Johann Gottfried, 24–5, 27
Herzog Paul Wilhelm von Württemberg bei den Indianern (unknown artist), 41–2
Hoffmann, Francis A., 66–8, 169, 171–2
Hohenemser, Wilhelm, 129–30, 133–4
Holy Roman Empire, 4–5, 22–3, 35–7
home
  as a cultural institution in US, 98–101, 106–8
  as social reform in Europe, 97–8, 104–5
  femininity and masculinity, 93–7
  Haus interpretation of, 92, 94–5, 98, 108–11
  patriarchy and matriarchy, 92, 101–3, 111–12
Homestead Act of 1862 (United States), 62–3, 65–6, 83–4, 166–7
Hudson River landing docks, 52, 54

incorporation, 11–12, 17, 116–17, 124–6, 130–1, 136–7, 199–202, 204–6, 208
industrialization (in Germany), 1–2, 11–14, 16–17, 113–15, 163–5
industrial modernity, 1, 12–13, 17–18, 45, 69, 91, 112, 138, 161, 183–4, 210, 214–19
Industrial Revolution, 1–3
inheritances, 47–9, 54–7, 59–61, 90, 149–50
Ireland, 1–2, 58–9, 82–3, 120–2
Italy, 1–2, 30, 216

Jefferson, Thomas, 14–15
Jewish people
  capitalist spirit and, 187, 189–90
  Jewish emigrants, 182
joint-stock corporation model
  Americans' perception of, 126–7
  appealing aspects of, 114, 190
  converting to from ordinary proprietorships, 190–1
  Deutsch-Amerikanische Handelsgesellschaft as, 132–6
  as enterprises of modernity, 115, 124–7, 131–2, 218–19
  Free Incorporation Act of 1870, 117–19, 136–8, 190–2
  versus GmbH model, 11–12, 17, 199–200, 202–8
  joint-stock banks, 116–18, 128, 130–1, 133–6, 173
  Joint Stock Corporation Act of 1884, 196, 201–2, 208
  new narrative around, 126–7, 136–7
  potential drawbacks of, 115–17, 191–2
  principle of limited liability and, 114–15, 198–9
  Prussian government and, 129–33
  Wilhelm Oechelhäuser's view on, 193–6
Jonas, Johann, 108–10

Kansas, United States, 41–2, 65–6, 165–6, 173
Kansas–Nebraska Act of 1854 (United States), 126–7
Kant, Immanuel, 29–33, 36
kapitalistischer Geist (capitalist spirit), 1–2, 16–17, 187–8
Kapp, Friedrich, 51–61, 119–20, 122–4, 144–54, 159, 161, 173–84, 210–13
Kessel, Regina, 59–61
Kladderadatsch, Der (magazine), 7–9
Kleindeutschland (little Germany in New York City), 148, 150
Klusemann, Friedrich August, 185–7
Know-Nothing Party (United States), 50–1, 64–5
Kommanditgesellschaft auf Aktien (variety of joint-stock corporation), 130–1

Krause, Albert, 48, 74–82, 84–9, 91–4, 99, 169–70, 218
Krause, Aurelius, 85–9, 91
Kuhn, Emil, 83–4

labor and enterprise
  American approach to, 76–8, 81–126
  breadwinner-homemaker model of domesticity, 11, 17, 97–9, 104–6, 110, 218–19
  dignity of labor, 32, 72–3, 92–3
  domestic labor, 97–8, 105–6, 111–12
  enslaved labor, 62–4, 106–7, 181–2
  free labor, 17, 64–6, 77–8, 126–7, 219
  lack of employment opportunities for women, 92–3, 103–4
  loss of labor to emigration in Germany, 179–80, 198, 205
  Neue Ära (period of reform in Germany) and, 71–4
  Revolution of 1848 and, 4–5, 49–52, 69, 71–2, 91, 119, 124, 144, 178–9, 182
Labor Exchange—Emigrants on the Battery in Front of Castle Garden, New York (unknown artist), 122–3
laissez-faire, 118, 187–8, 192
land agents, 57, 178, 183
landed independence, 14–16, 23, 49, 69, 210, 213, 215–16
land grants
  to the public, 62–3, 65–6, 83–4, 166–7
  to railroads, 166–8
Leuchs, Johann Carl, 70–4, 77–8
liberalism, economic, 11, 71–2, 118
life insurance companies, 123–4, 126–7, 129
limited liability protections, 114, 130–1, 190, 199–202, 205–8
List, Friedrich, 12, 19–22, 32, 37–40, 152
Locke, John, 14, 23–4

mail. *See* correspondence
Malthus, Thomas R., 169, 171–2, 203–4
manifest destiny, 105–6
Marcuse, Hermann, 128–31, 133–6, 139–43, 147, 154, 157, 159–60
Marx, Karl, 13–15, 51–2, 73
May, Karl, 214
Meinecke, Sophie, 99–103, 108
Meister, Barbara, 104–5
mentorship, 51–2, 91, 161
Mevissen, Gustav, 113–18, 124–6
migrant's spirit
  capitalist spirit and, 2, 187–8
  concept of, 2, 17, 217, 219
  decline of, 16–17, 216
  Reichtumsfieber (fortune fever) and, 189–90
  role of German nationalism in, 12, 33–4, 120–2, 148–50
Minnesota, 66, 170–1, 175–6
Missouri
  Hermann settlement in, 120–2
  immigrant recruitment in, 65–7
  life of Johann Bauer in, 61–2, 64, 169
modernity
  America and, 7
  capitalism and, 16, 213, 215–17
  economic, 3–4, 11–13, 210, 215
  French Revolution and, 27
  industrial, 1, 12–13, 17–18, 45, 69, 91, 112, 138, 161, 183–4, 210, 214–19
  joint-stock corporations and, 124–6, 132–3
mortgages, 46–7, 173–4
Möser, Justus, 22–5, 27
mutual aid, 49, 55–6, 123–4

Napoleon I (emperor of France), 30, 33–4
Napoleon III (emperor of France), 137–8
National Assembly (Frankfurt am Main), 49–50, 178–80

nationalism
  emigration and, 33–4, 42
  the migrant's spirit and German, 10–12, 219
  nation-state (Germany), 49–50, 120–2, 137, 141
  proponents of, 24–5, 27, 43–4, 146–8
  rival nationalisms, 11, 26–7, 146–7
  views on German national character, 30–2, 45
National Liberal Party (Germany), 143–4, 180–1, 202–4
Native Americans, 20–1, 31–2, 44–5, 65–6, 83–4, 105–6, 127, 209
nativists, 50–1, 64–5, 122
Naturalization Act of 1790 (United States), 82–3
Nazi Germany, 215–16
Neue Ära (period of reform in Germany), 71–4
Norddeutscher Bund (North German Confederation), 132–5, 155–6
Northern Pacific Railway Company, 57, 161, 167–8, 175–7, 180–1, 182, 212

Oechelhäuser, Wilhelm, 188–200, 202–6, 208
Olmsted, Frederick Law, 62–5, 68
Oregon, 56–7, 66–8, 171, 183–4
Osnabrück, Germany, 22–5

Pacific Railway Acts of 1864 (United States), 65–6, 126–7, 166–7
Pape, Heinrich, 111
Paris, France, 29, 33, 119–20, 128–9, 134–5, 138, 143–4, 146–7, 149–50, 155–6
Poland
  Polish workers, 75–6, 212
  as political party in Imperial Germany, 206
population growth
  American railroad corporations and, 168, 171, 175–6, 180–1

  European versus American, 5–7, 168–9, 172
  immigrants' contribution to US, 169–70
progress idiom, 216–19
Protestant ethic, 16–17, 213–14
Protestant Ethic and the Spirit of Capitalism, The (Weber), 16, 213–14
Protestantism
  coalition in the Seven Years' War, 22
  the greater Protestant world, 44–5
  Reformation in Germany, 16–17, 213
  values associated with, 81, 85
Prussia, 12, 58–9, 76–81, 88–9, 116–18, 124, 129–30, 132–3, 137–8
Prussian government, 117–19, 129–32, 136
Prussian navy, 86–9

Reichstag (Imperial Germany), 148, 177–82, 192–8, 202, 204–5, 210–11
Reichtumsfieber (fortune fever), 189–90, 197
Revolution of 1848 (Germany), 4–5, 49–52, 69, 71–2, 91, 119, 124, 144, 178–9, 182
Rosenthal, Adolph, 56–7

San Antonio, Texas, 62–4, 109–10
San Francisco, California, 56–7, 102–3, 127–9
San Joaquin, California, 102–3
Schaar, Christoph, 19–22
Schano, Anna Maria, 101–2, 108, 146–7
Scheuermann, Joseph Ignatz, 54
Schiller, Friedrich, 9–10, 15, 25–7, 29–31, 36, 178
Schlüter, Wilhelmine, 100–1, 110
Schulze, Paul, 56–9, 183
Schurz, Carl, 50–1, 122
Seven Years' War, 9–10, 22, 24–5
Shanghai, China, 150, 156–9
Siemens, Georg, 143, 154–61, 210–11

Sittengesetz (system of ethics), 72–3, 186–8
slavery, 50–1, 62–6, 68–9, 84, 106–8, 122, 126, 166, 181–2
Smith, Adam, 151–2
Social Democratic Party (Germany), 193, 203, 206–7
Société Générale de Crédit Mobilier, 11, 116–18, 129–30, 132–4, 142, 150–1
society
    capitalism and, 3, 16, 213, 215–17
    importance of land ownership in, 14
    migrant's spirit and German, 189–90, 197
    Naturalization Act of 1790, 82–3
    role of GmbH in, 206–8
Sombart, Werner, 3–4, 187
South America, 7–9, 16, 44–5, 127, 150, 180–1, 210–11
speculation, 57, 102–3, 143, 176–7, 186–7, 189–90, 213
Stockton, California, 100, 102–3
Strähle, Jakob, 32

Tacitus, Cornelius P., 23, 25
technology
    cultural and social implications of, 3–4, 14–15, 217
    effect on ability to stay in touch with Germany, 5–7, 214
    innovation of financed by German banks, 140–1, 164
    lowering risk of long-distance migration, 48, 57–8
    progress, 216–19
Texas, 15, 43–4, 62–3, 65, 109–10, 120–2, 149
Thie family, 110–11
trade protectionism, 157–8, 164
transatlantic connections
    emigration of forty-eighters and, 49–51
    Friedrich Kapp's work with immigrants, 51–6, 119–20, 122, 175–84
    immigrant recruitment in the US, 61–2, 65–9
    new legal and financial institutions, 49
    function of correspondence, 59–61
    requesting money from relatives in Germany, 47–8
    support system for immigrants, 55–7
    trade, 128–9, 154–5
transportation
    for European emigrants, 4–5, 37–8, 48, 171
    German laws proposed regarding transatlantic, 178–9, 182–3
    new technologies, 3, 48, 57–8
Turner, Frederick Jackson, 16, 209–10, 213–14

Union Pacific Railroad Corporation, 126–8
US securities
    demographic transformation and, 167–9, 175–7
    incomplete information concerning, 171–2
    misinformation concerning population growth, 169–71, 182–3
    railroads, 165–7, 172–5
    rationales for investing in America, 162–5, 177–9
    universal banking model, 11, 17, 141–2, 160. *See also* Deutsche Bank
University of Heidelberg, 51–2, 144, 158
US Civil War, 65–8, 76–7, 82–3, 101, 110, 126–7, 129, 162–3, 166–7, 173

Villard, Henry, 161, 165–6, 168–9, 172–7, 182–4, 210–12
Völkerwanderung (peoples' migration), 28–33, 36, 38–43, 210
von Bismarck, Otto, 133–4, 136–8, 179–82, 192–4, 204
von der Heydt, August, 131–3

wages, 46–7, 72–3, 75–6, 78, 106–7, 150
Wallich, Hermann, 155–60
Weber, Der (Liebermann), 94–5
Weber, Max, 16–17, 209–13, 215–17
Wesendonck, Hugo, 124
Wiesbaden, Germany, 134–7, 139, 144, 147
Wilhelm I (king of Württemberg), 20, 33–7, 40–2, 58–9, 100, 135, 178–9
Wisconsin Central Railroad Corporation, 165–7, 174–5
Witte, Auguste, 54
Woltze, Berthold, 4–5, 7–11, 74
women
    characteristics associated with in Europe, 92–3, 106
    expected to be "heroines," 92–3, 105–8
    Frau (cultural ideal in Germany), 104–5
    in wartime, 104–6
    independence of, 93, 98, 101–2
    lack of employment opportunities for, 92–3, 103–4, 106
    proponents of women's rights, 50–1
    See also breadwinner-homemaker model of domesticity
World War I, 43, 214
Württemberg
    conflict over constitution, 1815–1819, 33–6
    exodus of 1817, 9, 29–33
    Friedrich List's interviews conducted in, 19–22, 32, 37–8
    insights gathered from events of 1817, 41–5
    Wilhelm I stance on emigration, 36–41

Zitz, Franz Heinrich, 119, 144
Zollparlament (Customs Parliament), 143–4, 147–8